The Bodley Head History of
WESTERN MUSIC

BY THE SAME AUTHOR

The Orchestra and its Instruments

The Bodley Head History of
WESTERN MUSIC

CHRISTOPHER
HEADINGTON

THE BODLEY HEAD

LONDON SYDNEY

TORONTO

DEDICATION

This book is for Christopher Dovell,
Nicholas Guest, Andrew and Steven Kennedy
and Timothy Slaney

© Christopher Headington 1974
Musical examples © The Bodley Head Ltd 1974
ISBN 0 370 01581 9
Printed and bound in Great Britain for
The Bodley Head Ltd
9 Bow Street, London WC2E 7AL
by W & J Mackay Limited, Chatham, Kent
Set in 'Monotype' Ehrhardt
First published 1974

Contents

Preface, 9

1

MUSIC IN THE ANCIENT WORLD, 11

2

THE MIDDLE AGES, 27

3

THE RISE OF POLYPHONY AND

THE RENAISSANCE, 45

4

THE LATE RENAISSANCE, 65

5

THE SEVENTEENTH CENTURY, 91

6

THE LATE BAROQUE, 115

7

ROCOCO AND CLASSICISM, 131

8

BEETHOVEN, 155

9

GERMAN ROMANTICISM, 177

10

FRENCH ROMANTICISM, 200

CONTENTS

11

FRENCH AND ITALIAN OPERA
IN THE NINETEENTH CENTURY, 221

12

LATE ROMANTICISM AND NATIONALISM, 232

13

THE ROMANTIC TWILIGHT
AND THE EARLY TWENTIETH CENTURY, 258

14

THE ENGLISH RENAISSANCE AND
NORTHERN EUROPE, 288

15

TRADITION AND INNOVATION
IN THE TWENTIETH CENTURY, 300

16

NEW COUNTRIES AND SOCIETIES:
THE PRESENT DAY, 325

Acknowledgments, 341
Bibliography, 343
Index, 345

Illustrations

A blind harpist and other Egyptian musicians. Stone relief from Saqqara of approximately 1340 BC, *facing page* 32

This Attic *krater* for mixing wine and water dates from the fifth century BC and shows on its side the winner of a *kithara* competition, *facing page* 33

The manuscript of *Sumer is icumen in*, probably dating from the mid-thirteenth century and found at Reading Abbey in England. The notation, in longs, breves and semibreves, shows the rhythm; the key is F major, *facing page* 48

Guillaume Dufay and Gilles Binchois with portative organ and harp. From the fifteenth-century French *Champion des Dames* by Martin Lefranc, *facing page* 49

'Concert of Angels', by the fifteenth-century Flemish painter Hans Memling, shows (*from left to right*) a psaltery, one-stringed fiddle or *tromba marina*, lute, trumpet and shawm, *facing page* 49

In a Lutheran church the Cantor often conducted with a roll of music: a picture from Johann Gottfried Walther's *Musical Lexicon* of 1732. Walther was a relative and colleague of J. S. Bach, *facing page* 128

A baroque opera set by Giovanni Carlo Bibiena. The Bibiena family were the greatest designers of 'spectacle' of their day, and their talents were in demand all over Europe, *facing page* 129

A scene from Handel's opera *Flavio* (1723). In this contemporary caricature the singers are the *castrato* Senesino, the soprano Cuzzoni, and the bass Berenstadt, *facing page* 129

The title page of the six string quartets which Mozart composed between 1782–86 and dedicated to his friend Joseph Haydn. They were published by Artaria of Vienna, *facing page* 144

An instrument-maker's workshop in the mid-eighteenth century. Illustration from the *Grande Encyclopédie*, *facing page* 144

Mozart by Josef Lange: one of the few authentic portraits of the composer in adult life, *facing page* 145

The old Burgtheater in the Michaelerplatz in Vienna was built in 1741 and it was here that Mozart's *Entführung aus dem Serail*, *Nozze di Figaro*, and *Così Fan Tutte* were first performed, *facing page* 145

Beethoven walking in the streets of Vienna in about 1823. A contemporary drawing by Lyfer, *facing page* 208

An almost illegible, though typical, page from Beethoven's sketchbooks. This was eventually to become part of the 'Pastoral' Symphony, *facing page* 208

A musical evening at Ritter von Spaun's house in Vienna by Schubert's friend Moritz von Schwind. Schubert is at the piano and beside him sits the singer Vogl, *facing page* 209

Kriehuber's 'An Afternoon with Liszt' shows the great pianist surrounded by rapt admirers including his former teacher Czerny and (*standing left*) Berlioz. The score of a Beethoven sonata is on the music stand, *facing page* 209

Berlioz had a reputation for excess and so provided rich material for caricature. Here he conducts an orchestra in which the bass players have to compete with the blast of a cannon, *facing page* 224

Verdi, in his eightieth year, acknowledges the applause of the audience after the triumphant première of his last opera, *Falstaff*, which took place on February 9th, 1893, at La Scala, Milan, *facing page* 225

Wagner's festival theatre at Bayreuth, in Bavaria: a contemporary engraving, *facing page* 225

Bruno Walter talking to Mahler (*left*) in Prague, 1907, *facing page* 304

The critic, Eduard Hanslick, tells the composer Richard Wagner how not to compose. Silhouette by Otto Böhler, *facing page* 304

Two remarkable faces: Debussy (*standing*) and Stravinsky, not long before the outbreak of World War I. This was the time of *Petrushka* and *The Rite of Spring*, both of which received their premières in Paris, *facing page* 305

Paul Hindemith was a skilled practical musician as well as a composer. It was he who gave the first performance of Walton's Viola Concerto in 1929, *facing page* 320

Ravel in 1915. He composed at the piano, and enjoyed smoking cigarettes made of characteristically strong French tobacco, *facing page* 320

Benjamin Britten, listening intently, conducts. Recently he has won a high reputation in this capacity, *facing page* 321

Pink Floyd: a modern pop group whose electronic techniques are inseparable from their style and public image, *facing page* 321

Preface

The scope of this book will be plain even at a fairly cursory glance. I have tried to bring out those things which seem important not only historically but also artistically. I cannot claim to have been wholly objective – what historian can, or desires to be? – but I have done my utmost to be fair. Experience has shown that even where, as a musician, I am not in full sympathy with a composer or artistic movement, writing about it as a historian has brought a more positive response.

Inevitably, one is aware of omissions. I have written, for example, fairly fully on Bartók, yet Kodály is only briefly mentioned. But no book can be absolutely comprehensive, least of all one in a single volume covering several millennia of musical history, and furthermore I believe that a better view of the general scene is obtained by taking longer surveys of particular aspects rather than trying to fit everything in. This in turn explains why I have devoted an entire chapter to Beethoven. More than any other single figure, he stands at a turning point in the history of music, while he has had a deeper and longer-lasting influence than even the greatest among his fellows. That the latter half of the book is spent on what is a short period relative to the whole time span is best explained in terms of familiarity with the repertory: it is only a decade or so since most people's knowledge began around 1700 with Bach or Handel, and however many musical examples are provided in the text, history will be most meaningful to a reader in terms of music with which he has some further acquaintance.

Most of the musical examples are on two staves at most, and they may therefore be played on any keyboard instrument. They have been carefully chosen to illuminate points, and although it is tiresome to have to get up repeatedly from one's chair to try something over, I hope and believe it will seem worth the trouble. Their apportionment to composers is not, of course, intended to reflect the relative importance of those musicians: Grieg has three, for example, but J. S. Bach only one.

A note on nomenclature may be useful. Particular works always have capitals, but general references do not: thus 'Beethoven's Ninth Symphony' but 'his nine symphonies'. Nicknames are in quotation marks: Bach's Second 'Brandenburg' Concerto. Titles as such are italicised: Haydn's *Seasons* and Debussy's *La Mer*. The names of these two works remind us that the matter of translation of foreign titles is often vexing. We refer to Wagner's *Tristan and Isolde* but talk of Debussy's *Pelléas et Mélisande*. Such consistency as is found in this book is, as far as possible, that of current usage. There have been doubtful cases. Few would quarrel with *Death and Transfiguration*, but perhaps *Ein Heldenleben* need not have been translated as *A Hero's Life*. Where readers disagree, I hope they will be indulgent.

I wish at this point to express my deep gratitude to Jill Black, who as editor was critical and encouraging in the right proportions. I am grateful too for the generous allowance of musical examples which have been so skilfully drawn by Dr Malcolm Lipkin. Several individual friends have also read portions of the manuscript and their comments have been valuable. But here I owe the greatest debt of gratitude to Professor Arthur Hutchings; he read through the whole book and provided me with a full and richly written commentary. Numerous improvements have been the result; for those weaknesses or errors that may remain, the responsibility is, of course, wholly my own.

CHRISTOPHER HEADINGTON

1

MUSIC IN THE ANCIENT WORLD

The distant past. East and West. The Greeks and Romans.
Jewish music. Music among the early Christians.

THE DISTANT PAST

If we ask ourselves where the history of music begins, we find at once that it has played a part in human life from the earliest times. It had a central place indeed, for it was not a luxury but useful and even essential. Naturally mothers sang their children to sleep thousands of years ago, just as today. But there was more than this. In ancient Egypt farm workers struck sticks together to frighten birds away from the crops. In time these clappers came to be used rhythmically to accompany working songs in the fields, and besides this they featured in dances of a ritual kind intended to bring good harvests. These uses of the Egyptian clappers illustrate two uses of music which survive today: the work song and the music of a church service.

One early civilisation was in Mesopotamia, now Iraq, at least five thousand years ago, where an agricultural people called the Sumerians lived in lands between the rivers Tigris and Euphrates. They built temples for the worship of nature gods who needed to be propitiated with the right kinds of singing and playing; and a reed wind instrument and a drum were consecrated to the gods of weather and water. There was solo singing by priests and choral singing; and besides the instruments already mentioned, there were flutes, horns, tambourines, rattles and various plucked string instruments. We know something about this music from Sumerian sculpture and reliefs, and from their cuneiform (wedge-shaped) writing on clay tablets. An inscription of the reign of the priest-king Gudea about 2400 BC shows that music was also used for pleasure:

> To fill the temple court with joy,
> To chase the city's gloom away;
> The heart to still, the passions calm,
> Of weeping eyes the tears to stay.

The Sumerians seem to have had contact with the people of Egypt, where the Old Kingdom came into being around 2686 BC. Egyptian kings were revered both as gods and as earthly rulers, so that temple services were important in both national and court life. The goddess Isis was the protector of the harvest, and to her and to her husband Osiris, protector of the dead, long and complex chants were sung by priests and priestesses: one ceremony dedicated to Isis lasted five days. The Egyptians considered the human voice to be the most powerful aid in invoking the gods, so their priests were carefully trained in singing. But they had instruments, too, to accompany their chants, like those of the Sumerians. And, just as in Sumeria, music was also used purely for pleasure, its charms being considered one of life's principal delights.

The rise of Egyptian civilisation was matched by some decline in that of the Sumerians. But the great city of Babylon, on the banks of the Euphrates, became a major political and cultural centre whose first dynasty of kings was founded in 2105 BC. Assyria, on the Tigris, was at first a vassal state of Babylon but upon becoming more powerful declared itself independent and finally annexed that city in 729 BC. The Babylonians used music in temple services, including music for instruments alone, but now the warlike Assyrians increased the importance of secular music: that is, music not for religious use. Banquets and military occasions were incomplete without music, minstrels were respected members of society, and Assyrian dancing girls were sent to delight the Egyptians. But the Assyrians' rule did not last long: the Babylonians, helped by the Medes, overcame them just before the birth of the famous King Nebuchadnezzar II (605–562 BC). We can read in the Bible (*Daniel*, Chapter 3) of the band at this king's Babylonian court. The description suggests a horn, pipes (perhaps an early form of organ), a lyre, and harps of two different sizes.

Babylonia was by this time called Chaldea, and the scholars of the court – astrologers, mathematicians and magicians – were the leading thinkers of their age. They observed everything around them, looking for the relationships which they were sure must exist between earth, heaven, and indeed all the different parts of nature. This 'harmony of the spheres' could, they thought, be expressed in terms of numbers. Where music was concerned, they found that by dividing a length of vibrating string into halves, thirds, quarters and fifths they could obtain a satisfying sequence of notes: nowadays we call this sequence the 'harmonic series', and the resultant harmony the major chord. True to their philosophy, the Chaldeans related the unison, the octave, the perfect fifth and the perfect fourth (the melodic intervals of the harmonic series) to the four seasons of the year.

EX. 1

† *The 7th harmonic is not precisely in tune with the normal scale.*

The Chaldean approach to music by means of proportions and numbers profoundly influenced its development. The Chaldean scale, for example, probably had seven notes, like our own, for to this ancient people seven was a mysterious and important number. So was four – we may remember the very ancient division of the month into four weeks of seven days. The ancient Greek scale was based on four-note groups, and it seems that Pythagoras studied in Chaldea and Egypt before laying down, in the sixth century BC, the principles of melody and harmony on which Greek musical theory was based.

EAST AND WEST

Before considering the cultures of Greece and Rome, to which the Western world owes such a great debt, it is worth looking briefly at the music of the Orient. There are several reasons for doing this. First, it seems likely that the Mesopotamian culture was a common ancestor to Indian and Arabic music as well as to our own. Secondly, the symbolic and even magical ideas connected with music in the East are part of our heritage, since they feature also in that early Jewish history which we call the Old Testament of the Bible. Finally, Eastern music is today becoming of increasing interest to the Western world. It has changed far less with the centuries than our own music, and thus provides a link with the past and with other civilisations.

Eastern music can seem strange to our ears, one reason being that it is improvised, not written down, and so may sound disorganised or monotonous. Lacking our developed Western system of harmony and key-changing, it often seems static, rather like the music of bagpipes with their constant droning bass. And in Indian music, for example, the use of intervals smaller than a semitone, as well as unusual styles of voice production, presents obstacles to a listener unfamiliar with its characteristic sound.

Yet there are points of contact between Western music and the unfamiliar music of the East. The bagpipe provides a useful example. It uses a scale which cannot be played on the piano, for certain notes come between the semitones separating the notes of the keyboard. But the Sumerians and Egyptians had the bagpipe, or something like it, five millennia ago. The same instrument was played in the Spartan and Roman armies; and it survives today in nearly every country from China, Russia and India to Spain, France and Great Britain. A world-wide gathering of pipers might well understand each other's music better than more 'cultivated' musicians carefully trained in specialist national styles. Turning from instruments to scales, we find that the pentatonic scale (a scale of five notes, say C, D, F, G and A) is a characteristic feature of Chinese, Scottish, Bengali and Eskimo folk music. Is this pure coincidence, or is it a survival of a scale widely used in Bronze Age times? 'The Chinese scale, take it which way we will, is certainly very

Scottish,' as the English musical historian Dr Charles Burney wrote as long ago as 1789.

In China, there were flutes, drums and bells, which we know of from writings and archaeological excavation, and which probably date from between 1500 and 1000 BC. The Chinese, like the Chaldeans, were interested in relating music and numbers; and the philosopher Confucius, who died in about 479 BC, held the view that music expressed 'the accord of Heaven and Earth'. Since the number 3 corresponded to heaven and 2 to earth, notes whose frequencies of vibration were in the ratio 3:2 were thought to 'harmonise as heaven and earth'. This relationship exists between the notes C and G, the second of which vibrates half as fast again as the first; or, to put it another way, C vibrates two-thirds as fast as the G above it. This particular pitch interval between two notes is called a perfect fifth. If one starts on the note F and proceeds upwards by intervals of a perfect fifth – F, C, G, D and A – and then arranges these notes within the range of one octave, one has the pentatonic scale mentioned in the preceding paragraph, C, D, F, G and A.

EX. 2

But though the five-note scale formed the basis of Chinese music, by the first century BC there was a Chinese flute which could play two extra notes in the octave, making seven in all. By this stage of their history the Chinese also used small organs with bamboo pipes and plucked string instruments as well as the earlier bells, flutes and drums. Players of these instruments often formed themselves into bands for the entertainment of the nobility. In the early centuries AD a plucked string instrument called a *ch'in* became important in more learned music; this had five or seven strings arranged in a series of perfect fifths and was supposed to have an ennobling effect on the soul. One temple possessed a hundred and twenty of these instruments, which accompanied chants; however, these large forces seem to have been used with subtlety. In the words of Confucius, 'The music of a man of noble mind is gentle and delicate, maintains a uniform mood, enlivens and moves.'

In India, too, music had a philosophical significance. Around 1500 BC, an Eastern Mediterranean race called the Aryans invaded the country from the Pamir area in the extreme south of Russia. Thus began India's so-called Vedic period. The word *veda* means 'knowledge', and books of hymns and temple rituals date from the early part of this time. There is a book of hymns which emphasises the correct pitching of the voice on one of three levels: high, middle or low. Another book, called *The Veda of Chants*, shows that melodies were sung in unison by three priests; and the number three again

appears in connection with rhythm, for the notes were short, long or augmented. Like the ancient Egyptians, the Indians treated the human voice as
the most important form of musical expression, but they, too, had plucked
string instruments, percussion, and flutes and reed wind instruments; these
perhaps featured especially in music for entertainments and dancing.

The Indian musicians thought their chants were composed by the gods
and not by themselves. Since nature was also considered to be the gods'
creation, mystical links were established everywhere in the ancient world
between particular aspects of music and nature. In India and Arabia different
melodic styles were assigned – as indeed they still are today – to the time of
day, days of the week, seasons, and other things. For example, one Arabic
melodic style, or *maqam*, belongs to the zodiacal sign of the Ram, to sunrise,
and to the cure of eye troubles. To the Chinese, the metal bell represented
West, autumn and dampness; and each note of the pentatonic scale had its
meaning, that of the fifth for example being South, the planet Mars, fire, and
the colour red. The ancients went a good deal further than this. Indian and
Chinese stories tell of singers changing the seasons and creating fire or water;
while the Bible describes Jericho's walls falling at the sound of military
horns, and Jewish priests wore bells to enter a holy place, to ensure their
spiritual protection. Though Western music has abandoned all these ideas,
the story of the minstrel Orpheus taming wild beasts with his melodies
reminds us that the ancient Greeks also believed strongly in the magical
force of music.

THE GREEKS AND ROMANS

Somewhere around 3000 BC the Bronze Age began, and in its early stages
in Europe flourished most brilliantly in the civilisation of the island of Crete.
The Cretans produced ornamental jewellery in gold, silver and precious
stones, and their clothes were elaborate. Though they were in contact with
priestly-monarchical Egypt, they were a pleasure-loving race whose religion
was a happy affair and music naturally played its part in their lives: they
danced and sang to the sound of rattles, plucked strings and reed-pipes.
Sometime before 1000 BC Greek culture came to Crete: this, together with
earthquake, fire and flood, put an end to the Cretan civilisation as such.
Dorian and Mycenaean Greeks invaded the island and brought with them a
new language and way of life.

As Greek civilisation developed, it spread to the western coast of present-
day Turkey and to much of Bulgaria. By the eighth century BC the Greek
alphabet existed, and Homer's *Iliad*, appearing at this time, is the first known
example of European literature. There was already a heroic past, centred round
events such as the Trojan War, and there now grew up a national culture
in which minstrels lived in the houses of noble families and entertained

their audiences with songs accompanied by the lyre. These told of epic deeds of gods and heroes, and no doubt the latter were sometimes ancestors of the householders.

Greek musical style came partly from Egypt, through Crete. Thrace, a north-eastern part of Greece, was the birthplace of the greatest minstrel of Greek mythology, Orpheus; and the Greeks themselves claimed that Hyagnis and Marsyas, from Phrygia in Asia Minor, were among the founders of their music. These two were credited by the Greeks with the invention of the *aulos*, and another Phrygian called Olympos was supposed to have developed the style of its melodies. But the *aulos* was in fact known in Sumeria, Egypt and Crete long before. It was a pair of pipes, each having a double reed like an oboe's and with holes stopped by the fingers; sometimes, perhaps, the player played the melody on one pipe and a continuous bass note on the other. It had a shrill and penetrating tone, and probably its nearest modern equivalents are the shawm, still played in Spanish bands, and the bagpipe. It was popular in the theatre, at weddings and other festive occasions, and at banquets. Appropriately, the Greeks consecrated the music of the *aulos* to Dionysus, their god of wine.

The more refined lyre was the other principal Greek instrument and this was regarded as the instrument of the god Apollo. It had from three to twelve strings, the largest and most elaborate examples having the name *kithara*. Since the gentle tone of the lyre did not mix well with that of the powerful *aulos*, they were not often played together. In any case, the cults of Apollo and Dionysus were different and even opposed. Dionysus represented emotion and the joys of the senses, whereas Apollo was the god of the intellect, of enlightenment, self-control and balanced judgment. According to legend, Apollo protected his style of music, and made King Midas grow asses' ears for daring to prefer the sound of a shepherd's pipe to that of the lyre. The three spheres of life consecrated to Apollo were light, prophecy and the arts; and the light of human reason among the Greeks, brought to bear upon the mysteries of life and nature, created works of art of calm power and perfection. These were a heritage to the Western world, teaching the value of art which, while full of feeling, is still disciplined by the intellect.

Since reasoned thought was so important to the Greeks, it is not surprising to find that their music, like their architecture, conformed to strict principles of style and shape. Their word *nomos* referred to a musical form, but it also meant 'law'. Perhaps the simplest explanation of the Greek nomes is to say that they were principles of construction. Greek temples were built according to three 'orders' which can be recognised from the shape and decoration of the columns: the plainest is the Doric, the Ionian shows more graceful elegance, and the Corinthian is sumptuously ornamented. A musical nome was an 'order' of this kind, and each nome had a basic style of melody and rhythm, just as an Indian *raga* has today.

Greek architecture and music both owed a debt to the researches into numbers made by Pythagoras. Fairly recently, a Greek writer has pointed out a close relationship between the placing of temple columns and the Pythagorean theory of musical scales. In the sixth century BC Pythagoras restated the Chaldean discovery of the harmonic series: the notes obtained by dividing a vibrating string into halves, thirds, quarters and so on. These notes, when sounded together, gave the major chord and so suggested a keynote: this is the most important note in a melody, on which it can come to rest.

The basic Greek melodic interval was a perfect fourth, called a tetrachord – for example, G up to C, or A up to D. The two notes, being part of the harmonic series, were regarded as fixed. But two more notes were added in between the outside ones. A G-to-C tetrachord might therefore consist of the four notes G, A, B and C. But even in present-day Western music there are no fewer than six ways of pitching the inner notes, and the Greeks used other intervals which were smaller than a semitone. The two inner notes of the tetrachord could therefore be very freely pitched, and how this was done depended on the nome, or style of playing.

Of course a piece of Greek music used more than four notes. By joining one tetrachord on to another, some overlapping, and adding an extra note at the bottom, the Greeks produced the following scale, which they called the 'greater perfect system'. The inner notes of the tetrachords are written here as if the intervals were tones or semitones.

EX.3

Each note of this scale had its name, even where its exact pitch was not fixed. Some of the names show the fingering for a lyre-player: for example, the G in the lower octave was called *lichanos*, meaning 'first finger'. It was the octave in the middle, from E to E, that was most used both for singing and playing.

We know quite a lot about Greek musical theory, the most valuable writing on the subject being by Aristoxenos of Tarentum and dating from the fourth century BC. Sadly, hardly any actual music has survived, for in this as in other ancient cultures music was essentially an improvised art. Yet written music was not completely unknown; perhaps the notation was invented as a teaching aid for the schools. This notation was alphabetical, and fortunately it is explained in the writings of Alypios around the fourth century AD.

Three pieces of Greek music have survived as stone inscriptions, though only one is quite complete. This is an epitaph written by a man called Seikilos for his wife, dating from about the first century BC. It is transcribed here in modern notation. The Greek notation above the notes has dots and lines which indicate the rhythm, while the letters identify the notes.

This should correspond quite closely with what a Greek listener might have heard long ago. But we cannot claim more than this. Scholars continue to argue about Greek music; and in one historian's words, 'No field of music-ology has produced a richer crop of disputation from a thinner soil of fact.'*

Besides songs, music for instruments alone was fashionable among the Greeks, and brilliant performers competed for public acclaim at festivals. One young aulete called Harmonides, if we can believe the writer Lucian, was so determined to astonish the audience at his début that he 'began his solo with so violent a blast that he breathed his last breath into his *aulos* and died on the spot!' Another story is of Sakados, who played the *aulos* and won a prize at the Pythian Games of 586 BC. The piece he played, usually called the Pythic Nome, is the first known example of programme music. It had five sections depicting a fight between Apollo and a dragon, called *Preparation, Challenge, The Fight, Song of Praise and Victory Dance*.

The importance accorded to music by the Greeks cannot be doubted; and in fact the great Athenian philosophers Plato and Aristotle advocated a form of education in which music was one of the two main elements. The other was athletics, for they believed that while the latter created and main-tained physical health, music offered the best schooling for the mind. To understand this high place accorded to music by such sober men, we must remember the ancient Chaldean-Pythagorean view of it as expressing the harmony of the universe. In Plato's words, 'Just as our eyes are made for astronomy, so our ears are made for music . . . the two are sister sciences.'

Music was still widely believed to have a considerable power over men's minds. Plato thought Dorian melodies noble, but classed Phrygian ones as demoralising.† For Aristotle, the shaping of a man's character could depend

---

* Donald J. Grout: *A History of Western Music*, J. M. Dent & Sons, London, 1962.
† These were not the same as the modes of Christian plainchant having these names, as will be explained later in this chapter.

on his having the right kind of musical environment. The importance of music in education was no mere philosophers' theory: in Plato's Athens instrumental study and choral singing were general practice, while in Sparta musical education was believed to make people law-abiding. It may be added that the philosophers had no use for brilliant playing as an end in itself. As Aristotle put it: 'The right standard will be reached if music students stop short of the arts practised in professional contests, and do not try to acquire those fantastic marvels of performance which are now the fashion in such contests, and from these have passed into education. The young should practise just such music as we have prescribed, only until they are able to feel delight in noble melodies and rhythms.'

The Greek theatre was an important institution of public life which rose to great artistic heights with the plays of Aeschylus, Sophocles and Euripides in the fifth century BC. These dramatists used a chorus which both sang and danced. Actors occasionally sang instead of speaking; and the *aulos*, which accompanied all this, sometimes provided incidental music as well. Both text and music were closely connected: in fact it was the rediscovery of Greek drama in Renaissance times which brought about the birth of opera at the beginning of the seventeenth century, for at that time people believed Greek drama to have been sung throughout.

Though some of the Greek plays were lofty epics and tragedies, there was also a much lighter side to the theatre, provided by the works of comic writers like Aristophanes and Menander. In music, too, more popular styles gained ground. One poet-musician, Timotheos of Miletos, said, 'I don't sing about outdated things – new ones are much better. To Hades with the old Muse!' He fitted twelve strings to his lyre, instead of the usual seven, and played cheerful tunes which delighted the public but scandalised conservatives. One playwright called Pherecrates launched an attack on Timotheos by making Music appear on the stage as a woman in rags claiming that she had been dishonoured by modern composers caring nothing for her beauty and dignity.

The new-style music became more important than the words in the pantomimes which delighted Greek theatregoers in search of lighter entertainment. Here the *aulos* joined in ensembles with lyres, flutes and cymbals, and there was a good deal of dancing. One result was that music's status as a serious part of education lost ground. The teaching of it deteriorated, and it became unfashionable, at least among the upper classes, to have much to do with performance. The educated still had their musical interests, but a division had appeared, familiar to us today, between the professional performer and the amateur listener with critical pretensions.

Looking back, it is easy to think in terms of a decline, a falling away from Plato's lofty musical ideals. But in another way we may feel grateful to Timotheos of Miletos, for there is a need in music as elsewhere for good light entertainment as well as more exalted thought. All the same, one may wonder how Timotheos would have felt if he had known that a few generations later his own work would be forgotten by audiences whose idea of the musical theatre was that of a variety show with dancing, acrobatics and gross caricature.

Certainly the fourth and fifth centuries BC, when Plato and Timotheos lived, represent the highest point in the story of Greek civilisation. Driven on by local patriotism and mutual distrust, which saddened Plato and made him advocate a more peaceful order under the guidance of philosophy, the city-states came near to destroying their own achievements by fighting among themselves. A last great period was still to come: Alexander the Great of Macedonia led a united Greek army to conquer the Persians and create a vast Eastern empire. But at his early death his generals divided that empire, and in due course it was lost. In 146 BC Greece became a province of the rapidly expanding empire of Rome, taking the name of Achaea.

Yet, as a French historian has put it, Rome 'came under the influence of these Hellenes whom her arms had vanquished'. Greek architecture was imitated in the Roman world; education too was based on Greek ideas, and in higher education both languages were used as a matter of course. The Emperor Hadrian endowed Rome with an Athenaeum, a university on Greek lines; and Marcus Aurelius, who later inherited the empire, chose Greek as the language of his philosophical meditations.

Greek music took root in Rome so firmly that when we speak of Roman music we really mean Greek music as developed and practised there. Yet the story of Graeco-Roman music is not, as it happens, a very happy one. We have already seen how in Greece the art had steadily become more colourful, but also coarser, and now a rather vulgar Roman taste for the colossal brought about the development of a more powerful *aulos* and lyres 'as big as chariots'. Egyptian influence also reached Rome through Alexandria: in Egypt there were often large instrumental bands, and these became a feature of Roman music. The organ, worked by water pressure, came from Egypt, and so did powerful brass instruments. We know of orchestras, and the large choruses of singers which they accompanied, from Seneca, the tutor of the Emperor Nero. Even so, there was music of another, subtler kind: according to Cicero, thoughtful and knowledgeable amateurs played and sang in their homes, appreciating such finer points as crescendo and diminuendo.

The private practice of more cultivated music reached public attention because of that notorious emperor whose love of music seems to have been his only redeeming feature. In his early twenties, Nero introduced festivals of music and literature on the Greek pattern, to take place every five years in Rome, and the first of these was held in AD 60. He actually took part as a lyre-player in the Greek Olympic Games of 66 where, according to rumour, it was by bribery that he won the first prize; he then toured the country destroying statues of previous victors and collecting several other prizes in competitions, bringing them back to Rome triumphantly like a general with his spoils of war. Nero took care of his voice: he dieted and employed an official to warn him if he risked vocal strain, and if Nero spoke too loudly in spite of advice to the contrary this person had orders forcibly to restrain him! His voice was thin and slightly husky, perhaps what we should call a light tenor, but he must have had stamina, for his concerts, to which large audiences were invited, sometimes lasted for hours. Nobody was allowed to be inattentive or to leave before the concert was over, and when Vespasian, a future emperor himself, once committed both these crimes, only the inter-vention of important friends saved him from punishment. Nero must have been an extraordinary man. Even at the time of his death, forced to suicide by a military revolt, it is said that his mind turned to music and he exclaimed, 'What an artist is lost in me!'

Private education in music was given to other aristocratic Romans besides Nero – the historian Tacitus maintains that Nero's murder of the young prince Britannicus was largely due to the boy's excellent musical ability. Some later emperors, like Antoninus Pius, Caracalla, the boy-ruler Elagabalus and Alexander Severus, were talented singers and players. Hadrian, a musician and a patron of the art, commissioned choruses from Mesomedes, a Cretan composer who wrote funeral music on the death of the emperor's favourite Antinous, and also a *Hymn to the Sun*. The melody of this particular hymn, and of one other by Mesomedes, survived as early Christian chants. This is not so surprising as it may at first seem. Christianity, at this time a century old, drew upon the common musical language of the Roman world. To that same world of course, though uneasily, the Jewish people belonged, and the early Christians also derived much of their music from the Jewish heritage which provided the background for their new faith.

JEWISH MUSIC

The Bible provides such a detailed record of Jewish history that we can draw a wealth of musical information from it. The great leader of early times, Moses, was a musician: the early Church Father Clement of Alexandria tells us that the Egyptians taught him especially medicine and music. Moses instituted an annual musical event (*Numbers*, Chapter 29) which took place on the first day of September and was probably a harvest festival – 'it is a day of blowing the trumpets unto you'. These were made of rams' horns; and the same instrument, called the *shofar*, is still used by Orthodox Jews today on solemn occasions such as New Year. There was also a silver trumpet used for signals, called the *hazozra*. In *Numbers*, Chapter 10, we read of Moses being instructed by God to make the *hazozra*, which was probably similar to the Egyptian trumpet found in the tomb of Tutankhamun (*c.* 1352 BC). Besides such instruments of public ceremonial, there were three more domestic ones: the *ugab*, a reed pipe; the *kinnor*, a lyre; and the *tof*, a tambourine. The translators of the English Authorised Version of the Bible, working in the early seventeenth century, did their best with the Hebrew names of these three instruments, calling them organ, harp and tabret or timbrel. There was also the *nevel*, a large harp; while the *halil* was undoubtedly an *aulos*, for the Jews seem to have used the instruments generally available in the ancient world rather than inventing new ones.

The prohibition of 'graven images' restricted the role of the visual arts in Jewish worship. Music, on the other hand, flourished. The close connection between music, religion and even statecraft is illustrated by the story of King David. It seems more than coincidence that the prophet Samuel's friend Jesse had a youngest son who was devout, intelligent, resourceful, and a skilled player of the lyre. David was sent for by Saul's advisers, for only music, they said, would cure the King's strange, disturbed moods. David came and played his lyre, and 'Saul was refreshed, and was well, and the evil spirit departed from him.' But David was no mere court musician, since at this time Samuel had already anointed him as future king.

During David's reign (about 1010–975 BC) and that of his son Solomon, music seems to have acted as an inspiring force. According to the religious historian Eusebius of Caesarea, writing in the fourth century, David carried his lyre everywhere; as both prince and prophet, he sang his psalms as inspiration came to him. He is also said to have set out the basis of the Temple music. In *Chronicles*, we read that David appointed the Levites as Temple musicians; the prophet Amos (Chapter 6) believed, though probably wrongly, that he invented musical instruments.

Solomon, like his father, reigned for over thirty years. At the dedication in 950 BC of the magnificent new Temple in Jerusalem, there were 'an hundred and twenty priests sounding with trumpets', and also lyres, harps and cymbals (*zelzlim*), the Levite singers joining with the instruments 'to make one sound to be heard in praising and thanking the Lord'. We do not know if Solomon himself played or sang, but he had 'men singers and women singers, and the delights of the sons of men, as musical instruments, and that of all sorts'.

In 587 BC, Israel fell to the Chaldeans. The great Temple in Jerusalem was destroyed, and many Jews were sent as captives to Babylon. Their despair is illustrated by a poignant reference to music in Psalm 137: 'We hanged our harps upon the willows . . . they required of us mirth, saying, sing us one of the songs of Zion. How shall we sing the Lord's song in a strange land?' Fortunately the period of exile lasted only fifty years. Re-established in their homeland, the Jews resumed their community life and worship, rebuilding their Temple. Many Psalms belong to this period, and the Levites carried on their traditional office as Temple musicians. Alternate singing of half-verses of the Psalms was a common practice, just as it is in Christian churches today.

The established musical practices of Jewry remained, with certain changes, for many generations. By the time of Christ, the Temple had a choir of twelve Levite men, whose training period was five years. The Temple orchestra had nine lyres, two harps and cymbals, and to this basic ensemble of a dozen players, two performers on the *halil* were added on certain feast days. We do not know whether the orchestra accompanied the choir or played alone; probably it did both.

Between the return from exile and the time of Christ, Palestine had submitted to the Greeks under Alexander, and a further period of independence had been followed by Roman intervention. Roman rule seems to have been reasonably light. Yet the fierce independence of Jewry brought about rebellion which led to the destruction of the Temple in AD 70. Eventually Jerusalem itself was wiped out, and the very name of Palestine indeed erased from the map. Though Jews continued to worship where they could, their homeland was lost to them. As a symbol of sorrow they gave up the use of instruments in worship; only many centuries later were they to be re-established.

MUSIC AMONG THE EARLY CHRISTIANS

The early Christians existed alongside established Jewry, and so it was natural that music should also play a part in their worship. Christ himself, accusing the Jews of a lack of understanding, uses the phrase, 'We have piped unto you, and ye have not danced;' and the Greek verb used here means 'to play the *aulos*'. St Paul and a companion, lying in a Macedonian prison, 'prayed, and sang praises unto God', whereupon an earthquake loosed their bonds and burst open the prison doors. To the Ephesians, Paul recommended 'psalms and hymns and spiritual songs, singing and making melody in your heart to the Lord'. In fact the Greek writer Lucian, and the Roman Pliny the Younger, both comment on the enthusiasm for singing among Christians of the first and second centuries. Music was soon established as part of an ordered liturgy. By the fourth century, Bishop Eusebius of Caesarea was able to write that 'there was one common consent in singing the praises of God. The performance of the service was exact, the ritual of the church decent and majestic. There was a place appointed for the psalm-singers: youths and maidens, old men and young.'

The oldest and most characteristic form of Christian music, a form which is still in regular use today, is called plainchant, plainsong, or 'Gregorian chant'. In psalmodic plainchant, a melody of two phrases is sung without accompaniment. It is repeated for each verse of a psalm or other verse text, the two melodic phrases corresponding to the two halves of a verse. This style of singing came from the Christians in Byzantium, the great city which was the Eastern capital of the Empire that was later renamed Constantinople and is now Istanbul in Turkey. The Byzantines used eight melodic 'orders' called *echoi*; and each of their chants had its melody which belonged to one of these. The *echoi* were in due course superseded by a system of eight scales, arrangements of tones and semitones in order of pitch, called 'modes', and to the present day these are the basis of plainchant. Byzantine chant is thus the ancestor of music in the Christian Churches, Western and Eastern alike.

By the fourth century, Rome and Milan, an imperial residence, were the leaders among established Christian communities. Saint Ambrose was Bishop of Milan from 374–397; and there was a strong political and cultural link between his city and Byzantium. Ambrose introduced antiphonal singing of psalms and hymns to the West, with two groups of singers singing alternate verses; and where before only the trained choir had sung, Ambrose encouraged the whole congregation to join in, saying that 'Psalms are sweet for every age, and are becoming to both sexes . . . they create a great bond of unity when the whole people raise their voices in one choir.' Ambrose is also supposed to have composed the music and words of a number of hymns, some of which are still sung today. Legend even has it that he and St Augustine composed the *Te Deum* – both words and music – by improvising alternate verses; but this was probably written by Bishop Nicetas of Remesiana, now Niš in Yugoslavia, at around the same time.

It used to be said that St Ambrose established the first four of the modes used in plainchant, which were called Ambrosian modes after him, but nowadays scholars date them rather later. Certainly the application of Greek names to them belongs to a later period of history. These four modes are shown here, together with another version which was attached to each: these latter 'plagal' versions had the same keynote but covered a different range of pitch. Two hymn tunes by Jeremiah Clarke in the English Hymnal could be called plagal melodies in this sense. These are *St Magnus* (No. 147) and *Bishopthorpe* (No. 408); both are in the key of G and come to rest on G at the end, but have a compass from D to the D an octave higher.

EX.5

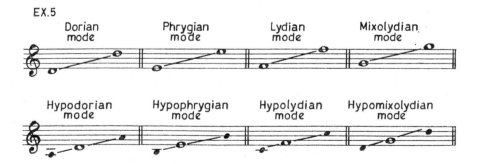

In fact the Greek names used for these modes are confusing, for we simply do not know the exact nature of Greek melodies. Modern books of plainchant use numbers only to identify the modes. But in the meantime the Greek names, though misleading, have become accepted terminology.

Why was plainchant unaccompanied, where the Jewish tradition, with its strong ceremonial element, had been so rich in instrumental colour? Most probably it was because Christianity, in its missionary stage, tried to avoid anything savouring of paganism. Theatre music made full use of instruments, but the nature of the stage action made such performances abhorrent to Christian teachers. St Basil commented, 'There are towns where one can enjoy all sorts of histrionic spectacles from morning to night;' and he added ruefully that, 'We must admit, the more people hear lascivious and pernicious songs, which raise in their souls impure and voluptuous desires, the more they want to hear.' Clement of Alexandria put the objection to the secular associations of instruments another way: 'We do not need the . . . trumpet, drum and flute, which are liked by those who prepare themselves for war.' He also echoed Aristotle's view of music's power over the character: 'It must be banned, this artificial music which injures souls. One must not expose oneself to the powerful influence of exciting and languorous modes, which by the curve of their melodies lead to effeminacy and weakness of will.'

Though common sense prevailed, helped by plentiful and approving references to music in the New Testament, music's place in worship could have been endangered by the austere views of some church leaders. St Augustine was 'inclined to approve of the use of singing in the church, that so by the delights of the ear the weaker minds may be moved to devotion'; yet sometimes he admitted himself to be more moved by the music than by the devotional words to which it was attached. Does music, in fact, distract the mind from worship? Christians did not, and still do not, agree. Fortunately, music had its influential champions, and St Ambrose was not ashamed to exclaim, 'Some claim that I have ensnared the people by the melodies of my hymns – I don't deny it!'

As its name suggests, much early plainchant was simple: one note to a syllable was the general rule. An exception was made for the elaborate runs of notes often sung to the last syllable of 'alleluia'. These runs had a special name, the *jubilus*. St Augustine accepted the *jubilus* on the grounds that it was a praise of God expressing things which words could not express; and his remark must have to some extent opened the way to musicians who were anxious to use their art more freely in church. Church music did in time become more elaborate, but the process was slow; and, as we shall see, the form it took was not so much the re-introduction of instruments into worship, but the growth of polyphony, the simultaneous singing of more than one melody.

Of course, instruments continued to feature in the secular music of this period. In Christian homes, the lyre was permitted, though the *aulos*, which in any case was too loud for ordinary domestic use, did not find a place. No doubt, too, the ancient association of these two instruments with the calm Apollo and the wild Dionysus respectively was one of which churchmen were aware.

The State required a form of pageantry, too, which was unnecessary to the early Christian Church. In Byzantium the organ was often played, and there was a band of wind instruments and cymbals for imperial ceremonies, as well as a choir. The Byzantine court had to impress visiting foreigners, and organs made of gold and silver were reported by travellers.

Though the Eastern Empire flourished, the fall of Rome to the Vandals in 455 meant the end of the Empire in the West. From now on, learning and the preservation of culture in Western Europe were largely in the hands of the Church. The professional musicians continued to make music, of course; many took their instruments with them on the roads of Europe, which were part of Rome's legacy, and became wandering minstrels. Some from the theatres were jugglers and acrobats as well. For about four centuries we lose touch with the music of these itinerant artists. Secular music has left little record. The Church, as well as being the repository of learning, was now the sole international authority; and the continuing story of music is for a while closely bound up with Christianity.

2

THE MIDDLE AGES

Europe after the Romans. Gregorian chant. Sequences and tropes. Notation. Troubadours and trouvères. Minstrels in Germany and Britain. Medieval instruments and musical forms.

EUROPE AFTER THE ROMANS

Though we sometimes think of a disordered, pagan world following the collapse of Imperial Rome, with a few Christian scholars bearing isolated lights of civilisation through the Dark Ages, history is not really so simple. Greek thought had for some time had its effect upon civilised pagans and Christians too; while the Gothic races had received the message of Christianity by the fifth century. It was because the new Europeans were no longer simple tribesmen that they could overcome Rome; and perhaps for the same reason, their Nordic gods began to yield to Christianity. In Britain, Ethelbert, King of Kent, married the Christian daughter of a Frankish king and himself became a Christian in 598. Canterbury was the first great centre of Christianity in England, but almost all the country was converted by 700.

Though the Goths, Franks and Saxons were not savages, it was in the Church that the heritage of traditional learning was mainly preserved. Many Christians in former Roman territories had Latin or Greek as their first language, and young men attended schools of rhetoric which kept up the old methods. Sometimes old ideas were mixed with new, Christian ones. For example, St Augustine wrote on music using the Pythagorean theory of numbers, so that the number seven now stood for a curious mixture of things: the planets, the strings of the lyre, the days of the week, the graces of the Holy Ghost and the notes of the scale.

Learning generally received a new impetus with the foundation of the first monasteries in the sixth century. Monks who had at first lived entirely by their hands later became richer through endowments from wealthy Christians and were thus enabled to devote themselves to study. Cassiodorus, who founded a monastery in Italy in 540, even recommended non-Christian learning. The purpose of this was supposed to be 'to confound pagan philosophy'; but be that as it may, Cassiodorus had a true scholar's curiosity. He was interested in new inventions, and one of his books described an organ worked by bellows: 'A kind of tower of pipes, which is made to produce a loud sound; . . . the player's fingers make the most pleasant and brilliant tones.'

This is the language of a real music-lover, for whom sound is always more important than theories. A more traditional scholar's view was that of Boethius, whose book *De Institutione Musica* is thoroughly scientific. For him, the musician was 'one who measures by reason'. Both he and Cassiodorus served King Theodoric the Ostrogoth in Italy. Their work helped keep alive an interest in music for its own sake and not only as an adjunct to worship.

Theodoric attempted to conserve the best features of the former imperial administration. He struck coins bearing an imperial inscription and was prepared to listen to the advice of the Church. But his death in 526 left Italy without leadership. In due course, however, a new kind of ruler emerged. Gregory the Great, who became Pope in 590, was the spiritual adviser of the West as well as a skilful and powerful statesman. Born in Rome, Gregory no doubt felt a pride in his city and resolved that the best of its older civilisation should continue. He strengthened the Church as an institution; like a prudent man who inherits land, he cultivated new fields and improved, where possible, the old ones.

Church music came into the latter category. Schools of singing already existed in Rome. People had often been given church offices for no other reason than that they possessed good voices, and one of the Pope's first acts was to curb this practice: music for him was to be the servant of worship, but not more than this. His celebrated interest in the art of music may have been due to real enthusiasm, but was also surely at least in part a cautious watch lest it should get out of hand. Whatever his motives, he spent a good deal of time on it. He supervised two singing-schools, one near St Peter's and the other near the church of St John Lateran. He founded an orphanage for the instruction of future choristers and went to hear choir practices. Three hundred years later, the school still had the couch on which he used to sit, and (according to one historian) a strap with which he occasionally threatened the inattentive!

GREGORIAN CHANT

Gregory's great achievement was that of organising church music and giving it a clear role in the liturgy. Plainchant style has already been briefly described in Chapter 1 (page 23). Melodies of this kind had to be provided to go with the different texts used throughout the Christian year; and there had to be a method of Latin singing appropriate for worship. Though Gregory was not the inventor of plainchant, his contribution was great enough for it to acquire his name, Gregorian chant.

His work was also timely: the Church had spread to North Africa as well as Northern Europe, and regional variations in the liturgy, carried too far, could have destroyed the common heritage which helped to unify the Christian world. As it is, plainchant remains to the present day the traditional chant of the Roman Catholic service; and the number of melodies used extends to nearly three thousand. The music of the Mass can be found in the Gradual, a standard liturgical book. To examine it is to recognise the common sense of the Gregorian arrangement. The sections of the service with invariable words, like the *Credo* and *Sanctus*, are provided with many different musical settings; but other parts such as the *Offertorium*, where the words change with the Christian year, have one setting only for each individual text.

Some plainchant texts, like the psalms and gospel readings, come straight from the Bible; while others like the *Kyrie*, *Te Deum* and hymns do not. The way of singing the chants varies: this can be with alternating choirs (antiphonal), alternate solo and choir (responsorial) or simple unison. Some chants have one note to each syllable, but the 'melismatic' kind have runs of notes without change of syllable. The *jubilus* was such a run, or melisma, sung to the last syllable of the word 'alleluia'. Alleluias were replaced, in penitential seasons like Lent, by short groups of psalm verses called tracts. A hint of the future expressive use of minor and major is found in their music: Mode II, with a minor third above the keynote, is used for the sadder texts, but Mode VIII with its corresponding major third goes with *Like as the hart*, the message of Easter hope on Holy Saturday.

The Emperor Charlemagne acknowledged the spiritual rule of Rome, and it was Pope Leo III from whom he received the imperial crown on Christmas Day 800, to mark his responsibility for territories which extended from Northern Spain to present-day Czechoslovakia. Long after Pope Gregory's death, it was still his name that Charlemagne invoked when settling an argument between Italian and French singers at a Roman Easter festival. The Italians accused the French of spoiling the chants, while they in turn, sure of the Emperor's support, insulted the Italians. But Charlemagne gave his compatriots little comfort, and told them to turn to the Italian style, the Gregorian tradition, which they had 'manifestly corrupted'; and he applied to the Pope for singing masters to put things right. One was sent to Metz and another to Soissons, and French musicians were ordered 'to conform in all respects to the Roman manner of performing the church service'. The French found Italian vocal methods difficult, and it was unkindly said that their attempts sounded like the cries of shivering goats. We do not know how far Charlemagne could have been called an educated man in the modern sense of the word, or even if he was himself literate; yet it is certain that this Frankish ruler consciously promoted the revival of intellectual life in Europe.

SEQUENCES AND TROPES

In northern France, England and Germany, musicians invented new ways of using their art in church, though the process was a slow one. One of these ways was to add something to the music and words of plainchant. Perhaps northern singers found the long vocalising of the *jubilus* awkward or un-attractive; at any rate they fitted suitable new words to this music. The result was called a 'sequence'. The next stage was for new music to be provided as well as additional texts. Where ordinary plainchant used one melody repeated with each verse, the new sequences had a much richer form. A single line was followed by a number of verse couplets, each consisting of a different musical phrase plus its repetition; and there was another single line at the end. The structure was thus A, BB, CC, DD, etc., followed by the last line N. Such music as this was obviously more inventive than the earlier plainchant, and it seems appropriate that at this stage in history composers' names begin to appear. It was a German monk, Notker Balbulus of St Gall in Switzerland (died 912), who claimed the invention of sequences.

Notker's colleague in the same Benedictine abbey, the Irish monk Tutilo (died 915), wrote melodies of definite individual character, according to a writer of the time who found them 'very distinguishable' with 'a certain sweetness of their own'. Tutilo is also a leading figure in the early story of additions to the traditional service, all of which are covered by the word 'tropes'. The sequence was the most important of these, but there were others. The short text of the *Kyrie* was often added to, for example; so that the words *Kyrie eleison* ('Lord, have mercy upon us') could become something like 'Lord, Almighty Father, Giver of Light and Life, have mercy upon us'. Sometimes words could be added with the original notes left untouched, while at other times additional music was composed. This *Kyrie* is of the former type, and is shown here in its original and troped forms.

EX. 6

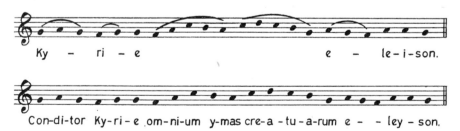

The special importance of the tropes is that they gave rise to what was really a new art form, the church musical drama. A Christmas trope, com-posed by Tutilo, began with the words, 'Who is this Child?', and in it different singers presented a little scene of the Nativity. One Easter trope was actually acted in church during the service. The women come to Christ's tomb, finding it empty, and an angel tells them that Jesus has risen from the dead. The music is of course still plainchant. But it is almost operatic in style; and the upward leap at the words, 'He is not here!' ('*non est hic*') must have been quite startling to the first listeners a thousand years ago.

EX.7

Between the tenth and thirteenth centuries musical plays of this kind became more and more popular, the favourite stories being those of Easter, Christmas and St Nicolas. The clerical actors and producers, and the congregations too, seem to have entered fully into the spirit of the stories. There are accounts of cards and dice right at the altar, and one 'Flight of the Holy Family into Egypt' even featured a pretty girl riding a donkey into church; popular songs, hymns and spoken dialogue jostled one another, and illustrations of the time show faces weeping and roaring with laughter. But almost inevitably, such goings-on brought reproofs from the church authorities. The dramas therefore moved out of church into the open air and became mystery or miracle plays; the local language replaced Latin, and spoken dialogue replaced the music. So ended the church musical drama of the Middle Ages. Yet its blend of drama, music and audience participation was to reappear with Bach's settings of the Passion story, to take an example from the eighteenth century, and with such a work as Britten's *Noye's Fludde* in our own time, this being a setting of the Chester Miracle Play. In India, incidentally, the tradition of enacting religious plays at such festivals as the Birth of Krishna has remained unbroken from early times up to the present day, troupes of travelling actors or students joining with villagers for the purpose.

NOTATION

In the seventh century Isidore, Bishop of Seville, wrote, 'If music is not retained by man's memory, it is lost, since it cannot be written down.' We are so used to seeing written music that we may forget the relatively short history of this skill. The art of writing words goes back to Sumerian times, and the Roman alphabet is, after all, our own. But though we now know that the Greeks had a form of musical notation, the Christian world had to start again from the beginning. In the sixth century Boethius named the notes of the two-octave scale, the recognised range of sounds, after the first fifteen letters of the alphabet; though later it was found easier to use the letters A to G for each octave, as we do now.

It may seem that the first major step towards modern musical notation had now been taken, for all musicians begin by learning the letter-names for the notes. But of course this is not so. We do not write music down in this way. Instead, we use more-or-less circular marks placed on or between five parallel lines called a stave. Their rise and fall on the stave represents the rise and fall of their pitch, thus:

EX. 8

The great advantage of this sytem is that we actually see pitch differences, indeed the whole contour of a melody.

Notation had to be developed. Without it, the plainchant melodies could only be transmitted and preserved through the memory of singers; inevitably these melodies would suffer change, and we know how anxious the Church was to preserve the Gregorian tradition. With the development of tropes, that is new compositions, there was a real danger of the older chants being forgotten or (perhaps worse) changed beyond all recognition. Indeed this very nearly happened; and written music arrived just in time to prevent it.

The first system actually to sketch the rise and fall of a melody used accent marks, similar to those used in the French language. There were three: ´ , ` , ^ ; and they were written above the words of a chant to remind singers that the melody ascended, descended or went up-and-down. In the tenth century, they were still thought of just as memory aids, for singers were after all supposed to know the chants. But something more exact was needed, so additional symbols were next introduced; and a helpful step forward was that of setting these marks, called 'neumes', at definite different heights above the words to show the precise pitch of the notes.

The famous teacher Guido of Arezzo in Italy (995–1050) now invented or perfected a stave system of up to four lines. A red line represented F, and

A blind harpist and other Egyptian musicians. Stone relief from Saqqara of approximately 1340 BC.

This Attic *krater* for mixing wine and water dates from the fifth century
BC and shows on its side the winner of a *kithara* competiton.

a yellow one C, and to show the pitch of other notes extra lines were drawn, not inked but simply scratched on to the parchment. Thus one might draw a yellow C line, a scratched A below, and a red F below that. With only these three lines, by putting marks above, below, between and upon them, a scale of seven consecutive notes could be written,

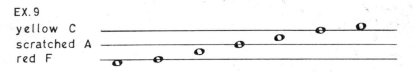

EX. 9
yellow C
scratched A
red F

From now on, progress was easy. In order to move the stave to another range of notes, musicians labelled one line and deduced the others from that. With four lines, a range of nine notes was available, enough for any particular chant melody. Four of these settings of the stave, such as we now call clefs, were sufficient for the whole plainchant repertory: the word 'clef' meant clue, or key.

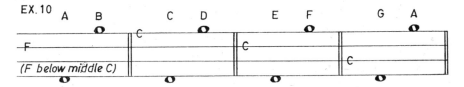

EX. 10   A   B   C   D   E   F   G   A

—F—

(F below middle C)

The old neumes were now, of course, no longer needed. They were replaced by the somewhat square marks still used in today's printed plainchant. The Latin word *punctus*, used for a note, survives as 'point' in 'counterpoint': originally it referred to the process of marking parchment with a needle.

The 'Guidonian Hand' and the hexachord were also Guido of Arezzo's innovations. The 'Hand' was a teaching method which became famous among choirmasters, and Guido claimed proudly that it allowed his choirboys to learn in days music which otherwise would take weeks. The full range of music at that time was twenty notes, from G at the bottom of the modern bass clef to E on the fourth space of the treble clef. Guido named twenty points on his left hand after each of these notes; then with his right forefinger he indicated these notes and his pupils responded by singing them. One has to admit that the positions of the notes seem rather odd, for the scale proceeds upwards in a spiral, but the method evidently worked (*See* Example 11).

Guido's hexachord had nothing to do with chords in the modern sense. It was a six-note scale; and this too was devised as a teaching method for his choir. The hexachord covered the interval of a major sixth, say G to E. Each step in the scale was a whole tone, except for the semitone between the third and fourth notes, B and C. Reference to the modern piano may be helpful here. The white notes of a keyboard instrument illustrate exactly the nature of the church modes; and this is not coincidence, for those modes formed the

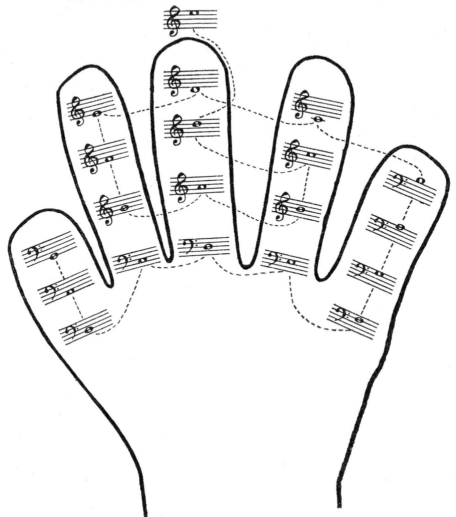

basis of European music. The notes of the octave from A to A are of course not the same as those between G and G, but the *nature* of these two scales is also different, because the sequence of tones and semitones is different. They are in fact Modes II and VII. The white notes of a keyboard allow us to play all the modes. But if we use *only* the white notes, we have to start on the proper note for each particular mode.

Guido used three pitches for singing his hexachord. These started on C, F and G. The pattern of tones and semitones remained the same, the semitone coming between the third and fourth notes. But on the keyboard this is impossible with the F hexachord unless we play the black note B flat. The hexachord opened the way to transposition, the shift of any scale to any pitch. This is only possible where every octave is divisible into twelve semitones, and so on a keyboard we have the five black notes as well as the seven white ones.

For the time being, however, only the note B was recognised as existing in two forms. In the G hexachord it was natural, called 'square B' and written ♮. In the F hexachord it was flat, called 'round B' and written ♭. These symbols are the prototypes of present-day natural and flat signs. An important step forward had been taken. No one would suggest that B flat had never been heard before Guido's time. But its theoretical definition led eventually to the establishment of the chromatic scale, of twelve notes to the octave.

In the tonic sol-fa system used by singers, notes are named not by letters but by their position in a scale; the first three notes of a major scale for example are always called Do, Re and Mi. It was Guido who developed this nomenclature in order to teach the hexachord. There was a plainchant hymn to St John the Baptist, whose first six phrases each began with a different note of the hexachord, in regular ascending order. The Latin syllable beginning each phrase of the text became the name of its note in this six-note scale. This hymn, which could actually be construed as a prayer for good singing, is shown here in both plainchant and modern notation.

EX. 12 A

EX.12 B

35

The fact that the hexachord and 'Guidonian Hand' were teaching aids reminds us that musicians in church aimed now at better standards of performance, worthy of their calling. The Belgian monk Hucbald (about 840–930) noted the skill of 'lyre players and other secular musicians and singers', and admitted that all had not been well in church music: 'We, who have the honour to utter the words of divine majesty, pronounce them without any art and with negligence.' Guido himself remarked that ignorant singers who lacked understanding and learned parrot-fashion were not true musicians. Quite properly, musicians now took a pride in their work, so making possible further developments. 'We should perhaps seek the beauty of art for the saintly things,' said Hucbald.

One obvious gap remained in the field of notation. Why was there no means of showing the length of notes? Without this, it seems impossible to guess their rhythm. In most familiar music notes are of several different lengths in relation to a steady pulse (the beat), and a strong beat occurs at regular intervals marked by bar lines. Rhythm is thus a matter both of duration and of emphasis. It is such a basic element in music that if we sing or play even a series of equal notes it is difficult not to accentuate them in twos or threes. Was there no definite rhythm in plainchant? This would at least explain the absence of a rhythmic notation.

Scholars do not agree. A modern piano student, of course, has to 'count', for long and short notes have to be fitted together; while a conductor's first task is similarly to show the pulse of the music. But no conductor is needed for plainchant, a single line of melody without accompaniment. Even so, we need not and indeed should not say that it lacks rhythm, remembering that the original Greek meaning of the word is simply 'flow'. Many people hold the view that the correct tradition of plainchant singing is best preserved by the Benedictine monks of Solesmes in France, who permit a sort of accentuation 'felt and intimated by tone of voice' with both swells and stresses. No special rhythmic notation is needed, since the Latin words themselves suggest accent, duration and even expression. In other words, the singers shape the melody just enough to avoid a flat and lifeless effect. Some scholars, however, go further and argue that since poetry has had established rhythmic patterns since Greek times a more clearly measured and accented form of singing might have been used at any rate in parts of the Christian world. Here is one scholar's version of the hymn quoted on page 35 'which might well have been sung a thousand years ago'.*

EX. 13 Hymn *Ut queant laxis*
(metrical accentual version)

Ut qué – ant   la – xis   re – so – ná – re   fi – bris

* Alec Harman: *Medieval and Early Renaissance Music*. Barrie & Jenkins, London, 1962.

Mí – ra ge – stó –rum   fá–mu–li tu – ó – rum,   Sól – ve pol–
–lú – ti   lá – bi – i   re – á – tum,   Sán – cte Jo – án – nes.

TROUBADOURS AND TROUVÈRES

The subject of rhythm leads us now away from music in the Church and towards the 'lyre players and other secular musicians and singers' whose skill, though not their 'vanities', earned the admiration of the monk Hucbald. Outside the Church, dance music was certainly rhythmical; and it was provided by minstrels. For in medieval times, as in all others, there were story-telling ballads, dances, work songs and love songs. The tradition of the minstrel, a poet-singer, stemmed from such legendary figures as the Greek Orpheus and the Gael Ossian, and it remained very much alive. Medieval dances and songs have melodic beauty as well as vitality.

The new French 'Roman Empire' of Charlemagne had allied itself firmly with the Christian cause. The First Crusade, which liberated Jerusalem from Moslem occupation in 1099, was led by French lords of France, Italy and recently-conquered England; these holy wars, ending with the Eighth Crusade in 1291, took the French to many lands, including Syria, Tunisia and Egypt. The crusaders' faith, energy and strength of purpose were apparently shared by others, for some of the great Gothic cathedrals and the universities date from this period.

An epoch such as this produced heroes and tales of brave deeds by chivalrous Christian knights. The 'Song of Roland' dates from the late eleventh century and is the oldest and most famous of the narrative poems called *chansons de geste*, 'songs of deeds'. That these poems were songs, and not merely stories, is significant. It was probably felt that spoken words were simply not enough for the telling of heroic deeds. The *chansons de geste* were in verse; and the lines were of equal length, those of the *Chanson de Roland* having ten syllables. There was a short melodic phrase repeated continually, with perhaps some slight variation at the end of a section of the poem, a form in fact similar to that of plainchant. This music may have been only a simple clothing for the words; but it was evidently suitable enough, the text itself being full of action. The only *chanson de geste* melody which survives is four bars long, and must have been sung to lines of eleven syllables.

EX.14

Latin remained the language of the Church, but most secular songs were in the developing European languages. The 'goliard' songs are however an exception, and were written in Latin by wandering students and even young churchmen who first appeared at the end of the tenth century, though the height of their fame came in the twelfth. The subjects of the poems were usually love, gambling or drinking. One boisterous song has these lines, translated here from the Latin:

> In the public house to die
> Is my resolution:
> Let wine to my lips be nigh
> At life's dissolution:
> That will make the angels cry,
> With glad elocution,
> 'Grant this toper, God on high,
> Grace and absolution!'

The *jongleurs* were less educated than the goliards, but they were more professional as musicians. They too were generally wanderers, going from town to town, though occasionally they gained places in noble households. They are known from the ninth century onwards and were the musical descendants of Roman mimes or entertainers: one Latin name for them was *joculator*. The English name, 'juggler', represents only one of their traditional skills; for they played and sang, made use of performing bears or dogs, and were acrobats. These strolling players sang popular folk songs and also the *chansons de geste*. At public occasions like princely weddings and Church councils, they would gather, sometimes in large numbers. By the eleventh century they had organised guilds, with regular meetings (in Lent, their off-season) at which they exchanged songs. The Italian poet Petrarch called them 'people of no great wit, but with amazing memory: very industrious, and impudent beyond measure'. Their social status, in spite of clerical distrust and disapproval, generally improved throughout the Middle Ages.

The social status of the troubadours of southern France, on the other hand, was not open to question; indeed, many of them were knights. Their name meant 'finder', or in other words 'inventor'; for the verb *trobar* in the language of Provence is the same as the modern French *trouver*. Some may have been poets only, whose words were set to music by professional minstrels, while others were no doubt composers as well. The characteristic troubadour poems are about courtly love. The chivalrous knight treated his beloved with the greatest delicacy, singing love songs from beneath her window, or indeed, if he were a crusader, from distant lands. Jauffre Rudel, in the twelfth century, sang of 'She, on whom my heart is set, far away . . . so fair is she, so noble, that I would accept captivity in pagan lands for one glance from her eyes.'

We possess about three hundred troubadour songs. Among the famous names of troubadours are those of William Duke of Aquitaine, Bernard of Ventadour, Marcabru of Gascony and Jauffre Rudel in the twelfth century, and Guiraut de Bornelh and Guiraut Riquier in the thirteenth. The latter, who died in 1292, lived at the end of the troubadour period, for the wars against the Albigenses, a heretical sect of southern France, ended the two centuries of troubadour culture there. Guiraut Riquier was conscious of this and wrote: 'Song should express joy, but sorrow oppresses me; and I have come into the world too late.'

The *trouvères* were the northern French equivalent of the troubadours. Their art dates from the marriage in 1137 of Duke William of Aquitaine's daughter Eleanor to the future King Louis VII. Eleanor was a patron of the troubadours and took Bernard of Ventadour to the North with her. The King of Navarre, Thibaut, was a famous *trouvère* who lived from 1201–53, and over sixty of his songs survive, many being love songs. The legacy of *trouvère* songs that have come down to us, in fact, is more than that of the troubadours, about eight hundred.

The music of these songs may have been derived from plainchant style, which was after all familiar to everyone who went to church. But another more probable theory is that secular music had its own tradition. Because of clerical disapproval, a *jongleur* could not marry in church or take communion, so these minstrels at least were not in constant touch with church music. Some secular music certainly survived from Roman times, and Druidic singing to the harp was reported from fourth-century Gaul. Secular music, unlike plainchant, was often built round the melodic interval of the third. Three of these intervals, plus one note, gave an octave, thus:

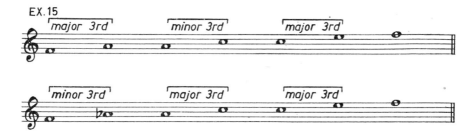

EX. 15

This idea of the 'secular thirds' is worth bearing in mind when we look at the next musical example. But first we should return briefly to rhythm. Troubadour and *trouvère* songs were written down in plainchant notation, which, as we know, does not indicate rhythm. But songs for dancing must have had definite groups of beats; and the same might be true for all songs, provided the natural rhythms of the words were reflected in the music. We know, too, that by the twelfth century even church music used definite rhythmic patterns borrowed from poetry: perhaps this technique was copied from secular music. Knowing these patterns, we can deduce the rhythm of a song from the natural accentuation of the words. In this example, by Thibaut of Navarre, the basic poetic rhythm is a dactyl; the musical equivalent of this is a bar of three beats with the rhythm ♩. ♪ ♩. The melody is also interesting. It is in the 'modern' major scale, not a church mode. The interval of the third is very prominent, more than half the bars having a phrase such as E, F, G or A, G, F. The top note, F, always falls to C. The whole effect is such that we can think in modern terms and regard F as the tonic (keynote) and C as its dominant.

EX. 16

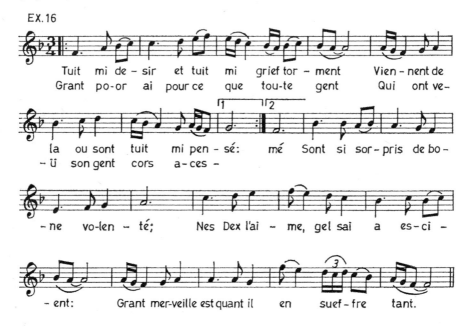

Tuit mi de – sir et tuit mi grief tor – ment Vien – nent de
Grant po-or ai pour ce que tou-te gent Qui ont ve-

la ou sont tuit mi pen – sé: mé Sont si sor-pris de bo –
– ü son gent cors a-ces –

– ne vo-len – té; Nes Dex l'ai – me, gel sai a es-ci –

– ent: Grant mer-veille est quant il en suef – fre tant.

MINSTRELS IN GERMANY AND BRITAIN

The great Italian poet Dante (1265–1321) mentions troubadours in Italy. But in that country poet-musicians were often Franciscan monks, for St Francis himself knew and loved the *chansons de geste*. His followers used plainchant notation to write religious songs of praise, called *laudi*, and earned the name of '*jongleurs* of God'. Troubadour influence also reached Spain and Portugal, but more important, because in some ways more independent, was the work of minstrels in Germany and Britain.

The German *Minnesinger* (the word can be singular or plural) sang of *Minne*, a word meaning chivalrous love. They appeared, under troubadour influence, in the twelfth century. They were often of noble birth, and their songs tend to be more sober and restrained, and sometimes also longer, than those of the French. The greatest of these grave poet-musicians was Walther von der Vogelweide (about 1170–1230), the author of a crusader's song which begins with the words: 'Now at last life begins for me, since my sinful eyes behold the Holy Land.' In his last years he wrote a farewell to 'Madam World':

> Thy caress has deceived me:
> It was so full of sweetness.
> May God grant thee, Lady, a good night:
> Now will I go to the sheltering inn.

A lighter kind of music did exist, however, in Germany. This was provided by the *Gaukler*, a German word for *jongleurs*. They wore red and yellow together, and had colourful nicknames, like *Regenbogen* (Rainbow) and *Saitlein* (Little String). A twelfth-century report tells us that they were expected 'to play the drum, the cymbals and the hurdy-gurdy; to throw small apples and to catch knives; to perform card tricks and to jump through four hoops; to play . . . many other instruments.'

In Britain, Roman occupation forced the Druids to retreat to Wales. They were both learned and musical, and there is a fourth-century Roman account of Druidic singing of heroic tales to the harp. Later Welsh minstrels, or bards, gathered in 517 to make music under the direction of Taliesin, bard to King Urien of Rheged. A similar occasion took place in Conway in 540, and no doubt there were many such meetings, forerunners of the *eisteddfod*. The Angles had come to England in the previous century, and they and the Saxons seem to have accepted the existing bardic tradition. Their own minstrels were called scops and gleemen: scops, the superior order, served noble lords 'with upraised song, loud to the harp'. King Alfred the Great (849-901) himself was a musician of some skill who, the story goes, once entered a Danish camp disguised as a minstrel, to spy out military secrets.

At the Battle of Hastings, Taillefer, a minstrel to William the Conqueror, was in the forefront of the battle, singing the *Chanson de Roland*, but was at once killed by the defending Anglo-Saxons, to whom even such a musical invader was unwelcome. But the local traditions survived the Norman Conquest, and in 1159 Thomas à Becket, on a mission to France, had boy choristers who performed 'English songs after the custom of their country'. The Norman occupation did bring the troubadour style to Britain, though; for Eleanor of Aquitaine married King Henry II in 1152, and brought Bernard of Ventadour to the English court. In spite of church disapproval of 'romances and similar folly', troubadour love songs were preserved at Romsey Abbey. Genuinely English songs of the time are usually religious, both in words and musical style.

Queen Eleanor's son, Richard Coeur de Lion, was a distinguished poet-musician. While captive in a fortress of the Duke of Austria, he composed a song describing himself as 'the wretched prisoner of a powerful foe'. A charming legend tells how his minstrel Blondin de Nesle discovered his whereabouts by going from one fortress to another singing a song known to them both; when the King heard it he replied in song from his prison. The English minstrels, like the French, formed guilds. In due course minstrelsy became such a feature of English life that Edward II issued a decree in 1315 restraining musicians from arriving uninvited at castles and houses and expecting not only food and drink, but 'gyftes' as well.

Music continued to flourish in Wales. A feast held at Cardigan in 1176 featured a contest for harpists, bagpipers and players of the *crwth*, the Welsh lyre. But during the reign of King Edward I (1272–1307) Wales became a subject nation, and no further *eisteddfod* seems to have taken place for a hundred years or so.

From Scotland, instrumental music is reported from the twelfth century. For a journey to London in 1278 King Alexander III brought with him nine musicians, including a harpist and two trumpeters. Scottish minstrels at a royal wedding in 1328 were paid sixty-six pounds, a large sum in those days; but the bridegroom's father was Robert the Bruce, and he was evidently anxious to put on a good show. Since he himself was of Norman origin, no doubt French songs were familiar to his court.

MEDIEVAL INSTRUMENTS AND MUSICAL FORMS

The ancient Greeks knew instrumental music as an independent art: that is, not merely as an accompaniment to voices. In medieval Europe, however, instruments were used mostly in this latter way, and even dancing took place to dance songs.

Plucked string instruments, popular in Charlemagne's time, were joined and in some cases replaced by bowed ones as these developed. For example, the Welsh *crwth* was a small lyre which from the eleventh century was played with a bow as well as plucked. It had a finger-board, which meant that several notes could be played on one string. The slender, pear-shaped rebec was of this same kind, and held to the player's chin like a violin. The commonest *jongleur* instrument was the five-stringed *vièle*, or 'fiddle', which was held upright on the player's lap. Both the rebec and *vièle* were bowed.

The psaltery and dulcimer were both ten-stringed and of triangular shape. The strings of the psaltery were plucked, and those of the dulcimer struck with small hammers, so that these two instruments are prototypes of the harpsichord and the piano. St Dunstan (925–88) was not only the Archbishop of Canterbury but also a keen musician; he played the psaltery, as well as the organ, harp and chime-bells, and he also astonished people with his Aeolian harp, which was designed to play by itself, apparently, as the wind set its strings vibrating – an effect rather like the 'singing' of telegraph wires.

Indeed most of our present-day instruments were by the tenth century established, though in their earlier forms. There were flutes and recorders, shawms with their double reeds, and trumpets and horns. Percussion instruments often appear in medieval pictures; and castanets, cymbals and triangle all bear witness to the vivid colour and rhythm of music in the Middle Ages. Most people were unable to buy rich houses or clothing, or to travel, but they therefore took all the greater pleasure in the more accessible delights of music. Sound must have played a great part in their lives. Being without clocks, they would listen for the church bells signalling the time of day and, with the curfew, the time to retire for the night. They may even have been more sensitive to sounds in general, including music, than people are today.

Instruments could sometimes be made by village craftsmen, as they still are among primitive peoples. But the more complex ones required skill and time, and so were confined to the wealthy. In 757 the Byzantine Emperor sent an organ to Charlemagne's father, Pépin, and organs were made in Germany and Britain in the first half of the following century. They were small, with a range of only one octave, and each note was produced by moving a little lever or slider and thus letting the wind through to the pipe. Much larger instruments were soon built, with Church resources, such as the famous English organ at Winchester, which had forty notes and ten pipes to each note. An account written in the tenth century tells us that seventy men perspired as they worked the bellows, and its writer, a deacon called Wulstan, seems to have suffered! 'Like thunder the iron tones batter the ear . . . everyone stops with his hand his gaping ears . . . The music is heard throughout the town, and the flying tone thereof is gone out over the whole country.' One interesting feature of this description is the fact that two performers played at the same time; and we know from the manuscript called the Winchester Troper that two-part writing was a feature of the music there: this was *organum*, to be discussed in the next chapter. The organ was used not only for accompanying singing but also as the 'merry organ', mentioned in Chaucer and elsewhere, which expressed joy at festivals.

There were also much smaller organs in later medieval times, small enough in some cases to be moved about. There were two kinds: the portative organ was held by the player, who also pumped the wind as with a modern accordion, while the positive organ needed a 'pumper' as well as a player. Sliders, such as the Winchester organ had, gave way to keys in the modern sense which were pressed down; though these were sometimes long and of thick wood. Since fists and elbows had to be used, the Latin phrase *organum pulsare*, 'to strike the organ', meant just what it said.

With the organ, we at last reach the re-introduction of instruments into Christian worship, even though other instruments were not generally approved of for this purpose because of their secular associations. The organ was fortunate, for like church architecture, its development was supported by ecclesiastical finance and prestige. Some of the most cultivated men of the time were in the Church, and now they had a greater opportunity of devoting their inventive talents to music. The organ developed rapidly: in the thirteenth century it had a range of three octaves, and by about 1325 a complete chromatic scale of twelve semitones to the octave was available.

It is not to the Church however, but to secular music, that we owe developments in musical form. Plainchant texts dealt with eternal things and the music had a 'timeless' quality; but this was not true of village dances. The dance songs of the Middle Ages led in time to sets of dances and the modern suite, and these were to embody fundamental principles of structure.

The word 'form' has a particular meaning when applied to music. Just as the different parts of a sculpture are arranged in space, so the different parts of a piece of music are arranged in time. However good a composer's ideas may be, we cannot rearrange them in a different order, for without its structure the piece cannot exist; and indeed for many people the 'form' of, say, a Beethoven sonata is its chief feature and claim to greatness. Yet a medieval musician would not have understood this, unless perhaps dimly in the case of dances. Music was so closely linked to words in the Middle Ages that the idea of it requiring its own independent form was slow to develop; and just as each verse of a poem resembled the next in rhythm and rhyme, so its musical setting, with few exceptions, used the same melody. This form is called strophic, after the Latin word *stropha*, a verse. It is of course a perfectly good one, and is still used by song composers right up to the present day.

There was, however, a small seed of future development that was to grow. Each verse of a song may have had the same melody, but within the tune itself there were different structural possibilities. Musical form depends on repetition and contrast: the first of these gives symmetry or balance and the second gives variety. In medieval dance songs, a leader sang some lines and a chorus the others. Calling one melodic phrase 'a' and a second 'b', a *rondeau* with six-line verses had this form, with the choral lines in capitals: a, A, a, b, A, B. In the eight-line *virelai* there were three melodic phrases: A, B, c, c, a, b, A, B. In this latter case the soloist entered with a new idea like a middle section, so that the music resembles a miniature minuet and trio, a piece built up by the use of contrast as well as repetition.

Instruments and musical form, the subjects of this final section to the present chapter, were one day to forge ahead together in a field of 'pure', non-vocal music. But this was still a long way off, during the Renaissance. Something else happened first: the discovery of polyphony. So far this book has dealt with monophony; for ancient and oriental music, plainchant and secular song all represent melody writing without independent accompaniment. But in the next chapter we come to polyphony, the use of more than one melody at a time.

THE RISE OF POLYPHONY AND THE RENAISSANCE

Harmony and polyphony. Organum. Rhythm and its notation. Polyphonic forms. The Renaissance and the 'New Art'. Burgundy, the Netherlands and Britain.

HARMONY AND POLYPHONY

The composer Grieg used to tell the story of how he discovered harmony for himself at the age of five, sitting at the piano and adding notes together. Eventually he came to the combination G, B, D, F, A: 'My happiness knew no bounds,' he said. This particular chord is called the dominant ninth; and it is just one of many different chords, each with its own character. The study and use of chords is what we call harmony.

Polyphony also involves the sounding together of different notes, but concerns melody instead of chords. In polyphonic (that is, 'many-voiced') music we hear not one melody alone, but two or more sung or played at the same time:

EX.17

From the polyphonic point of view, we have here two simultaneous melodic phrases, an upper and a lower part or 'voice'. From the point of view of harmony, on the other hand, we have three chords belonging to the key of C major, namely the tonic, the dominant and again the tonic.

Nowadays a student of music learns harmony before beginning to study polyphony. But in the history of music this order was reversed. Firstly, melodies were put together. Then, though very gradually indeed, there grew up a sense of chords and their uses. This historical order of events, as it happens, creates problems for a modern listener to early polyphony; and they have become acute in our own time, for early music which was formerly little known has in the last few years reached the concert platform and recording studio.

The attitude of the Church towards music was largely responsible for the way in which it developed. Instruments were, as we have seen, for a long time banned from worship, while plainchant itself positively aimed at simplicity. All the inventiveness of musicians was channelled into melody; and polyphony, when it appeared, was after all only a new way of treating this aspect of music.

Even so, to understand the beginnings of polyphony we must go back very briefly to a harmonic idea, the series of intervals called the octave, perfect fifth, perfect fourth and major third. Two notes an octave apart are so closely related that we even give them the same letter-name. From the most ancient times, men and women singing the same tune together have sung in octaves, and indeed we are not at all conscious of harmony when singing in this way. But with the next interval of the harmonic series, the situation changes. This example shows an upper and a lower voice a perfect fifth apart.

EX.18

Odd though this may sound to modern ears, it is an actual example of folk song from Iceland. Such singing can still be heard at times among untrained singers, for example in church congregations. Mozart, visiting Venice in 1771, heard 'a duet in pure fifths sung by a man and woman in the street without missing a note'.

ORGANUM

Two-part singing of this kind, applied to plainchant, was called *organum*. In the words of the monk Hucbald, this was 'the judicious and harmonious mixture of two tones which, from different sources, meet in one joint sound'. The first full description of *organum* of which we know occurs in a work called *Musica Enchiriadis* written by an unknown ninth- or tenth-century theorist.

The simplest kind of *organum* had a tune in one voice duplicated by another voice a perfect fifth, or a perfect fourth, below. The main part was called the principal voice, the other the organal voice.

EX.19

Principal voice

Organal voice

In four-voice *organum*, octave doublings were used. The principal voice sang the alto part, and the organal voice the tenor; while the bass duplicated the principal voice an octave lower, and the treble the organal voice an octave higher.

EX.20

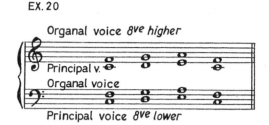

Soon there were other intervals in *organum* besides the octave, fifth and fourth. Here, two voices begin on the same note, the unison. The principal voice then moves up to the interval of a fourth, step by step, and after this the voices continue in fourths but finally come together again on a unison.

EX.21

Principal voice

Organal voice

In the eleventh century, Guido of Arezzo wrote about *organum*, and he made it clear that he preferred a style with as much melodic independence between the voices as possible. These could move in three ways. Oblique motion had one voice remaining on a note while the other moved; contrary motion had the voices going in different directions; and there was also simple parallel motion. The parts were even allowed to cross each other. This eleventh-century example has the principal voice below. The bar lines show the length of the phrases.

EX.22

All this music was in rhythmic unison, note against note. But in the twelfth century a new kind of *organum* appeared. It is usually called 'St Martial *Organum*', after the Abbey of St Martial in south-western France, whose library preserved manuscripts in this style. Here the lower voice sang the words and music of a chant in long, sustained notes; but the upper voice, a solo, had long runs of quicker notes, often twenty or more against one note of the lower part. Sometimes the upper voice sang the same text, sometimes it sang other words.

RHYTHM AND ITS NOTATION

With the appearance of such rhythmically independent parts as those of 'St Martial *Organum*', there was obviously a problem to solve, namely that of keeping the voices in time with each other. The difficulty was much greater where *three* melodic parts were sung together, as in one Spanish pilgrims' song of about 1140. As a thirteenth-century writer put it: 'The notes they had in the old books were excessively ambiguous, because the simple materials were all equal, and they were occupied solely with the intellect, saying: I understand this as a long note, I understand this as a short one.'

By the twelfth century definite rhythms were used in church music, which borrowed six rhythmic patterns from poetry. The simplest of these consisted of a long note followed by a short one half the length of the first: ♩♪. When repeated, this pattern is like modern triple time, or compound duple time; and this twelfth-century music (in modern notation) shows the pattern being quite freely varied.

EX. 23

All six of these rhythmic patterns were arranged so that they could be counted in threes: for example the poetic dactyl, ♩♫, became ♩. ♪ ♩. This meant, for one thing, that it was easy to change from one pattern to another during the course of the music.

But the development of a notation for rhythm was rather slow. Notes were linked together in groups called 'ligatures' which indicated which pattern to adopt. But when this system had been added to in order to accommodate new rhythms, it became so complicated that a memory aid of no less than ten verses about it had to be written for singers! By the thirteenth century, when duple rhythms were used, the rhythmic patterns became outdated. In *The Art of Measurable Music*, Franco of Cologne distinguished four lengths of note: the double long, the long, the breve and the semibreve. The breve was the basic time unit as the crotchet is for us, and so these note-lengths correspond to the modern semibreve, minim, crotchet and quaver. Yet unlike present-day time values, they did not always have the same relation to each other. For example, the long could equal three or two breves, depending on whether it was 'perfect' or 'imperfect'. One other necessary development was

The manuscript of *Sumer is icumen in*, probably dating from the mid-thirteenth century and found at Reading Abbey in England. The notation, in longs, breves and semibreves, shows the rhythm; the key is F major.

Guillaume Dufay and Gilles Binchois with portative organ and harp. From the fifteenth-century French *Champion des Dames* by Martin Lefranc.

'Concert of Angels', by the fifteenth-century Flemish painter Hans Memling, shows (*from left to right*) a psaltery, one-stringed fiddle or *tromba marina*, lute, trumpet and shawm.

that of the rests corresponding to the various note-lengths.

In about 1325 Philippe de Vitry, in a famous book called *The New Art*, described some further developments. Now time signatures showed the rhythmic shape of the music: a circle indicated a measure of three beats, while an upright half-circle indicated two. This latter sign, looking like a C, has come down to us as the signature for 'common time', four crotchets to a bar. There were also shorter notes, the minim and the semiminim. The symbols for note-lengths were, not surprisingly, the forerunners of our own modern ones. They were: ▗ double long, ▜ long, ▬ breve, ◆ semibreve, ♦ minim, and ♪ semiminim.

POLYPHONIC FORMS

The thirteenth century showed quite new currents of thought in Western Europe. The broad, massive solidity of Romanesque art gave way to the Gothic style, and great spires sprang heavenwards as if their stonework were light as flowers. The cathedrals of Gerona in Spain, of Chartres and Notre Dame de Paris, of Canterbury and Salisbury, symbolised both faith and confidence. The troubadours' art flourished; and the new languages replacing Latin emphasised the differing characters of individual nations. The thirteenth century was the time of St Francis of Assisi, of the theologian St Thomas Aquinas, and of the English scientist Roger Bacon. The European universities now came into being and taught theology, the arts, law and medicine; the men of this Gothic period had both inventiveness and individuality, faith in humanity as well as in God.

Music, reflecting the spirit of this age, developed rapidly. Indeed, composers' ideas nearly outstripped the craft of writing them down. Over a period of about two hundred years, musical forms grew more complex and even 'scientific'. During this time, too, sacred and secular music grew very much closer together, so that the same style could serve for a hymn or a love song.

The Parisian cathedral of Notre Dame, and the church which preceded it, had two choirmasters whose names became famous. These were Léonin, called the 'greatest composer of *organum*', and Pérotin, who succeeded him in about 1180 and held office for nearly half a century. Léonin wrote a *Great Book of Organum*, settings of music for the whole church year. Here straightforward plainchant sung by the choir in unison alternated with *organum* for two soloists; some of this *organum* had both solo voices singing in definite rhythm, this being called 'descant' style. A whole section in this style was a *clausula*.

Pérotin wrote *clausulae* for up to four voices. The lowest voice was the 'tenor', while the others were designated *duplum*, *triplum*, and *quadruplum*. The tenor sang in plainchant; but no words were written for the upper voices, who may have followed the tenor text as best they could. But the text itself was by now creating problems. Plainchant melodies were usually short: as the upper voice parts became more and more elaborate, words had to be prolonged to quite unnatural lengths. Allowing the tenor to repeat the chant was only a partial solution.

The obvious way to solve problems posed by the use of traditional chants was to abandon them in favour of free composition. This happened in the *conductus*, a setting of devotional words, often for three voices. These hymns were simpler than the *clausulae*: the voices were rhythmically closer to each other, and there were fewer runs of notes on one syllable. The effect was therefore more chordal. Franco of Cologne advised the composer of a *conductus* to compose the tenor part first, making it as beautiful as he could. After that he was to add the two other parts in turn.

Nevertheless, traditional plainchant remained the basis of polyphony. In a new form called the motet, which succeeded the *clausula*, the tenor still sang plainchant, but the upper voices had their own words, which in church were rhymed commentaries on the plainchant text. This was the starting point for a strange medieval practice, the singing of several texts at the same time, which in its most extreme form could result in a mixture of sacred and secular words in two languages. A motet from Montpellier in the South of France, for example, has a French love song in the upper voice, a Latin hymn in the middle voice, and plainchant in the tenor.

The use of simultaneous texts seems odd to us simply because our ears cannot really take in the meaning of both. But the medieval technique in the motet was to emphasise contrast, not to blend or unify ideas. The upper voice might sing a cheerful love poem in quick notes, while the middle voice had a sadder love poem in long notes. In some tritextual Montpellier motets, one voice has four syllables to a bar, and the others three and two syllables respectively.

Complexity like this puzzles us. Are these motets perhaps among the highest achievements of polyphony? The question is not easy to answer. We can at least define polyphony, the art of combining different melodies; and 'counterpoint' has the same meaning. Two truly independent melodies will not have identical rhythm, any more than they have identical notes. But all must lead to what modern textbooks call 'a result of uniform coherent texture', 'a harmonious texture'. This last point is the crucial one. Even if two good tunes have the same key, time signature and speed, it is very unlikely that they can be heard simultaneously in a way which satisfies our ears. The modern student of counterpoint has first to learn about harmony; because for musicians today polyphony depends on harmony, on the chords formed when melodies are combined, which must be pleasant and meaningful in themselves and also move in ordered sequence.

Scholars remain divided as to the intrinsic, artistic worth of the Gothic motets. By modern standards the harmony may be haphazard and full of clashes. But should we apply modern standards? Another view is that 'One should never think in this case of primitive form and technique; it is all highly rational polyphonic construction.' Let a specific musical example make some points clearer.

EX.24

Here are three phrases of two-part polyphony. The first seems perfectly acceptable to our ears, for each melodic strand moves quite naturally, both in itself and in relation to the other. This is also true of the second phrase, from the point of view of melody; but the harmony now strikes us as un-pleasant, with its clashing E and F. To the medieval musician, however, both phrases might be equally good. The third phrase is the last two bars (upper voices only) of a thirteenth-century motet; and here it is the combined rhythm which is doubtful. The not-quite-similar rhythms of the two parts are almost impossible to grasp, as we find if we try to play the phrase on the piano.

Certain other forms known in the thirteenth century must be mentioned more briefly. The *cantilena* was secular and to one text only, in three voice parts of which the lowest was fairly simple. It was often a dance song, and six examples of *cantilenae* survive which were written by the *trouvère* Adam de la Halle. One is a *rondeau* with a verse of eight lines. With capital letters for choral phrases and small letters for solo ones, the form is A, B, a, A, a, b, A, B. The words begin: 'As long as I live, I shall love only you.' The 'A' phrase is the first five bars, and the 'B' phrase the remaining nine.

EX. 25

The hocket was a form of motet or *conductus* in which a melody could be divided between two voices. The most extreme use of this device had alternate notes sung each in turn; and if the British National Anthem were sung in this way, the second voice would have a text beginning: 'save . . . gra- . . . Queen'! This technique was something of a last straw where Church tolerance was concerned. The singer's 'ridiculous interception of his voice' was unbearable, said Abbot Aelred (*c.* 1109–66) of Rievaulx, the Cistercian abbey in Yorkshire. 'Music defiles the service of religion,' thundered John of Salisbury, Thomas à Becket's friend. Finally Pope John XXII issued a decree in 1324–25: 'They chop up the melodies by hocket, mollify them by descant and *triplum* so that they rush around ceaselessly, intoxicating the ear without calming it, falsify the expression, and disturb devotion instead of evoking it.'

The Pope might have been less distressed about the state of church music had he known of a gentler, more euphonious style which existed in England. It was chordal, even harmonic, and may well have arisen through improvisation of added parts to go with a plainchant melody. If we imagine *organum* technique of the parallel kind with the chant in the middle voice, an upper voice a perfect fourth above, and a lower voice a third below, we arrive at a sequence of three-note chords of the same shape. They are called 'triads', and this particular shape is a 'first inversion'.

EX. 26

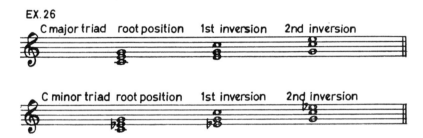

Whether or not the English descant style arose in this way, this thirteenth-century example shows it used more freely than the description above would suggest. The chord of the first inversion is certainly prominent; the other chords are in root position, mostly with the middle note of the triad missing.

EX. 27 *In te Domini speravi*

(In te   Do-mi – ne spe – ra – – – vi

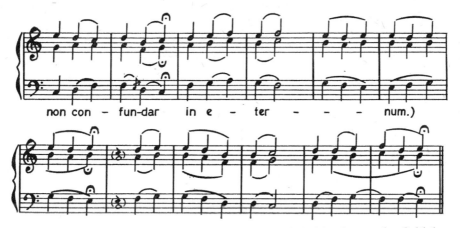

non con – fun–dar in e – ter – – – num.)

The simplicity and ease of this music is paralleled in the secular field by a *rota*, or canon, dating from the thirteenth century, or perhaps the early fourteenth. This is in no less than six polyphonic parts, of which the upper four sing the main tune; it antedates by at least a hundred years any other known examples of six-part polyphony. The effect of this canon, *Sumer is icumen in*, is fresh and dance-like, and the polyphonic skill of the unknown English composer does not seem contrived, but on the contrary delightfully natural.

EX. 28 *Sumer is icumen in*   (The numbers indicate the canonic entries of the four upper parts)

1.
Su-mer is i - cu-men in,   Lhu-de sing cuc-cu,   Grow-eth sed and

4.
bloweth med, And springth the w - de - nu   Sing cuc-cu,   Aw - e bleteth

af- ter lomb, Lhouth - af-ter calve cu   Bul-loc sterteth, bucke verteth

Mu – rie sing cuc–cu   Cuc – cu   Cuc –cu   wel singes thu

cuc– cu   Ne swik thu na–ver nu.   Sing cuc – cu nu

sing cuc – cu   Sing cuc – cu   sing cuc – cu cuc–cu.

Example continued

THE RENAISSANCE AND THE 'NEW ART'

The word 'renaissance' means 're-birth'. But when historians use it for the period following the Middle Ages, they mean something more like a renewal, a re-shaping of human thought and customs; the modern phrase 'a wind of change' is perhaps an apt definition. In music, this wind started to blow gently as early as the fourteenth century. We speak of a 'new art', echoing the title of a book by Philippe de Vitry (1291–1361). This French bishop, composer, musical theorist, poet and diplomat was, according to a contemporary, 'the flower of all the world of musicians'; and the little music of his that survives shows a more harmonic style, a new expressive quality and a breaking away from the harness of the standard rhythmic patterns.

The Gothic world had been one of the infinite, of eternity. Church spires rose to unguessable heights, while church music itself attained a complexity impossible to grasp. Even simple plainchant was an unending song, the voice of the eternal Church raised in continuous prayer. What this age lacked was an art of completion. A cathedral could never be seen all at once; the words and music of a polytextual motet could not be grasped all at once; even a simple song was constantly varied in music and words.

A painting is of course a finished work of art, and it was now that European painting began to stride forward; and indeed in the work of the Florentine artist Giotto (about 1266–1337), it has been said that Christian art speaks for the first time 'in terms of human feeling'. The change in intellectual climate was partly due to a series of catastrophes. The Church itself, the ultimate authority, showed itself weakened. King Philip IV of France defied and insulted the Pope in 1303; six years later a Frenchman became Pope and resided at Avignon instead of Rome, and after 1378 there was the sorry spectacle of rival Popes, each claiming divine office. In 1337 the grim Hundred Years' War broke out, and the English took Calais in 1347; in that same year bubonic plague, the Black Death, came to Europe and killed roughly one quarter of the population. Italy had left the Empire and her cities were in continual conflict, while the Empire itself was riven by civil war. The symbol of triumphant Christendom, the liberated Holy Land, finally fell back completely into pagan hands in 1291. In England John Wycliffe (1320–84) attacked the papacy and asserted the right of every man to examine the Bible for himself.

The moral and social order only survived these disasters through the will of men to live, to grapple with disorder or natural calamity, refusing to accept suffering as the natural order of things. As the plague raged in Avignon, it was the Pope himself who ordered intensive medical research in an attempt to diagnose the cause and halt the epidemic. But the will to defy death was expressed in many ways. In the *Decameron*, Boccaccio described a group of people in plague-stricken Florence joining together to dedicate what might be their last days to pleasure: to love, literature and music. 'Some of them could both play and sing excellently well . . . Dioneo took a lute and Fiammetta a fiddle . . . they sang sundry other songs and danced.'

Fourteenth-century Italy, independent now of the Empire, was full of a new, vigorous spirit. The Italians had never built mysterious Gothic cathedrals with stained-glass windows; nor had they written polyphonic motets. But now, at last, Italian polyphony appeared: and it was simple and sunny, with no rhythmical complexities, mixed texts or plainchant melodies. The commonest type was a canon, a form in which two voices sang the same tune but started at different times. One voice thus always followed the other, and the Italians called this kind of secular song a *caccia* or chase.

The words and music of these *caccie* often bubbled over with brilliant and vivid life. 'Crabs, fresh crabs! Give me crabs for two people! Let's shell them first. I want five! Anna, go and shell them. None for me! Good lemons! Are they really fresh? How much?' In Italy at least, the answer of fourteenth-century men to the problems of life was to assert its positive qualities, to live

55

it to the full and to make the most of every human situation. With this music, melody was all-important. Whereas in earlier polyphony the main tune (plain-chant) had been in the lowest part, in the Italian style the melody was on top, to modern ears its natural place. The lower part or parts were now more in the nature of supporting harmony. 'No one had ever heard such beautiful har-monies, and their hearts were almost broken,' wrote Giovanni da Prato in 1389. He was referring to the music of Francesco Landini (1325–1397), the blind composer who is the most famous of fourteenth-century Italian musi-cians.

The 'new art' in France was less obviously a break with the past. We find its first great exponent in Guillaume de Machaut (about 1300–1377). A priest, poet and composer, Machaut served King John of Bohemia, at whose two courts of Prague and Paris some of the old traditions of chivalry lived on. He wrote songs in the old forms, such as *virelais* and *rondeaux*, which were often love songs. As well as these, he composed twenty-three motets, of which nineteen are in three polyphonic parts and the rest in four.

The new quality in Machaut's music is a certain smoothness and sweet-ness, an increasingly harmonic approach to polyphony. There is also a greater definition of form, of those features which bind the music together and give it a unity of style. One of these features is isorhythm, a development of the older rhythmic patterns; in Machaut's isorhythmic motets phrases are repeated in their rhythm, though not necessarily in their melody notes. A more important unifying feature is the use of a short fragment of melody. This technique provides the structural basis of his Mass for four voices written in about 1364, the earliest known complete polyphonic setting by one com-poser. Because his harmony was normally smoother and more consonant than that of his predecessors, Machaut was able to use discord as a deliberate effect: such clashes occur as the words describe the Crucifixion. This music has expressiveness as well as beauty.

With Machaut's forty-one *ballades*, too, we find a new approach to music. His characteristic texture was that of a solo voice with two instrumental parts underneath forming an accompaniment. His phrases come to definite ends, called cadences, which are the musical equivalent of punctuation marks. These cadences are sometimes simple and sometimes more ornamented. The last example given here is of the ornamental kind, and is taken from one of his *virelais*.

EX. 29

Machaut's 'smooth' harmony is largely due to his use of thirds and sixths: for example the chords C and E, and C and A. Though he was an ingenious craftsman, the actual sound of the music mattered to him as much as its construction. He once sent a new composition to a friend, writing, 'I have listened to it several times and it pleases me very well.' One of his pieces, appropriately called *My End is my Beginning*, is in three polyphonic parts. The lower has the same notes as the upper, in reverse order, while the middle voice has a tune which, on reaching the middle, reverses itself until the end. Yet in listening, one hears only smoothly graceful music; there is no feeling of awkwardness or fussy contrivance. Machaut's watchwords were beauty and feeling, and he once said that without true feeling both words and music were merely false.

BURGUNDY, THE NETHERLANDS AND BRITAIN

We have already seen how English music was flourishing by the fourteenth century; and Chaucer (about 1340–1400) makes many references to music in the *Canterbury Tales*. John Dunstable (about 1385–1453) lived in France in the service of the English Duke of Bedford, who became Regent of France in 1422. This Duke was Henry V's younger brother, and he married the Duke of Burgundy's sister in 1423, remaining in France till his death twelve years later. He lived like a king; and Dunstable was his court composer.

We possess about sixty pieces of music by Dunstable. These include secular songs, settings of the Mass and other religious words; there are twelve motets of which the most famous is *Veni sancte Spiritus* – 'Come, Holy Ghost'. Here Dunstable uses the technique of similar rhythmic phrases (isorhythm) as well as traditional plainchant and free added parts. But for all the technical complexity, the listener's impression is of a natural flow. We may gain some idea of the gracefulness of Dunstable's style from his song to Italian words, *O Rosa Bella*.

EX. 30

57

Dunstable influenced the Burgundian composers Guillaume Dufay (about 1400–1474) and Gilles Binchois (about 1400–1460). A contemporary poem says of them:

> The English guise they wear with grace,
> They follow Dunstable aright,
> And thereby have they learned apace
> To make their music gay and bright.

This is a Frenchman writing, and it is pleasant, because rather rare, to receive a compliment to English music from the other side of the Channel. Dunstable was of course French by adoption, though his noble patron was English and he himself was buried in England.

Reading Chaucer reminds us that the English nobility was still to a large extent French in speech and outlook. Indeed, frontiers themselves changed often enough, and empires rose and fell. Burgundy ruled territories in north-eastern France and what are now the Benelux countries, and though it is now the name only of a French district, in the fifteenth century it was a powerful near-nation and famous for its culture. Duke Philip 'the Good' reigned for nearly fifty years, and maintained at his court at Dijon the most magnificent musical establishment of the time. Charles, his heir, was not only a patron of music but a composer as well.

The Burgundian ducal chapel employed many musicians. At first they came mostly from Paris; but later arrivals tended to come from the Netherlands, though the language of the court was always French. The great number of foreign musicians who visited the court quickly spread the Burgundian style far and wide. It influenced the royal courts of France and England; it reached Germany and even the Papal Chapel in Rome. For we have now come to the period in which noble households took the lead over the Church in developing music. In these circumstances, religious and non-religious music could come closer together; so that as well as his twenty or so chapel musicians, Duke Philip of Burgundy employed players of the trumpet, *vièle*, lute, harp and organ. At this time, too, choirs became larger. In 1416, King Henry V of England employed for the Chapel Royal (the royal musical establishment) over thirty voices, including nine trebles. And while in 1436 the Papal Chapel used only nine voices, later in the century the number rose to twenty-four.

Large choirs brought about an increase in choral polyphony. Previously the full choir had sung only in unison passages, the polyphonic ones being taken by groups of soloists. But the choirmasters of noble households held the most coveted musical posts of their time, and their work was very much under their patrons' eyes – or ears; they had every incentive to produce good results. After all, the brilliant effect of a full choir singing rich polyphony

was entirely appropriate to a court, though it might not have been thought
so in a monastery. Choral polyphony is much more difficult than unison
singing; and since the court musicians set an example to all who heard them,
general standards of performance improved. Various choir schools were
founded at this time, those of Dijon and Lille by Duke Philip of Burgundy
himself.

It was both natural and easy for musicians, and their ideas, to move freely
about Europe. Bitter wars were indeed being fought, yet in some ways
Europe was more unified than it is now. Travel, though slow and uncomfortable, was not restricted. In cultured circles at least foreigners were not
resented, but on the contrary welcomed if they brought new and interesting
ideas with them. During the years 1470–1550 musicians from France and the
Netherlands were to be found working in all the capitals and other great
towns of Europe, from Madrid and London in the west to Warsaw, Budapest
and Riga in the east. Indeed, educated people were internationally-minded:
Chaucer studied French and Italian literature, and Shakespeare was later to
set his plays in many of the countries of the known world, from Denmark to
Cyprus. The general communication and sharing of ideas had its effect on
music. The process was greatly aided by the invention of printing, which
eventually replaced the laborious copying by hand of precious manuscripts.
It was a significant event in the history of music when, in 1476, books of
plainchant were printed in Rome.

Guillaume Dufay (about 1400–1474) was born in what is now Belgium,
and became choirmaster of Cambrai Cathedral in France; as a young man
he had been a member of the Papal Chapel choir and travelled in Italy. In
Dufay's music we can find combined together a sense of harmonic richness
learned from Dunstable, a graceful Italianate sweetness of melody, and a
polished conservatism of form inherited from his French Gothic predecessors.
But whatever the influences, Dufay synthesised them into a style which was
his own; for while all composers grow up against a background, the mature
and original artist expresses himself in a personal way. Dufay's music is often
both gentle and touchingly beautiful. He was greatly admired, and Lorenzo
de' Medici, known as 'the Magnificent', once requested him to set to music
a poem he had written – in fact Lorenzo's sonnet on the death of a famous
musician may refer to Dufay. Though we know little about his personality as a
man, two scraps of information suggest that he loved life and yet had a strong
religious faith. Once before moving house he wrote a regretful musical
farewell to the good wines of the district; and at his death he asked for one
of his motets to be sung which included the words 'have mercy on dying
Dufay'. The harmony in Example 31 would have made good sense to J. S.
Bach, nearly three hundred years later. The C minor chord, which occurs on
the first syllable of *'miserere'*, 'have mercy', is a dramatic piece of word-
painting.

EX. 31

Gilles Binchois of Mons (about 1400–1460) was the chief composer of the Burgundian court at Dijon, where he served from 1430 until his death. He came from a wealthy family, and was a soldier before taking holy orders and devoting his life to music. Though Binchois was a priest, it is for his secular songs, or *chansons*, that he is remembered. Tinged with tender melancholy, they have been described as standing on the threshold between a past era and the modern world.

Four composers of the next two generations were also Burgundian, born in or near what is now Belgium. These were Johannes Ockeghem, Jacob Obrecht, Heinrich Isaac and Josquin des Prés. Ockeghem, called by contemporaries the 'Prince of Music', contributed most to music by his skill in imitative counterpoint, where different voices in a choir sing the same melody, but starting at different times, and thus seem to imitate each other. The technique was not new, but Ockeghem's mastery of it was such that it influenced the whole course of music: it is the basis, for example, of Palestrina's vocal style and Bach's fugues. But the actual effect of Ockeghem's music is usually such that the listener does not perceive its structure; it flows along in a mystical contemplation of heavenly matters, and in this way it looks back to the older Gothic style.

Jacob Obrecht (1452–1505) was closer to the new humanist thought, more warmly spontaneous and fresh in style, for he spent part of his life in Italy. Like many other composers of the time, he used secular melodies as an alternative to plainchant in polyphonic church music: one of his Masses includes about twenty melodies borrowed either from *chansons* or folk tunes. This seems odd to us, but people rarely recognised a popular tune once it was woven into polyphony, and in any case the tunes were regarded as ennobled by their association with religious words.

Heinrich Isaac (about 1450–1517) also lived in Italy, where he served Lorenzo de' Medici, and later he worked for the Emperor Maximilian I in Austria. Writing polyphonic vocal music to French, German, Latin and Italian texts, he was a master of styles from the homely to the most complex, both sacred and secular.

Josquin des Prés (about 1450–1521) was the outstanding composer of his time, and recognised as such. 'He is the master of the notes,' said Martin Luther, and his genius in music was compared with that of Michelangelo in the visual arts. A pupil of Ockeghem, he later worked in Italy; then in middle age he moved to the French royal court, and he finally returned to the Netherlands. Josquin did for harmony what Ockeghem had done for polyphony. For, having mastered the older style of his teacher, he learned in Italy the value of clarity, brightness and brevity. His music is clear in shape, punctuated by cadences (see page 56) which are approached by purposeful progressions of chords. Little by little the church modes were beginning to give way to our modern major and minor scales with their associated harmony.

Josquin and his followers brought a new sense of proportion into the art of music. There are clear paragraphs, each leading to the next within an overall shape which can be perceived by the listener. One idea is balanced against another, either by imitation or by contrast. The method was that of the secular medieval forms described at the end of Chapter 2, but its application to polyphonic music meant a step forward in the development of musical technique.

Besides much church music, Josquin wrote seventy *chansons* and other secular pieces. It was difficult to follow the words in polyphonic music, but in secular music they were important: so he wrote in such a way that although the voices sang different notes, they sang the same words at the same time. The style thus became chordal, harmonic rather than polyphonic; and listeners as well as later composers learned to think in terms of chords and sequences of chords. With the new importance given to words, more trouble was also taken to find a suitable musical setting for them. Medieval composers had not always bothered very much about the natural accentuation of speech. But all this was to be changed: this aspect of the words, and their meaning too, now received their proper due. This new approach was important enough to receive a special name, *musica reservata*; and Josquin, called the 'painter' in music, was recognised as its inventor.

All this brings the music of Josquin into realms whose language is more familiar to us, less remote-sounding, than that of earlier periods. He has been called the first composer 'whose music appeals to our modern sense of the art'. We can see what is meant by this when we look at his lively little song called *The Cricket*, in which the poet describes the insect as an excellent singer who lives on dew alone.

EX. 32　Josquin　*El grillo*

Josquin des Prés was one of Anne Boleyn's favourite composers. In fact the history of music in Britain is often closely tied to the court and even to the names of individual sovereigns. While Dunstable served Henry V's younger brother, the Duke of Bedford, in Burgundy, that king himself is said to have led his victorious soldiers in the *Agincourt Song* of 1415. If this polyphonic song was truly improvised on the spot, the musical culture of the time must have been remarkable. But legends aside, Henry V did have a musical talent which was compared with that of King David in the Bible.

He paid generously for music at his wedding, and when on campaign in France he had trumpeters to play outside his tent. Under him the Chapel Royal grew to a choir of thirty voices, and he founded a choir school at Durham in 1420. He even composed a few sacred pieces, being the otherwise unknown musician 'Roy Henry' whose work appears in a collection called the Old Hall Manuscript. English music was the richer for his reign. In the striking contemporary phrase of King Sigismund of Hungary, this was 'blessed England, full of melody'.

Henry V's son, Henry VI, founded Eton College as well as King's College, Cambridge; the choir at Eton was associated with the Chapel Royal at Windsor and the Eton Choirbook of about 1490 is another famous manuscript. Since 1464 the University of Cambridge had awarded degrees in music, and skilled composers were becoming more numerous: no less than twenty-five are represented in the Choirbook. Most of the music is in five polyphonic parts; but nine-part writing is also to be found, exceptionally, something only possible with large choirs and advanced compositional skill. Usually a whole piece was based on plainchant, but sometimes the writing is quite free.

The composers of the Eton Choirbook include two leading names of the time, William Cornyshe and Robert Fayrfax. Cornyshe (about 1468–1523) was the first musician to hold the post of Choirmaster at Westminster Abbey, and then became a Gentleman (a chorister) of the Chapel Royal, probably a promotion in those days even though it does not sound like one. Eventually he became Master of the Chapel Royal under King Henry VIII. Italian visitors who heard his choir in 1515 thought them 'more divine than human', sounding more like angels than mortals. Both Cornyshe and Fayrfax accompanied the King to his meeting with Francis I of France on the Field of Cloth of Gold in 1520. The talent of Fayrfax was of rather a sober and restrained kind compared to that of Cornyshe, and most of his music was written for the Church. By some he was 'accounted the prime musician of the nation'; and his thoughtful, harmonically smooth music helped to establish a characteristic English style and thus to prepare the way for men like Tallis and Byrd.

Henry VIII himself played the virginals, lute and clavichord as well as the recorder; and he was something of a composer also. It was he who persuaded Cardinal Wolsey to part with his best choirboy for service in the Chapel Royal, much to the satisfaction of Cornyshe, who tactfully complimented Wolsey's choirmaster on his teaching. Perhaps this gifted boy sang in one of the King's 'two goodly masses, every one of them in fyve partes, which were songe oftentymes in hys chapel'.* It was Wolsey who appointed the outstanding young musician John Taverner as a choirmaster to his own

* Hall's Chronicle of the year 1520.

foundation, Christ Church (formerly Cardinal College) in Oxford. However, when Taverner was locked up briefly on religious grounds Wolsey released him on the rather slighting, mitigating plea that he was 'but a musician'.

Yet music and its practitioners were to play their role in the important events of European history which were imminent at this time. The Reformation had a profound effect on many aspects of life in England, and music was not least among these. The rich tradition of sacred music to English words, for example, dates from the sixteenth century and was brought about by political as well as religious developments having nothing to do with the arts as such, but affecting them nonetheless.

4

THE LATE RENAISSANCE

Luther and Calvin. Church music in Britain. Church music in Italy. Instrumental music. The madrigal. The Renaissance spirit.

LUTHER AND CALVIN

The last chapter covered about five hundred years of musical history, but this one deals with only a hundred years or so. This period, the sixteenth century, is a rich one. Old techniques were improved and new ones developed. Polyphony and harmony, vocal and instrumental music, all took great strides forward. This was not because the century was one of peace and affluence; if anything, the opposite is true. But after all, music springs from the minds and hearts of people living their lives to the full. Art is often the product of powerful feeling and even of conflict. The rise of Protestantism was followed by religious wars, but it also gave us the Lutheran chorale and the English anthem; while it is to the Counter-Reformation in its turn that we owe the austere riches of Palestrina's sacred music.

In German lands, the medieval *Minnesinger* were succeeded by the *Meistersinger* of the fifteenth and sixteenth centuries. These latter claimed a musical descent from their famous forerunners, but they were less aristocratic, and Hans Sachs, immortalised by Wagner in *The Mastersingers*, really was a shoemaker. Yet Sachs was no simple rustic: indeed, as well as composing music, he wrote poetry and plays. Such a man was the proud product of the German Renaissance. The printing press was a German invention, and by the beginning of the sixteenth century some nine million printed books existed as against the few thousand manuscripts of former times. As the world's accumulated wisdom became available, learning, and a pride in learning, quickly spread. Hans Sachs (1494–1576) belonged to a new middle class, craftsmen and traders possessing knowledge and self-assurance, often prosperous and proud of their financial integrity. These sturdy people were independent enough to do something quite extraordinary, namely to establish a new kind of Christian worship. Martin Luther, the son of a peasant, was a philosopher and then a monk and choirmaster. In 1517 he called for reforms in the Church's monetary policy, and after three years of bitter argument he was expelled from the Church to become the leader of the Protestant movement.

Hans Sachs was a follower of Luther, and many Protestant hymns derive from *Meistersinger* tunes. They have a character of their own; for since the Lochamer Songbook of 1452, which had both polyphony and solo songs, there had been a distinctive style to German music. This matured and came to have virtues of warmth and solidity which befitted the burgher musicians, and it was admirably suited to the new approach to Christianity. A melody which had had secular words could still be borrowed for a sacred text; and Luther remarked, probably with a chuckle, that he did not see why the Devil should have all the best tunes. Thus *O Innsbruck, I must leave thee* became *O world, I must leave thee*; and the wonderful Passion chorale *O Sacred Head sore wounded* actually uses the melody of a love song. Both of these were to become traditional church melodies, and as such they feature prominently in Bach's Passion music.

It is interesting to compare the style of Lutheran music with the nature of Protestantism itself. Luther translated the Bible into German, for it was in the nature of Protestantism to remove barriers of obscurity which seemed to stand between the faithful and their Saviour. In the same way, the hymns of the Lutheran Church offer humanity and comprehensibility in place of the contemplative and complex polyphony of medieval times. The Renaissance showed that plain speaking need not mean ordinariness or triviality. The Dark Ages were past, and people now looked for enlightenment to be placed within reach of the humblest believer. In this sense at least education itself was a religious movement. The achievement of the Lutheran hymn was that its style could appeal to the simplest listener while remaining dignified, noble and lofty.

This achievement was greater than one might think at first. Reformation could have meant simple reaction: in musical terms, a return to the dignified simplicity of plainchant, unaccompanied unison melody. But these sixteenth-century musicians did something more difficult. They reconciled the techniques of many-voiced music – harmony and polyphony – and placed them at the service of clarity and directness. They created satisfactory chord progressions while still paying heed to the melodic shape of each voice part. They were craftsmen, but they served their fellow citizens as well as their art, for they wished neither to baffle a listener by complexity nor to bore him by monotony. Theirs was the 'art which conceals art', and where advanced techniques were used this was to delight the ear and not to mystify it. Luther thought it wonderful that one could sing a simple tune while other voices enveloped it 'with exultation, playing and leaping around and embellishing it wonderfully through craftsmanship as if they were leading a celestial dance, meeting and embracing each other amiably and cordially'. Brotherhood and good fellowship, a kind of guild of melody: this approach to music was a humanistic one that was also typically and warmly German.

Luther himself was a musician, a composer and a performer on the flute and lute; and he contributed both words and music to Protestant worship, which he liked to be richly ceremonial where possible, with an orchestra as well as an organ and choir. The characteristic hymn was the chorale or 'church song', with a German text and a verse structure like an English hymn. Beginning as a tune which the congregation could all sing together, it became a four-part piece with the melody at the top; there are usually four beats to a bar. Some of these tunes are very fine, and indeed even Catholic churches in Germany used them on occasion. The one on the following page has words and music by Luther himself and is sung in England to the words 'A safe stronghold our God is still'.

Several sets of chorales were published in the second half of the sixteenth century. Towards the end of the century, 'chorale motets' were composed by such men as Hans Leo Hassler (1564–1612), born in the *Meistersinger* town of Nuremberg, and Michael Praetorius (1571–1621). In these, the traditional chorale melodies were used freely as the basis for polyphonic pieces, suitable however only for trained choirs. Hassler studied in Venice, and both he and Praetorius explored the Venetian style of using more than one choral group in alternation. Hassler's Italian training is significant; for in spite of religious divisions, music in Germany did maintain contact with new Italian developments. This was fruitful for the German tradition, which went from strength to strength and indeed led directly to J. S. Bach.

Luther wrote: 'He who despises music, as do all the fanatics, does not please me. Music is a gift of God, not a gift of men. Music drives away the Devil and makes people happy . . . after theology I grant music the highest place and the highest honour.' But he knew well that Protestant extremists saw all art as ungodly vanity, and already in 1524 he warned against 'the opinion that all the arts should be crushed to earth and perish through the Gospel, as some bigoted persons pretend'. Unfortunately Luther's liberal views found little echo in the hearts of those Huguenots who later burned down Orleans Cathedral, or those English Puritans who defaced statues; and the cathedral organist of Zurich was to weep as he saw his magnificent instrument destroyed in the name of religion.

Yet even the extremist reformers were followers of a spiritual leader who regarded music as God's gift, the first among 'things which are proper for recreation and pleasure'. This was John Calvin (1509–64), whose teachings took hold in his native France as well as Switzerland, Holland, Britain and (with the *Mayflower* in 1621) the future United States. Calvin permitted only the singing of biblical texts in church, and those without accompanying harmony, and Calvinist music consists mainly of psalm settings. A complete psalter, with the words put into verse form, appeared towards the end of Calvin's life, with music selected or specially composed by Louis Bourgeois (about 1510–61). The later four-part harmonisations of Claude Goudimel (about 1510–72) remained famous for centuries, and in this form the French

EX.33 *Ein' feste Burg.*

psalter influenced the whole Protestant world. It contains some of the greatest hymn-tunes we know, including the 'Old Hundredth', sung in England to the words 'All people that on earth do dwell'. The melody was originally a Flemish folk-tune; but once a tune was taken up for church use, it was regarded as sacred, and poor Bourgeois was actually briefly imprisoned for daring to alter some melodies without permission. It was Calvin himself who obtained his release; but even so, he removed himself eventually from austere Calvinist Geneva and settled in Paris. France, however, proved unsafe for Protestants, and in 1572 Claude Goudimel was tragically killed there, in a massacre of Huguenots which took place in Lyons.

CHURCH MUSIC IN BRITAIN

The story of religious change in England was a very different one, and when King Henry VIII declared himself head of the Church in 1534 his reasons were political and personal. To the end of Henry's life, Lutherans suffered execution for heresy, while Roman Catholics also died, for treason.

The Reformation in England affected music deeply. Here, as elsewhere, new attitudes to worship called for new styles of composition. The wonderful language of Cranmer's Prayer Book provided fresh English texts for musical setting. The closure of over a thousand religious foundations, many having both choir and organ, put many lay musicians out of work. And although in 1542 a cathedral choirmaster was still required 'to keep Our Lady's Mass and Anthem daily, Jesus's Mass every Friday', the refusal to acknowledge the Pope's supreme authority inevitably opened the doors wide to Protestantism. Much of the monasteries' wealth came the way of the nobility, who thus had a vested interest in anti-papal feeling, while Henry VIII's Chancellor, Thomas Cromwell, openly sympathised with Protestant Germany.

The story of John Taverner (about 1495–1545) reflects the problems of the times he lived in. At the end of the last chapter we noted that in 1528 he fell into disfavour on religious grounds. His Masses, Magnificats and other church music are among the finest to have been written in England at that time. Yet while still a young man, on leaving his Oxford choirmaster's post in 1530, he gave up music and repented 'very much that he had made Songes to Popish Ditties in the time of his blindness'. He became a fanatical reformer and a paid agent of Cromwell; but fortunately his music was not lost, and later some more moderate reformer provided two of his Masses with English words. Life was not more peaceful at the other end of the religious spectrum. The strongly Catholic Richard Sampson (about 1470–1554) was Dean of the Chapel Royal, and as such he was close to King Henry VIII. The King made him Bishop of Chichester, yet that did not save him from being accused of treason and committed to the Tower of London by Cromwell, though he was released upon Cromwell's own downfall.

On the whole, musicians did better for themselves by keeping out of the limelight and avoiding controversy. Even among those who lost their monastery posts, the most talented might find places in a cathedral or even the Chapel Royal. Thus John Byrchley moved from the monastery at Chester to the cathedral there, and as organist had the doubtful privilege of boarding the eight choirboys at a shilling a week each. Yet even cathedrals were not absolutely secure refuges, for in 1552 Protestant feeling temporarily silenced the organ of St Paul's.

A question at issue was the old one which had so much bothered St Augustine long before: how much music was proper for worship? 'The song should not be full of notes, but, as near as may be, for every syllable a note so that it may be sung distinctly and devoutly,' wrote Archbishop Cranmer to King Henry. Cranmer's English liturgy benefitted from the gifts of John Merbecke, who composed 'playne tunes', unison plainchant which is sung to this day in many English churches. But Merbecke's musical reforms did not catch on: choirmasters hardly wished to reduce their carefully trained choirs to unison singing. Harmonised plainchant to English words was more to their taste, and this became what we now call Anglican Chant. Merbecke became disillusioned, condemned music as 'vanity' and gave up composition.

'From Cranmer's time composers were urged to write syllabically (that is a note to a syllable) and with plain chordal progressions rather than counter-point.'* On the other hand, 'The doctrinal requirements of Cranmer could not eradicate from the English composers' imagination the wonders of poly-phony.'† They managed to compromise, to reconcile different methods, by finding a style which could embrace them both. The example opposite shows two passages from the *Lamentations of Jeremiah*, by Thomas Tallis (about 1505–85), who came from an organist's post at Waltham Abbey in Essex to Canterbury Cathedral and, eventually, the Chapel Royal.

The first of these extracts is polyphonic. The five vocal parts enter in turn, using imitative technique, and the interest here is in the interplay of melodic lines. The second is harmonic or chordal. Here one melody, in the upper part, is accompanied by chords shared between the other four, and no one would claim that the first tenor part, for example, is intended as anything more than a participant in these chords.

This beautiful and expressive music deserves closer examination. In the first passage the imitation between the voices is obvious, yet it is still subtle. The voices enter at the irregular interval of five beats. Furthermore, no two of them actually start on the same note, for although they sing the identical phrase of melody, it is at different pitches. This had to be so because of different vocal ranges. But even though the reason was a practical one, the result was a greater freedom of movement between one tonal centre, or

* P. Scholes: article, 'Cathedral Music' in *The Oxford Companion to Music* (9th Edn.)
† P. H. Lang: *Music in Western Civilisation*. J. Dent & Sons Ltd, 1942, p. 281.

EX. 34 A   Tallis *The Lamentation of Jeremiah II*

Example continued

EX. 34 B

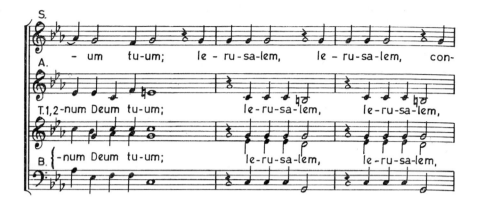

'key', and another. We call this modulation; and the feeling of different keys, each with its keynote (tonic) and its appropriate harmony, took a firm hold on music in Tallis's time, the sixteenth century.

In the eighth bar of the first passage of Example 34 there is a cadence signalling the key of B minor; but the soprano's A sharp immediately changes to A natural, and in the following bar another cadence confirms that we have modulated to F sharp minor. The cadence which clinches modulation is called a perfect cadence, moving from the dominant chord (on the fifth note of the scale) to the tonic (the keychord). Usually this form of cadence contains a note belonging in the new key, but not in the old, like the E sharp in bar nine. In cadences of this kind the seventh note of the scale rises by a semitone to the tonic; and the church modes were altered in these and certain other circumstances, eventually giving way altogether to the major and minor scales. But in the meantime there were some odd dissonances. There was no reason in theory for Tallis to avoid the clash between the E natural (first tenor) and the E sharp with which the alto immediately follows it. In terms of harmony this is uncomfortable and we cannot conceive of Mozart or Beethoven writing it; but as polyphony the writing is quite in order. A time was to come when the claims of harmony were to dominate music, but this had not yet happened. We enjoy the bold clashes of the sixteenth century, which seem especially to occur in English music and often increase its expressiveness. Yet they were not due to any revolutionary tendencies: it is truer to think of them as marking a conjunction of old and new methods, and this was to last well into the following century.

By the middle of the sixteenth century it was generally accepted that Latin *or* English was proper for church use; though in colleges it was Latin that was sung. Tallis, and his fellow composers Christopher Tye and Robert Whyte, chose Latin or English texts as they pleased; and Tye composed a six-part Latin Mass but was also the author of an *Actes of the Apostles* (1553). Tallis's younger pupil and friend William Byrd (1543–1623) even composed music for both the English and the Roman Church, being a steadfast Roman Catholic who nevertheless served the Chapel Royal of the Protestant ruler Queen Elizabeth.

Byrd has been called the greatest figure, after Shakespeare, of the English Renaissance. He wrote Anglican church music in its two main forms, the service and the anthem. The service consisted of settings of the *Venite, Te Deum, Benedictus, Kyrie, Creed, Sanctus, Gloria, Magnificat* and *Nunc Dimittis* – all, of course, in English. It could be 'short' or 'great' according to whether the style was chordal or elaborately polyphonic: Byrd's *Great Service*, with its rich and noble style, is justly famous. The anthem was the English equivalent of the motet: a 'full' anthem was polyphonic and for choir alone, while a 'verse' anthem was sectional, with solo and choral sections accompanied by the organ or a consort of viols, these latter introduced by Byrd himself. His pupil Thomas Morley said that Byrd was 'never without reverence to be named of the musicians'; and another pupil, Thomas Tomkins, called him his 'ancient and reverenced master'. Byrd himself approached the Scriptures with devotion: 'I have found there is such a power hidden away and stored up in those words that – I know not how – to one who meditates on divine things . . . all the most fitting melodies come as it were of themselves, and freely present themselves when the mind is alert and eager.'

Byrd's treatment of discord is freer than that of Tallis. It is also more deliberate, and he once wrote that his printer should not be blamed for 'any jarre or dissonance'! These closing bars of alleluias, from a work of 1605, show the vigour and ease of his melodic imitation; and there is a clash between F natural and F sharp at the final cadence. This is of just the same kind as the Tallis cadence to the first passage on page 72, and in fact it is sometimes called an 'English cadence'.

EX. 35 Byrd *Sacerdotes Domini*

Byrd's greatest successor in the field of church music was his pupil Orlando Gibbons. Gibbons (1583–1625) was among the first English church music composers to set only English texts. His twenty-five verse anthems, for solo and choir with string and/or organ accompaniment, including the famous *This is the record of John*, set the high standard of Chapel Royal music in his time. Gibbons's untimely death at the age of forty-one took place on a journey to Kent with the young King Charles I, and he was buried in Canterbury Cathedral.

CHURCH MUSIC IN ITALY

Adrian Willaert (about 1480–1562) was a Netherlands disciple of Josquin des Prés who made his home in Italy as *maestro di cappella* of St Mark's Cathedral in Venice, holding the post from 1527 till his death and becoming widely renowned. His influence spread through his pupils, one of whom was Andrea Gabrieli, whose own pupil Hassler took the so-called Venetian style to Germany. This style, which lies behind the development of the concerto, was really Willaert's discovery. St Mark's Cathedral had two organs, and he apparently decided to use two choirs opposite each other as well, in order to achieve all kinds of effects of alternation and combination, including contrasts between soft and loud: Italian churches often had a spatial layout which favoured this kind of writing, for instruments as well as voices. Willaert's music proved to be so colourful and expressive that one contemporary listener exclaimed that he never knew what music was until he heard this new 'answering groups' style. This composer was not the last great Netherlander to work in Italy, but he was perhaps the most influential.

The Venetian technique, in the hands of later composers, like Andrea Gabrieli and his nephew Giovanni Gabrieli, became grand and splendid. A Venetian motet might have three, four or even five vocal groups, chosen for particular blends of high and low voices, and of soloists and chorus. The Venetians used instruments freely in church music, and the organ, brass and strings were mixed with voices in a wonderful variety of ways. A work such as Giovanni Gabrieli's *In ecclesiis* was literally stereophonic: its sounds echoed from all sides of the cathedral. Venice was of course independent, powerful and rich, a city-state in which the East and West met, with an eleventh-century Byzantine cathedral, whose music, like its golden mosaics, had to be rich and sumptuous. There were some thirty singers and twenty instrumentalists, chosen with care, and these numbers rose on the numerous festive occasions.

The other great musical centre of Italy was of course Rome. But the artistic character of the Sacred City was more restrained than that of Venice, and the Counter-Reformation of the mid-sixteenth century affected it more. This was partly the consequence of Protestantism, but the movement towards Church reform had begun before Luther, who indeed was part of it: it was directed away from worldliness towards greater spirituality and even mysticism. The composer who above all represents this revived devotional spirit was Palestrina, whose music was later to be described by Wagner as both timeless and spaceless, 'a spiritual revelation throughout'.

Giovanni Pierluigi was born in about 1525 near Rome, in the town of Palestrina, by whose name he is always known; and he died in Rome in 1594. He was organist and choirmaster of his local cathedral at the age of eighteen; and on his Bishop becoming Pope Julius III, he was invited to the Vatican as choirmaster of the Julian Chapel. He spent a happy and prosperous life in Rome, where one of his friends and artistic collaborators was St Philip Neri, at whose oratory there were performed sacred musical plays which later gave us the name of oratorio.

We associate Palestrina with the reforming Council of Trent, which spent from 1545 to 1563 in the dual task of correcting abuses within the Church and reasserting the Church's authority in the face of Protestantism. The complaints which were made about church music included irreverence on the part of choirmen and the use of secular tunes with religious words. Most important of all, the sacred words could not be understood. In a poor choir this might be due to careless pronunciation; but with a good choir it was the fault of over-elaborate polyphony. The Council decreed in 1562 that singing should be used 'not to give empty pleasure to the ear, but in such a way that the words may be clearly understood by all'. This stopped short of a complete ban on polyphonic church music. But some cardinals were nevertheless altogether opposed to polyphony. However, among the music considered was Palestrina's, and polyphony was saved; although the story that by composing the six-part *Mass of Pope Marcellus* Palestrina became the sole saviour of church music is only a legend.

Palestrina habitually used plainchant as the basis for the music of a Mass. But while many of his predecessors had woven elaborate counterpoint *around* a plainchant melody, Palestrina's 'reformed' style makes its polyphony out of the melody itself, broken up into short and recognisable phrases used in imitation between the voices. The music is free of strong dissonance, flowing onward in a way reminiscent of Ockeghem, and was thus somewhat 'old-fashioned' for its time. 'Nothing is noticed as you go along, but at the end of the road you find yourself carried to prodigious heights:' that is how a later composer, Gounod, put it. This is the first phrase of the plainchant melody on which Palestrina based his *Missa Regina Caeli*, followed by the opening of the *Sanctus* in that Mass; each of the four voices enters with the first notes of the chant.

EX. 36 A

Re-gi-na cae-li lae-ta-re, Al-le-lu-ia;

EX. 36 B

(Sanc - -

- tus_____)

Tomás Luis de Victoria (about 1549–1611) and Roland de Lassus (about 1532–94) are also associated with Italy though not Italian, the former by residence and the latter by training. Victoria was born at Avila in Spain, the city of the great Catholic mystic St Teresa, but lived for some years in Rome. He wrote only sacred music, which alternates dramatically between shadow and light like the illumination of the mystic's vision. Lassus, some would say, is greater still. While Palestrina excelled in settings of the Mass, Lassus is the master of the motet, and he seems to sum up the best of two centuries of Flemish culture. He wrote about two thousand compositions, including Masses and motets, Italian madrigals, French *chansons* and German chorales. He knew the Venetian style and composed double-choir works for the Ducal Chapel of Munich, whose music he directed from 1560 until his death. This Netherlander was a true European who spoke every musical language of his time with ease. He is impossible to classify, equally at home in a vulgar Neapolitan part-song and a Mass in 'reformed' style such as Palestrina's.

INSTRUMENTAL MUSIC

At the beginning of the sixteenth century, instruments still occupied a position in music secondary to the human voice. Isaac and Josquin des Prés wrote a few pieces in polyphonic style in which instruments simply replaced voices: in fact these pieces were called *carmina*, a Latin word meaning 'songs'. But instruments could not convey words. Compared to voices they lacked flexibility of sound. Their tuning was in some cases unreliable or at any rate unsuitable for ensembles; they certainly could not blend together as naturally as voices.

In the sixteenth century this situation changed. Families of instruments were made, ranging from treble to bass, which made a well-blended sound. Two such families or 'consorts' were those of the recorders and the viols: some music was indeed designed to be 'apt for voices or viols'. Recorders, viols and voices blended well between the families, too; so that, for example, a viol and a recorder could replace two missing voices in a madrigal, and the term 'broken consort' meant a mixed instrumental group. This discovery of a satisfactory blend of strings, wind and voices had far-reaching effects. By 1607, Monteverdi was able to use an orchestra of about forty players for his opera *Orfeo*.

There were more wind instruments at this time than there are today. The shawm, crumhorn and rackett (whose German name means 'sausage-bassoon') had double reeds, like the modern oboe and bassoon. There were trumpets and trombones, which had a softer tone than their modern counterparts. A treble-range instrument which blended with the trombones was the cornett: this has nothing to do with the modern military-band cornet, but was made of wood or ivory even though it worked like a brass instrument.

The cornett was used also to strengthen the treble line in the Chapels Royal of both England and France; and it was said that 'nothing comes so near, or rather imitates so much, an excellent voice as a cornet pipe'. There was a tenor-range cornett also, while the nearest thing to a bass member of the family was the serpent, made of wood covered with leather in a series of sharp curves.

By the sixteenth century the organ was in all its main features the instrument which we know today. A century before, some large churches had had a second, smaller organ to accompany the choir as well as a 'great' one for impressive solos; and it was then found that two keyboards placed one above the other would function in the same way when connected to different sets of pipes. Some instruments were made with up to three of these 'manuals'.

Certain string instruments also now had a keyboard, each note having its corresponding string, or strings. Those of the harpsichord (called in England the virginals) were plucked, and those of the clavichord struck by small metal 'tangents', or touchers. The clavichord had only a very gentle sound, but the harpsichord's tone was much more powerful. One of 1590 by the Flemish maker Hans Ruckers had five fully chromatic octaves and two keyboards. Such keyboards possessed the short 'black' notes, though without the colour contrast of modern ones. The virginals often stood on a table, in a sort of box or chest, instead of on legs.*

In the home, the chief instrument was the lute. Its strings were tuned to six notes. There were frets, as on a guitar, these being markers under the strings which were felt by the fingers and indicated the position of the notes. The strings were plucked and the tone was sweet and expressive. The lute could play chords as well as melodies, and even some polyphonic music was possible to a really skilled player. John Dowland (1563–1626) was the leading lutenist of his time, and many people thought English lutes the best available.

The viols also had frets, and six strings tuned over two octaves like a guitar's. There were three sizes – treble, tenor and bass – the latter also being called the *viola da gamba*. The tone was more intimate than that of the violin family. The violins themselves appeared at the end of the sixteenth century in a recognisably modern form, but lived alongside the viols for a long time before eventually superseding them, so that as late as about 1720 Bach wrote three sonatas for *viola da gamba*.

New instruments went together with new performing and compositional skills. Yet the idea of writing especially for instruments was still quite a bold one, after the centuries in which music had been tied to words. Without words to provide meaning and continuity, a simple flow of ideas was not enough. Music needed its own kind of architecture to stand unsupported. Various structures were tried out, and the best of them led quickly on to

* This was the instrument which Queen Elizabeth played: almost all English composers of her reign wrote for it.

others which were still more effective and capable of development.

Dances made a good starting point. A Venetian printer called Petrucci brought out collections of these in 1507 and 1508. Two and sometimes three dances (*pavane*, *saltarello* and *piva*) followed one another, making what we should now call a suite. Often a slow dance with two beats in a bar was followed by a quick one with three; the *pavane* and *galliard* in France and the German 'walking dance and leaping dance' were pairs of this kind. Other dances were the *allemande*, *sarabande*, *courante* and *bransle*, called by Shakespeare a 'French brawl'. A keyboard piece of about 1525, by Hugh Aston, is a hornpipe: this dance seems to have been entirely English.

By the end of the century, suites of up to five movements were common. Sometimes they were intended for a group of instruments; but usually they were for a solo lute or harpsichord. The preliminary tuning-up of the lute became a prelude which was itself part of the suite. It was really more 'warming-up' than actually tuning the strings: a few impressive chords and runs were improvised by a skilled player. When such pieces were written down, they were sometimes called preludes or fantasias, and the latter name suggests the flights of fancy in which the player-composer indulged.

Organists at this time, since they played in church, could do little in the field of dance music; and so they contributed in a different way. The practice grew up of allowing the organist, during a service, to play in place of certain sung passages. What he usually did was to improvise counterpoint above plainchant melodies, a technique like that of later chorale preludes. Among the earliest composers of these preludes or voluntaries was John Redford, organist of St Paul's Cathedral from about 1530. Finally, there was the important innovation of variation form, where a melody was played several times, each time with different counterpoint. Into this category fall the *chaconne* and *passacaglia*, both of which were originally dances. The blind Spanish organist Antonio de Cabezón (1510–66) was the first notable variation composer.

The *ricercar* and the *canzona* have Italian names which reflect their country of origin. Both were based on vocal forms and could be solo or ensemble pieces. The former, whose name meant 're-search', a seeking-out of a theme's possibilities, was a piece of learned polyphony in imitative style, and it is easy to see how this technique too led to Bach, who in fact sometimes called complex fugues ricercars. Canzonas were literally songs without words; another name for them was *canzon da sonar*, a song to be played. Their strongly melodic style and their use of contrasting sections allow them to be regarded as forbears of the classical sonata.

The development of melody and of dramatic contrast must have been encouraged by public interest. The organ was after all a public instrument, and great acclaim was to be won by skilled players. When Claudio Merulo (1533–1604), the organist of St Mark's Cathedral in Venice, came to Rome to play at St Peter's the audience was so excited that it had to be restrained from getting crushed. Merulo wrote toccatas with contrasting middle sections which displayed his skilful 'touch', as the name implies. He once even tested his virtuosity in a friendly 'duel of two organs' with Andrea Gabrieli (about 1520–86), his successor at St Mark's. In Gabrieli's own music and that of his nephew and pupil Giovanni Gabrieli (1557–1612) we find a definitely established instrumental style. The great Amsterdam organist Jan Sweelinck (about 1562–1621) was another Andrea Gabrieli pupil, whose Netherlands background and Italian training made him very versatile. Sweelinck delighted audiences with weekday recitals including variations on dances and folk-songs. Skilled in polyphony and also in the sectional use of themes and keys, he has been called the first composer to write fully worked-out organ fugues and he was among the first to compose pedal parts with different notes from those played by the hands. Sweelinck leads to J. S. Bach by a direct link of three generations of pupils, through Scheidemann and Reinken.

John Bull (about 1562–1628) was a friend of Sweelinck. Though, one need hardly say, an Englishman, he was organist of Antwerp Cathedral from 1617. Coming from Queen Elizabeth's Chapel Royal, where he began as a choirboy and ended as organist, he was the subject of the lines:

> The bull by force in field doth raigne:
> But Bull by skill good will doth gayne.

A great virginals player, he contributed to the first printed book of music for the instrument, called *Parthenia* and published in 1612. The later Fitzwilliam Book of about 1620 contains nearly three hundred pieces: among the composers are Byrd, Bull, Gibbons, Tallis, Morley, Giles Farnaby and John Dowland.

As well as the fantasias, dances and preludes in the Fitzwilliam Book, there are several sets of variations which alone would make it historically important. The themes are usually short and song-like, with regular phrases; then follow about six to twenty variations, each of which presents the theme in some new and interesting way. A common scheme was to make the variations more decorative as they progressed, so that with an increasing number of notes to a bar the effect was one of steadily greater brilliance; but the final variation might be in a rather broader style in order to sum up the whole set. This cumulative method has influenced most composers of variations right up to the present day.

THE MADRIGAL

Madrigals flourished in the late sixteenth century in both Italy and England. The name had already been used in the fourteenth century for vocal compositions to secular words such as the two-part madrigals of

Landini. Now in the sixteenth, Willaert and his pupil Cipriano de Rore (1516–65), Netherlanders working in Italy, revived the name and gave the form a more definite character. The music was carefully fitted to every shade of meaning which the text offered: in fact words and music were more closely allied now than they had ever been. Human expression being the main ideal of Renaissance artistic thought, we find vocal music, as well as instrumental music, achieving a new maturity at this time. The madrigal was for a small group of voices, often in four or five parts. Traditionally there was no accompaniment, though the later madrigals of Monteverdi are an exception to this rule.

The Italian madrigal composers vied with one another in the portrayal of complex and extreme emotions. If the poem which was being set to music spoke of dying of love, it was no longer sufficient just to write quiet and solemn music: the music had to portray the full anguish of the unfortunate lover. Composers had to stretch the existing musical vocabulary to heighten its expressive power. They did so mainly by means of chromaticism, a word which comes from the Greek and means the use of 'colour' in the same way as we speak of 'shades of emotion'. In technical terms, chromaticism meant the employment, as a definite feature of the musical style, of the semitones lying between the notes of a scale; thus while the major scale beginning on C reads C, D, E, and so on, the equivalent chromatic scale is C, C sharp, D, D sharp, E. The West Country composer John Daniel was writing in the new convention when he composed this phrase in 1606:

EX. 37

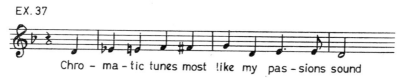

Chro - ma - tic tunes most like my pas - sions sound

The bold use of these 'extra' notes led composers to move very freely out of one key into another; in fact some of them probably saw the key system itself as a mere transitional stage between the old church modes and a new and completely free chromatic language. Carlo Gesualdo (1560–1613) was one of the most adventurous musicians of his time; he was also a man of strong passions who murdered his unfaithful wife. Being a Neapolitan prince, he escaped punishment. He composed a large number of madrigals, as well as some church music, and the daring of his chromatic style is exemplified in the extracts on pages 83 and 84 from the madrigal called *Moro lasso al mio duolo* ('I die, prostrate with grief').

Gesualdo was admired by a great innovator of our own time, Stravinsky, who arranged three of his madrigals as a tribute to 'one of the most personal and most original musicians ever born to my art'. Stravinsky praised his harmonic 'riches' and the way they grew from polyphony: 'His harmony is trained by his part-writing exactly as a vine is trained by a trellis.'

EX. 38 A   Gesualdo *Moro lasso al mio duolo*

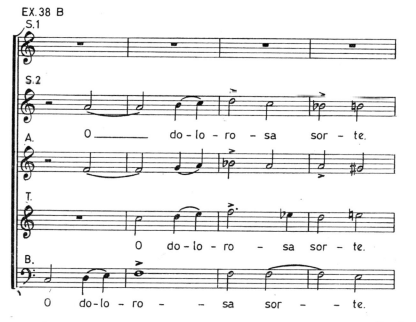

EX. 38 B

Example continued

The outstanding Italian composers of madrigals are Marenzio and Monteverdi. Luca Marenzio (1553–99) probably studied in Rome; he spent most
of his life there, though in his last years he served at the Polish court at
Cracow for a short time, finally returning to Rome to die. According to
Henry Peacham, writing his book *The Compleat Gentleman* in 1622, Marenzio
was small and dark-haired. 'He went into Poland, being in displeasure with
the Pope for overmuch familiaritie with a kinswoman of his . . . but returning,
he found the affection of the Pope so estranged from him, that hereupon he
took a conceipt and died.' One of his last madrigals, *Love's hard Decrees*, is
so sadly expressive that one might well believe Peacham's melancholy story.
It is in the last of his published collections, which together make up over two
hundred madrigals. Marenzio set to music words by the best Italian poets
both past and present: from Dante and Petrarch up to Tasso, whom he may
have known. His command of musical techniques was matched by such skill
in capturing the spirit of a text that he won universal admiration, and his
madrigals appeared in French, German and English editions.

The madrigals of Claudio Monteverdi (1567–1643) are of a rather different
kind. To us, they have a skill and beauty equal to Marenzio's; yet certain of
them, written around the turn of the century, were attacked by the learned
author of a textbook on polyphony, for this scholar, who was anxious to
establish principles, found himself in conflict with a creator looking towards
new artistic ideals. Monteverdi took the criticism seriously and explained
that he aimed to satisfy both the intelligence and the ear, composing 'on the
basis of truth'. His madrigals tend to have a harmonic texture, a tune with
chordal clothing as opposed to equally-important voice parts; and there is a
semi-dramatic interplay of almost conversational phrases. One is reminded
of the innovatory work of Josquin a hundred years before. Indeed an un-

broken line joins these two men from teacher to pupil: Josquin, Jean Mouton, Willaert, Cipriano de Rore, Ingegneri and finally Monteverdi himself. Monteverdi's later madrigals are accompanied vocal pieces. The new features of Monteverdi's style really belong to the baroque period, of which he was the first great master; and since this is the subject of the next two chapters, we may leave Italy for the time being and turn elsewhere.

In France, sixteenth-century *chansons* were much like madrigals; though there is a difference, since these French pieces avoid serious and solemn words and aim at refinement and delicate charm. The *Dictionnaire Larousse* characterises the madrigal as 'refined, tender, gallant', a description which would much restrict the dramatic range of the Italians. Perhaps the most important French 'madrigalist' was Josquin's pupil Clément Jannequin (about 1475–1560). He made a speciality of 'programme music' and composed four-part vocal pieces with titles like *The Hunt* and *The Battle*, as well as *The Calls of Birds* and *Hear the cries of Paris*; and these are so vivid and picturesque that they look forward to the new form, as yet unborn, of opera. But Jannequin's last words were settings of psalms and proverbs, for Calvinist influence was now strong in France, and after him little more madrigal-type music was composed there.

In Spain, a number of madrigals were written from about 1560 onwards, though Victoria wrote none. Germany has one important madrigalist, Hans Leo Hassler, who studied in Italy and wrote madrigals both to Italian texts and to his own German words.

It is to England that we must turn to find madrigal composition which not only compares in every way with the work of the Italians, but possibly surpasses it. Madrigals by Willaert and Lassus were sung there in the 1560s; Thomas Tallis composed one called *Fond love is a bubble*. There was a long English tradition of polyphonic music stretching back to *Sumer is icumen in*; one Italian madrigal composer, Alfonso Ferrabosco, lived in England and became a friend of William Byrd; and English musicians of Shakespeare's time could hardly be indifferent to poetry. It is not surprising that the madrigal took root in this country and flourished brilliantly and abundantly for about twenty years. This period began in 1588, when a volume called *Musica Transalpina* was published containing fifty-five madrigals by Italian composers, with texts translated into English. Significantly, it also contained two by Byrd. In the following year Byrd himself published some madrigals in his *Songes of Sundrie Natures* and in 1593 came Thomas Morley's *Canzonets to Three Voyces*.

Morley (about 1557–1603) was Byrd's pupil and almost certainly acquainted with Shakespeare, for whose plays he composed songs. He is probably the best-known and most attractive of all the English madrigalists, and his *Plaine and Easie Introduction to Practicall Musicke* (1597) is full of useful advice, delightfully expressed. For example, the would-be composer is reminded of the principles of word-painting: if the text refers to 'descending' it is ridiculous to let the music rise, and vice versa. And there is a little parable of a gentleman covered with confusion when, as a guest, he is asked to sing and has to confess he knows nothing about music – a story calculated to make any musically ignorant reader hasten to improve his knowledge. A few titles of Morley madrigals will give a fair idea of their subject matter: *Lady, those eyes, Say, dear, will you not have me?, Clorinda false, Blow, shepherds, blow, Springtime mantleth every bough, Those dainty daffadillies.* In other words, the two main subjects are love and nature – sometimes both at once, as in *April is in my mistress' face.*

Thomas Weelkes and John Wilbye are the most important madrigalists of the generation after Morley, being in their twenties at the turn of the century. Orlando Gibbons, a few years younger, wrote nobly serious madrigals: among these are *What is our life?* and *The silver swan,* which ends with the sad comment that 'More geese than swans now live, more fools than wise'. Gibbons also composed two *Cries of London* – not precisely madrigals, perhaps – for voices and strings; he might well have known Jannequin's similar piece on Parisian street calls. These are beautiful and fascinating tapestries, loosely woven and of very varied words and music: the second of them begins with the phrase 'A good sausage it is'! This organist of Westminster Abbey obviously loved his city.

The most famous collection of English madrigals, *The Triumphs of Oriana,* was published in 1601. Thomas Morley was its editor, and apart from an extra one by himself each madrigal was by a different composer. There were twenty-five composers in all, and the fact that there are no weak members of the team bears witness to the high standard of English composition. The collection was modelled on a similar Venetian book of 1592, and one composer (the only foreigner) is actually represented in both by the same madrigal in translation, this being the Venetian Giovanni Croce (about 1557–1609), who with Marenzio was especially admired by Morley. 'Oriana' was a poetic name for Queen Elizabeth, in whose honour the book was published, and each madrigal ends with the same couplet:

Then sang the shepherds and nymphs of Diana:
Long live fair Oriana.

Thomas Weelkes (about 1575–1623) wrote the madrigal which is probably the best known in the 'Oriana' book, the six-part *As Vesta was from Latmos hill descending.* The word-painting here is very detailed. 'First two by two, then three by three, together' is set to music so that two voice parts, three voice parts and finally the whole consort of singers take the appropriate words; and the last two words of 'Leaving their goddess all alone' are given to one voice part only. Of course there would be no virtue in this use of musical metaphor if the effect sounded merely contrived, but here it is both charming and natural. Though Weelkes excelled in the portrayal of pastoral scenes with nymphs and shepherds, he was also a master of intense musical expression – which meant the use of chromaticism and very free modulation; he and John Wilbye were the boldest of their generation in this respect. The opening bars of Weelkes' *O care, thou wilt despatch*, written in 1600, are often quoted; the music begins on G and then moves within seven bars (and basically seven chords only) to B minor, via C minor and A major. Each key is established according to the rules of modulation (see the remarks on page 74) but it serves only as a starting point for a new change.* Even to ears accustomed to more modern music, this has a very restless quality.

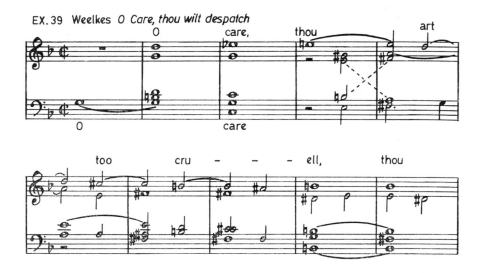

EX. 39 Weelkes *O Care, thou wilt despatch*

But Weelkes did not rely only on chromaticism and modulation to achieve expressive effects. In *Death hath deprived me*, written in memory of his friend Morley, the second half of the example on page 88 has a straightforward sequence of chords. Though the opening chord of D major plunges abruptly and poignantly towards B flat ('is dead'), the return to the final chord, again D major, is gentle and even resigned. The smooth sound of the full consort contrasts with the sharper, more plaintive tone of the upper voices used alone at the beginning; and the two bass parts, very low and in thick, close harmony, convey a feeling of darkness. How much more subtle it is to have a descent

* The simple sounding of a chord cannot establish a key, for to do this all seven notes of the new scale have to be heard or at least implied. The major triad on F – F, A and C – could be part of a passage in F major, C major, A minor and other keys besides. But when it is preceded by F major's dominant chord, the major triad on C, plus the note B flat which makes the so-called dominant seventh, that F major triad will be clearly established as the key-chord. The E in bar 7 is a seventh of this kind.

into the grave 'painted' not by the conventional upper part, whose brighter sound Weelkes decides to silence, but by the lowest voice, which sinks through six notes of the scale to the final D. One also notices the repetitions of certain words: 'is dead' and 'in grave' (first bass and the two middle parts). And the way 'dead' is heard in different voices on successive beats (bars 4–5) seems to suggest the tolling of a funeral bell.

EX. 40

When they remember how much the madrigal in England owes to its Italian originators, English musicians often feel guilty about lavishing praise on it and think that patriotic pride has carried them away. So it may be worth quoting a German scholar, Alfred Einstein, who spent forty years writing a three-volume book on the Italian madrigal composers. 'It would be a mistake to regard the English madrigal as a mere imitation of its Italian forbear . . . we find a more personal spirit, a more robust and more natural emotion, not to mention a greater certainty, instinctively acquired, in the handling of harmony and rhythm.'

We note Einstein's reference to 'harmony', the use of chords and keys. But we may also ask, why are the 'personal spirit' and 'more natural emotion' qualities especially to be admired? After all, a work of art is not natural but artificial, a word whose meaning the dictionary gives as 'made by art'. Do we really want anything 'personal' in a cathedral, say, or in Beethoven's Ninth Symphony, in which the composer aimed to speak for all mankind? The answer given by men of the Renaissance was 'yes': what an individual man had to say must be fully human, and fully personal. With the Renaissance, and subsequently too, it is individual expression that counts: the unknown craftsmen of medieval times have no place in the modern world.

So, with the Renaissance, great individual names appear in the arts. But it seems that in this respect music lagged behind, although one would not wish to exaggerate this. However, while names like those of Michelangelo and Shakespeare already stand out at the point in history which we have reached, the earliest musician of comparable popular fame, Bach, lived over a century after Shakespeare and longer still after Michelangelo.

Did music 'miss the boat' at the start of the Renaissance? The first truly Renaissance music had been the Italian *caccie* – the 'catches' of the fourteenth century, brilliant and strongly melodic pieces with plenty of human interest, which indeed sounded a new note. And yet though the old polyphonic complexities were from now on tempered, polyphony was still far too new to be abandoned, for developments were still going on which were to lead to the all-important mastery of harmony. That things moved slowly must be admitted. The approach to music as a kind of science still survived in many quarters: the medieval idea of eternal truth as opposed to the Renaissance one of human expression. To put it crudely, the cleverest music was the best according to that way of reckoning. Another problem was that of form. Music could be built upwards in a towering polyphonic structure – and indeed the fact that 'bass' and 'base' are the same word makes us think of architecture. But the idea of a structure spaced out in time, which the trained ear can grasp as it passes, was slow to develop; composers wishing to demonstrate their skill built up instead large structures of dense polyphony. Tallis's motet with forty vocal parts, though shorter in length, contains more notes than many a symphonic movement.

This would not have been so, perhaps, if everyone had known the music of Josquin des Prés. It is he who was called in his lifetime the Michelangelo of music and in ours the first whose music appeals to our modern sense of the art. Josquin had indeed been a clarifier, and yet he was an innovator too. Martin Luther, himself a sweeper-aside of obscurities who preferred enlightenment to mystification, knew exactly the compliment he was paying when he said that Josquin was 'master of the notes; others are mastered by them'.

Though there was recognition of Josquin's genius, its nature seems to have been misunderstood. His ideas, handed down in an unbroken line from teacher to pupil, eventually reappeared in the 'harmonic' madrigals of Monteverdi. The opposition which they still encountered after a century was serious enough for Monteverdi to feel obliged to justify himself, for his critics recognised that if his ideas were generally adopted, the whole art of music as they understood it was in danger. Polyphony was for them the supreme mode of musical thought; but their music was a private art and was inevitably to yield before the demands of the new humanism. The earlier madrigals, in Professor Dent's words, 'were written more for the pleasure of the singers than for that of an audience'; Monteverdi, on the other hand, used his singers to convey a personal utterance to a listener. The madrigal era marked the end of a period of history. Just in time, music had caught up with the rest of Renaissance thought. Often thought of as the purest of the arts, it was actually the last to shake off the impersonality of the medieval world. Having done so, it found itself suddenly upon the threshold of a new era: the uneasily mature world of the baroque.

5

THE SEVENTEENTH CENTURY

Baroque style. Italian opera and oratorio. France and Germany. England. Techniques, instruments and forms.

BAROQUE STYLE

The word 'baroque' probably comes from a Portuguese word '*barocco*', meaning a misshapen pearl, and it can still mean something like 'irregular'. The reason for its appearance in music seems to have been that it was used to describe an ornamented style in Italian art found from about 1600 onwards, and it then (though only quite recently) came to be applied to the period generally as a convenient label. The baroque period begins with the seventeenth century and the appearance of opera, and it ends with Bach and Handel. When Handel died in 1759, Haydn as a young man in his twenties was already composing string quartets whose style belongs to a later era, that of classicism.

The baroque era was in many ways an unsettled one. The liberating ideas of the Renaissance had brought about the breakdown of many forces which had held society together, and the religious division of Europe proved to be permanent. Troubled churchmen reacted with severity; and thus the baroque period began with the burning in 1600 of the Italian philosopher Giordano Bruno, condemned as a heretic. Though to suppress knowledge is surely wrong, we too today are sceptical of the optimistic and humanistic doctrine of the Enlightenment – that the replacement of ignorance by knowledge made for a better world. But this belief was passionately held, in conflict with the Church, and the philosopher Descartes (1596–1650) went so far as to claim that to find truth men must rid themselves of received doctrines and begin the search afresh.

The dramatic tensions and contrasts of this period were reflected in various ways, in music as elsewhere. Ultra-conservative Spain nipped Protestantism in the bud with sentences and executions carried out after judgment by the Inquisition and beginning in 1559 at Valladolid; this town was not far from Avila, whence the composer Victoria went to Rome in 1565, and Victoria's music often seems to us intense and even anguished. It has been said that 'The man of the Baroque loves unrest and tension and the overwhelmingly pathetic . . . he wants to present us with drama.'* Handel knew how to achieve the kind of musical drama which Beethoven later admiringly called 'great effects': thus in *Messiah* the grandeur of 'Glory to God in the highest' is immediately followed by the quiet of 'and peace on earth'. Another baroque master, Monteverdi, wrote: 'Contrasts are what move our souls, and such is the aim of all good music.'

Roger North, an English writer who was James II's Attorney General as well as an amateur musician, expressed a generally held view when he wrote that music's two aims were 'first to please the sense, and that is done by the pure Dulcor of Harmony, which is found chiefly in the elder music . . . and secondly to move the affections or excite passion.' The German composer and theorist Heinichen went further and blamed his forbears for 'exaggerated metaphysical contemplation', claiming that all that mattered was 'how the music sounds and how the listeners like it'.

As a matter of fact, there was a good deal of practical sense in a view of this kind. With increasing education and the growth of the comfortably-off merchant class, there now appeared a public which was prepared to pay for music. There were numerous music clubs or societies founded in the seventeenth century in most countries; and since people were spending their money on music, their tastes naturally had to be taken into account. In Italy, this new audience was first and foremost an operatic one. It was in wealthy Venice that the first public opera house, the Teatro di San Cassiano, opened in 1637. In the same city, eleven new theatres opened during the remainder of the century, and the total of operas performed there came to three hundred and fifty-eight. This most dramatic and spectacular form was one which characterised the baroque spirit.

ITALIAN OPERA AND ORATORIO

The Renaissance made Western Europeans passionately enthusiastic about antique art. Buildings like St Paul's Cathedral in London and St Peter's in Rome represented a deliberate attempt to revive ancient styles. The French dramatists Corneille and Racine drew on antiquity for their plots and even observed rules of construction which had been formulated by Aristotle. Yet while in architecture and literature actual examples of antique styles were common, these were virtually non-existent in music. There was speculation about the nature of ancient music; and an Italian called Nicola Vicentino wrote a book on the subject and composed some madrigals demonstrating his theories – though these were polyphonic and written out, whereas we now know that ancient music had no polyphony and was improvised.

Vincenzo Galilei, the father of Galileo the astronomer, was one of a

* P. H. Lang: *Music in Western Civilisation.*

society of artists and intellectuals who met at the Bardi Palace in Florence to discuss a possible revival of the methods of the Greek theatre, with its vital but tantalisingly mysterious musical element. What finally emerged from their speculations was what we now call accompanied recitative. This is a musical style nearer to speech than conventional singing, and thus more direct in its expression of feelings. Galilei's first attempt at this form of writing was a setting of words by Dante to the accompaniment of a viol, which he himself performed.

Giulio Caccini (about 1550–1618), though thirty years younger than Galilei, was a member of the same Florentine group, and he too composed recitatives which he sang to his own lute accompaniment. His aim, he said, was 'A sort of music in which a noble restraint was placed on singing (in the strict sense) in favour of the words.' The accompaniment was entirely chordal – and thus harmonic rather than polyphonic – and it was indicated only by the lowest note of each chord, marked with figures indicating the kind of chord to use. Another member of this society (called the *Camerata* or 'fellowship') was Jacopo Peri (1561–1633); he too, like Caccini, was a singer and lutenist as well as a composer.

The *Camerata* believed that Greek drama had been sung throughout, and their first 'musical drama' in 1597 was of this kind, the music being mainly by Peri and the words by Ottavio Rinuccini, a nobleman and poet. It was called *Dafne*, and in this classical pastoral Peri himself, who had long blond hair, played the part of Apollo. The success of *Dafne* was so great that a new opera was quickly commissioned for performance at a royal wedding, that of King Henry IV of France and the Florentine Maria de' Medici. *Euridice*, the first opera whose music survives complete to the present day, was performed in Florence on October 6th 1600. The story chosen was again a classical one: drawing on antiquity for opera plots became a universal practice.* *Euridice*, in which Peri and Caccini collaborated, was like its predecessor *Dafne* remarkably successful. It was no coincidence that Orpheus, played originally by Peri, was a wonderful singer, for this feature of the story made it good propaganda for the new operatic style.

In a preface to *Euridice*, Peri declared that he aimed at a musical rendering of speech, with all its shades of emotion; and the singer's note and accompanying harmony might only change when the meaning of the text justified this. These were revolutionary views, for not only polyphony but melody itself seemed reduced to a subordinate role. But for better or worse, this was the new recitative style, the *stile rappresentativo*. In fact the musical interest of Peri's work is pretty slight, and one feels that it must have been the novelty of the whole thing, as well as the excellence of the singing and production, which made *Euridice* such a triumph.

* It even survives today in works such as Milhaud's *Medea* and Orff's *Antigone*.

The first great opera composer was Claudio Monteverdi (1567–1643). The sheer expressiveness of his style may be exemplified by a passage from his *Lettera amorosa* or 'Love letter'. This song for soprano with accompaniment is in recitative style and 'to be sung without any beat', in other words with great rhythmic freedom. At first the harmony does not change and the voice hardly leaves the note B; then a brief excursion to new harmony and melody notes comes as the beloved one is addressed, the trill even suggesting a voice trembling with emotion.

EX. 41   Monteverdi

Monteverdi's first opera was *Orfeo* (1607), in five acts and, as the name suggests, similar in story to Peri's *Euridice*, though musically of far greater stature. The emotions expressed in the text are strongly brought out in the music; and, more important, the lightly-accompanied recitative is varied with true songs (arias), duets and madrigal-like choruses. Also, while Peri gave his small ensemble of seven players only a few bars of independent music, Monteverdi's forty or so musicians played a prelude and numerous interludes. They were not precisely an 'orchestra', in that various instrumental groups were used in turn for scenes of differing character – pastoral, Stygian and so on – but the imagination of the instrumental writing marked a major step forward towards a true opera orchestra.

The stage works Monteverdi wrote after *Orfeo* have unfortunately been largely lost. But *The Return of Ulysses* (1641) and *The Coronation of Poppea* (1642), despite his advanced age when he composed them, are masterly and of striking beauty. The final love duet between Nero and Poppea, though these two persons have been quite unscrupulous in achieving their wedded bliss, provides a suavely charming ending to a work which is surprisingly modern in its reliance on psychological interest rather than spectacle.

Oratorio developed from operas using religious subjects. *The Representation of Soul and Body*, by Emilio de' Cavalieri, a former member of the

Florentine *Camerata*, was not so much an opera, however, as a morality play set to music. *Saint Alessio*, by Stefano Landi, was given in Rome in 1632, and contained dances and comic scenes although dealing with a sacred subject. The established form of oratorio appeared with Giacomo Carissimi (1605–74). It is a setting of a sacred story for performance in a church or concert hall, rather than a theatre, for solo voices, chorus and orchestra, and though individual singers take dramatic roles there is no stage action. A narrator sometimes links the events of the plot, and the chorus also comments on the action or indeed participates in it – in Carissimi it can represent victorious Israelites, guests at Belshazzar's feast or sailors on board Jonah's ship. Carissimi's best-known oratorio is *Jephtha*. Vigorous six-part choruses such as we find here were important in giving oratorio its own particular style, and this composer's influence – as well as his mastery – may be judged from the fact that Handel, a century later, borrowed whole scenes from him with success.

In a sense, the antique solemnity of the early Florentine operas gave them a certain sacred character, and in fact comedy was banned from opera in Florence. This was not, however, the case in Rome. The librettist of Landi's *Saint Alessio*, with its comic scenes, was in fact Cardinal Rospigliosi, who later became Pope Clement IX.* He was also the librettist of the first comic opera as such, a three-act work called *Chi soffre, speri* ('He who suffers, hopes') with music by a pair of composers called Mazzocchi and Marazzoli; at its premiere in the Barberini Theatre in 1639 the audience included Cardinal Mazarin and an English visitor, John Milton. The same Cardinal Rospigliosi was the librettist of *Dal male il bene*, or 'From evil comes good' (Rome, 1653), which again had music by two composers, Marazzoli and Abbatini. The first and third acts, by Abbatini, had ensemble finales in which all on stage participated; and this feature, along with the clear distinction between recitative and aria, and the spirit of sharp-witted but good-natured mockery and fun, clearly set the style of Italian comic opera or *opera buffa*, such as we still recognise in much later works like Mozart's *Marriage of Figaro* and Rossini's *Barber of Seville*.

In Venice, where Monteverdi was *maestro di cappella* of St Mark's from 1613, it was the new public opera house of San Cassiano which housed the première of his *Return of Ulysses* in 1641. One of Monteverdi's singers in the cathedral choir, who gradually rose to become organist and eventually choirmaster, was Pietro Francesco Cavalli (1602–76). Cavalli composed forty-two operas during the thirty years following his first, *The Marriage of Teti and Peleo*, given in the San Cassiano in 1639. The great majority of these were performed in Venice; and *La Calisto* (1651), a sophisticated tale of intrigue between gods and mortals, has quite recently enjoyed a successful revival.

* It was later to be said of him that he neglected his sacred office in favour of his operatic interests!

The use of a chorus remained rare in opera, partly for economic reasons; but Cavalli followed Monteverdi in writing melodious songs and reducing 'realistic' but dull recitative to a subordinate role.

Indeed, an age of great singers was approaching, in which vocalism itself became of the greatest importance. A similar tendency towards this later style of *bel canto* (literally 'beautiful song') is found in the operas of Antonio Cesti (1623–69). These were heard not only in Venice but also in Austria, mainly Vienna and Innsbruck, where this composer served the Archduke Ferdinand. Cavalli too was performed abroad, his *Hercules in Love* being given in Paris in 1662.

FRANCE AND GERMANY

Musical culture under the 'Sun King' Louis XIV bore little relation to public demand and taste; for it was that of the court and was required to reflect the magnificence of court life and the palace of Versailles. A tradition of amateur theatricals or masquerades led in time to danced *ballets de cour* and songs called *airs de cour*. By the middle of the seventeenth century, the dance scenes were commonly linked by *récit* or narration, and this blend of drama and music paved the way for the development of opera itself.

The first operas heard in France were brought from Italy by the Italian-born Cardinal Mazarin, who became France's leading statesman. Rather similarly, an Italian who came as a boy to France in the service of the Duchesse de Montpensier became a French citizen and the leading composer of French opera. This was Jean-Baptiste Lully (1632–87), whose violinistic talent and lively personality brought him to the notice of the young Louis XIV. At first Lully was a member of the royal string band of 'Twenty-four Violins', as they were called, but the King soon gave him a small orchestra of his own, *Les petits-violons*. In the meantime he studied to acquire the training in orthodox skills which he needed as support for his brilliant natural gifts. In 1653 he was appointed court composer of ballets, sometimes even dancing side by side with the King himself. It was he, too, who composed additional ballet music when Cavalli's opera *Hercules in Love* was performed at the opening of a splendid *salle des spectacles* at the Tuileries. By studying Cavalli's methods Lully gained insights into operatic technique which were to stand him in good stead later. In the meantime he composed numerous ballets, several in collaboration with the great comic dramatist Molière.

However, his enormous and undisputed success as a court composer did not altogether satisfy Lully. When an Académie de Musique was established in 1669 and an opera called *Pomone* by Robert Cambert (1628–77) had a great public success and an eight-month run, he evidently became jealous, managed to gain control of the Académie for himself and established what amounted to a monopoly of operatic performances in France. Now master of a theatre, the Paris Opéra, he composed a series of operas during the last fifteen years of his life. France already had her own literary and dramatic traditions, so that French opera soon established its artistic independence, above all retaining the French language with its special character and quality.

Lully called his operas *tragédies-lyriques*. Their texture is more sumptuous, but also perhaps less varied, than that of the Italian operas; recitatives and arias blend into one another in a flexible style and have rich orchestral clothing, while the music itself is dignified if sometimes staid, with full use of a chorus. The orchestra plays alone for dances and for the overture.

Lully's death was the result of an infection caused by striking his foot with a long stick, or baton, while conducting. In these times, a conductor often did literally beat time with a stick, either on the ground or a desk. An alternative method, closer to that of our own day, was to wave either a stick or a roll of paper – usually music – in such a way as to indicate something of the character of the music as well as its pulse. The essential thing, of course, was to keep a group of performers in time with each other. If some idea of expression could also be conveyed by gesture, this was all the better. Naturally it was not only in the opera house that this kind of conducting was practised. There is a picture of the Cantor or musical director of St Thomas's Church in Leipzig in 1710 wielding a paper roll in front of a group of strings, wind, organ, drums and singers. Later in the eighteenth century people were to complain of the desk-striking conductors whose banging spoiled the music itself, and the use of gesture only, whether or not the conductor was seated at a keyboard instrument, as was often the case, became universal.

It is often said that Lully was unscrupulous, even villainous. His contemporary Boileau called him a 'hateful court jester'. But however he may have achieved and maintained his success, we cannot doubt his genuine ability. This most versatile of men, who delighted the King in the role of Moliére's Monsieur de Pourceaugnac, was a master of dramatic effect as well as of the difficult art of setting French to music. In spite of his unpopularity among fellow-artists, the musical quality of his works allowed them to dominate the French musical theatre for a full half-century after his death. The cultural authority and *réclame* of the court and the Académie, with responsibilities for the arts and dating from the seventeenth century, ensured a widespread and lasting influence for French music, from minuets and gavottes to larger forms like the overture.

Protestant Germany at this time possessed neither the intellectual vitality of Italy nor the splendid court life of France. Much suffering was caused by the Thirty Years' War, which began in 1618 with attempts to uproot Protestantism in Bohemia and then spread throughout the German-speaking lands. This was a considerable setback to German culture and made conditions hardly suitable for the establishment and growth of opera.

The first opera actually heard north of the Alps may have been *Andromeda* by Girolamo Giacobbi (1567–1629), a leading composer of Bologna in North Italy. The first opera to German words was given at Torgau on the River Elbe at the wedding of a Saxon princess in 1627: this was *Dafne*, by Heinrich Schütz (1585–1672), with a text taken from the original Italian *Dafne* of 1597 but translated into what was still a fairly new literary language by its chief scholar, Martin Opitz. Schütz's music has unfortunately been lost; but it must have been in the Italian style since he had studied in Venice under Giovanni Gabrieli and published madrigals to Italian words. The earliest surviving German opera, published in 1644, is *Seelewig* by the Nuremberg organist Sigmund Staden. Written for solo voices and small orchestra, this is a pastoral morality play set to music described by the composer himself as 'in the Italian style'.

A truly German style in opera was still a long way off. For opera *was* Italian, it seemed, rather as in our own time jazz seemed for many years essentially American. In centres like Munich and Vienna, therefore, opera was simply imported from Italy, both the music and the singers; this was also true of Salzburg, creating a tradition in which it was natural that Mozart, born in that city a century later, should himself compose Italian operas. A more individual character developed further from Italian influence in the rich city of Hamburg, which resembled Venice in being a semi-independent port and which had its own opera house from 1678: in fact this was the only one at that time apart from Venice.* The Hamburg opera house opened with a sacred work called *Adam and Eve* by Schütz's pupil Johann Theile (1646–1724), produced in 1678; and though this music is lost, eleven arias survive from another opera called *Orontes* which Theile wrote in the same year.

Though German-language opera established itself in Hamburg, this was against a background of semi-official Lutheran disapproval of the theatre – hence the frequent choice of sacred subjects – and a conflicting public demand for lighter, secular entertainment. Among a group of composers associated with Hamburg during the last twenty years or so of the seventeenth century were Nikolaus Strungk, Johann Franck and Johann Förtsch. The first of these three also opened a new opera house in Leipzig in 1693 with a performance of his own *Alceste*. Reinhard Keiser (1674–1739) is the great name among the composers of the Hamburg opera, with over a hundred operas to his credit: though these are virtually forgotten nowadays, they had great expressive range and dramatic sincerity. But for much of the time, the story of German opera is one of a simple struggle for economic survival. Significantly, Handel, after beginning his operatic career with *Almira* in Hamburg (1705), soon departed for Italy to triumph with Italian opera upon its home ground, and then after that he established himself not in his native Germany but in England.

* A Roman opera house opened in 1671 but survived only five years.

If the Protestant spirit handicapped the growth of opera, it encouraged a vital and continuing growth in church music. In Rome the Church was already on the defensive: the austerities of unaccompanied choral singing suited its mood better than the rich Venetian style of the previous century. Indeed, the baroque splendours of Venice crossed the Alps to find new expression in the Protestant north: Schütz, a former Gabrieli pupil, revisited Venice in 1628 to meet Monteverdi and study his methods, and the following year he published a set of *Sacred Symphonies* to Latin texts, with instrumental accompaniment. Later he produced two more collections with the same title, but to German words. The last collection, of 1650, includes a dramatic *Saul, Saul, why persecutest thou me?*: this is for six solo voices, two choirs, two violins and organ, and the repeated cries of 'Saul' echo from one vocal group to another in effective, indeed dramatic, style.

The church musical drama of the Middle Ages was to find fresh expression in the settings of the Passion story which became characteristic in Protestant church music, among them four by Schütz himself. The narrative of Christ's Passion as given in the Gospels had been told to church congregations during Holy Week from very early times. Its treatment became increasingly dramatic and musically elaborate, and by the fifteenth century plainchant and polyphonic choral singing were used together as in a Passion by the Englishman Richard Davy around 1500. About a quarter of a century later, Luther's friend Johann Walther (1496–1570) composed the first Passion to use the vernacular. Schütz also used the German language, as did Bach and Handel later, though his four settings are unlike theirs in being for unaccompanied voices. The best-known of these is the St Matthew Passion of about 1664: the words of Christ are given to a bass, while the part of the narrator or Evangelist is for tenor, and these two soloists alternate with sections for chorus. The recitative style of the solos owes something to that of Italian opera, and something too to plainchant, while the choruses are dramatic yet mainly sober in character. The choral body of singers also provides soloists for the shorter dramatic roles, such as those of St Peter and the Maid who questions him.

With their grave spirituality, and at the same time their dramatic force, Schütz's Passion settings represent a fine blend of German sobriety and Italian richness. This Venetian-trained Saxon reconciled Protestant and Catholic feeling in a way that perhaps no theologian could have done. He was around eighty years old when he composed his Passion settings; and in his old age, confined to his home by illness, he spent much of his time reading the Bible and other sacred literature. Schütz understood how simple truths exist alongside divine mysteries: his music shows this and so may move us deeply. He left a considerable legacy in artistic riches. Bach's St Matthew Passion of sixty-five years later, perhaps the greatest work of this kind ever to be written, owes much to him.

ENGLAND

England in the time of Shakespeare (1564–1616) had a national character which was wholly her own. Nevertheless in artistic matters at least, she was closer to Italy than to France or Germany. John Dowland (1563–1626) was a contemporary of the English madrigalists, but he specialised in accompanied solo songs which are forward-looking in style. He studied with Marenzio in Rome, and the 'ayres' which he wrote are stylistically somewhere between Italian aria (the same word) and recitative. These songs to lute accompaniment appeared between 1597 and 1612 and are thus contemporary with the first operas. In Italian opera such as Monteverdi's, recitative blossoms into song where the music must become richer and more expressive; Dowland was especially skilled in maintaining flexibility of style between these two modes of delivery, hitherto separate. He is one of the great song composers, and it is interesting to compare Monteverdi's celebrated *Lament of Arianna* (1608) with his *In darkness let me dwell*. They are strangely similar, and surely Dowland is the equal of the Italian master in expressive power.

EX. 42 A   Monteverdi *Lasciatemi morire (Arianna)*

in così du-ra sorte, in così gran mor – ti-re, la-scia – te-

–mi mori – re, la-scia – te – mi mo – ri – – re.

EX. 42 B

The earliest Italian recitatives relegated music to a secondary role: considered purely as music (which of course they were not meant to be) they are frankly dull. The newer lyrical song, ayre or aria was a very different matter, reflective rather than narrative, dramatically static when used in opera but serving to crystallise a mood, like the soliloquies of Hamlet in Shakespeare's play. With the ayre, whether by Monteverdi or Dowland, song came fully of age as a powerful, yet intimate, form of human expression.

Perhaps the spoken drama was too well-established in England for its musical equivalent, the opera, to gain popularity. Instead England had the masque, a form of colourful entertainment which resembled the French *ballet de cour* but had its own flavour of pageantry and extravagance. Thomas Campion (1567–1620), second only to Dowland as a song composer, and a poet too, composed several court masques. Among typical subjects for these spectacular musical plays were tales featuring witches and fairies; there was even science fiction, and Ben Jonson in 1621 used the exploration of the moon as a subject! Jonson's *Lovers made Men* in 1617 had music by Nicholas Lanier (1588–1666), later to be Master of the King's Musick: this was according to Jonson 'after the Italian manner, *stylo recitativo*' and so perhaps the first example of English recitative.

John Milton's masque *Comus* dates from 1634, with music by Henry Lawes (1596–1662) who, Milton claimed:

> First taught our English Musick how to span
> Words with just note and accent.

– high praise from the great poet. Of course these plays, with their dancing and elaborate costumes and scenery, were very expensive to put on: *The Triumph of Peace* (1633), with music by Henry Lawes' brother William, cost the London Inns of Court about a quarter of a million pounds in modern money. Such lavishness inevitably incurred Puritan disapproval, as did the subject-matter of some masques: the Puritan pamphleteer George Wither wrote in 1641 that 'Scurrilous and obscene songs are impudently sung, without respecting the reverend presence of Matrons, Virgins, Magistrates or Divines.' But some of the more cultured Puritans did not object to music as such; Cromwell enjoyed Latin motets and had his daughters taught music, and Milton, himself a Puritan, produced in his masque *Comus* a moral work perfectly acceptable to most Puritan taste.*

An attempt to establish opera in England was made by Sir William Davenant, Ben Jonson's successor as Poet Laureate and, some said, a son of Shakespeare. His 1656 production called *The Siege of Rhodes* had music by five composers: one of these, and possibly the main contributor, was Henry Lawes. *The Siege of Rhodes* was described as a 'Story sung in Recitative Musick', a style 'unpractised here, though of great reputation among other nations'. This production marks the first known professional appearance of a woman singer on an English stage, the wife of the composer Edward Coleman. Samuel Pepys, the diarist, wrote that she sang finely, referring to Davenant's theatre as 'the Opera'.

* Restrictions placed upon public music-making during the Commonwealth period (1649–60) did at least encourage chamber music, which flourished in people's homes.

When Charles II came to the English throne upon the Restoration in 1660, he quickly changed the nature of the musical scene. This 'brisk, and Airy Prince comeing to the Crown in the Flow'r, and vigour of his Age,' said the composer John Blow, 'was soon if I may say so tyr'd with the grave and solemn wayes and ordered the Composers of his Chappell to add Symphonys etc. with Instruments to their Anthems.' The diarist John Evelyn wrote that there was 'rare music, with lutes, viols, trumpets, organs, and voices' at the Coronation, while a sermon delivered by a King's chaplain was followed by a string orchestra playing 'after the French fantastical light way, better suiting a tavern, or playhouse, than a church'.

In fact the King, returning from France, had quickly established a string band upon the model of the French 'Twenty-four Violins'. He enjoyed music which was colourful and rhythmical, sang to his brother James's guitar accompaniment and, says Pepys, was not above requesting 'all the bawdy songs they could think of' from folk musicians. But church music flourished too, for the King had learned in France the value of royal pomp and ceremony. Captain Cooke, the choirmaster to the children of the Chapel Royal, was an excellent trainer: his boys, according to Pepys, could read 'anything at sight', sang in Latin and Italian as well as English, and even composed. One of them was Pelham Humfrey (1647–74), whom the King sent to France when about seventeen. He returned, if we are to believe Pepys, 'an absolute Monsieur . . . full of form, and confidence, and vanity'! Before his death, aged only twenty-seven, he managed to compose anthems, royal birthday odes and music for Shakespeare's *Tempest*; he also taught the greatest English composer of the baroque period, Purcell.

Though London and the court attracted the finest talents, the provinces too were rich in music. There were municipal waits whose bands of shawms, cornetts, recorders, trombones and other wind instruments were best suited to festive outdoor occasions. These waits were trained musicians with official posts; the father of Orlando Gibbons was both a wait and a town councillor of Oxford. There was also an urban folk music, and in this healthy culture no one worried much about distinguishing 'cultured' from 'popular' art: Pepys, an amateur musician who moved in court circles, also frequented the taverns of East London. At *The Dolphin* he 'sang and sometimes fiddled' and at *The Dog* a friend provided a bass for one of his songs; while at *The Green Dragon*, 'We sang all sorts of things, and I ventured with good success upon things at first sight, and after that I played on my flageolet.'* At a lower level of skill, the humorist Ned Ward described 'the catterwauling scrapes of thrashing fiddlers, the grumbling of beaten calves-skin, and the discording toots of broken organs' which were to be heard at St James's Fair, held in May in what is now called Mayfair in London.

* This was a recorder or end-blown flute. It had six holes (two of which were at the back) and was a favourite instrument with amateurs.

Since music was to be found at all levels of society, it is perhaps not surprising that England had the first fully established, non-operatic, public concerts of Europe. These began in 1672 at the house of a former court musician called John Banister; there were daily performances in the afternoon, given by a small group of professional musicians, to which admission cost a shilling. Another enterprise of this kind, promoted by the music-loving merchant Thomas Britton, began in 1678 and continued for thirty-six years. Concerts became frequent, and a concert hall near Covent Garden was specially opened and enjoyed royal patronage.

Thus Henry Purcell (1659–95) was fortunate in his environment as well as his remarkable gifts. Born at the time of the Restoration with both his father and his uncle employed as court musicians, he grew up to serve the royal music himself at a time when money was available for lavishly festive occasions, both sacred and secular. As a treble in the Chapel Royal choir, he wrote the music for an *Address of the Children of the Chapel Royal to the King* when only eleven; while in his early twenties he became organist of Westminster Abbey and from 1682 he served the Chapel Royal in a similar capacity.

Naturally Purcell wrote a good deal of church music: sixty-two anthems, settings of the Morning and Evening Services, psalms in English and Latin, hymns and so on. As a court composer he also wrote festival odes for occasions like royal birthdays. Since the Restoration court did not take a gloomy view of religion, the brilliant style of these pieces could find its way into his church music. This sort of writing caused him to be thought by some people rather frivolous as a composer of sacred music:

EX.43

Al - le - lu - ia, Al - le - lu - ia, Al - le - lu - ia, Al - le - lu - ia.

As it happens, not many of Purcell's sacred works are brilliant in character. The double-choir anthem called *Hear my Prayer, O Lord*, with words taken from Psalm 102, is austere and deeply moving: here baroque musical thought is seen in its maturity as chordal and polyphonic effects blend and contrast in the eight-stranded texture. The melodic style ranges from simple repeated notes to rich chromatic phrases; and while sometimes there is one syllable to each note, elsewhere a syllable may last through several notes in a more flowing style.

This was a time of instrumental innovation too, when wind instruments and drums found their places alongside the string band. In his ode of 1692,

Hail, bright Cecilia, Purcell used flutes, oboes, trumpets and timpani as well as strings and harpsichord; there were also five solo singers and a chorus. Though this was written when Handel was a mere child of seven, it strikingly anticipates that great composer's 'English' style, and without disrespect to either Handel or Bach one might consider Purcell to show the outstanding orchestral imagination among these three baroque masters. The overture to this ode has brilliant imitative polyphony, while its sections are like those of a classical symphony in miniature. Nothing if not versatile, the composer himself sang in the première of this work, taking the counter-tenor solos, according to a journal of the time, with 'incredible graces'.

There is a certainty of touch in Purcell which is striking, a kind of precision of thought. He knew what he was doing in discarding the old church modes once and for all, writing in 1694: 'There are but two Keys in Musick ... To distinguish your Key accordingly, you must examine whether the Third be sharp or flat.' He advised young composers to write in either of the two 'natural keys' of A minor or C major, from which 'all the others are formed, by adding either Flats or Sharps'. Harmonically speaking, Purcell looks forward to Handel and Bach; it would be fascinating to discover the extent of his influence on them. Handel undoubtedly studied Purcell's music after settling in England; but the only scrap of evidence of Purcell being known to Bach was the appearance of a toccata of his 'in the style of a Fantasia and Fugue' in a collected edition of Bach's works.

Purcell composed one opera only, though it is a masterpiece: *Dido and Aeneas*, written for a girls' school in London in 1689. Although there were a few works such as Matthew Locke's *Orpheus and Eurydice* (1671) and John Blow's *Venus and Adonis* (1685), operas were still not in public demand in England; so that *Dido and Aeneas* is the only work with continuous music among Purcell's many dramatic pieces, his *King Arthur* and *The Fairy Queen* being more akin to masques.

The libretto for *Dido and Aeneas*, by the Poet Laureate Nahum Tate, is sometimes criticised in terms of literary quality; yet it is absolutely right for its purpose here, and Purcell was able to make it his own, transforming it into that unique alliance of drama and music which the word opera implies. The work might have been called, like a later opera of Verdi, *The Force of Destiny*: for the word 'fate' is constantly used at key moments in the story. Dido, the Queen of Carthage, declares that fate forbids her love for Aeneas of Troy, yet her counsellor and the chorus assure her that 'fate your wishes does allow' and that a royal marriage would bring triumph over 'their foes and their fate', and Aeneas tells her that he has 'no fate but you!'. But the sorceress reminds us that the prince is bound by fate to seek the Italian shore, and she and her witches bring about the downfall of the lovers. Aeneas is ordered by a spirit disguised as Mercury to leave at once: 'How can so hard a fate be took?' he groans, forgetting that he declared himself ready, for Dido's sake, to 'defy the feeble stroke of destiny'. For the abandoned queen, only death remains: 'Remember me!' she sings, 'but ah, forget my fate!'

EX.44 Purcell *Lament from "Dido and Aeneas"*

These last words end her final lament, and the orchestra continues alone with sighing and profoundly moving harmonies; yet for all the apparent freedom of the music it is strongly built upon a repeated bass phrase five bars long which has been used throughout the whole song.

The author of the funeral inscription for this great English composer seems to have spoken from a heart full of the memory of his music, saying that he 'left this Life And is gone to that Blessed Place Where only his Harmony can be exceeded'. A more matter-of-fact tribute is that of a modern composer, Benjamin Britten, but it is all the more striking coming as it does no less than two and a half centuries after Purcell's death. 'I recall a critic once asking me from whom I had learned to set English poetry to music. I told him Purcell.'

TECHNIQUES, INSTRUMENTS AND FORMS

In baroque times harmony established itself as essential to music. From now onwards, people listened to melody against a kind of harmonic clothing, a chordal background. If there is no accompaniment this background is supplied mentally: thus there are folk tunes from Eastern Europe which end on the supertonic, one scalic step above the key note, and sound un-finished to our ears because we expect a note corresponding to a final tonic chord. In this way, harmony is closely bound up with form itself, and even the nature of melody was changed by the harmonic approach. Since the old church modes were unsuited to harmonisation they quickly became obsolete. From now on, as Purcell wrote, there were 'but two Keys in Musick', the major and the minor.

The major and minor scales are shown here with their three principal chords, those of the tonic, subdominant and dominant (the first, fourth and fifth degrees of the scale):

EX.45

While the major scale rises and falls through the same sequence of notes, the melodic minor does not. The reason is that the final upward step from the seventh note to the tonic is harmonically better as a semitone than as a tone; this necessitated the raising of the sixth note also in the ascending form of this scale so that an awkward gap of three semitones between the sixth and seventh notes could be avoided. The harmonic minor scale, as the name implies, is not used for melody: in a sense it is artificial, representing as it does simply the notes used in the three principal minor chords.

The new importance of harmony is exemplified in the music of the baroque masters. Both Purcell and Bach were masters of chaconne form, in which the theme is not a tune at all but a sequence of chords. Rhythm too was affected by harmony; for chords move more simply than melodies, and even in complex music like Bach's fugues the harmonies are clearly related to the bar-lines. Indeed the division of music into bars was partly due to this unobtrusive but ever-present harmonic rhythm.*

Bars are regular measures of two, three or four beats, the first beat of a bar being strong. Balanced groups of bars, called phrases, measure out music like the sentences into which we divide words. The parallel continues through paragraphs, chapters and so on, corresponding to sections and movements in a piece of music. For with music as with words, there is a natural progress from one idea to the next within a balanced overall shape. With the new structural awareness, a fully independent language of instrumental music was within reach. Free at last from words, music could go its own way; and thus in the seventeenth century it may be said to have come fully of age. This did not mean that it became divorced from human expression. On the contrary, it was seen as a more powerful expressive medium than words themselves.

Advances in instrumental music were due not only to composers and performers, but also to fine, inventive craftsmen. Among these were the Ruckers family of harpsichord makers in Antwerp, Antonio Stradivari of Cremona and the Amatis and Guarneris also in the field of violin making, and the Harris family of organ builders in England. The Silbermanns in Germany were famous for organs both majestic and delicate, as well as clavichords and the first German pianos. The construction of both woodwind and brass instruments was steadily refined, with better tuning and greater control over the dynamic range, from soft to loud. All these instruments served the professional musician: the church organist in ecclesiastical employ, the hautboy-playing waits of England and Scotland serving a municipality, or the simple member of a French or German guild or union of free-lance

* A side effect of this was that the once-popular percussion instruments, no longer necessary to mark the beat, declined: they play almost no part in Bach's music, and even with the dynamic Beethoven a century later their use is limited compared with that of medieval times.

players who entertained the public. There were teachers too in the growing profession of music: seventeenth-century London had a number who offered lessons in organ and string playing as well as singing.

The early baroque instrumental forms may seem only forerunners of those of later, better-known composers, in the sense that we might compare the Wright brothers' aeroplane of 1903 with a jet airliner. But while technological progress may be measured in terms of efficiency, this is not true of art. No one can measure beauty. The organ fugues of Pachelbel may be less sophisticated than Bach's, but they deserve to be listened to in their own right. Fifty years ago many people thought of Mozart as little more than Beethoven's predecessor: nowadays his own individual genius is recognised.

Variation form, discussed in the last chapter, was important because it involved the deliberate exploration of a theme's possibilities. In the same way, the organ fantasias of Jan Sweelinck were not simply the flights of fancy suggested by the name, but carefully worked-out treatments of a single musical idea. Organ hymns of this kind by Michael Praetorius (1571–1621) and Samuel Scheidt (1587–1654) helped to establish a German style ranging from elaborate chorale fantasias to shorter and simpler pieces.

Scheidt's chorale prelude on *Our Father*, a tune possibly by Luther, is in four parts or 'voices', and the soprano has the complete hymn melody. Its entry is preceded by the other voices in turn, each with the first seven notes of the tune: an introduction serving to build up the texture in true polyphonic style. Yet the imitation is not merely mechanical, and in fact the alto and bass enter with the melodic phrase inverted; while after bar seven the lower voices tend to imitate each other rather than the soprano. The bass line is not cumbersome but moves as freely as the others, yet towards the end it has longer notes which give a feeling of broadening out: with the sounding of the final chord, there can be no doubt that the music has reached a close.

EX.46 Scheidt *Vater unser im Himmelreich*

Example continued

The toccata with its freer style originated in Italy, where the celebrated organist Girolamo Frescobaldi (1583–1643) evidently attracted huge audiences. Imported into Germany, organ toccatas developed into fine examples of the baroque spirit, with sections of free and fanciful character alternating with others in stricter polyphonic style. An influential composer of toccatas was Dietrich Buxtehude (1637–1707): he was a Dane born at Helsingør, the Elsinore of *Hamlet*, but spent most of his career at Lübeck in Germany, near the Baltic Sea, achieving such a reputation that Bach as a young man walked two hundred miles to hear him. Indeed both Handel and Bach applied to succeed him in his Lübeck post. Part of the Lübeck organists' tradition was the joining together into a pair of a toccata, or prelude, and a fugue.

The dance suite also symbolised a tendency to build long pieces by grouping together several shorter ones. German suites, more than French, used definite schemes; and those published in 1617 by the Saxon Johann Schein (1586–1630) consisted of a pavane, galliard, courante and allemande. While French composers added new dances, the Germans made connections of melody and key which helped create unity; and a German who died in France, Johann Jacob Froberger (1616–67) combined the best ideas from both countries, so that he is sometimes called the 'father of the suite'. With him, the allemande, courante and sarabande became standard components.

If the suite was international, with dances from different countries (including, later, the English jig or gigue), the sonata was very much an Italian invention. The violin sonatas of Biagio Marini (about 1595–1665) borrowed quasi-vocal display elements from operatic style. Purcell's twelve violin sonatas of 1683 were in his own modest words an attempt at 'a just imitation of the most fam'd Italian Masters'. The term 'sonata' in itself simply meant something played instead of sung, but it was applied to more or less definite forms by the latter half of the seventeenth century. The *sonata da camera* and *sonata da chiesa* were the main types, and both are represented in the works of the Italian violinist-composer Arcangelo Corelli (1653–1713).

Of the two kinds of sonata as understood by Corelli, the 'chamber' or *camera* type was really a suite. But the 'church' sonatas had independent movements in alternating slow and quick tempo, not dances as such. What all these sonatas had in common was their 'Italian' layout for two violins and accompaniment for string bass and a keyboard instrument, usually the harpsichord. The accompaniment was the figured bass, also called continuo, described earlier in this chapter on page 93. The keyboard player filled in the texture above his bass part, and musicians skilled in this improvisatory art were praised by connoisseurs. The bass was thought of as one part, even though two players were involved, so that these pieces for two treble instruments with accompaniment were always called trio sonatas: the distinction between 'church' and 'chamber' types eventually disappeared. Purcell composed twenty-two such sonatas, all for two violins and this kind of bass. Most baroque sonatas were ensemble pieces. Even so-called solo sonatas required the two accompanying players as well as the soloist. True solo sonatas requiring only one performer were a later development on the whole, though Johann Kuhnau (1660–1722) published in 1700 a set of six Biblical Sonatas for solo harpsichord describing events such as the fight between David and Goliath.

The thirteen string fantasias which Purcell composed in 1680, when he was only about twenty, were for their time old-fashioned, since they were written for viols rather than the more modern violin family and have no keyboard accompaniment. Yet they are so fresh and beautiful that they must be mentioned briefly. In Example 47, from the first half of the three-part Fantasia in G minor, each instrument enters in turn with the theme, but at different pitches and with some variation. The middle part modifies the tune so that we are not led into another key; while the bass, though entering like the treble an octave lower, has yet another version which seems to lead to D minor but turns back on itself in bars 11–12 to give a gentle surprise.

EX.47   Purcell   *Fantasia No.3 for three viols*

The baroque practice of holding an ensemble together by means of a keyboard accompaniment became especially important as the number of players increased. In Italy and Germany suites and sonatas were composed for larger groups of instruments with this kind of accompaniment. Suites with five string parts were published in 1670 by Johann Rosenmüller (about 1620–84). These begin with an overture: as it happens, Rosenmüller lived in Venice and must have been influenced by the operatic overtures he heard there. Several players share each part in this music, just as in a modern orchestra, and indeed these suites are orchestral in conception.

It was in baroque times that the orchestra as an organised body began really to take shape. Instruments had played together from the earliest times; but this kind of music-making was not the kind of balanced, calculated writing by a composer which takes into account the strengths and individual characteristics of instruments and instrumental families so as to make the best use of them in a particular piece. Giovanni Gabrieli's *Sonata pian' e forte*, composed for Venice in 1597, made dramatic use of wind and strings divided into two groups. Ten years later Monteverdi used about forty players for his opera *Orfeo*, treating them both as individuals and groups and achieving various dramatic effects by orchestral means. The predominance of string tone, with the idea of the violin family as the basis of the orchestra, came later. The 'Twenty-four Violins' of the French court in Lully's day, the middle of the seventeenth century, marked a new stage in the development of homogeneous, flexibly expressive yet well-disciplined large groups of players. When Lully added flutes, oboes, bassoons, trumpets and timpani to his well-trained strings, something like a modern orchestra had come into being.

Much of Lully's orchestral writing was for the opera house, and perhaps it was because of its dramatic potentialities that the orchestra developed above all in this field. Italy, too, had a contribution to make. For example, it was the operatic overture in three sections, fast–slow–fast, such as Alessandro Scarlatti composed around the start of the eighteenth century, which provided a model for independent works in sonata form later in that century, concertos as well as symphonies.

6

THE LATE BAROQUE

*Concerto form. Vivaldi. Handel. Bach. Opera and
church music.*

CONCERTO FORM

The concerto was the characteristic orchestral form of baroque times. The name itself, like most names of musical forms, has changed its meaning a good deal over the years. Early in the baroque period there were 'church concertos' for voices with instrumental accompaniment. But Bach's *Italian Concerto* is for harpsichord solo and his 'Brandenburg' Concertos use a variety of orchestral groupings; while on the other hand such works as his violin concertos are consistent with our modern use of the term for music written for a solo instrument and orchestra.

The original meaning of the term concerto was simply a joining together of musical forces, in the sense of a 'concerted effort'. In form it quickly became a sonata for several players. The baroque *concerto grosso*, as composed by Corelli among others, consisted of a group of movements in which the music was divided between a small group of solo players and the main orchestral body. Corelli's pupil Francesco Geminiani (1687–1762) carried on this scheme, working within the four-movement form of the church sonata that his teacher had helped to establish, with alternate slow and quick tempos.

It was an obvious step forward towards greater contrast to use a single soloist. Furthermore all the brilliance and individuality of some skilled performer could be displayed. Usually it was the violin that was chosen, because many composers themselves played it well, Geminiani among them.* Solo concertos by Giuseppe Torelli (1658–1709) usually have three movements, the slowest being placed centrally, and Torelli also gave the soloist themes of his own which were discreetly accompanied by the orchestra. These were separated by varied orchestral statements of the main theme of a movement: it was called the *ritornello* since it kept returning throughout.

In the hands of the violinist-composers of the early eighteenth century, the concerto went from strength to strength, mainly of course in Italy, the home of violin-making and performance. A new standard of technical

* He was the author of the first important book on the art of violin playing, one which helped the development of better performance standards.

accomplishment was demanded in the works of Pietro Locatelli (1695–1764). Like Geminiani, he was a Corelli pupil: both these men spent much of their lives outside Italy and so helped to propagate the art of violin playing as well as that of composition for the instrument. Other concerto composers of this time were Francesco Maria Veracini (1690–1750) and Giuseppe Tartini (1692–1770); in time the work of such musicians as these was to lead away from the sturdy idiom of the baroque towards the melodiousness and elegance of rococo style and the classical period.

VIVALDI

Antonio Vivaldi (about 1678–1741) was the outstanding master among the concerto composers. Vivaldi was a Venetian, the son of a violinist serving the Chapel of the Doge and also the great Cathedral of St Mark which stood close by the ducal palace. The splendours of the Venetian court were very different from the vast but colder world of Versailles, where Lully served Louis XIV. Venice had more intimacy, and her wealthy citizens of both the aristocracy and merchant class took a pride in their cultural as well as their monetary riches. Fine architecture contributed to the unique blend of water, light and stonework which inspired the painter Tintoretto; there were paintings by Titian, Giorgione and Veronese as well as the music of Monteverdi and his operatic successors. Domestic music-making existed on every scale from the smallest to the largest, and with the ever-present songs of the gondoliers and street-sellers the city was perhaps the most musical in Europe.

Though Vivaldi's brothers were of the working class – one was a hairdresser and another was banished for a knife brawl with a grocer's boy – he himself received a good education and became a priest. He was ordained quite young, in 1703, but a chest ailment which may have been asthma prevented him from saying Mass; and his real career was that of a brilliant director of music in a school, the Conservatory of the Ospitale della Pietà, at which orphans and other poor girls were educated at the expense of the state. They learned to sing, and the instruments taught included strings, flute, oboe, bassoon and organ. Vivaldi seems to have enjoyed a degree of freedom, and he travelled quite widely. In fact he went as far as Amsterdam to perform his own music, though it was laid down that in his absence he should send two concertos a month back to Venice. He seems to have retired from the school in 1740, and it was actually in Vienna that he died in the following year. Sad to say, he was evidently in rather poor circumstances, for his funeral obsequies were humble.

In spite of his comparative ill-health, Vivaldi had a reputation for composing 'furiously and prodigiously'. One of his friends once remarked: 'I have heard him undertake to compose a concerto with all its parts faster than a copyist could copy it.' His solo concertos in fact amount to over four hundred, a notable achievement considering that he wrote plenty of other music as well. But of course it is not their quantity but their quality which matters, and this is often very high. Vivaldi did not owe much to Corelli's structural methods when he composed his concertos. Their form is more akin to that of elaborate operatic arias of the time, with contrasting sections. The orchestral passages are richer in themes than in earlier concertos by other composers where they seem mainly to provide a rest for the soloist. There is a true feeling of dialogue, even at times argument, between the solo player and the orchestra. The themes themselves are often striking yet simple, so that their development during the course of a movement is all the more interesting. At the same time the music is easy to follow, clear in form, with harmony and changes of key which are assured and purposeful. Of the three concerto movements, it is the slow central one in which Vivaldi aims to move the listener's feelings with lyrical beauty: more often than not, it is in a minor key by contrast to the preceding allegro movement in the major. The finale is another allegro, rather shorter and more lively than the first.

One feature of Vivaldi's style which is worth special mention is his rhythm. There is a vitality which moves the music forwards and holds the attention, but this is prevented from sounding mechanical by subtlety and flexibility in phrase-lengths and orchestral textures. The feeling of onward movement which we note in his music, a confident narrative style as it were, is one to be found in later masters, Beethoven being an obvious example, but in few before him. Vivaldi's descriptive instrumental music too was in-fluential. The bird imitations in Beethoven's 'Pastoral' Symphony are antici-pated by a century in the unaccompanied cadenza below, occurring after only a dozen bars of his flute concerto called the *Goldfinch*.

Perhaps Vivaldi's best-known descriptive music is a set of four concertos for violin and orchestra representing the seasons of the year. Each of these is accompanied in the score by a descriptive poem on the same subject.

Example continued

Whether or not the poems were actually written after the music, as has been suggested, there is some quite detailed tone-painting. In the 'Spring' Concerto repeated viola notes are marked with the words 'the barking dog' and the players are asked to emphasise them; while at the same time the soloist's soothing melody depicts a sleeping goatherd in a flowery meadow amid the orchestral violins with their 'sweet rustling of leaves'. This particular concerto became very popular. In France, Louis XV once asked especially to hear it, and Vivaldi was praised as the best musical 'painter' of the time. These 'Seasons' Concertos were dedicated to a neighbour of the Esterházy family whom Haydn served, and Haydn's predecessor composed an *Instrumental Calendar*; so it may be no coincidence that Haydn himself later wrote an oratorio called *The Seasons*.

HANDEL

English history is full of paradoxes. The English Church parted from Rome and yet claimed to remain Catholic, though Queen Elizabeth as its head declared herself to be Protestant. James II observed the Anglican rite at the Chapel Royal, but kept a second chapel in Whitehall at which there were Roman Catholic services. The diarist John Evelyn went there on Christmas Day 1686 'to heare the Musique of the Italians in the new Chapel . . . & so I came away: not believing I should ever have lived to see such things in the K. of Englands palace, after it had pleas'd God to inlighten this nation.' But the Italians were not the only foreigners to make their home in England, for soon even the throne was to receive them. King George I, while Elector of Hanover, had employed a musical director: he like his royal patron came to England and took up a position of great eminence on the national scene. George Frideric Handel was born in 1685 in the Saxon town of Halle, but he became an English citizen and died in London in 1759. He was supremely cosmopolitan: a man of the world who was equally at home in different countries and different musical styles, from Italian opera to the German suite and the English anthem or royal birthday ode.

Handel's father was a prosperous citizen of Halle, a surgeon who was already over sixty when his son George Frideric was born. The boy's exceptional musical gifts were not encouraged to the extent of music being considered as a profession. Handel was destined for the law, and even though his father died in 1797, when he was still a boy, he went ahead and entered his local university. But by now he was so proficient musically that when the chance came of an appointment as principal organist of Halle Cathedral he took the post and finally decided on a musical career.

Almost at once he moved on again, into the more stimulating and varied musical environment of Hamburg. There he became a violinist in the orchestra of the famous opera house; soon he was able to take on the more important job of playing the harpsichord. At the age of nineteen he composed a setting of the Passion story according to St John, for Holy Week in 1704; and within a year his first opera was performed. This work, *Almira*, was the success of the Hamburg season. Designed for North German audiences, it had German-language recitative in the interests of comprehensibility, while Italian (considered to be more singable) was used in some of the arias. It may have been that his sheer brilliance caused a certain hostility towards him on the part of other musicians. One called Johann Mattheson fought a duel with him in which Handel's life was saved by a metal waistcoat button which deflected his opponent's sword; it is pleasant to be able to add that the two made up their quarrel (which was over a musical matter) and remained good friends thereafter.

Even Hamburg could not hold a young man so spectacularly gifted, especially when a future operatic career was in question. In 1706 Handel set off for Italy, and the following year a Roman writer noted the arrival of 'an excellent harpsichordist and composer' who played the organ to an admiring audience in one of the Roman churches. He met Corelli there, as well as the opera composer Alessandro Scarlatti. He also went to Venice, where he may have met Vivaldi. In Florence, the very birthplace of opera, his opera *Rodrigo* was a success; while in Venice in 1709 *Agrippina* was another triumph. 'Long live our dear Saxon!' the audience shouted, and the opera received twenty-seven performances.

While in Italy Handel was a master among masters, but in his native Germany he was supreme. And so in 1710 he became *Kapellmeister* or musical director to the Elector of Hanover. The post carried considerable status, and no doubt it was well paid. But it offered no scope for Handel's operatic gifts, and having tasted the joys of public success he may have felt frustrated at being confined to a dullish German court. Within a very short time he obtained leave and arrived in London in 1710 to find that at long last Italian opera was becoming popular there. Perhaps this was because Purcell's death fifteen years before had left audiences with a taste for dramatic colour and brilliance that no native English composer could satisfy. At any rate Handel found himself more than welcome. A new opera called *Rinaldo*, written in a fortnight, was produced with great success at the Queen's Theatre in the Haymarket on February 24th 1711, the day after his twenty-sixth birthday, with the composer himself directing from the harpsichord.

Handel returned to his duties in Hanover; but already he was dreaming of a return to England and had set to work studying the English language. In 1712 he went again to London, taking a second leave from which he never returned. Henceforth England was to be his home, and musically London laid her heart at his feet. He conquered professionally to an extraordinary extent, and not only in the field of opera. It was he, rather than an Englishman, who was entrusted with the composition of Queen Anne's birthday ode in 1714, even though he had never set English to music before; and no local musician seems to have complained when the Queen awarded him an annual stipend of two hundred pounds, not merely for a limited period but for life.

It must have been worrying for Handel when his former employer ascended the English throne in 1714. He had, after all, every reason to feel angry with the *Kapellmeister* who had treated his court appointment in such cavalier fashion. As it happened, good relations between George I and Handel were quickly re-established, but not, however, through the *Water Music*, in spite of the story to that effect. The King attended performances of Handel's operas, took him on a visit to Germany in 1716 (the *Water Music* was written the following year), doubled his royal allowance and made him the teacher of his daughters.

From 1717 Handel set about diversifying his style. He composed English anthems for a wealthy patron, the Duke of Chandos, at the Duke's palatial house at Edgware, as well as the oratorio *Esther* and the pastoral opera *Acis and Galatea*, both to English words; and he also turned his mind to instrumental sonatas and suites, such as the Suite in E major containing the set of variations called (though not by him) *The Harmonious Blacksmith*. Nevertheless it was as a composer of operas that he became most celebrated. When he went off to the continent to recruit a company of singers, Bach, hearing of his presence in the neighbourhood, went to Halle, where Handel was visiting his family, to try and see him but arrived too late. The two great composers never met. Back in England again, Handel set about directing an opera company.

Handel wrote nearly forty operas, all in Italian: the idea of writing an opera in English, or even his native German, probably would have seemed to him an odd one. These works show the form of *opera seria* in a state of rich maturity, with a widely ranging vocal style and highly imaginative orchestral writing. It is only in the sphere of drama itself that a weakness shows. The public were interested above all in the singing, and the story was frankly secondary; in fact the lights stayed on during the performance and people would stroll in or out, and chat to their companions, in a way that nowadays would be regarded as intolerable. The singers were highly trained, expensive, and fully conscious of their public standing, which at times was higher than that of the composers and librettists. Handel, being their employer as well as a composer, was less subservient to their temperament than most, and he is said to have held one leading lady out of the window and threatened to drop her if she did not sing correctly. Female roles were sung by women: one famous soprano was Faustina Bordoni (1700–81), who after singing in Handel's company married another opera composer, Hasse. But the leading men of this *bel canto* or 'beautiful song' age were usually male sopranos or altos whose unbroken boys' voices had been artificially preserved; and the voices of these *castrati*, far from being piping and effeminate, were often fine, powerful and used to great effect.

In Handel's operas there are relatively few ensembles and choruses. Dialogue is in recitative with light accompaniment; but arias, where the real singing is done, have a fuller orchestral clothing and, in more important items, a three-part form in which the final section is a repeat of the first with added decorations from the singer such as are prized by connoisseurs of the vocal art. It is easy to see how these operas fell for a period into neglect: they needed both performers who could do them justice – and we had no male sopranos – and audiences prepared to overlook elements of conventionality in the plots. For a long time enthusiasts had little hope of reviving them successfully, but in quite recent times this has been done with audiences who are sophisticated in their historical sense and aware of the wealth of music which might otherwise remain unheard. Singers in their turn are learning how to perform the often demanding roles, with male soprano parts given to women or sung an octave lower.

No kind of special sophistication, however, is needed to enjoy Handel's instrumental music or his oratorios. Handel took over forms used by Corelli such as the trio sonata and the concerto. One splendid set of twelve *concerti grossi* for strings and harpsichord, published as his Opus 6, were written in a few weeks in 1739 and contain a variety of movements, from dances to fugues. He also composed true solo concertos for oboe and for organ. In the suites called *Water Music* and *Music for the Royal Fireworks* his orchestra has woodwind and brass instruments as well as strings: from Purcell's time, English pageantry had been well served by skilled players. Though Handel was one of the finest vocal writers of his age, his instrumental imagination was also remarkable, so that as early as his first London opera, *Rinaldo*, he used small recorders to represent bird song, while in the oratorio *Saul* (1739) the appearance of a ghost was enhanced by the sounds of two bassoons at the bottom of their range.

The oratorios which Handel composed in the latter part of his career, when the public began to tire of *opera seria*, are among the great sacred works of music: they include *Messiah*, *Belshazzar* (1745) and *Jephtha* (1752). When

Messiah received its first performance in Dublin in 1742 it was rapturously hailed in the local press: 'The best Judges allowed it to be the most finished piece of Musick. Words are wanting to express the exquisite Delight it afforded to the admiring crouded Audience. The Sublime, the Grand, and the Tender, adapted to the most elevated, majestick and moving Words, conspired to transport and charm the ravished Heart and Ear.' In this, the most famous of his oratorios, Handel managed effectively to combine the styles of Italian operatic melody, German Passion music and English choral writing.

The profits from performances of *Messiah* were given to charity. Indeed, Handel, while becoming a fairly wealthy man, remained a generous one. He was generally amiable, devout, a lover of pictures and other fine things (he owned some Rembrandts), and of good food and wine. Towards the end of his life he suffered from increasingly poor eyesight, and when he played his organ concertos in public he had to do so from memory or simply improvise; the sight of him being led to the organ or towards the audience to make his bow 'was a sight so truly afflicting,' wrote the musical historian Dr Burney, 'as greatly diminished their pleasure in hearing him perform.'

When Handel died on April 14th 1759 an anonymous poet wrote:

> O! for the glorious Change, great Handel cry'd.
> Messiah heard his Voice, and Handel dy'd.

He was indeed a great composer, with an unsurpassed command of the majestic and dramatic style of the mature baroque. These qualities were recognised by Haydn, who on hearing the *Hallelujah Chorus* wept and exclaimed, 'He is the master of us all!' Ever since King George II rose to his feet for this chorus, the tradition has been kept in England of standing for it.

BACH

Johann Sebastian Bach was born in the same year as Handel, 1685, in the German town of Eisenach in Thuringia. But in most ways they were very different. Handel was unmarried and could take financial risks on theatrical enterprises; he was a man whose life was a public one of concerts and the opera house; he moved amid wealthy society in great cities, travelling and composing to texts in as many as five languages. Even his religious music has a public quality, and his oratorios were first performed in theatres, not in churches. Bach, on the other hand, was married and had a large family; he once said of them with pride that they could put on between them a complete vocal and instrumental concert, but they also had to be provided for out of an income which, though regular, was small. Bach's employers in the various provincial posts which he occupied were middle-class merchants who had no special interest in brilliant artistry. His music often seems to look not towards a public but inwards, to have a mystical spirit not only in sacred vocal works but also in such pieces as the chorale preludes for organ. Yet strangely enough, these two great lives which began together but developed differently converged again at the end: both Bach and Handel were operated on, unsuccessfully, by the same oculist.

Bach came from a family of musicians. His father was a professional violinist and a town musician of Eisenach, and it was he who gave the boy lessons on the violin and viola. He was also a devout Lutheran* who was well aware of Luther's love of music. But both he and his wife died while Johann Sebastian was still a young boy, and the orphan went to live with his brother Johann Christoph, fourteen years his senior, and the organist at Ohrdruf, a town thirty miles distant. His brother was a good teacher, himself a former pupil of the organist-composer Pachelbel, and gave him lessons in harmony as well as tuition on the three keyboard instruments, the organ, harpsichord and clavichord. His progress was rapid: it was said that no sooner had his brother given him one piece to play than he requested another more difficult one.

After five years with his brother, Bach became a choral scholar at a choir school in Lüneburg. The music at St Michael's Church there was of a high standard indeed: not only was the choir an excellent one, but there was also an orchestra and a good music library. He got to know an organist called Löwe, whose teacher had been Schütz, born exactly a century before him in 1585. Another acquaintance was Georg Böhm, an organist and composer whose music he had already studied while living with his brother. He walked the thirty miles to Hamburg to hear Böhm's teacher Reinken play. Böhm admired French music, so it may have been on his advice that Bach also visited Celle, about sixty miles distant on the Hanover road, where the ducal court orchestra was made up mainly of Frenchmen playing French music.

Trained as a singer, organist and string player, with a knowledge of harmony, Bach was now equipped as a fully professional musician. In 1703 he was playing the violin in a court orchestra at Weimar, then soon after that he took up another post as a church organist at Arnstadt in his native Thuringia. It was not altogether a success, since his choir were unwilling to submit to discipline from a mere eighteen-year-old. Not only that, after a visit to Lübeck to hear Buxtehude, the finest organist-composer he had so far met, he returned with his head full of unconventional inspirations. The church authorities were not best pleased with their gifted young organist: not only had he overstayed his leave, but he now treated the congregation to what they called 'wondrous variations and strange sounds'.

Already Bach had shown his ability as a composer. There were chorale preludes; and there was also a piece of remarkable programme music, the

* Luther began work on his translation of the Bible into German at Eisenach.

Capriccio on his brother Johann Jakob's departure to join a Swedish military band as an oboist. Here, in one of Bach's first harpsichord pieces, sighing chromatic phrases in both hands depict the sorrows of the friends and relatives left behind.

EX.49

But most of Bach's early music was for organ. As well as the chorale preludes, he soon produced a number of variations, toccatas and fugues, and fantasias. All show the exuberance of his invention, his youthful delight in the discovery of his creative powers. This part of his career brought into being works such as the celebrated Toccata and Fugue in D minor (BWV 365), with its majestic opening using every dramatic device from bare descending melody to rich chords building themselves upwards like great cathedrals of sound, only to vanish into brief silences full of expectancy. The Passacaglia in C minor was perhaps modelled on one by Buxtehude but is much longer and grander: it begins with an eight-bar theme stated quietly on the pedals alone, and then follow twenty variations leading to a final fugue.

These two works actually date from the second major appointment of Bach's career. After a year at Mühlhausen, where he married his cousin Maria Barbara, he moved to Weimar to serve in the musical establishment of Duke Wilhelm Ernst. There was a small orchestra which accompanied the choir on Sundays: Bach and his fellow-musicians had to dress up in uniform and perform in a cold gallery under the high chapel roof. Though he was better paid than in his previous posts, he was by no means in charge of the ducal musical establishment, and even on his appointment as 'concert-master' in 1714 remained second-in-command to the elderly *Kapellmeister*. But this new appointment did entail his writing a new cantata each month. Henceforth he was to be a composer of church cantatas, exploring and mastering new creative realms to set beside those which were already his in the field of organ music. *Jesu, Joy of Man's Desiring* is an early cantata from these Weimar years.

When the Duke's *Kapellmeister* died, Bach naturally enough expected to be given his post. Since this did not happen, he felt that it was time to leave, and accepted an appointment as *Kapellmeister* to another nobleman, Prince Leopold of Anhalt-Cöthen. This new position proved a happy one, with an employer who loved music and played both the harpsichord and violin as well as the larger *viola da gamba*. This was the time of Bach's suites and sonatas for violin, *viola da gamba* and cello, of the first book of the 'Forty-eight' Preludes and Fugues written for his sons to study,* the French and English Suites for harpsichord and the six 'Brandenburg' Concertos of 1721 named after the nobleman, the Margrave of Brandenburg, to whom they were dedicated.

The 'Forty-eight' demonstrate the use of all the major and minor keys formed on the twelve notes of the chromatic scale; the name of *Well-Tempered Clavier* applied to the first book refers not to good humour but to the fairly newly-adopted system of tuning keyboard instruments with twelve exactly equal semitones to the octave, a system in which Bach believed and which permitted the greatest possible freedom in key-changing. The preludes often seem to be studies in technique or in expression; but the fugues however cannot be described so briefly. Fugal writing found its supreme master in Bach. There have been attempts to classify his fugues into types, to establish rules which composition students can themselves follow. Yet his treatment of his fugue themes or 'subjects' is nearly as varied as the subjects themselves, of which the shortest is four notes long (C sharp minor in Book I) and the longest over forty (E minor in Book II). The composer Vaughan Williams told a story of a pedantic teacher who forbade the study of Bach's fugues because they were against 'the rules', and went on to cite the remark of a better scholar that fugue was a matter 'of texture rather than of design'. The variety of Bach's procedures in the 'Forty-eight' is paralleled perhaps only by Beethoven in his thirty-two piano sonatas, sometimes called the New Testament of music following Bach's 'Old'.

We can say of fugues, at least, that they are polyphonic, based on a single subject (very occasionally, more) and cumulative in interest. Usually there are three or four parts or 'voices' which enter in turn with the subject. This section, called the exposition, is followed by changes of key and new treatments of the subject with incidental, episodic material leading to a final section in the main key. This final section is the climax of a building-up of concentration, a kind of raising of the musical temperature in many cases. Sometimes a fugue is said somehow to typify the baroque spirit, to exist as a kind of musical essay as opposed to the more narrative sonata form of later times. There is some truth in this, but we may remember that Beethoven introduced fugues into his sonatas: an example of genius reconciling apparently contradictory forms.

Bach's orchestral music may not have the same important standing in his work as a whole as that of Handel, but this is simply because the circum-

---

* Bach married twice and had children by both his wives; the male children include several composers in their own right such as Carl Philipp Emanuel Bach (1714–88) and Johann Christian Bach (1735–82), who made his home in London.

stances of his career did not require him to compose regularly for the orchestra. When he did so, the richness of his imagination worked as fully as in his other music. Each of his six 'Brandenburg' Concertos is differently scored, a proof, if one were needed, of his interest in varied instrumental textures. On the other hand, it is true that in the Second 'Brandenburg' Concerto, just after the opening, the same phrase is given to each soloist in turn – violin, oboe, flute and trumpet – though it is perhaps not equally suited to all of these and sounds uncomfortable when the trumpet plays it in a very high register. *The Art of Fugue*, a monumental work begun in 1749 and left unfinished at his death the following year, does not indicate the instruments needed for performance, and so it can be argued that tone quality, the nature of the sound, was less important to Bach than the interplay of the polyphonic parts. On the other hand, he used instruments colouristic-ally in many works, for expressive reasons: the violins in the *Agnus Dei* and the horn in the *Quoniam*, both in the great Mass in B minor, are only two examples of this.

The Mass in B minor was a work dating from the period of his last and longest appointment. In 1723, after his prince married a wife who cared less for music than he did, Bach moved to St Thomas's Church in Leipzig to become Cantor or director of church music to the city council. Once again he was a church musician, and his two great Passion settings, the St John and St Matthew, date from this part of his life, as do the *Magnificat* and the *Christmas Oratorio*. His duties included responsibility for music at St Nicolas's Church as well as St Thomas's. He was also required to compose over fifty cantatas a year: we possess nearly two hundred of these, though another hundred or so have been lost. Bach was a devout member of the Lutheran church in whose faith and tradition he had been brought up; and the cantatas were essentially highly developed forms of Lutheran church chorales, the simple yet profound character of which is reflected constantly in Bach's later art. His cantatas have something in common with opera, with their recitatives and arias and their dramatic use of the chorus – in fact the secular, light-hearted 'Coffee' Cantata and 'Peasant' Cantata can be staged successfully. There was never a 'cantata form' in the sense that we speak of sonata form, except that Bach's usually end with a harmonisation of a chorale verse. His cantatas last anything between ten and thirty-five minutes, and were vocal-orchestral pieces originally performed as part of the service, before the sermon. Their variety of layout makes them all the more interest-ing and valuable, offering striking proof of their composer's inventiveness in a situation where he might easily have fallen back on routine methods.

When setting words to music, Bach sought for musical ideas suitable to the texts with as much care as any madrigal composer. In the *Magnificat*, 'He hath scattered', 'lowliness' and 'the proud' all receive appropriate treat-ment: for example, 'he hath put down' (in Latin *'deposuit'*) is set to a quick descending scale. At times indeed he carried word-painting to such a degree that it almost became a private matter, introducing double sharps with their cross-shaped sign where the text referred to the Crucifixion, a kind of musical metaphor which might be seen but could hardly be heard.

The Passion story, as set to music by Bach, uses a German poetic text for the arias and choruses, with the biblical text as a basic narrative. Bach shows such sensitivity to every shade of meaning in the words that the total effect is more dramatic than in most operas. The chorus can represent the crowd demanding the release of Barabbas, or the faithful Lutheran congregation meditating on these events; and similarly the music itself is narrative and reflective by turns. The final chorus of the St Matthew Passion, 'In tears of grief', is really in a dance form, a sarabande sung almost as a lullaby to the sleeping Saviour; yet Bach, while using the musical language of his own time, transcended it. His mastery and the sublimity of his thought have made him a universal figure, one of those artists whose message crosses with undiminished force the barriers of religious creed, nationality and time.

Bach's stature was unknown to most of his contemporaries. When he went to his Leipzig post the authorities would have preferred another, more 'progressive' composer, Telemann; and indeed his music came to seem old-fashioned as baroque style was gradually superseded by the rococo of which Telemann was a fine early exponent. Yet Bach's work came as a revelation to both Mozart and Beethoven. Then in Berlin in 1829, the young Mendelssohn conducted the first performance of the St Matthew Passion to take place for a century. The musical world marvelled at Bach's genius, and the great task of collecting and publishing his music began. Now this music seems likely to last as long as our civilisation itself. Every superlative has been bestowed on Bach by music-lovers awed by the richness of his genius. It was Debussy, in our own century, who commented, 'Bach alone divined eternal truth'; while before him, Mendelssohn declared, 'We are never at an end with Bach. He seems to grow even more wonderful, the oftener he is heard.'

OPERA AND CHURCH MUSIC

We left the story of Italian opera with Cavalli and Cesti, composers born in the first quarter of the seventeenth century. One of their successors was Agostino Steffani (1654–1728), who went to Germany as a young boy and helped to establish the Italian operatic style there. He became a friend of Handel and certainly influenced him. In Venice, Vivaldi wrote nearly forty operas, but was always more admired for his instrumental works. But *opera seria* as understood by Vivaldi or even Handel was steadily giving way to a lighter style. Even the operas on serious subjects written for the Naples opera house showed an increasing concern for elegance and charm. Alessandro

Scarlatti (1660–1725) is the leading composer of this Neapolitan school: he was a master of graceful melody and of shapely harmony, who wrote lighter operas as well as *opera seria*, a hundred and fourteen in all. Other Neapolitans followed his lead and developed the *bel canto* style in which the singing of arias became the main interest of operatic connoisseurs, at the expense of both the music and the drama; at its most extreme, operatic form degenerated into a mere series of elaborate vocal 'concertos' separated by perfunctory recitatives.

This was not always the case, especially where finer composers were involved such as Handel or Hasse, who married one of the singers from Handel's company. Johann Adolf Hasse (1699–1783) was a German pupil of Scarlatti, whom the historian Dr Burney called 'the most natural, elegant, and judicious composer of vocal music' among living musicians – this was in 1775, after Handel's death. Hasse wrote about eighty operas as well as eleven oratorios. In 1771, when his last opera was produced at Milan, he met the fifteen-year-old Mozart. In spite of the great difference in age, the two composers became friends; and with prophetic insight, as well as generosity, Hasse said, 'This boy will cause us all to be forgotten.' In fact Mozart's father wrote in a letter home that his young son's music had quite put Hasse's opera in the shade; with several symphonies already to his credit, Mozart represented the advent of the new classical period and the elderly Hasse must have known that times were changing around him.

The influence of operatic style was pervasive. Viennese church music by Johann Fux (1660–1741) and Antonio Caldara (1670–1736) shows this influence clearly. Both served the Imperial court, as well as writing operas; and the Emperor Charles VI's austere musical taste caused both also to compose learned pieces of a strictly contrapuntal kind. Fux's textbook of counterpoint called *Gradus ad Parnassum* ('Steps to Parnassus', the legendary home of the Muses) was for a long time after its appearance in 1725 used for teaching purposes, which has caused his name to be linked with academic dryness and dullness. But this is hardly fair to this kindly and well-liked man, the composer of pieces with such titles as *Aurora's Wedding*, whose harmonies were described as gorgeous. That the Austrian Fux and his Venetian assistant Caldara wrote in a similar style reminds us how far musical idioms were international in the eighteenth century. Hasse's very operatic oratorio *The Conversion of St Augustine*, given at the Saxon court of Dresden in 1750, has an Italian text and could have been composed by an Italian for his own compatriots.

In the Protestant North, however, something like a 'national' style did exist, for the Lutheran chorale lent an unmistakable character to church music. The church cantata was a regular part of Sunday worship, though the use of recitatives and arias with their secular, operatic associations disturbed the most extreme elements of Protestant opinion; yet Bach's music

In a Lutheran church the Cantor often conducted with a roll of music: a picture from Johann Gottfried Walther's *Musical Lexicon* of 1732. Walther was a relative and colleague of J. S. Bach.

Above A baroque opera set by Giovanni Carlo Bibiena. The Bibiena family were the greatest designers of 'spectacle' of their day, and their talents were in demand all over Europe.

Below A scene from Handel's opera *Flavio* (1723). In this contemporary caricature the singers are the *castrato* Senesino, the soprano Cuzzoni, and the bass Berenstadt.

was surely enriched both technically and spiritually by this 'Italian' feature which he made so much his own.

The Italian style also influenced church music in France under Louis XIV, through the oratorios and other sacred works of Marc-Antoine Charpentier (1634–1704), a pupil of Carissimi. Charpentier also collaborated with Molière and the Théâtre-Français, and his dramatic style has earned him comparison with his contemporary Purcell. Lully's few church pieces have a feeling of massiveness and dignified ceremonial which can verge on dullness, but his *Te Deum* has its own kind of magnificence. A rather lighter and more varied style than Lully's was that of Michel Richard de Lalande (1657–1726), master of Louis XIV's Chapel Royal from 1704: his *Symphonies for the King's Suppers* are charming. Though he is much better known for his instrumental music, François Couperin (1668–1733) composed delicately beautiful motets for the Chapel Royal. His three *Leçons des Ténèbres* (1713–15) for soprano voice with instrumental accompaniment, settings of the Lamentations of Jeremiah for performance in Holy Week, have an autumnal melancholy well suited, perhaps, to the declining years of the Sun King.

The Italian oratorio after Carissimi, with the brilliant exception of Handel's work, passed through what seems to have been a rather undistinguished period. The twenty-four oratorios by Alessandro Scarlatti are musically hardly different from his operas, and his *Assumption of the Most Holy Virgin* (1710) ends with a duet in *siciliana* rhythm for the 'Heavenly Bride and Bridegroom' which might be an operatic love scene. Alessandro Stradella (1642–82) wrote the oratorio *St John the Baptist* which has been praised as an important step between Carissimi and Handel: according to Dr Burney he was Purcell's favourite composer. Stradella's death was untimely though romantic, at the hands of hired assassins after his elopement with a Venetian lady: according to one story, which later provided the subject for an opera by Flotow, some of the villains abandoned their purpose after their hearts had been melted by his music.

The Passion story was also treated by Italian composers, and Scarlatti wrote a St John Passion. However, in Catholic countries the musical style was fairly simple and the words restricted to those of the Latin version of the Gospels. Passion music is thus perhaps the special province of Germans, from Schütz to Keiser, Handel and Bach. Keiser, the opera composer of Hamburg, wrote music of distinction in this field which may well have influenced Bach; though virtually unperformed today, he may well be a major composer of his time whose music still awaits rediscovery. Telemann composed no less than forty-four settings of the Passion: but he was a particularly prolific composer of whom Handel once said that he could write a motet in eight parts as easily as another man might write a letter.

Like oratorio, the Italian and French chamber cantata of the late seventeenth century came into being as an offshoot of opera. It was a domestic form, one which replaced the madrigal in musical homes and which had nothing to do with the Bachian type of orchestral cantata. Chamber cantatas developed from recitative style and lasted perhaps ten minutes or a quarter of an hour, resembling operatic scenes for solo voice with instrumental accompaniment. The words were usually about love, though Carissimi among others also set sacred texts. Alessandro Scarlatti wrote six hundred of these cantatas, their typical form being of two arias, each preceded by a recitative; Stradella composed nearly two hundred, and Handel seventy-two.

Handel's death in 1759, with that of Bach nine years earlier, marks the end of the baroque period. The lighter rococo style and the still newer classical style of Haydn and his successors were now what interested both musicians and public alike. The movement towards enlightenment and enjoyment of life which had begun with the Renaissance now continued with increasing force. These forces of change brought about a greater secularisation, as well as a general questioning of the structure of society. The French Revolution was only three decades away. Neither Mozart nor Beethoven were ever to know the sense of spiritual purpose of Bach's world, nor the social ease of Handel's.

7

ROCOCO AND CLASSICISM

Rococo style. Opera in the late eighteenth century.
Sonatas and symphonies. Haydn. Mozart.

ROCOCO STYLE

In baroque times people had turned back, with the *opera seria*, towards the ancient world of heroes, gods and goddesses. But this was a secular art, and in social terms it was an aristocratic one. Its humanistic philosophy was distrusted by the Church; while the paying public, on the other hand, came to demand a more homely form of entertainment. Thus the Handelian kind of opera had to give way to the lighter topical humour of Pergolesi's *The Maid-Mistress* (1733) and *The Beggar's Opera* (London, 1728), the latter indeed parodying *opera seria*.

It seems a contrast when we turn from *The Beggar's Opera* to the aristocratic and refined world of François Couperin (1668–1733), the French composer of delicately ornamented harpsichord pieces whose very titles are alluring – *The Bees, Delights, The Nightingale in Love, The Little Windmills, The Eel*. This kind of music is called 'rococo', a word taken from the French *style rocaille* of shell and scroll work that was entirely decorative and charming. Couperin has been compared to the great rococo painter Watteau, for in the art of both these men beautifully costumed shepherds and shepherdesses seem to inhabit an idealised, courtly countryside in which, one feels, such real-life annoyances as nettles and mosquitoes could never exist.

Of course the realism of *The Beggar's Opera* (with its popular tunes arranged by the poet John Gay and the composer Pepusch) is very different from Couperin's world. Yet both had in common the desire to entertain: in one case the London paying public, in the other a cultured and leisured class in France. Rococo art was lighter than that of the baroque. Where baroque musicians sought to exalt the hearer, those of the rococo reasserted qualities of charm and delight. We should not call the rococo decadent, though. After all, 'the pursuit of happiness' was thought a proper aim by the founders of the United States of America in the late eighteenth century.

The invigorating keyboard music of the Italian Domenico Scarlatti (1685–1757) also represents the rococo ideal in its individual way. His harpsichord sonatas, over five hundred in all, are short single movements full of vitality and feeling. They have an alternative name of 'studies'; but they were certainly written to delight as well as to instruct Scarlatti's pupil, the Queen of Spain. Though he was a contemporary of Bach and Handel and friendly with the latter, these pieces, composed when he was around sixty, clearly belong to the new era rather than the old baroque one. And their use of brilliant effects like crossing of hands and repeated notes led to advances in keyboard technique.

Another composer of this generation who matured late was the Frenchman Jean-Philippe Rameau (1683–1764). Like Couperin, he composed short and picturesque harpsichord pieces, but his main achievement was in music for the theatre. His first major dramatic work, written when he was fifty, was the opera *Hippolyte et Aricie*. This noble yet emotional music took people by surprise, for Rameau's reputation at the time was mainly that of a *philosophe* or learned scholar in the theory of music. The use of the orchestra, too, was startling and well in advance of its time, for Rameau was able to make it suggest not only deep human feelings but also thunder, earthquake, the appearance of a monster and so on. A disciple of Descartes and a man of lofty ideals, Rameau had some baroque characteristics and was a worthy successor to Lully; but with the lilting pastoral tunes of the ballets *Les Indes Galantes* (1735) and *Les Fêtes d'Hébé* (1739) he became more an exponent of rococo ideals. From 1745 he held a royal appointment, and after that most of his music was written for diversion and delight. *Platée*, the comedy–ballet given that year at Versailles, and later in public with equal success, is positively frivolous. The philosopher Rousseau, himself an exponent of rococo thought, considered it his masterpiece.

Rameau had doubts about the way in which his art developed. 'From day to day,' he said, 'I acquire more taste – but I no longer have genius.' But still he wished to move with the times. 'Were I twenty years younger . . . but after sixty one cannot change . . . the mind refuses to obey.' One is reminded of Telemann's saying that art 'must always go onwards, ever onwards'. Yet perhaps Rameau's apparent admission of failure is a mark of his greatness. This author of an important textbook on harmony (the first of its kind and still studied a century later by Berlioz) became a richly humanitarian artist who was able to move, or simply to charm, court and public alike. Exactly the contemporary of Bach and Handel, he is dramatically their equal. His influence is to be felt in the operas of Gluck and, still later, Berlioz.

The rococo was at least to some extent a Parisian invention, and Georg Philipp Telemann (1681–1767), after a visit to Paris in 1737, brought the style to Germany. At the end of the previous chapter he has been mentioned only briefly as being prolific. But that is hardly a fault, since most great composers have been fluent creators. The writer of an article on him in Grove's Dictionary claims that he lacked any earnest ideal and had 'a fatal facility naturally induced to superficiality'; but this is like judging Beethoven by the standards of Palestrina, for Telemann's aims were different from those of his contemporary Bach. We tend also quite unfairly to disparage him because the Leipzig authorities would have preferred him to Bach as Cantor of St Thomas's Church. Yet Bach himself admired him. Telemann had his own ideals. He said: 'He who writes for the many does better work than he who writes only for the few . . . I have always aimed at facility. Music ought not to be an effort, an occult science.' He studied Lully's works and composed forty operas as well as a great deal of church and instrumental music, mainly in Hamburg. Significantly, Bach chose Telemann as godfather to his son Carl Philipp Emanuel, named Philipp after him, who in turn was to become one of the main founders of the classical school to which Haydn and Mozart belong, and to whom both these great composers paid tribute.

OPERA IN THE LATE EIGHTEENTH CENTURY

Near the end of the previous chapter, the meeting in 1771 between Hasse and the young Mozart was mentioned. Both composed operas to Italian words, as Handel had done, though neither was Italian. Yet the supremacy of Italian opera was open to challenge, and we have seen how with Lully and Rameau a national French opera was established. But in 1752 an Italian company visiting Paris performed a comic opera by a brilliant but short-lived Neapolitan, Pergolesi (1710–36), called *La Serva Padrona* – 'The Maid-Mistress'. This had the lightness and freshness of the best comedy; it amused without being empty-headed, its laughter being that of warm and intelligent humanity. In comparison, the over-familiar and long-drawn-out myths of 'serious opera' seemed antiquated and fusty. A couple of months after the great success of Pergolesi's comedy, the influential and versatile philosopher-musician Jean-Jacques Rousseau (1712–78) scored an equal success with a comic opera of his own, set in the countryside and called *The Village Soothsayer*. Both text and music were his; the first performance pleased Louis XV and his court at Fontainebleau, while the Parisian public were equally delighted by it a few months later.

Rousseau next produced a publication called *Letter upon the Subject of French Music*, in which he declared that melody was the basis of composition and harmony therefore less 'natural'; that polyphony was a useless and perverse complexity, and instrumental writing merely the servant of song and expression. Furthermore (though this came oddly from the pen of a successful French opera composer) the French language was basically un-musical compared to Italian: therefore 'the French have no music, and never will have any'. The reaction to all this was quite a violent one: the supporters of Lully and Rameau hanged and burned Rousseau's effigy. The controversy, which divided even the royal family, was actually more good-humoured than this would suggest. Rousseau wrote a witty reply to his attackers; and it is clear from his later writings and his admiration for Gluck's French operas that some of the *Letter* was deliberately provocative and exaggerated. The quarrel involved several well-known names and has become famous as the *guerre des bouffons* – literally the 'comedians' war', but probably better translated as 'controversy over the comics'.

French comic opera eventually established itself, appropriately enough, with a joke played on the public. In July 1753, a 'French adaptation of an Italian comic opera' called *Les Troqueurs* ('The Swappers') was presented successfully to a Parisian audience, who were then informed that it was the entirely original work of a French librettist and a French composer, Jean-Joseph Vadé and Antoine Dauvergne. With François André Philidor and the Belgian André Grétry, French comic opera moved into a new phase, gaining in depth without losing its power to entertain. Philidor (1726–95) is best known for *Tom Jones*, produced in 1765 and based on Fielding's picaresque novel; while Grétry (1741–1813) in his *Richard Coeur de Lion* (1784) treated a heroic theme, Blondel's rescue of his master from captivity. This story helped set the fashion for 'rescue operas', among which Mozart's *Seraglio* and Beethoven's *Fidelio* are famous later examples.

To mention Grétry's works, linking one of them to Beethoven's highly serious *Fidelio*, is to be reminded that the term 'comic opera' should not be taken too literally. One French dictionary defines *opéra-comique* simply as a theatrical piece in which singing alternates with speech. *Opéra bouffe*, on the other hand, is always humorous, the equivalent of the Italian *opera buffa*. Eighteenth-century comic opera, appearing in different languages in different countries, represented a reaction against the *opera seria* or 'tragic' opera and dealt with more topical subjects in an entertaining way. This did not by any means imply that the stories were necessarily superficial. Piccinni's *The Virtuous Maid* (1760), based on Richardson's novel *Pamela*, was a sentimental drama; while Paisiello's *Barber of Seville* and Mozart's *Marriage of Figaro* (1782 and 1786) make serious comments on society as well as providing first-rate entertainment.

In England *The Beggar's Opera* of 1728 established the form called ballad opera, which interspersed popular tunes with spoken dialogue – as John Gay put it in his preface, with sharp wit, 'I hope I may be forgiven, that I have not made my Opera unnatural, like those in vogue, for I have no recitative.' Dr Thomas Arne, the composer of *Rule, Britannia*, composed comic operas of which *Love in a Village* (1762) is a typical example. In America, *The Beggar's Opera* was given in New York in 1750.* There were operatic tours, so that the largest cities such as Baltimore, Philadelphia and New York heard various European works, including Paisiello's *Barber of Seville* sung in English.

---

* French opera was performed in the French-speaking city of New Orleans towards the end of the century.

The Devil to Pay was an English comic opera to popular tunes which was produced with German words in Berlin in 1743 and afterwards in Leipzig. Johann Adam Hiller (1728–1804) made a new version of this in 1766 which was so successful that he followed it with ten more comic operas – the German word is *Singspiel* – mainly adapted from French originals of a romantically pastoral kind. Mozart called his own *Seraglio* a *Singspiel*; but *The Magic Flute*, though it also has German words, goes beyond conventional definition of this sort.

Late eighteenth-century Spain was musically almost swamped by Italian influence, supported by the court. But here as elsewhere a popular form of opera came to flourish in the *tonadillas*, fairly short, colourful entertainments including spoken sections and sometimes dances.

A comic opera to French words, *The Unexpected Meeting*, was composed for production in Vienna in 1764 by a German-Bohemian, Christoph Willibald Gluck (1714–87). Gluck, in fact, was a complete cosmopolitan, and we are not even sure what language was truly his mother tongue. As a boy he learned to play the harpsichord and organ; then he studied singing, the violin and cello in Prague. By 1740 he was in Milan and writing Italian operas which were successfully produced both there and in Venice. In 1745 he went to London, calling on Rameau in Paris on the way, and while there he produced two operas in some haste. His talents were still developing, and the sixty-one-year-old Handel criticised these works adversely, though treating Gluck personally with kindness. In the 1750s, having married a wealthy wife, Gluck settled in Vienna. There he composed Italian operas and, when the fashion came in, French comic operas on mainly pastoral themes.

There was an unconventional quality about Gluck's music which caused the librettist Metastasio to describe him as a composer of 'surprising fire, but mad'. He became more and more concerned with the relationship between music and drama, reacting against the Italian style and responding to French views such as those held by Charles de Brosses, who said of the arias inevitably occurring at the end of operatic scenes that 'while they enchant the ears they permit the interest to cool off', or by Beaumarchais – 'there's too much music in theatre music'. Gluck's answer was to attempt a restoration of a proper balance between dramatic action and musical beauty. Writing a ballet, *Don Juan* (Vienna, 1761), he discovered in himself new resources of symphonic drama. These he put to good use the following year in his opera *Orfeo ed Euridice*. Here too he enjoyed the collaboration, the importance of which he willingly acknowledged, of his new librettist Calzabigi. He, Gluck said, 'enabled me to develop the scope of my art'.

Gluck's reform of the classical opera consisted mainly of avoiding extravagant musical display at the expense of the story and dropping prosaic recitatives so as to achieve better continuity. In so doing, he made the well-

worn mythological plot of *Orfeo* into a movingly human story. The scene
in the Elysian Fields, with its 'pastoral' flute, creates a memorable atmosphere
of space, peace and light. Gluck found the musical equivalent of what the
art historian Winckelmann, writing in the same decade, called the 'noble
simplicity and quiet greatness' of Greek art. In his preface to *Alceste* (1767),
the opera in which he next collaborated with Calzabigi, he made his purposes
clear. 'I tried to restrict music to its proper function of serving poetry
through expression and following dramatic situations . . . I have aimed to
abolish all the abuses against which good sense and reason have for long
vainly protested.'

Orfeo and *Alceste*, in French versions, reached Paris, where the Dauphine
Marie-Antoinette was Gluck's former singing pupil from Viennese days: her
husband Louis XVI ascended the throne in the year of *Orphée et Eurydice*'s
performance at the Opéra, 1774. Earlier in that year Gluck's *Iphigenia in
Aulis*, based on Racine's play, had received great acclaim at the same theatre.
Thenceforth he composed operas only for Paris.

After suffering a stroke in 1781, Gluck composed little more, though that
little included some church music. He admired Mozart, who returned the
compliment by attending rehearsals of one of his operas and improvising on
a theme of his. He and his wife were Gluck's dinner guests in 1783. But as
he wrote to his father, the older composer's health was 'in a very precarious
state'. In 1787, against doctor's orders, Gluck drank a glass of liqueur and
not long afterwards suffered another stroke while out in his carriage. He was
brought home unconscious and died, aged seventy-three.

As a 'French' opera composer, Gluck influenced Berlioz, born some
ninety years after him in 1803. Mozart too shows his influence, especially in
the solemnities of *Idomeneo* and *The Magic Flute*; he too wrote a *Don Juan* and
in the statue scene at the end makes a near-quotation from Gluck's score.
Even so, in many respects Mozart belonged to a different musical climate;
and to understand how different it was, we have to look at the development
of instrumental music, which Gluck himself hardly affected.

SONATAS AND SYMPHONIES

Rococo music was intended to give pleasure. The delicate prettiness of
French court music is summed up by the term *style galant*, though its spirit
was not confined to France and J. S. Bach called some of his keyboard dances
galanteries. In Germany the homely warmth of the *Singspiel* represented the
somewhat different, middle-class *style bourgeois* or *empfindsamer* (sentimental) style, also exemplified by solo songs or *Lieder*, of which over seven
hundred collections were published in the second half of the century.

This second type of rococo music was addressed to the public, and with
success. As the philosopher Leibniz had put it, what experts thought the

best failed to touch the heart, and simplicity 'had more effect than embellishments'. By these standards, the supreme craftsmanship of Bach went for nothing; one critic remarked in 1737 that he 'clouded beauty with over-elaborateness'. Bach's own pupil Johann Doles said that fugues were outdated academic exercises. The ideal of the new song composers was to write 'as simply and clearly as possible', to quote one of them, J. A. P. Schulz of Berlin. Bach's sons Carl Philipp Emanuel and Johann Christian became important figures in a transitional period of rococo style which was to lead to the new heights of craftsmanship and expression reached by such classical composers as Haydn, Mozart and Beethoven.

Classicism is hard to define. The term 'classical' is often used in antithesis to 'romantic' or 'modern', the latter two being reserved for the nineteenth and twentieth centuries respectively, and the former for all earlier periods. It is also inaccurately used by some for 'serious' music as opposed to 'popular', or for established as opposed to ephemeral works. But here 'classical' is used as historians often employ the word, to refer to the period of the so-called Viennese classics, beginning with Haydn and ending with Beethoven: that is, the second half of the eighteenth century and the first two or three decades of the nineteenth.

But even when we set limits upon the period to be called classical, a definition still has to be made of the nature of classicism. Like the baroque or rococo, there is an artistic climate which we can recognise. This was an art of mature humanism and enlightenment in which, as with the original 'classics' of ancient Greece, disciplined and balanced thought came to terms with the free expression of individual human feeling. In the words of one historian, 'Instinct made peace with the law, form triumphed over matter, order over chaos. Classicism beatified life and gave it lastingness by viewing it from the heights of the ideal ... its principal object was man living in consort with nature, man beautiful in body and soul, in bearing and in deed, man who became aware of his own inner harmony, and who was the measure of all things.'* To some extent at least, we may well feel that the classical spirit as exemplified in Mozart's music realises the ideals of the Renaissance.

In the classical period, one instrumental form dominates the scene – the sonata. It was written for any number of instruments, but rather confusingly it was not always called by this name. That is, a sonata for one or two instruments is so-called; but a sonata for three, four, five and so on is referred to as a trio, quartet, quintet, etc. An orchestral sonata is called a symphony, but where there is a soloist we talk of a concerto.

Sonatas normally have three or four movements, mostly the latter in the case of quartets and symphonies. The first movement is fairly fast, and commonly the longest; the second is slow and the finale lively. If there are four movements, the third is a minuet or scherzo. Obviously this is only a

* P. H. Lang: *Music in Western Civilisation.*

general scheme lending itself to all kinds of treatment. All the same, it is a stricter framework than that, say, of a three-act play, for principles of structure govern each movement, even if they are principles rather than rigid rules. Contrasts of mood, texture, key and so on are used for eventfulness and drama, while in slow movements a composer can display his talent for melodic charm, emotional expression or tone-painting. In a sparkling last movement there can be an exhilarating, lighter effect produced by the composer's inventiveness and the performer's skill, suitable for the end of a longish work requiring close attention from a listener.

A minuet or scherzo is in ternary form: that is, with a contrasting middle section. The same structure is often used for a slow movement, obvious examples being those of Mozart's D minor Piano Concerto and Beethoven's 'Pathétique' Sonata in which we move from gentleness to agitation and back again; but a slow movement may also be a set of variations or, as in Haydn's 'Oxford' Symphony, a mixture of variation and ternary form where lyrical invention and expression together produce a freedom which seems gently to reprove any attempt at strict analysis. A finale is often in rondo form, in which the principal theme returns at intervals, each statement of it separated from the next by a contrasting 'episode' – this, incidentally, is the same as the *ritornello* technique of the last movement of Bach's E major Violin Concerto.

The first movement of a sonata is almost always written in 'sonata form'. This is a confusing term since it applies to a single movement and not to the structure of a sonata as a whole. A sometimes-used alternative name is 'first-movement form', but this is also misleading since other movements may use it – the finale of Mozart's G minor Symphony, No. 40, for example. A sonata-form movement has a basic three-part shape. Its exposition section consists of two main ideas contrasted in mood and key, the first vigorous and the second gentler; then comes a 'development' based on material from the exposition; and finally there is a recapitulation of the opening material without the key change between the two main ideas. There may also be an introduction to the whole movement: this is usually slow and sometimes of a fair length, as with Beethoven's Seventh Symphony. More common still is the coda, a rounding-off section at the very end of the movement, normally short and brisk and in the nature of a final flourish.

The symphony had a prototype in the Italian operatic overture, such as those composed by Alessandro Scarlatti, which had three sections with contrasting speeds. Some early symphonies in three movements ended with a minuet or variations; this was a form used by Johann Stamitz (1717–57). Stamitz is an important figure here, whose orchestra at Mannheim on the Rhine was justly famed. This city, whose Duke was lavish in his spending on the arts, also had fine performances of opera, a fact which must have contributed to the vigorous and dramatic qualities of Stamitz's symphonies. Stamitz and his work became known and influential even in Paris, where he spent a year shortly before his untimely death. He introduced the clarinet into the orchestra, now complete with woodwind, brass and strings, giving the wind instruments as a whole greater importance and so making a feature of contrasting tone-colours; his orchestral crescendo, still a novel effect, upset Mozart's conservative father, who warned his son against it. However, the historian Dr Burney visited Mannheim in 1772 and said of Stamitz's music that it had original genius: 'invention, fire, and contrast, in the quick movements; a tender, graceful, and insinuating melody, in the slow... great effects... refined, but not repressed by cultivation.' Beethoven himself modelled the scherzo of his Fifth Symphony on a Stamitz movement written over half a century before – a tribute to this innovator more eloquent than any words.

Stamitz's importance in the realm of symphonic music is paralleled by that of Carl Philipp Emanuel Bach (1714–88) in the rise of the classical piano sonata. The pianoforte, invented just before his birth, was a harpsichord with 'soft and loud' as its name indicated: its strings were struck lightly or strongly according to the pressure of the player's fingers on the keys, and this gave it an expressive power of a kind which was unavailable on the organ or harpsichord and which brought it into line with the violin or even the voice. C. P. E. Bach spent many years at the Berlin court of Frederick the Great, then in 1767 he moved to Hamburg, a city which welcomed 'this great master of piano playing', where he spent his remaining years. Dr Burney visited him there and found him 'of a cheerful and lively disposition', his playing however being that of a man 'possessed ... he not only played, but looked, like one inspired'. A short passage from one of his sonatas shows the intense and passionate expression that was a feature of his style, seeming to look forward even beyond Haydn and Mozart, to Beethoven. Indeed Beethoven called him a 'true artist' and studied his music.

EX.50 C.P.E.Bach *Sonata in C minor*
Molto adagio

Haydn and Mozart too paid generous tributes to C. P. E. Bach, the former saying that he owed him all he knew and the latter with a famous phrase, 'Bach is the father, we the children.' Bach himself summed up his aims as a 'mixture of brilliance and simplicity, sadness and joy, the singing and instrumental styles'. This forward-looking genius respected his illustrious father's art, yet turned himself to something utterly different. His work looks so much towards the future that even a younger, 'advanced' composer – Hiller, the founder of the *Singspiel* – had doubts about such a style, writing that a 'mixture of the serious and comical, the sublime and lowly, so frequently blended in the same movement, often creates a bad effect.'

It was left to later geniuses to make the mixture work, to impose emotional and structural unity upon the stirring, but strange and wild, inspirations and inventions of this most interesting of Bach's composer sons. Haydn and Mozart were able to place the ornamental charm or homely simplicity of the rococo alongside the lofty drama of the baroque – one thinks of the playfulness, and of the solemnities, of Mozart's *Magic Flute* – but in their work there is also ample expression of the individualistic drama and energy of Stamitz and C. P. E. Bach. They gave the world a musical language which cannot be summed up simply as aristocratic, avant-garde or merely popular. It was intelligible to everyone; yet in such works as Haydn's string quartets or Mozart's 'Jupiter' Symphony it reaches sublime heights of craftsmanship as well as human expression. According to one historian, Wilfrid Dunwell in his book *Music and the European Mind*, the great composers of the period 'brought European music to a summit from which only descent was possible'.

HAYDN

Haydn was a great composer, and yet he was a simpler man than either Mozart or Beethoven. He kept a sturdy humanity throughout his life, and he was less self-questioning, less of a rebel, than the majority of great creative artists. He had few serious battles to fight, either within himself, like Beethoven, or with his employers, like Bach, or with fellow-musicians and critics, like Liszt. His main trial was his shrewish wife, who gave him no children and cared nothing for his music; but instead of allowing this to make him morose, he simply admitted, 'I was therefore less indifferent to the charms of other women.' He was a superb craftsman and inventor, yet even at the height of his fame he remained a man of common sense as well as sensitivity. In Haydn's music we find warmth of feeling and a sunny personality, so that it is not surprising to learn that he was loved as a man as well as being respected as an artist.

Joseph Haydn was born in 1732 at the village of Rohrau in eastern Austria, the eldest son of a wheelwright – a maker and mender of wooden wheels for farmers' carts. In later years he said that he was grateful to his

parents for bringing him up to be thrifty, hard-working and God-fearing.
It was a musical schoolmaster, a relative, who set him on the path of musical
training. Living with this uncle and his family in the town of Hainburg ten
miles north of his birthplace, he sang in church and played the violin and
keyboard instruments. One day the choirmaster of the Imperial court came
to the town in search of new talent. Haydn, the treble soloist in church, was
sent for, given a few cherries and made to sing a trill, a thing he had never
done before. At the third attempt he succeeded. 'Bravo! You shall come with
me!' said Herr Reutter; and Haydn thus became a choirboy of St Stephen's
Cathedral in Vienna. He said in later life that singing a trill always reminded
him of the taste of cherries.*

When his voice broke his place in the choir was in danger. Though the
Empress herself said she enjoyed his singing, nobody was much concerned
what would happen to him after he lost his post. At the age of seventeen he
found himself suddenly penniless and unemployed, spending a November
night on a bench in the open air. He was fortunately befriended by a tenor
singer called Spangler who took him into his own small household, and over the
next few years he made a living by teaching and a little singing. As a boy,
what he had learned of composition was largely his own doing: he had studied
textbooks and filled manuscript paper with ambitious ideas. Now he continued his studies with steady purpose, often working far into the night. One
day he got hold of C. P. E. Bach's sonatas, took them home and played them
right through at a sitting: 'I played them time and time again for my own
pleasure, especially when I was discouraged and depressed by worry, and
always got up from the instrument cheered and in good spirits.' The structure
and the emotional impact of these sonatas influenced his own development,
and Bach later returned the compliment by describing Haydn as 'the only
one who fully understood his work'.

At this time, aged twenty-two, Haydn found himself living in the same
house – really a block of flats – as the famous opera librettist Metastasio.
Through him he acquired a brilliant pupil, the ten-year-old Marianne
Martinez, who was a singer, keyboard player and later one of the first known
women composers. Marianne's singing teacher, the fashionable Nicola
Porpora, brought Haydn further work as a keyboard performer, as well as
giving him lessons in composition. In 1759 Haydn became director of music
to a certain Count Morzin. Two years later, in May 1761, now the composer
of symphonies and string quartets, and having also married his former pupil
Maria Anna Keller, he joined the service of Prince Esterházy, the head of the
greatest family of the Hungarian nobility, at his castle at Eisenstadt.

Haydn stayed in this post of director of music for nearly thirty years,
retiring in 1790. For almost all of this period he served Prince Nikolaus

* Many of the direct statements attributed to Haydn come from his first biographer, Georg
August Griesinger, who was on close terms with him in his latter years.

Esterházy, who succeeded his original employer, Prince Paul Anton, within months of his appointment. Their relationship was a congenial one, for although Haydn only had the status of a skilled servant, the music-loving prince came to appreciate his qualities both as an artist and as a man, so that over the years respect ripened into a genuine and lasting friendship. The vast Esterházy palace, built in 1683 and according to a French traveller comparable only to Versailles, boasted an opera house, a puppet theatre and concert rooms. Haydn was in charge of an orchestra of strings and wind which expanded to over twenty players during his time, as well as six singers who sang operatic roles and also performed as a choir for Sunday Mass.

Haydn's hundred and four symphonies span a period of nearly forty years: the last, known in recent times as the 'London' Symphony, dates from 1795 and like the first, it is in D major, a favourite key of Haydn's. Among the early symphonies is a sequence of three (Nos. 6–8) called 'Morning', 'Noon', and 'Evening'. Each has the standard order of four movements: the slow introduction to 'Morning' depicts dawn, while the finale of 'Evening' is a storm, though not a very furious one.

In these works, written at the beginning of the 1760s, there are features borrowed from operatic recitatives, arias and finales, as well as from the outdoor serenades in which the composer played as a youth, and of course from the vigorous and expressive music of C. P. E. Bach. Perhaps the most Bachian symphony is the first to be written in a minor key, No. 26 in D minor, composed in about 1768; this 'Lamentation' Symphony evokes the Passiontide story by its sombre emotional colour and the use of plainchant melodies written for Holy Week.

Yet Haydn imitated no one, so that for example C. P. E. Bach's contempt for 'learned' music did not prevent him from writing a fugue as the finale of his Symphony No. 40 in F major. This is now known to have been composed earlier than its number suggests, in 1763. In fact, it followed No. 13 in D major, which has a fugal finale in sonata form, such as Mozart composed twenty-five years later for the finale of his 'Jupiter' Symphony. Even the strict imitative style of canon, which to C. P. E. Bach represented 'dry and despicable pedantry', appears in the minuet of No. 44, while the minuet of No. 47 is composed *al rovescio*: that is, with whole sections repeated in reverse.

What Haydn never fails to show is that devices of craftsmanship need not impair a feeling of naturalness and freedom, a truth which the more revolutionary C. P. E. Bach, necessarily reacting against his father's great and learned art, could not fully know. Yet truth it is, none the less, so that for example with a Shakespeare sonnet the fourteen-line form seems the perfect shaping of the inspiration. Content without form is as unsatisfactory as the opposite; so that there is some truth in the comment made by a modern scholar, Basil Lam, that in C. P. E. Bach we find 'the too-easy surprises of a style where anything may happen'. With Haydn we find both a wider scope and a greater sense of balance. His was the greater genius, trying out new ideas of all kinds, but with an unfailingly critical ear. 'My prince was always satisfied with my works; I not only had the encouragement of constant approval, but as the director of an orchestra I could make experiments, observe what produced an effect and what weakened it . . . and be as bold as I pleased; I was cut off from the world, . . . and I was forced to become original.'

In the winter of 1781–82 Haydn met Mozart, and from then on the two men had the highest mutual respect, while their friendship was musically fruitful for both. Haydn's fame had spread widely, and in fact his music had reached France and England as early as the 1760s. As soon as he retired from his Esterházy post in 1790, he found himself receiving all kinds of offers of work, most of which came from high places and must have been difficult to refuse. He was tempted by an invitation to go to Italy, a lifelong ambition, in the service of the King of Naples. The offer he did accept was one which left him a free-lance as well as being financially attractive, and came from the impresario Salomon. This was to come to England as an orchestral director and composer, writing six new symphonies and other music for performance there. Mozart and other friends were against the plan, pointing out that Haydn was nearly sixty, unused to the rigours of travel and no linguist; but they received the brisk retort that he was still fresh and vigorous and that 'all the world understands my language'. In fact, Haydn was longing to try out his powers in the wide world – Mozart, over twenty years younger, had travelled far more. Yet Mozart was anxious for his friend, and both men shed tears at their parting. 'I fear, father, that this will be our last farewell,' Mozart said, and he was right – yet it was he, thirty-four years old, and not Haydn, who had less than a year to live.

Haydn's journey to England took seventeen days, and he had a day-long crossing from Calais throughout which, he wrote, 'I stayed on deck to gaze my fill at that vast monster, the sea . . . most of the passengers were sick and looked like ghosts.' Once arrived in London, he rested for two days in the Holborn household of a friendly publisher; and then he began in earnest what was to prove an enormously successful visit. The former peasant's son was fêted by the nobility, including the future King George IV. Dr Burney reported: 'I have had the great Haydn here, I think him as good a creature as great musician.' Modest as always, and moved to tears by *Messiah*, he declared that the music of Handel had sent him back to study as if he were a beginner.

His grand opening concert, which he directed from the piano, aroused (according to Burney, who was present) enormous enthusiasm, the slow movement of his new symphony (No. 96) being encored. But he was living at high pressure, and very quickly had to move from the noisy streets of central London to the comparatively rural Marylebone area. He suffered from eye-strain and had some sleepless nights because of incessant work, writing in his sixtieth year that, 'Never in all my life have I written so much in one year as I have in the past twelve months.' The news of Mozart's death upset him greatly, and he wrote to the widowed Constanze Mozart, offering his free services as a teacher of her child. He was also at times homesick: 'I am looking forward like a child to being home again and embracing all my old friends.' Even so, London brought him one special happiness, for he fell in love with a widow called Mrs Schroeter, who became his piano pupil. Though she was no longer young, Haydn said of her in later years that she was charming and still beautiful, and 'Had I been free, I would certainly have married her.' And he had memorable experiences as a tourist: a London fog 'so thick you could spread it on bread', the loveliness of Cambridge in autumn, Guy Fawkes's Day celebrations, the 'divine' view from the terrace of Windsor Castle – and, not least, the races of Ascot Week, of which he wrote a vivid description in his diary.

In that same month of June 1792 he left for home. As on the outward journey, he paused at Bonn. There the young Beethoven showed him a cantata and Haydn agreed to take him on as a pupil: this he did in Vienna at the end of the year. The city was troubled, however, with the continually worsening news from France: for this was the year of the abolition of the monarchy and the establishment of the Republic, and in the following year Louis XVI and his queen, born a Viennese Archduchess, went to the guillotine. Nor was this a happy period of Haydn's personal life. Mozart was 'irreplaceable'; and early in 1793 Marianne von Genzinger, another dear friend, died aged only thirty-eight. The lengthy negotiations for the purchase of a house bored him, particularly since his wife had suggested that this would be suitable for her widowhood. She herself was not in the best of health or humour. Even his brilliant young pupil Beethoven, divided between a desire for strict academic training (which his teacher was too fine and gentle a musician to offer him) and a creative impetuosity manifesting itself in 'errors', presented him with a difficult task.

So instead of settling down at home, Haydn left once again for London, arriving in February 1794 for another visit of eighteen months. England was now at war, but the visit was a success; Haydn was welcomed as an old friend by London society, and presented to the King by the Prince of Wales. This was the period of his last three piano sonatas and his last five symphonies, as well as songs to English words including twelve 'canzonets'. At this time also his second set of fifty Scottish folk song arrangements appeared, and indeed over a period of fifteen years from 1791 he arranged numerous Celtic (rather than English) folk songs. One wonders how much of the words he could have understood, with titles like *My mither's ay glowran o'er me* or *Fy gar rub her o'er wi' strae*; but he may have appreciated *What can a young lassie do wi' an auld man* and Burns's topical and political *Does*

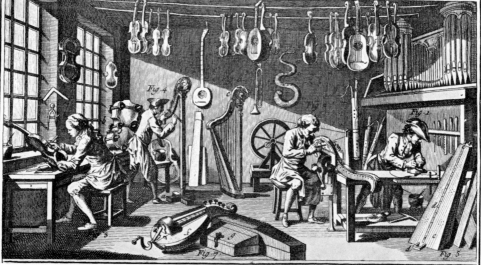

Above The title page of the six string quartets which Mozart composed between 1782–86 and dedicated to his friend Joseph Haydn. They were published by Artaria of Vienna.

Below An instrument-maker's workshop in the mid-eighteenth century. Illustration from the *Grande Encyclopédie*.

Mozart by Josef Lange:
one of the few authentic
portraits of the composer
in adult life.

The old Burgtheater in the Michaelerplatz in Vienna was built in 1741 and it
was here that Mozart's *Entführung aus dem Serail*, *Nozze di Figaro*, and *Cosi Fan
Tutte* were first performed.

haughty Gaul invasion threat?; for this last probably dates from the year before French forces occupied Vienna. To that city he returned in the late summer of 1795, wealthy enough now to be free of financial anxiety for the rest of his life.

Apart from a few string quartets, completing his notable achievement in that form, he now turned mainly to choral music. From his last years date two oratorios which certainly owe their existence to England and Handel's example, *The Creation* (1798) and *The Seasons* (1801), the German text of the first being drawn from Milton. He recognised *The Creation* as a task to crown his career and, devout man that he was, began each day's composition with prayer. In 1808, now truly an old man, he attended a performance of it and was heard to say, 'Not from me – it came from above'; he was too moved to stay till the end and left during the interval. As he was helped out, Beethoven came up and kissed his forehead and hands. It was in the following year that he died, peacefully on May 31st. His last visitor was a young French officer, who sang to him the aria *In native worth* from *The Creation*; the young man and the old were moved and embraced upon parting.

Haydn's long life takes us from the late works of Bach and Handel to Beethoven's Sixth Symphony. We cannot sum up his achievement in a few words. He did not invent the symphony, the sonata or even the string quartet – though in the latter case he has the strongest claim. But by the time he was about forty he had established sonata form in a way which is difficult to define, but might be thought of as its early maturity. 'Maturity' implies the creation of masterpieces, works of genius with nothing of uncertainty or experimentation about them. This maturity is 'early' only in the sense that while J. S. Bach seems to sum up a chapter of musical history, Haydn opened a way forward for his successors. For classicism was a dynamic, driving force which was to lead onward into the turbulent world of the nineteenth century.

MOZART

When Wolfgang Amadeus Mozart died in 1791, Haydn wrote that 'the world will not see such a talent again in a hundred years.' He was right in recognising Mozart's genius as unique. He had told Leopold Mozart: 'I say to you before God, as an honest man, that your son is the greatest composer I know, either personally or by repute: he has taste and the greatest craftsmanship in composition.' Later, he wrote: 'Friends often flatter me that I have some genius, but he stood far above me.'

Haydn's natural modesty was well known; but even so, such considered tributes were generous indeed. Could this master really have intended to praise the younger man in such terms? It seems that he did, weighing his words soberly: the last remark quoted above, for example, formed part of an expert opinion requested by a publisher. And if imitation is the sincerest form of flattery, Haydn's most sincere tribute was his assimilation at the age of fifty of Mozartean features into his own style: a compliment which was returned, for Mozart himself was influenced by Haydn and acknowledged the fact.

Mozart was born in the Austrian town of Salzburg in 1756, his father Leopold being a professional musician of some eminence in the service of the Archbishop of that city. The boy was an infant prodigy as a keyboard performer, violinist and composer. His father, having become his teacher too, took him thousands of miles through Europe so that the musical world might learn of his talents; and he was constantly on public show from the age of six until his mid-teens. In 1764, by way of Louis XV's Versailles, he reached George III's court in London. Here he came under what proved an important influence: that of Johann Christian Bach (1735–82), sometimes called the 'London' Bach and Johann Sebastian's youngest son. He had studied in Italy and become a Roman Catholic and organist at Milan Cathedral, but finally settled in England where, among other things, he wrote sonatas, symphonies and keyboard concertos. There is a story of Bach and the eight-year-old Mozart sharing in the performance of a sonata and then, interestingly, a fugue; for J. C. Bach, this form may have been old-fashioned but was obviously still of importance. Mozart's own first symphony dates from this time, though he was still not quite nine years old!

Unlike Haydn, whose travels took place late in life, Mozart came into contact during his formative years with the finest examples of European music-making, and like J. S. Bach he had the habit of making copies of music that interested him. His formal training culminated in lessons from the celebrated Italian teacher Martini. And Italy was in some sense his obvious goal, for here was music both learned and of wonderful beauty, Italian singing and violin playing being justly celebrated. In Bologna, aged fourteen, he was elected a member of the select Philharmonic Society, having passed an examination in which his contrapuntal technique* was thoroughly tested; apparently he had no trouble in doing this, and in the academic sense there was literally nothing left to teach him.

Mozart's technical skill, acquired so young, was truly second nature to him. His prodigious learning was worn lightly, so that he could only pay polite compliments to one composer whose music lacked charm, even though 'the poor fellow must have taken a great deal of trouble and studied hard enough'. His last symphony, the 'Jupiter', contains astonishing contrapuntal feats presented in an atmosphere of sublime playfulness: 'perfect, as if created by a god', said the composer Grieg, feeling this symphony to have been well named by posterity. He was also an artist of cosmopolitan culture, and not only because of his travels. For his birthplace, Salzburg, was in the

* 'Counterpoint' and 'contrapuntal' were terms which by this time were more often used than 'polyphony' and 'polyphonic' for many-voiced music.

Catholic and thus Italianate part of German-speaking Europe, and from the age of thirteen his letters often mix Italian and even French with his native German. He wrote operas in Italian and German. Yet he is always unmistakably himself, whether he is writing sonatas, church music or opera. In him all trends seem to meet: not even Beethoven has this universal range of utterance. If Mozart has any weakness, it lies quite simply in his absolute musicianship. His music could be said to lack the common touch, the peasant humour which Haydn and Beethoven could display. Only in some of his German songs and dances, and the lighter parts of *The Magic Flute*, do we find a more 'popular' style; though there is ample tenderness and humanity elsewhere. 'Nature' however, other than human nature, meant little to him.

Like Handel, Mozart started his professional career as a court musician and then in his mid-twenties gave up his employment in favour of independence. But where Handel had been a businessman, an impresario as well as an artist, Mozart had to rely on music alone. After his marriage in 1782 to Constanze Weber, he found things very difficult. It was only a year since his appointment at the Archbishop of Salzburg's court had ended with embarrassment and anger ('I hate the Archbishop almost to fury,' he wrote to his father), and he had no intention of trying to return there;* while the idea of searching for another court post was not attractive. After all, he was an expert composer and keyboard performer as well as a fine violinist and an experienced teacher: surely he could make a decent living in Vienna.

Yet somehow circumstances seemed from the very start to be against the young composer and his wife, who soon became pregnant. Neither he nor Constanze seem to have brought any financial resources to their marriage, nor were they good at managing money. Mozart gave concerts and lessons, writing piano concertos to play himself and also improvising before enthusiastic audiences; but he had to apologise to his sister for writing only seldom: 'Hasn't a man without a penny of secure income enough to do and think of day and night in a place like this?' The Emperor, who knew and admired his gifts, could have offered him some official court position with only nominal duties but commanding a good salary, which by now he would gladly have accepted; his friends, he told his father, were 'much vexed at the little value the Emperor places on men of talent'. Failing such an appointment, he seriously thought of trying his fortunes in London or Paris. He began negotiations with the director of the *concerts spirituels* in the latter city, where he had had a success five years previously; but his father persuaded him to abandon his plans in view of his family responsibilities. Though his father had been against his marriage, he was now determined that his son should properly fulfil his role as a husband and father.

Of course Mozart had splendid isolated successes, such as his opera *The*

* The Archbishop had him forcibly removed from his presence in order to terminate an interview.

Marriage of Figaro in Prague in 1786, and *Don Giovanni*, composed the following year for the same city. Yet financially he gained little, receiving only 'the usual fee of one hundred ducats' for *Don Giovanni*. Outright payment was the rule of the day, for though the idea of copyright in literature was already formulated in Mozart's lifetime, music was not safeguarded, while the performing rights which provide most of a modern composer's income did not exist. Where Handel, as an operatic impresario, shared in the profits of a successful opera, Mozart's only gain from repeated performances was an enhanced reputation and a greater demand for his services. But the story of Mozart's finances generally is a sad one. When at last in 1787 the Emperor gave him an appointment as court composer for imperial dance music, the salary was little more than a hundred pounds annually. 'Too much for what I write,' he wrote bitterly, 'and too little for what I *could* write.' The following year he wrote to his friend Michael Puchberg that he was 'unavoidably obliged to raise money somehow'. Among the many and pitiful letters requesting the loan of money which he addressed to this same friend between now and his death in 1791 there are continual references to his worsening situation: 'Unfortunately Fate is so much against me, though only in Vienna, that even when I want to, I cannot make any money.' Mozart's age may have been a golden age of music, but to him it must have seemed otherwise.

Had Mozart lived longer, into an age which valued individual genius, his fortunes could well have changed: *The Magic Flute* became widely popular and was played even in England. During his tragically short career, he produced a vast quantity of music. His compositions include over forty symphonies, around a dozen full-length operas, numerous concert arias for brilliant vocal display, a great deal of church music for the Roman Catholic Church into which he was born and which culminates in the magnificent, unfinished Requiem (completed by his pupil Franz Xaver Süssmayr), nearly forty songs with piano, of which those with German words come into the category of *Lieder*, innumerable dances and serenades, divertimentos and marches, over twenty piano concertos, concertos for other instruments including violin and horn, string quintets and quartets as well as trios and duos, trios and quartets for piano with strings and the Piano and Wind Quintet K. 452, sonatas for violin and piano, and piano sonatas as well as variations and other pieces for the same instrument.

The emotional quality of some of Mozart's music still reveals nothing of his personal life, as a romantic composer's does. For example, his last three symphonies were written within a period of only eight weeks, during which his baby daughter died and he was so poor that he had to write begging letters; yet these masterpieces show a variety of moods ranging from pathos to joy, as well as the unsurpassable craftsmanship which with Mozart we take for granted. In similar personal circumstances most creative artists would be unable to work at all, much less produce work of this quality. In fact it is only of this composer that a scholar can say, as one did of the piano Adagio in B minor (K. 540), that it 'may simply have flowed from Mozart's pen in an hour at once tragic and blessed': a comment which seems meaningless until one actually hears this moving and beautiful piece. In the same way, some claim his opera *Don Giovanni* to be a comic work, others a tragic one: such is the depth of this music.*

The 'K' numbers usually attached to Mozart's works are those of Köchel's catalogue.† This lists them from K. 1, a piano Minuet and Trio written when he was six, to K. 626, the Requiem of 1791 which was not quite finished at his death. Sometimes it is felt that a man who could write so much so effortlessly before dying at thirty-five must have lacked depth. But neither in music nor in the other arts has facility, or ease of creation, necessarily meant triviality. Bach's output rivals Mozart's; and even Beethoven's, in spite of his struggles with the act of creating music, is considerable. In fact Beethoven admired and played Mozart's music, for example the powerful D minor Piano Concerto, and referred to Mozart and Haydn as 'these two great men'.

Poor Mozart! Beethoven and Haydn may have recognised his genius, but it all too often eludes lesser mortals. Even now we listen to the *Eine kleine Nachtmusik* – a serenade and thus entertainment music, even if the finest example of the type – or we remember the 'easy' piano pieces learned at school, and we may think of him as somehow a light-weight. But exactly the opposite opinions were voiced by contemporaries, friends and foes alike. Haydn said, with tears in his eyes, that Mozart's playing touched the heart unforgettably. But he was too much for Viennese taste, leading listeners, it was said, 'among steep rocks into thorny forests few in flowers' and into 'impenetrable labyrinths'; while the orchestral writing in *Figaro* was alleged to be 'artificial, weighty and overloaded', and in Berlin a critic wrote that 'caprice, ambition but not heart created *Don Giovanni*'.

So much for the idea of Mozart as the wonderfully gifted entertainer, casually placing his talents at the disposal of a painted and powdered society which was soon to be swept away by the French Revolution and Napoleon's armies! And for all his facility, composition was not invariably easy. He once had to give up work on a commission because he found himself 'engaged on a very difficult task . . . the ode is too exaggerated and pompous for my

* Mozart's mature operas are as follows: *Idomeneo*, *opera seria*, Munich 1781; *Die Entführung aus dem Serail*, German *Singspiel*, Vienna 1782; *The Marriage of Figaro*, Italian comedy, Vienna 1786; *Don Giovanni*, *dramma giocoso*, Prague 1787; *Così fan tutte*, *opera buffa*, Vienna 1790; *The Magic Flute*, grand opera, Vienna 1791; *La clemenza di Tito*, *opera seria*, Prague 1791.

† Ludwig von Köchel (1800–77) lived in both Salzburg and Vienna. As an amateur botanist and music-lover, he was distressed by the lack of any proper classification of Mozart's work and, in his retirement, made the chronological and thematic catalogue which was published in 1862.

fastidious ears. But what is to be done? The golden mean of truth in all things is no longer known or appreciated. To win applause one must write stuff which is . . . empty.' He explained that his 'golden mean' lay between triviality and the pseudo-highbrow.

Mozart practised what he preached. The opera *The Marriage of Figaro* is certainly superb entertainment; yet it is also both beautiful and tender, and it makes, as do all great comedies, serious comment on human nature. Even so, it was asserted after Mozart's death, in 1793, that he 'was a great genius, but he had no real taste' – exactly the same comment that Voltaire as a young man made about Shakespeare. And while Mozart's friend Haydn succeeded in pleasing his contemporaries, the six string quartets which Mozart dedicated to Haydn ('most celebrated and very dear friend'), the very works which elicited Haydn's 'greatest composer' tribute, were for one critic only 'grave and unusual . . . Mozart's compositions do not unanimously please.'

For modern ears, however, Mozart is not so difficult. After all, we are accustomed to stranger sounds even than those of the mysterious slow opening of the 'Dissonance' Quartet (K. 465), in C major but bristling with both flats and sharps, or the Minuet in D major for piano (K. 355), quoted here:

EX. 51

And passages like these are not really typical of Mozart. He is possibly the easiest of the great composers to enjoy. Yet he is also the hardest to appreciate; and scholars, after years of studying his music, have commonly felt that they have taken only a few steps towards the real understanding of his art. Even other composers, his fellow-professionals, have regarded Mozart with something like awe. For Grieg he was 'like a god', for Wagner a 'divine genius', for Richard Strauss the 'most sublime of all musical masters'; while Tchaikovsky wrote, 'I idolise him . . . this pure and ideal artist.'

In the light of all this, it would obviously be both impertinent and foolish to attempt an 'explanation' of Mozart's style here. Even so, it seems worth looking at a passage chosen almost at random, the opening of the Piano Sonata in B flat major (K. 333):

EX.52

This graceful music, with its effortless flow, is a perfect example of an art which conceals art. The rippling left hand supplies harmony in the highly pianistic form of broken chords, while the right gives us the first paragraph of a melody. There is nothing in the way of a preliminary: the music simply starts. The melody begins with a little falling scale followed by a broken chord curving upwards and then falling again; this is at once answered by a balancing phrase in which both melody and rhythm are similar but not identical. The falling scale now leads to a new rhythmic idea, in bar 5, answered by a brilliant scalic run and then, in bar 6, by a decorated version of itself. In the following bar a scale flies upwards to the highest and loudest point so far; then the melody falls to rest on the key chord through a version in longer notes of the opening scalic figure.

Anyone who cares to look at this whole movement can see how the music grows, with supreme naturalness, from the music of the first bars. Even the contrasting second melody (bar 23) begins with a phrase whose contours are very like those of the first:

EX.53

Key, texture and rhythm are all so different that no resemblance is noticed, and this is as it should be, since contrast is essential in a sonata movement. Yet the similarity makes the second subject belong with the first, so that the movement holds together from first note to last.

As we have already noted, Mozart lived in something like a golden age of music. He did not have to struggle to escape from old forms and find new ones, for the sonata and the opera were fully established when he grew up: as far as form is concerned, his main innovation may have been in his serenades for orchestra, and similar pieces called divertimentos, which lie in a region somewhere between suites and sonatas. Of course, this is not to suggest that he failed to create new ideas in his quartets, concertos and symphonies, only that these forms were ready for his genius in a way which had not been the case with Haydn. In the same way, the symphony orchestra was ready for him at just the right time, both in the concert hall and the opera house; while the more expressive piano replaced the harpsichord just as he reached manhood.

Mozart once wrote to his father that he found the thought of death consoling rather than frightening. Neither he nor his wife enjoyed good health. His membership of a Freemasons' lodge seems to have had a calming effect on him as well as eliciting some masonically-inspired music, of which the opera *The Magic Flute* is the most celebrated example. Yet when in July 1791 he was approached with a somewhat mysterious commission to compose a Requiem he was so overworked and overwrought that he began to see this as an omen of his own imminent end. He suffered from fainting fits and general depression, even fearing that he was being poisoned. He took to his bed, but continued to work at the Requiem, discussing the music with his pupil Süssmayr. A few hours before his death he was still talking about the work; and even after receiving the last rites he tried to sing some of the music. His death was probably of uraemia, a form of kidney failure, and his funeral was simple. While his wife lay at home ill with grief, a violent rainstorm drove the half-dozen mourners away before the actual burial, which thus took place without friends or music. A rather grander memorial service took place later and was well attended.

No account of Mozart's life would be complete without a reminder that though his music may be of god-like quality, he himself had human and lovable qualities. He was short, with fair hair and blue eyes, and liked to dress carefully. He appreciated a good table and once wrote of 'angelic cooking and glorious Moselle wine'. He enjoyed riding for a time and did not neglect to take active exercise, which probably to some extent compensated his health for his habit of working far into the night. He liked dancing, and he had a billiard table at his house where he played skilfully with friends, with his wife – or even alone, when his thoughts turned to music and whole compositions took shape in his head, to be written down later at leisure in his neat hand.

Thus even a description of the man comes inescapably back to the music. In the composer's own words to his father, he was 'swallowed up in music . . . busy with it all day long – speculating, studying, considering'. His belief in it was as a means towards beauty, and he once declared that it 'must never offend the ear, but must please the hearer, or in other words must never cease to be music'. We must approach his works in this light, and not as personal documents of his brief and troubled life. It is beauty we find in them: the beauty of vocal or instrumental tone displayed in shapely melody, of contrapuntal interplay or harmonic audacity. Yet the warmth of Mozart's own humanity is always there to be felt. It is present in the music he gave to the neglected Countess in *Figaro*, to the young and sweetly impetuous Cherubino, to the sparklingly vital Figaro and Susanna, even to the arrogantly egotistic Count. There are no real villains in Mozart's operas, even though this meant his having to read dozens of stories before finding one to suit him. The rake Don Giovanni is far from hateful, even though we may deplore his actions; for since Mozart was incapable of writing ugly music, even his 'bad' characters are redeemed from loathsomeness.

The writer Stendhal said of *The Marriage of Figaro* that in the composer's hands Beaumarchais's satirical comedy changed entirely: 'All the characters were turned towards the tender or the passionate. Mozart's opera is a sublime blend of wit and melancholy which is without any parallel.' An interesting comment from the literary world upon this 'musicians' musician'. Perhaps we may equate beauty with warmth of heart and agree with Professor Lang that Mozart's dominant characteristic was 'an inexhaustible capacity for love'. This quality showed itself in thirty years' free outpouring of beauty, until Mozart burnt himself out like a moth which flies too close to a flame.

8

BEETHOVEN

Beethoven's importance. Early life and first-period music.
The second period. The final years. Plaudite amici.

BEETHOVEN'S IMPORTANCE

When Rameau said that in the process of acquiring more taste he had lost his genius, he was obviously seeing the refinement of mid-eighteenth-century music as a limitation. On the other hand, Mozart was accused, towards the end of that century, of possessing genius but lacking taste. Mozart, we know, desired to please the public, though not by descending to triviality. There is a real problem here. 'One *ascends* to the public' – this dictum of a present-day Marxist, Cuba's leader Fidel Castro, has been approvingly quoted by the German composer Hans Werner Henze. But can a mass audience respond to the highest examples of human thought?

No history of music can offer a simple answer. But it can draw attention to Beethoven, a composer whose work attracts experts and public alike. In this, his art resembles that of Shakespeare.* Beethoven believed in the message of the choral finale of his last symphony, 'Be embraced, ye millions!' For him, all men were brothers under God.

The Renaissance spirit had been one of faith, even pride, in mankind. As we have seen, a reaction took place in baroque times as it was realised that knowledge did not necessarily bring wisdom and goodness: there is a certain sobriety in Bach and even Handel, composers from Protestant Germany. Next came the more extreme expressive style of 'storm and stress' and the homeliness of Italian comic opera, as well as the dainty and perhaps escapist art of rococo. These differing trends were to merge in the emotionally rich yet disciplined beauties of classicism. Even so, the sublime art of Mozart stood on a knife-edge. History was at a turning-point, and not only in music. Strangely enough, Mozart never once mentioned the French Revolution in any of his letters. But in any case he did not live long enough to learn of its worst excesses. These events meant a setback for Rousseau's creed of the 'noble savage'; and many artists like the poet Wordsworth, who at first

---

* Asked once to 'explain' his 'Appassionata' Sonata for piano, he said, 'Read Shakespeare's *Tempest*.'

welcomed the Revolution, suffered a lasting shock to their faith in natural goodness.

Beethoven, born in 1770, was the exact contemporary of Wordsworth – and of Napoleon Bonaparte. Indeed Beethoven and Napoleon are often compared: as it happens, they even looked somewhat alike. The composer admired Napoleon, and he too was a child of the turbulent times in which he lived. Unlike Mozart, who was unconcerned with politics, he believed passionately in the republican and democratic cause. Liberty, equality, brotherhood: the watchwords of the Revolution were also Beethoven's. His sheer forcefulness, the feeling in his music of struggle and heroic achievement, seem to reflect the birth-pangs of the new century. But his battlefield lay in his own soul and he used to pray for the strength to conquer himself; the wild young man whom Haydn nicknamed 'the Great Mogul' always remained in certain respects what Goethe called him, an untamed personality. In his music, however, he triumphed over anarchy, becoming a master of form: that is, of musical order.

This allows us to think of him as a classical composer. Yet for the romantics of the nineteenth century – Berlioz, Liszt, Wagner and others whose ideals were no longer classical – Beethoven was a father-figure; and regarding him with awe, they sought to follow in his footsteps. To see where Beethoven stands in the history of music is to understand why a whole chapter of this book is devoted to him. He is neither classic nor romantic, at least, not without so many qualifications that the labels themselves become useless. He accepted the established classical forms of sonatas and variations, and even the fugue, which was much older. Indeed he inherited the classical ideal of structural beauty, and could write 'eighteenth-century' minuets of impeccable grace and charm. On the other hand, his intense individuality suggests romanticism, a self-surrender into autobiography such as we may find in later works like Tchaikovsky's 'Pathétique' Symphony.

But when we think of Beethoven's Fifth Symphony beside Tchaikovsky's work we immediately sense a profound difference between these two composers. Beethoven reaches out beyond himself to a universal ideal: he speaks to mankind at large, even to God. Music was for him 'a higher revelation than all wisdom and philosophy', offering entrance to a spiritual world. He saw his work, quite consciously, as a humanitarian vocation in a religious sense. This is perhaps why he has been called 'too great an artist to be left to the musicians'. Nevertheless, even in the strictly musical sphere, it is safe to say that no composer before or since has had greater influence. Even today, two hundred years after his birth, the 'advanced' composers Boulez and Stockhausen have acknowledged their debt to him. Tippett's Piano Concerto of 1956 was inspired by Beethoven's Fourth, while Bartók's string quartets and the symphonic dramas of Shostakovich are inconceivable without Beethoven's own quartets and symphonies as part of their historical background. Thus it is possible to see Beethoven not only as a link between classical and romantic styles, but also as the father of modern music. A great modern master, Stravinsky, declared him to be supreme among musicians.

It is a convenient custom to divide Beethoven's work into three periods. To the first belong the first two symphonies, the first three piano concertos, the six string quartets of Opus 18 and the first ten or eleven piano sonatas – works written after the end of his early student days and up to about the age of thirty. After this comes the second period: the unmistakably individual and fully mature personality of the Third to Eighth Symphonies, the Fourth and Fifth Piano Concertos, the Violin Concerto, the 'Kreutzer' Sonata for violin and piano, the 'Moonlight', 'Waldstein' and 'Appassionata' Piano Sonatas, the incidental music to Goethe's *Egmont*, the 'Rasumovsky' String Quartets and the opera *Fidelio*. The third and last period begins around 1818, after something of a pause in Beethoven's output. It includes the great Mass in D, the Ninth Symphony, the 'Diabelli' Variations for piano, and the last five or so string quartets and piano sonatas.

These three periods, musically distinguishable one from another, were also separated by turning points in the composer's life. The first was his agonised acceptance of the onset of incurable deafness. This dreadful psychological blow came just at the time when a brilliant career seemed assured, well earned after the hardships of his youth. It presaged the end of his life as a performing musician, cutting him off at the same time from his fellow human beings and from the sound of all music. He confessed that it was only his consciousness of his vocation as a composer which gave him the courage to endure his existence; he feared that he would never know 'one day of pure joy' again. We can never know what it cost him to fight back against his tragedy, though the 'Eroica' Symphony, which now came into being, must tell us something of the struggle and final heroic victory. The second turning point in his life was a more mysterious inward and spiritual crisis. He emerged more isolated from his fellow-men than before, yet with a capacity for love and humanistic feeling in the wider sense which seemed to have increased in proportion to his withdrawal from society.

EARLY LIFE AND FIRST-PERIOD MUSIC

Ludwig van Beethoven was born in 1770 in Bonn; his grandfather and father were professional musicians in this fairly prosperous and artistic North German town. His mother was an intelligent, rather serious woman, whose marriage was not a happy one – she called it 'a little joy followed by a series of sorrows' – for Beethoven's father was a heavy drinker. Still, he set his son to music early, making him do daily keyboard and violin practice. He saw for the boy a career as a child prodigy, another Mozart, and even falsified his age, deducting a year, so as to make his talent seem the more

spectacular. Though what we know of him hardly suggests a likeable character, at least he gave Ludwig the best musical education he could, though that
included such harshness as waking him at night for lessons. If Beethoven had
learned to hate music in these circumstances, he could be forgiven for it.
As it was, the strain certainly told on him, and to his school fellows he evidently appeared dirty and unkempt, showing no sign of future greatness. In
1781 his schooldays ended so that he might concentrate on music; and soon
he held a small post as an assistant organist.

At this time the organist Christian Gottlob Neefe became his teacher. As
early as 1783 this good man wrote publicly of his pupil's talent as a performer
and composer, adding that 'This youthful genius is deserving of help to
enable him to travel;' perhaps he also felt that Beethoven needed to escape
from an unhappy home. It was Neefe who introduced Beethoven to Bach's
'Forty-eight', that celebrated set of preludes and fugues which has been
called the Old Testament of keyboard music.* He valued Neefe's teaching
and wrote to him some years later, 'If I ever become a great man, yours shall
be a share of the credit.' In 1784, in his fourteenth year, he got a job as an
organist at the Electoral court in Bonn, thus becoming a proper wage-earner.
He may even have managed to save some money. At any rate, in 1787 he
was able to visit Vienna, the great musical centre which must have seemed a
Mecca to him. There he met and played to Mozart, who was impressed by
his powers of improvisation and urged the others present to keep an eye on
this young talent, saying that, 'Some day he will give the world something to
talk about.' Apparently Mozart gave Beethoven a few lessons, and another
service he performed was to arouse Haydn's curiosity in this brilliant
newcomer.

Beethoven returned to Bonn to find his mother on her deathbed: for
although she was only forty, her hard life seems to have worn her out. She
had borne seven children; three of them had already died, and a fourth died
soon after. Beethoven called her 'my best friend among women', and these
words were later engraved on her tombstone. It seems likely that his mother
asked him to look after the family; and this charge became legally his in 1789,
his father's state of health having so degenerated that he was obliged to retire,
though still only about fifty.†

Fortunately Beethoven was not friendless in Bonn. The wealthy and cultured von Breuning family gave him access to their home. He found another
friend in the young Count Waldstein; and these two made music together for
hours, all differences of rank forgotten in a manner which was exceptional
for the time. Waldstein gave him a piano; he earned the composer's trust
and friendship, and gained a place in history as the dedicatee of the Piano

---

* Beethoven's own thirty-two piano sonatas being the New.
† Upon Johann van Beethoven's death in 1792, the Elector himself remarked sardonically
that the revenue upon alcoholic drinks would be noticeably lessened.

Sonata, Opus 53, which bears his name. Beethoven now also played the viola in the orchestra of the Electoral court, and in this capacity took part in performances of operas by Gluck and Mozart. He must have worn the orchestra's red uniform trimmed with gold: perhaps he even took a pride in his appearance. He seems to have been genuinely happy at this time, and was popular among his colleagues, good-natured, yet, for all his talents, modest and unassuming.

It was during this time that Beethoven helped to entertain Haydn, who paused at Bonn on both the outward and return journeys of his first English visit. It was agreed that Haydn should teach him in Vienna. A few months later, in November 1792, he took his leave of Waldstein and the von Breunings, as we know from their good wishes written in his autograph book; and then he set off on his great journey. He never returned to Bonn; from now on, Vienna was to be his home.

In theory he was on leave of absence granted by the Elector, with a salary. But Austria and France were now at war, and a French revolutionary army marched into Germany. The Elector had to leave Bonn and relinquish his office. Needless to say, the payments to Beethoven eventually ceased. He might have known poverty had it not been for his rapid rise to fame in Vienna. Haydn probably helped him with good advice, charging little or nothing for lessons, and the young newcomer was soon the darling of the cultured aristocracy. Perhaps some of the more thoughtful among these people wished to demonstrate their egalitarian principles in those troubled times. Certainly Beethoven from now on was never treated, as Mozart and Haydn had been, as anyone's servant. He lodged with the musical Prince Karl Lichnowsky, who provided him with money, a horse and groom, and the privilege of having his bell answered by the servants before the Prince's own.

It was only a year after Mozart's death that Beethoven arrived in Vienna. How, we may ask, did this young unknown musician manage to keep his head above water financially when his famous predecessor could not? Several factors were, however, on Beethoven's side. He seems to have received his small salary of a hundred thalers from Bonn for about eighteen months. He was given free lodging and some kind of an allowance by Prince Lichnowsky, to whom in return he dedicated his three Piano Trios, Opus 1. He did not, like Mozart, have family responsibilities or the expenses of frequent travel. He certainly received good fees for his piano performances at aristocratic *soirées*: these were frequent, though public piano recitals were still unknown and public orchestral concerts rare. His standing as a pianist, from the first, ensured him a supply of well-to-do pupils. The same higher ranks of society yielded a good supply of persons to whom he dedicated his works and who in some cases rewarded him financially: his chamber music, for example, includes works dedicated to four princes, five counts and countesses, two barons, a professor, an archduke and the Empress Maria Theresa herself. Sometimes a patron would 'own' a Beethoven work for an agreed period, with sole rights of possession and performance, and would pay well for the privilege: this happened with Prince Lobkowitz and the 'Eroica' Symphony which is dedicated to him.

Publication was another source of income. Beethoven even became his own publisher in one sense, in that he would himself pay for the printing of a work and its publication by a reputable firm, and then sell the copies at his own price, the finance for this being provided by subscriptions which he collected from his friends and patrons.

It was in this way that the three Piano Trios, Opus 1, were placed on the market in 1795, though they appeared under the imprint of the publisher Artaria, a firm founded in 1778 and one of several important firms whose foundation dates from around the end of the century. Haydn admired these Trios, though he had doubts about the boldness of the last of the three and advised Beethoven against publishing it unaltered. Beethoven did not take the older composer's advice: he already had ample confidence in his own judgment. But he valued and admired Haydn, who in fact received the dedication of his first three piano sonatas, published in 1796.

The first of these sonatas is in the key of F minor. Neither Haydn nor Mozart ever used this key for a piano sonata, though Haydn employed it for a set of variations dating from 1793 which may have influenced Beethoven's choice. This F minor Sonata begins with a phrase reminiscent of the finale of Mozart's late G minor Symphony:

EX. 54 Beethoven *Piano Sonata Op.2 no.1*

It is characteristic of Beethoven that the headlong energy of the music, after rising from *p* to *ff*, is instantly reined in. The effect is one of an increase in tension to a high point: it is achieved not only by an increase in loudness but also by a speeding-up of harmonic change. There is one chord for bars

1–2, another for bars 3–4, one each for bars 5 and 6, and two in bar 7. The second melody (or second subject) brings the necessary contrast of key and texture, with a flowing accompaniment instead of staccato chords and an unusual note, F flat, which gives a pathetic 'minor' feeling to a tune which is otherwise in the major. But just as in the Mozart sonata movement referred to in Chapter 7 (pages 151–2), there is a similarity between the first and second subjects. The latter is not just a new tune; it has somehow grown out of what has gone before. In fact its smooth descending five-note figure, which then turns upwards, corresponds to the contour of the first subject in what is called imitation by inversion, the tune turned upside down.

EX.55 Beethoven *Op. 2 no.1*

The slow movement of this F minor Sonata is clearly indebted to Mozart. Indeed this could be Mozart, for the energetic young Beethoven had not yet found his own way of writing gentle, lyrical music of the kind expected at this point in a sonata:

EX.56 Beethoven *Op. 2 no.1*

The very existence of the next movement, however, shows the composer's originality. A minuet was a regular feature of Mozart's and Haydn's symphonies, but not of their piano sonatas, which thus have three movements. Beethoven's first four piano sonatas have a minuet or scherzo (which is faster) before the finale, four movements in all. The effect was broader, more symphonic perhaps, than had hitherto been common in piano music. His originality did not stop there, though; for him, a new procedure was not an end in itself but a single step in a continuous voyage of discovery. The Fifth Piano Sonata, in C minor, has only three movements; its first is in sonata form, but with its triple rhythm and general style it sounds much like a scherzo, which therefore became unnecessary to the scheme of movements. On the other hand, the Sixth Sonata has no slow movement but a minuet instead, and the fact that it is not at once recognisable as such is due to Beethoven's no longer being content to repeat the opening section exactly. Though the 'repeat' section is of the same length, it is fascinatingly varied.

We may return briefly to the minuet of the First Sonata in order to make another point. Beethoven was the first to write for the piano like this, and even thought it worth while to provide a fingering to show how the passage might be played:

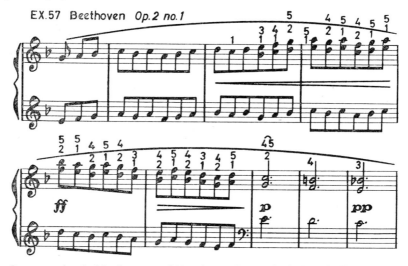

EX.57 Beethoven Op.2 no.1

One unmistakable feature of Beethoven's music is its vitality. Obviously this is most apparent in moments of humour or drama. But even his gentler music is more profound, less relaxed, than that of other composers: thus the slow movement of the Ninth Symphony might be some sublime lullaby written as it were for an infant Zeus. Beethoven's writing often approaches extremes of one kind or another. Thus the finale of this First Piano Sonata is marked *prestissimo*, as fast as possible, and the contrasts between loud and soft, *legato* and *staccato*, are as breathlessly vivid as they can be:

EX. 58   Beethoven   Op.2 no.1
Prestissimo

Even a lyrical second tune is accompanied by the galloping left-hand triplets, though Beethoven does not risk monotony by maintaining them throughout the whole movement. By the end, however, they have returned. The closing bars of the movement, and thus also of the whole sonata, are typically effective.

EX.59 Beethoven *Op.2 no.1*

Example continued

Beethoven is fond of wittily abrupt endings like this. Similar examples are the closes of the Piano Sonatas in D, Opus 10, No. 3, and in A flat, Opus 26.

This kind of abruptness at the end of a work suggests that Beethoven does not need to complete his sustained mental effort, like a long journey, with any relaxation of pace. His creative energy is as unflagging as ever, and has simply been switched off. No wonder Goethe said of him that he never knew a more energetic artist. His vitality is even shown in music which he marked to be played *grazioso*, gracefully. Here, surely, one would expect a feeling of leisure: but the relaxation is still of the Beethovenian kind. The finale of the Second Piano Sonata begins with four bars which could have been written like this:

EX. 60A Beethoven *Piano Sonata Op. 2 no. 2*
Rondo. Grazioso

But Beethoven gives us, instead, a great leap upwards and downwards. Incidentally, though these first sonatas were published as 'for harpsichord or piano', the piano's sustaining pedal is obviously needed to link the melody notes across the downward leap. Or perhaps not so much a leap as the step of a giant:

EX. 60B

This is a rondo-form movement, so that this theme must return several times. Should the composer have begun with something like our imaginary simple version and saved his arpeggio for a return of the tune? We need not underrate his powers of invention, though. This is the same tune on its second appearance:

In its third version, it has become this:

And the final form of the tune is:

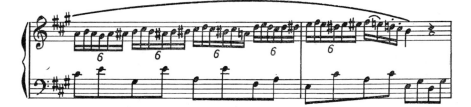

THE SECOND PERIOD

'Your Beethoven is living an unhappy life, quarrelling with nature and its Creator, often cursing the latter because He surrendered his creatures to the merest accident which sometimes broke or destroyed the most beautiful blossoms. Know that my noblest faculty, my hearing, has greatly deteriorated.' So Beethoven wrote to a friend in 1801. Yet, 'Plutarch taught me resignation. If possible, I will defy my fate.' Two works of this time symbolise the parts played by the world of classical gods and heroes, and by the Christian message, in the composer's struggle back to balance and a mode of living. One was the ballet *The Creations of Prometheus*, in which a godlike spirit endows men with the blessings of culture. 'I,' said Beethoven, 'am Bacchus who presses out this glorious wine for men and makes them drunk with the spirit.' The other was the oratorio *Christ on the Mount of Olives*, which emphasises the heroic acceptance of suffering in the Garden of Gethsemane, rather than its mystical aspects. It is said that Beethoven also thought of writing a similar piece on Christ's sojourn with the souls in Purgatory, a subject which has not so far tempted any other composer.

Heroism is of course the theme of a far more famous work: the Third Symphony, the 'Eroica', was written in 1803 and remained his favourite. It seems to have been intended to portray Napoleon, who 'at this time appeared to Beethoven as a hero in the antique mould, a character out of the Plutarch whom he had been reading, and a politician who would realise Plato's ideal of the philosopher-king.'* The dedication was angrily withdrawn when the composer heard that his hero had proclaimed himself Emperor of the French. 'Is he then, too, nothing more than an ordinary human being? Now he will trample on the rights of man and become a tyrant!' But Beethoven seems to have forgiven Napoleon and he considered dedicating his Mass in C to him in 1810. His ideals were in some ways contradictory. A hero, after all, is not, as he said, an ordinary human being; yet as the finale of the Ninth Symphony reminds us, Beethoven held throughout his life to his belief in mankind's brotherhood and equality. Alexander the Great was one of his heroes, and incidentally also one of Napoleon's; he considered Alexander's life as a possible subject for an opera. Yet the heroic stories of Alexander and Napoleon could have been written in the blood shed during their campaigns. Greatness, genius, excellence – the very words exclude ordinariness and, it seems, ordinary virtue as well as equality. The problem, seen in purely human terms, seems insoluble.

Yet if we move on to a spiritual plane, the ideal world of the philosophers and the mystics, such paradoxes may be understood at least partially. From the Crucifixion came resurrection and redemption; the martyrdom of Socrates or Thomas à Becket advanced men upon the long road to wisdom;

---

* Martin Cooper: *Beethoven: the last decade*, 1817–27. Oxford University Press 1970, p. 92.

and Beethoven himself had to pass through his personal agony to become the musician whose art brings us joy and hope. In Aeschylus's play, Prometheus declares that he overcame man's fear of death by bringing him hope: Beethoven's music offers us the strength and the example of a man who has suffered yet triumphed.

The 'Eroica' Symphony itself presents us with a mystery, unless we admit the existence of some spiritual level onto which the drama of the music moves. Why should the slow movement, a mighty funeral march, be followed by an exhilarating scherzo? Berlioz suggested funeral games around the hero's grave such as are described in Homer's *Iliad*, and since Beethoven knew Homer's work the idea is at least plausible. But then how do we explain the triumphant finale? The best clue comes from Beethoven himself. For this finale he used an important theme from *Prometheus*; so perhaps his hero has now been translated to a higher, godlike sphere. We remember that Beethoven copied into his diary Kant's phrase, 'The moral law in us, and the starry sky above us.' As for the question whether such a literary programme as this is likely, we have the composer's own note for a projected later work: 'In the adagio the text of a Greek myth – or *Cantique ecclésiastique* – in the allegro a Bacchic festival.' Not many people would think of mixing a Christian hymn with a pagan festival in the same work. Nor would they equate a Greek myth with a hymn as alternatives for the slow movement; but for Beethoven, on whose shelves the Bible (in two languages) and the Christian mystic Thomas à Kempis stood beside the writers of the ancient world, both were valid attempts made by Man to commune with his Creator.

The most striking novelty about the music of the 'Eroica' Symphony is its sheer size. Lasting about three-quarters of an hour, it is roughly double the length of a symphony by Haydn or Mozart. Indeed the first movement, except for that of the Fifth Piano Concerto which shares the same key of E flat, is the longest he ever wrote. The composer was aware of this, and even perhaps a little embarrassed by the fact. He was therefore willing to omit the customary repetition of the first movement's exposition; but, as his own brother said, 'It was found that the omission of the repeat was harmful to the work.' Of course, for to omit the repeat is completely to alter the movement's proportions. So Beethoven suggested that because of its unusual length, this symphony should be performed near the beginning of a concert, when the audience's ears would be fresh and not 'already wearied' by other music.

Naturally, length alone does not ensure grandeur. But Beethoven's whole design is grand; we are never reminded, as we sometimes are by ambitious works of lesser men, that the great prehistoric dinosaurs were sluggish creatures with tiny brains. As a matter of fact, in many ways the 'Eroica' offers examples of economy. Was there ever a shorter introduction to a symphony than these two chords, compared by Leonard Bernstein to 'two mighty pillars at the entrance to a great temple'?

EX.61 Beethoven *Eroica*
Allegro con brio

Two simple chords of the tonic, E flat major. Of course, any student could have written them. But we will surely concede that Beethoven was capable of writing an elaborate introduction had he felt it appropriate to do so; and we remember his admiration for Handel's power of achieving 'great effects with simple means'. As it happens, the composition of this introduction – short, simple, and enormously effective – cost him a good deal of thought, as we know from his sketchbooks.

The first subject, beginning in bar 3, also required considerable effort. There were several preliminary versions before it reached its present form:

EX.62 Beethoven *Eroica*

These are the first five bars of the melody. It starts in the bass; but the soft entry of the first violins with the high G in the last bar quoted, insistently repeated and swelling in tone over three bars, prepares us for a shift of the melody into the treble. Soon wind instruments take over the melodic line, in dialogue with the violins. This kind of change, from low to high register or from one instrument to another, even in the first statement of a tune, is characteristic of the composer. So is a drop to soft tone just as a crescendo is apparently about to reach its climax on a loud chord. The fact is that Beethoven is always surprising us, so that the music characteristically sounds dramatic and exciting. Yet however unlooked-for an effect may be, somehow we feel the rightness of it.

For example, the last melody note quoted above, the C sharp, is not at all what would be expected here. It does not belong in the key – far from it – and nothing could have been harmonically simpler than what has gone before. This odd note, as if faintly embarrassed by its sudden appearance on the scene, slips back obediently via D to the tonic, E flat, four bars later. Even so, it foreshadows conflict; in this movement we may always expect the unexpected, though there is purpose in everything Beethoven does. Later in the movement, when the recapitulation begins, we expect to hear the first subject as before. But the mysteriously intrusive C sharp now turns downwards to C. We are carried into an exploration of other keys before the expected tonic, which arrives nearly thirty bars later. By this time, Beethoven no longer bothers to give us the theme in its complete original form, but after a blaze of E flat major moves straight on to something else, namely thirty-eight bars leading to the second subject which, apart from their conventional transposition to the home key, are identical with the corresponding passage in the exposition. Again this is typical of the composer: at a moment when we are perhaps slightly disorientated, in danger of losing our bearings, he reassures us by putting us back firmly on familiar ground.

But the whole of the 'Eroica' Symphony's first movement repays close analysis. Every original stroke is convincing, yet the degree of boldness is unique. For example, a completely new tune appears in the development section, something even Beethoven could hardly make a habit of, since the very idea is foreign to sonata form. Yet it works in this particular movement. Beethoven does not break the sonata-form structure, but extends it in scope while retaining its essential nature. Three more striking passages from this same movement should be at least mentioned. One is the apparently premature, dissonant horn entry four bars before the recapitulation. The effect of simultaneous tonic and dominant chords which results was thought to be a mistake (to the composer's annoyance) at the rehearsal. Then there is this unprecedented violence of dissonance and syncopated rhythm:

EX. 63 Beethoven *Eroica*

Finally, there is the use of consecutive chords of E flat, D flat and C at the beginning of the coda: the sort of thing that Debussy is supposed to have invented a century later. Beethoven has no intention that we shall overlook the effect, either. He emphasises the boldness of the harmonic progression by equally violent changes in dynamics, from loud to soft:

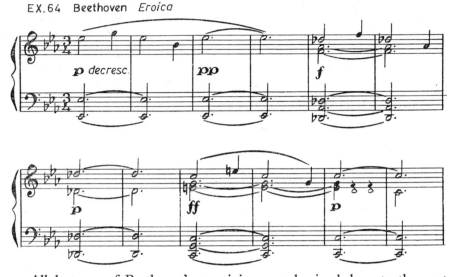

EX.64 Beethoven *Eroica*

All but one of Beethoven's remaining symphonies belong to the next decade, and thus to this second period of his career. He evidently went straight from the 'Eroica' to the mighty Fifth, but then put it aside to write the delightful and humorous Fourth, a work of altogether lighter character, though of no less mastery and with a lovely slow movement. The Sixth Symphony is the 'Pastoral': its five movements tell of the serene happiness to be found in the countryside, of streams and bird song, of a thunderstorm and the rain-washed freshness of the sunny weather following it. 'More expression than painting,' was how Beethoven described this most lovable symphony. For despite the obvious portrayal of natural sounds like the cuckoo's call and the thunder, the music tells us mainly about the composer's emotional reaction to his pastoral surroundings, and is thus a tone-poem in the sense understood by Berlioz, Liszt, or Debussy in *La Mer*.

The finale of the Seventh Symphony was described by Sir Donald Tovey as 'unapproached in music as a triumph of Bacchic fury'. This often-quoted remark is always misinterpreted. For there is no rage here; and the word 'fury' is used in the older sense of what the Oxford Dictionary calls 'inspired frenzy, as of one possessed'. This wonderful dance is wild, but not destructive, Dionysiac in a positive sense; it has a modern counterpart in the finale, in the same key, of Ravel's Greek-inspired ballet *Daphnis and Chloe*.

After the Seventh, the Eighth Symphony appeared a light-weight. There were people who had disliked or distrusted the tumultuous energy of the former work; even the composer Weber thought Beethoven mad or nearly so, and he was a younger man and a sensitive, progressive musician. But now the Eighth was found too Mozartian, even trivial. When he was told that it was liked less than the Seventh, the composer remarked with typical humour that this was because it was so much better. In fact the Eighth is one of his happiest works.

Thus each of the symphonies has its own, quite distinctive character; for Beethoven was not the man to be content with simply repeating himself. The same applies to the concertos of this period. The Fourth Piano Concerto is lyrical rather than grand. Its slow movement is said to have been inspired by the story of the musician Orpheus calming hostile creatures; the soloist's exquisitely pleading phrases and the initially harsh answers of the orchestra certainly fit the literary theme. The Fifth, his last piano concerto, is a work of truly imperial splendour – its nickname of 'Emperor' seems justified, even if Beethoven, in republican mood, might not approve. The Violin Concerto of 1806 came between these two works. It is even more lyrical and song-like than the Fourth Piano Concerto. The slow movement has an ethereal beauty, while even the spirited rondo-form finale is delicate rather than roughly boisterous.

The so-called 'Moonlight' Piano Sonata, in C sharp minor, is among the earliest sonatas of the middle period, and yet full of originality: in fact the composer called it a fantasy-sonata. The slow opening movement, like a nocturne, is profoundly emotional and yet of infinite restraint. Nothing could be further from the forceful utterances of the 'Eroica', yet this music too could be by no other composer. Beethoven never again attempted anything quite like it, except perhaps for the magically nocturnal passages in the slow movement of the last-period 'Hammerklavier' Sonata, composed about seventeen years later.

So far we have concentrated on Beethoven's instrumental music. Indeed, this is so powerfully expressive that it seems at times almost to 'speak' like vocal music. Here is such a moment, the instrumental 'recitative' in the D minor Piano Sonata, Opus 31, No. 2:

EX. 65 Beethoven *Piano Sonata Op.31*

Example continued

However, one supremely important vocal work is the opera *Fidelio*. It dates from the same time as the 'Eroica' Symphony and also deals with heroism. The title is the symbolic name, 'Faithful', taken by a young wife, Leonora, who disguises herself in order to gain employment in the prison where her husband Florestan is wrongfully confined for political reasons. She saves his life and brings about the prisoners' liberation by a visiting minister of state. The theme was one to fire this composer's imagination. 'Married love', the opera's sub-title, is a rare enough subject for the theatre, for is there any other operatic love story which is not about courtship? But it was typical of the idealist Beethoven to choose it. In his music at least he could celebrate marriage, though he never enjoyed it in life.

THE FINAL YEARS

The soloist's role in the first performance of the Fifth Piano Concerto, written in 1809 and thus a work of the second period of Beethoven's career, was entrusted to his pupil Carl Czerny. In 1814 Beethoven played for the last time in public. It is said that by 1817 he could no longer hear music; yet the degree of his deafness seemed to vary, and indeed loud noises gave him more pain than ordinary people. He was reluctant to give in. As late as 1822 his attempt to direct a dress rehearsal of *Fidelio* resulted in embarrassment for all concerned. He was described as 'with a bewildered face and unearthly, inspired eyes . . . with the strangest gestures, uttering the most uncanny sounds.' Soon it was clear that he could no longer control the orchestra. His friend Schindler tells us that Beethoven called him and handed him the conversation notebook in which his friends' remarks had to be written down. 'Hastily I wrote, "Please do not continue; more at home."' Beethoven sprang down at once, and though now over fifty, set off at a run to his lodgings. 'Once there he threw himself on the sofa, covered his face with his hands . . .'

No one can read of Beethoven's last years without pain, for their story is only too full of incidents like this. A lesser man might have fought less, or he might have dulled his misery with alcohol. Yet to have done so would have affected his creative work, and though not a teetotaller he drank sparingly. He struggled on, though at times he seems to have been near the brink of a mental breakdown.

The immensely difficult 'Hammerklavier' Sonata for piano, Opus 106, dates from 1818 and marks the full revelation of third-period Beethoven. It is a colossal work, not only in length but in the nature of its utterance. Here, he announced, was a sonata that would give pianists something to do, 'a work that will be played in fifty year's time'.* Yet it looks back as well as forward, with a fugal finale which is in itself a tribute to the art of Bach. Beethoven even used the highly academic device of having a reversed version of the fugue subject, a technique barely used even by Bach since it is almost impossible for any listener to be aware of it without preliminary study – though the ears of a Prometheus, outside time, might be.

But the mood of awe-inspiring striving of the 'Hammerklavier' Sonata's finale, fugal though it may be, is worlds removed from Bach. It is literally aggressive, with its shrilling trills and melodic leaps of terrifying purpose. Nobody could call this comfortable music, in spite of a gentle interlude a little beyond the halfway point which offers a brief respite from the conflict. Even so, as always with Beethoven, the wild energy and emotion are subject to order: this finale is a masterpiece of structure. The same may be said of the *Grosse Fuge*, Opus 133, for string quartet, in the same key of B flat and in some ways a similar work.

Another powerful late work is the D major setting of the Mass, usually called the *Missa Solemnis*, which occupied Beethoven at intervals from about 1819–22. When composing it he was described as oblivious of everything earthly; at one point in the score he wrote 'God above all – God has never deserted me.' In this work he is once again aware of his baroque predecessors and indeed as close as he ever was to Handel, a composer to whom he often paid tribute. The Ninth or 'Choral' Symphony dates from about the same time. In the finale of this, his last symphony, words – and thus voices – were brought in for the full expression of his thought; it is a setting of lines from Schiller's *Ode to Joy*, a hymn to the brotherhood of man. Beethoven's religious feeling, at times expressed with deep humility, found in Schiller's words, which he had known all his adult life, a link with his humanistic and

---

* Hitherto it had been rare for composers to think in terms of posterity. The 'latest thing' was for the musical public usually the only thing. Though Mozart and Beethoven themselves studied Bach they did not expect or attempt to interest the public in him, and Beethoven saw nothing odd in the fact that while Homer and Shakespeare were revered this great artist was allowed to remain in obscurity. However, in his last years Beethoven, perhaps with a conscious historical awareness, planned an overture on Bach's name. The letters of this, in the German nomenclature, corresponded to these notes, subsequently used in the same way by Liszt and others:

EX. 66

'revolutionary' creed.* The symphony as a whole sums up so many aspects of his art and of his philosophy that it provides one important key to the understanding of this complex personality and genius.

The solution to conflict, a long-sought peace, is approached in certain others among the last works. One thinks, for example, of the serenity of the closing pages of the last piano sonata, Opus 111 in C minor. We find an almost superhuman calm in parts of the last string quartets, such as the slow 'thanksgiving hymn of one recovering from illness' in the A minor Quartet of 1825. The opening fugue of the C sharp minor Quartet, Opus 131, is sad but at the same time extraordinarily calm: it possibly has some connection with a Mass or Requiem in the same key which was an idea in Beethoven's mind at the time. This C sharp minor Quartet has no less than seven movements. The fourth movement's theme and variations may be described in Wagner's words: 'A vision of perfect loveliness, the incarnation of pure heavenly innocence, revealed in countless different aspects, transformed ever-anew by the light shed upon it.'

Such works as these leave one with few words. All the struggles had not been in vain, though the ultimate victory seems to have been achieved on a level beyond common human experience. Beethoven fulfilled the vocation of which he wrote in 1823 to his friend the Archduke Rudolph, to whom the *Missa Solemnis* was dedicated: 'There is no loftier mission than to come nearer than other men to the Divinity, and to disseminate the divine rays among mankind.'

PLAUDITE AMICI

What sort of a man was this, whom the German critic Paul Bekker described as one 'crucified and descending to hell and rising again', whom Antonie von Brentano, a close friend, called 'even greater as a human being than as an artist'?

Beethoven was capable of writing the noblest of love letters. But it seems that his romantic adventures involved conquests dubious enough to cause disease; recent medical views suggest, however, that this was not of a serious nature such as would permanently affect his general physical and mental health. In particular, there is no evidence that the cause of his deafness can be traced to this and thus no question of Beethoven's feeling his disability to be any kind of divine punishment. Indeed he keenly felt the apparent injustice of his sufferings.

Yet contradictions do abound in this most complex man. He washed incessantly and at times seemed obsessed with personal cleanliness; yet he could become so absorbed in his work that he would tolerate extremes of

* The French Revolution was not wholly atheistic, and worship was addressed to a 'Supreme Being'.

dirt and disorder symbolised by an unemptied chamber pot underneath his piano! The noble humanitarian was capable of rudeness and even violence, not only towards his brother but also to people less able to defend themselves, such as servants, or the unfortunate waiter at whom he threw a plate of stew.

His friend Stephan von Breuning said in his obituary that, 'While possessing lofty musical genius, a great and cultured mind and rare depth of soul, Beethoven was from a boy perfectly helpless in all economic and financial matters.' This may explain his sometimes apparently sharp practice with publishers and his distrust of business associates and employees. That he was somewhat unorthodox and even eccentric is beyond question. Children jeered when they saw him standing trouserless by an open window while composing, and he was more than once taken for an old peasant. In 1820 he was arrested and locked up as a vagrant; and to his protested 'I am Beethoven,' the official reaction, till he was eventually identified, seems to have been the equivalent of 'Oh yeah? Says you!' in the Viennese dialect.

But the composer's eccentricity had a long history. When only sixteen he suffered from asthma which he feared would turn to consumption; confessing this, he added a more worrying fact: 'Furthermore I have been suffering from melancholia, which in my case is almost as great a torture as my illness.' Then things improved for a while; he met Haydn and came to Vienna, where his strong individuality, coupled with his brilliance, actually helped him in making friends. Yet there is little doubt that throughout his life he experienced extremes of emotion. He must have known that he would be difficult, if not impossible, to live with, and that a happy family life was unattainable.

His one extraordinary attempt to share his home has puzzled all his biographers. This was his acceptance of the guardianship of his nine-year-old nephew Karl, in response to a request contained in his brother's will. The boy's mother not unnaturally opposed this, having in any case been appointed a co-guardian in a codicil added at the last minute. The case went to court and dragged on for five years from 1815, for Beethoven distrusted the mother. She was evidently less than honest, and of doubtful morality; but at any rate she wanted her son back, and Beethoven was determined that she should not have him, though he tried to be fair and was willing to let her see the boy at intervals and to give her financial help. In the meantime, as one biographer has put it, he tried to be 'both father and, in his clumsy way, mother' to Karl. The legal wrangling and his altogether changed circumstances drained his energies. For two years, 1816–18, he composed almost nothing, describing himself in a letter of 1817 as 'so often in despair that I should like to end my life, for there is never an end to these afflictions. God have mercy upon me, I think myself as good as lost.'

Until quite recently Karl has had short shrift from biographers. Anyone who caused Beethoven worry, and above all creative impotence, is of course a villain to those who idolise the great musician. Yet the lad had to put up with a great deal. There was a letter saying 'I can never trust you again,' and signed 'Your father, or better still, not your father'; then another, 'Only come to my arms, you won't hear a single hard word . . . only come, come to the faithful heart of your father,' and then in clumsy French, 'If you don't come you will surely kill me.'

Yet Karl seems to have been a reasonable enough boy, well behaved as well as clever, dutiful too as the conversation books show. He was even intelligent enough to help with the manuscript score of the Ninth Symphony, and he played piano duets with his uncle – though how much could Beethoven have heard, one wonders?

Karl once wrote pathetically in Beethoven's conversation book: 'Too much I cannot endure . . . You must remember that other people are human too.' He felt himself a prisoner.* He tried to shoot himself, and upon recovering said that Beethoven was responsible: 'I grew worse because my uncle wanted me to be better.' This particular, and tragic, incident could not be hushed up, the police having been called in. Beethoven's appearance suddenly became like that of a man aged seventy. This was in fact the beginning of the end, for he died within eight months of Karl's suicide attempt.

The composer died on March 26th 1827, a full ten days after the doctors gave up hope and after two days' unconsciousness. The actual moment of death was during a storm; after a clap of thunder, he opened his eyes and lifted his right fist as if in defiance; when it fell back he was dead. The cause of death was a liver complaint. The physician, Dr Edward Larkin, writing quite recently, has advanced the view that this may have been a final outcome of a chronic disease dating from early adulthood, an allergy to one's own proteins such as might be successfully treated today with the drug cortisone. Should this theory be correct, there would be an explanation for occasional confusion and emotional instability. It would also account for the disfiguring facial rash, often commented on, which was another of Beethoven's afflictions which could not be hidden: there is no record of his ever having had smallpox, to which the scars on his face used sometimes to be attributed.

Beethoven's will left everything to Karl. On the day he signed it, March 23rd, he said something which was a common closing line in the Roman theatre, and also reputedly used by the dying Emperor Augustus in AD 14: '*Plaudite amici, comoedia finita est.*' It was typical of his indomitable spirit, of his sense of history and of drama too, even of his sense of humour. 'Friends, you may applaud. This is the end of the play.'

---

* As indeed he evidently was: 'Will you let me go out a little today? I need a break. I will come back later . . . Will you let me go to my room?'

9

GERMAN ROMANTICISM

The romantic spirit. Schubert. Weber and German opera.
Mendelssohn. Schumann. Brahms.

THE ROMANTIC SPIRIT

'Romanticism is beauty without bounds,' wrote the German novelist Jean
Paul in 1813. In the same year, another German writer, E. T. A. Hoffmann,
declared: 'Haydn's music reminds us of a blissful, eternally youthful life
before the Fall; Mozart takes us into a spirit world of love and melancholy,
of inexpressible longing; while Beethoven's music sets in motion the lever
of fear, of awe, of horror, of suffering, and awakens just that infinite longing
which is the essence of romanticism. He is accordingly a completely romantic
composer.' But Hoffmann, a composer himself, added that though Beethoven's imagination might seem boundless, he had the 'self-possession inseparable from true genius . . . The internal structure of the movements,
their execution, their instrumentation, the way in which they follow one
another – everything contributes to a single end.'

In fact the romantic music of the nineteenth century was still subject to
well-tried artistic laws or principles. In the English romantic poet Wordsworth's phrase, emotions must be 'recollected in tranquillity', for the
artist's thoughts have to be put into shape in order to make their effect.
Romanticism represented a change of mood, but not of the fundamentals of
composition. Symphonies and sonatas were still written, and opera continued
its development; the piano was as suitable an instrument for Chopin as it
had been for Mozart.

Romanticism in fact was not as revolutionary as it seemed to those who
were caught up in its first flood. But it did offer something new: a sense of
free self-expression, of adventure, the pioneer feeling shared by artists who
set out to explore the mysterious heights and depths of the human spirit.
For mystery was an important feature of this art, and the essayist Walter
Pater defined romanticism as 'the addition of strangeness to beauty', echoing
Byron's remark that 'There is no excellent beauty that hath not some strangeness.'

The price to be paid for such an ideal was sometimes that of isolation
from the listener. Schumann said, 'I should not like to be understood by

everybody,' while Berlioz declared that his own music was aimed at those listeners possessing unusual perception and intelligence. There was also perhaps a cost in personal terms; and Schumann's lifelong cultivation of a fantasy world, though it enriched his music, seems to have contributed to his later mental decline. For if 'strangeness' excludes routine, it also involves the loss of comfort and contentment. The young lover of Schubert's *Schöne Müllerin* song cycle cannot marry and settle down while still remaining a romantic youth. In this sense, adulthood is at some odds with the romantic spirit. 'The romantic ego is eternally in formation, for it is that endless driving itself which is its soul.'*

The first musical prophets of romanticism, Beethoven and Schubert, were German-speaking, and the movement had originated in German literature and philosophy. The philosopher Kant believed that art derived not from intellect but from feeling, and he defined music as 'the art of the beautiful play of emotions'. Goethe, the only contemporary artist whom Beethoven wholly admired, wrote an influential novel in 1774 called *The Sorrows of Young Werther*, in which the hero kills himself for love of a married woman; and Goethe also showed the scholar Faust mortgaging his soul in exchange for knowledge and power. The spirit of total emotional involvement also had its heroic side: thus the patriotic hero of Goethe's *Egmont* gives his life for his people. On the other hand, the gentle dusks and peaceful churchyards of the writer Hölty symbolise an equally romantic attempt to escape from life's harsh realities into some twilight pastoral world, and this particular mood brings us closer to Schubert.

Love, heroism, death: these were all subjects to attract romantic artists, and it is not surprising that these artists idealised Shakespeare. The tragic young lovers of *Romeo and Juliet* inspired Bellini, Berlioz, Gounod and Tchaikovsky to compose music; *A Midsummer Night's Dream* was a source of Weber's opera *Oberon*; *Macbeth*, *Othello* and the character of Falstaff provided Verdi with opera subjects; Schumann wrote an overture to *Julius Caesar*; and both Liszt and Tchaikovsky composed symphonic poems on *Hamlet*.

No one doubts the emotional power of Shakespeare. Yet with both Shakespeare and Beethoven, emotion was always subject to structural control, for its unbridled rule is no more possible in art than it is in life. This control seems less firm with a composer like Berlioz, and there are people who feel that the strongly emotional appeal of a Berlioz work, however exciting at first hearing, wears thin rather quickly, preferring the more disciplined and 'classical' romanticism of Mendelssohn or Brahms. This argument is really one of personal taste. But what should be avoided is the idea that highly expressive music is necessarily 'sentimental' and thus inferior to the more

* P. H. Lang: *Music in Western Civilisation*, p. 809.

'intellectual' art of earlier times, for both Bach and Beethoven made it clear that they intended their music to move the emotions. Still, when we hear such a work as the *Fantastic Symphony* by Berlioz after a symphony by Mozart, we do seem to undergo a different kind of aesthetic experience, and are carried into a more intensely personal world. Indeed, we find a richer variety of styles in the nineteenth century than in any earlier period. Every artist now had to find his own unmistakable, unique voice in which to address the listener. Each of the romantic composers does more than create beautiful music: he offers us a different kind of emotional experience.

SCHUBERT

Franz Peter Schubert was born in 1797 and died in 1828. All his short life was spent in Vienna, where he remained a virtually unknown figure over-shadowed by the great Beethoven. It was only during Beethoven's last illness that he was introduced to Schubert's music, examining about sixty songs. He was delighted, exclaiming repeatedly that this young man had genius, 'the divine spark'. He wanted to see Schubert's piano music and operas, but was too ill, though the young composer did visit him on March 19th 1827. When Beethoven died a week later, Schubert took part in his funeral as a torch-bearer.

More than Beethoven, Schubert belongs to the romantic era. Yet he too had classical qualities: he greatly loved Mozart's work, but certain features of Beethoven disturbed him, and he once said that Beethoven's mixture of tragedy and comedy, saintliness and clownishness, caused confusion in a listener's mind. But he was then still under twenty. Anyone who tends to think of Schubert as a merely gentle composer may remind himself of the finale of his Ninth Symphony, which almost outdoes Beethoven in its feeling of boundlessness and of which Schumann said, 'How refreshing is this feeling of overflowing wealth!'

If one remembers how short Schubert's life was, and then looks at a list of his compositions, one may guess correctly that he was both an early starter and very prolific – had Tchaikovsky died at the same age, *Romeo and Juliet* would be the only one of his popular orchestral works to exist. In fact, Schubert wrote songs and piano music in his early 'teens, and he had composed a symphony and fourteen works for string quartet before reaching his seventeenth birthday.

He was, however, fortunate in his upbringing. He was born in Vienna, the city of Haydn, Mozart and Beethoven. His schoolmaster father was a good enough musician to give his eight-year-old son violin lessons. He also had lessons in singing, and gained a choral scholarship at the Imperial Choir School. This was the school which Haydn had attended and which supplied choristers for St Stephen's Cathedral. He received tuition in violin and piano playing as a matter of course; he played Mozart on the piano and became the leader of the school orchestra, while at home he played the viola in a family string quartet. At school there was an eight-hours' gap between what he called the 'mediocre lunch' and 'miserable supper', and though the music practice room was cold, he was able to spend plenty of time there. When he told a friendly fellow-pupil that he would compose more if he could afford manuscript paper, this was provided for him. The school's training prepared him for the teaching profession as his father intended, but two unhappy years of schoolmastering showed him clearly that his vocation lay elsewhere.

Schubert made long-lasting friendships; and like Beethoven he was lucky in his friends. His life after he left school, and teaching, was not that of a court or church musician engaged in training an orchestra or choir, but was spent in his friends' company, a company of equals. These rather Bohemian and impoverished young men made up a circle of varied talents, not all of which were musical. A great deal of Schubert's music was first performed for his friends in private surroundings, and so has a domestic and intimate character. His songs he could sing himself to his own piano accompaniment; they required no expensive or elaborate means of performance.

It is probably above all for these songs, around six hundred in all, that Schubert is revered by the musical world. There have been other great composers of symphonies and quartets, but as a song-writer he stands supreme. His individuality comes out strongly already in the songs to Goethe's words written before he was nineteen: *Gretchen am Spinnrade*, *Erlkönig* and *Heidenröslein*. In the first of these, a young girl sits alone at her spinning wheel, thinking of her lover. As she recalls the pressure of his hand, and his kiss, she stops her work and the hum of the wheel ceases; then she resumes her spinning, at first falteringly and then once again steadily.

EX.67 Schubert *Gretchen am Spinnrade*

The evocation of that fatal forest spirit, the Erl King who steals away the soul of a child, is no less remarkable: the night ride and the galloping horse, the anxious father, terrified son and uncannily alluring demon are all unforgettably drawn. *Heidenröslein* is subtle and delicate. The story of a boy who must pluck a rose – though, as it warns him, he will be wounded by its thorns – is naturally and beautifully told. Neither poet nor composer bothers to point out the obvious moral, which makes the song all the more effective. In such music as *Heidenröslein*, Schubert comes very close to folk art. Time and again, he seems to find a great and profound simplicity. What could be more simple and yet absolutely right than his song called *An die Musik*, a setting of a poem in praise of the art he served?

An die Musik was the work of one of his greatest friends, Franz von Schober. Yet this same Schober confessed to liking only *Der Lindenbaum* out of the twenty-four songs in the *Winterreise* song cycle which Schubert composed ten years later, in 1827. This song sequence tells of a jilted lover who wanders alone through a grey and icy landscape in a hopeless search for peace, finally joining an old itinerant musician. The ending of this wonderful though mysterious work is hardly a happy one. Yet it is not quite tragic either. For the romantic wanderer, who cannot find contentment, at least remains free, sensitive and above all a poet. He may even find joy just around the next corner.

The 'Wanderer' theme is one to which Schubert, like other romantics, often returns: four of his song titles include the word. One of these songs provided a melody for the 'Wanderer' Fantasy (1822), which is a long piano work in four linked sections, like those of a sonata. Schubert here uses a principle of modifying a theme as the music proceeds, to evoke different moods. This technique became important in the symphonic poems of the later nineteenth century; and it is no coincidence that Liszt, the composer who was to establish the symphonic poem, made a version for piano and orchestra of this particular Schubert work.

Though he was never a brilliant performer like Mozart or Beethoven, Schubert wrote a good deal for the piano. There are over twenty piano sonatas and many shorter pieces, as well as piano duets: he wrote more duets than any other among the really well-known composers. Most of the piano music, which includes dances and marches, was intended for the home and not for the concert hall. It helped establish a tradition of short, tuneful pieces which were not too difficult for amateurs. Thousands of these compositions were to appear in the nineteenth century, designed for the delight of musical and piano-owning families.

Among Schubert's chamber works, the 'Trout' Quintet is for piano and strings and includes variations on his song of that name, while the Octet for strings and wind of five years later (1824) matches the 'Trout' in its mainly sunny mood. More compellingly stirring and obviously romantic than either of these are the four string quartets of 1820–26 and the great String Quintet of 1828. The Quintet is justly celebrated, but the Quartets in A minor and G major are quite as fine. Here Schubert disciplines his expansive and lyrical tendencies; and this control makes the ideas all the more thrilling and significant. Two quotations from the G major Quartet show the dramatic nature of the music, the interrelation of themes (these are the openings of the first movement and the finale) and the composer's love for major–minor alternation:

EX.68A

Allegro molto moderato

EX. 68 B

Schubert wrote no concertos. But he composed symphonies: like Beethoven and several other later musicians, he left nine. The early symphonies remind us often of Mozart, though that composer's bitter-sweet quality is here replaced by an irresistible youthful gaiety. Schubert shows his greatest individuality and mastery in the last symphonies. It is a tragedy that another symphonic work has been lost: this 'Gastein' Symphony (named after its place of composition) was composed between the 'Unfinished' Symphony of 1822 and the 'Great' C major six years later. The 'Unfinished', the Eighth, is in two movements only. Schubert certainly intended to continue with a scherzo, but laid it aside. Perhaps he felt, consciously or otherwise, that the work did not sound incomplete in spite of its unconventional shape, for the slow second movement is an entirely adequate complement to the first. In this 'Unfinished' Symphony Schubert showed himself a worthy successor to Beethoven, not by imitating him but by adapting his own different genius to symphonic ends. His warmly flowing melodic sense is abundantly present, but this lyricism is not allowed to hold up the progress of the musical thought. The mysteriously romantic atmosphere, too, is an even more significant pointer towards the late nineteenth century than Beethoven's 'Choral' Symphony, which dates from the following year. Schubert never heard this Eighth Symphony performed, for it was not played until nearly forty years after his death; nor indeed did he hear his Ninth Symphony, for that too had to wait some years for performance.

Like Beethoven, Schubert remained a free-lance composer. But where the older man had his own household, even if an unconventional one, and managed to amass some money, Schubert did neither of these things. He moved around in Vienna a good deal, staying with this or that friend. In the morning he composed, then he had a café lunch and perhaps a walk. His evenings were usually spent in cheerful, music-loving company. His life in some ways seems to have been happy-go-lucky, rather like that of a perpetual student. But after all he was only thirty-one when he died: and of course the quality as well as the quantity of the music he brought forth makes it ludicrous to think of his life as casually spent.

In fact, at the time of his death, Schubert was planning to undertake a course in counterpoint with a theorist called Simon Sechter. He was evidently ready for some new development in his style, and even said that he intended to turn away from song composition. So it was no idle sentiment that prompted the famous inscription on his memorial stone: 'Music has here entombed a rich treasure, but still fairer hopes.' What Schubert might have written had he lived only till fifty, no one can ever know. Even so, his work as it stands places him among the great composers.

WEBER AND GERMAN OPERA

Mozart, born in Austria, composed operas to German and Italian words; while Beethoven, a German, used his own language for *Fidelio*. Yet there is nothing specifically national about these German works, whose subjects have nothing to do with the country itself. German opera of a serious kind became established as a distinct form early in the nineteenth century. Its roots were in the comic operas or *Singspiele* with German words which appeared in the latter half of the eighteenth century, light-hearted ballad operas which included spoken dialogue and featured some kind of local, pastoral interest.

To the homely character of the *Singspiel*, the romantics added something exotic, the mysterious forces of nature and indeed of the supernatural, which after a century of rationalism re-awakened pleasantly primitive shudders among cosily-seated audiences of the comfortable merchant class patronising German theatres. There are some famous lines by the German romantic poet Ludwig Tieck:

> Magic night in moonlight shining,
> Captivating eye and mind,
> World of wondrous fairy tales,
> Rise again in splendour, as of yore.

The spirit world of old half-forgotten legends proved a rich source for operatic stories. As well as the Erl King whom Schubert evoked in his song, Germanic tales provided stories of the water-spirits called Undine or Lorelei which inspired Hoffmann, Lortzing and Mendelssohn as operatic subjects. Shakespeare's Oberon and Titania, the rulers of fairyland, also found their composers, so that Weber's last opera was called *Oberon*.

Carl Maria von Weber (1786–1826) bears the same relation to German opera as Haydn does to the symphony. That is, he was not the first composer in the form, but he was its first outstanding and influential figure. He was the son of a musical director in a theatre, and had literary as well as musical talent. He was only thirteen when he composed an opera called *The Forest Maiden* that proved good enough to be performed in the three great cities of Vienna, Prague and St Petersburg.

Beethoven once recommended that Weber should write 'operas, many operas'. But Weber composed a good deal of other music too: works for symphony orchestra and wind band, chamber music and piano music (including four sonatas), works for the church, and songs with piano or, unconventionally, guitar accompaniment. His most important instrumental composition is probably his *Concert Piece* of 1821 for piano and orchestra. Its four sections have titles containing the words 'tender', 'passionate', and 'joyful'; and these remind us of the German philosopher Hegel's remark that music should show the way in which 'the inmost being, according to his subjective nature and ideal soul, is moved'. In fact there was a whole narrative in the composer's mind here, which he related to his friends. The music describes a lady awaiting her husband's return from a crusade; she fearfully imagines him dying on some distant battlefield, but then at last he appears. 'She sinks into his arms. Love is triumphant. Happiness without end. The very woods and waves sing the song of love; a thousand voices proclaim his victory.'

It was in his operas that the dramatic tendency of Weber's thought had its fullest outlet, and it is mainly as the composer of *Der Freischütz* (1821) and *Oberon* (1826) that he is remembered. The latter was his last work, written for what is now the Royal Opera House at Covent Garden. He wrote to his wife from London, 'I obtained this evening the greatest success of my life.' It was a triumphant ending to his career. But he had accepted the commission against doctor's orders, and he died in London, aged only thirty-nine, seven weeks later. Eighteen years later Weber's body was taken back to his native Germany to be reinterred at Dresden, and it was the youthful Richard Wagner, his natural successor in the field of German opera, who spoke his funeral oration.

Of course, it takes more than literary subject-matter to make a truly romantic opera, and Weber's music itself is full of atmosphere. Even after a century and a half it can thrill audiences accustomed to the conventional 'suspense' music of films and television. The scene in the Wolf's Glen in the second act of *Der Freischütz* ('The Marksman')*, when the wicked forester casts magic bullets with the help of the Devil, is an especially effective one: the opera as a whole is a pastoral love story with a strong supernatural element. By way of contrast, what could be more warmly yet delicately poetic than the opening of the *Oberon* overture in Example 69? It prepares us for the rise of the curtain upon a fairy garden filled with flowers, butterflies and birds, in which Oberon himself reclines attended by elves.

Operas, obviously, must succeed as drama. It is not generally realised that Schubert wrote about the same number of operas as Weber; yet though their musical quality ensures an occasional hearing, they lack dramatic tension. In particular, Schubert did not possess Weber's art of swift transition from one situation to another. Another, though lesser, contemporary of Weber,

* Sometimes also called *The Magic Bullet*.

EX. 69 *Weber Oberon Overture*

Adagio sostenuto

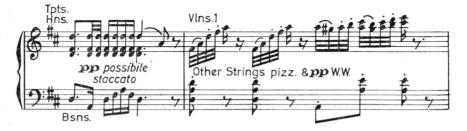

whose work has stood the test of time, is Heinrich August Marschner (1795–1861), who composed his *Hans Heiling* in 1833. Hans, half man and half earth-spirit, falls in love with a mortal, like Wagner's *Flying Dutchman*. Marschner set his supernatural tale in the German countryside, as Weber did in *Der Freischütz*, so making an effective blend of the mysterious and the homely-familiar.

An opera more directly in the comic and robust *Singspiel* tradition is Gustav Albert Lortzing's *Tsar and Carpenter* (1837). This composer liked to write his own librettos; in this he anticipated Wagner, as well as in writing an opera called *Hans Sachs* about the sixteenth-century Nuremberg shoemaker and musician who also appears in Wagner's *Mastersingers*. Another light-hearted work is the Shakespearian *Merry Wives of Windsor*, the last opera by Otto Nicolai (1810–49), which is best known today outside German-speaking countries for its sparkling overture.

MENDELSSOHN

Felix Mendelssohn (1809–47) was the son of a banker; and though he was born in Hamburg, he was brought up in Berlin, where his family moved in 1811. The Mendelssohns were partly Jewish and partly Christian: two of the composer's aunts became Roman Catholics and his parents had their children baptised as Protestants, later accepting Christianity themselves. The family was not only wealthy but cultured. Felix received a very full education, though it was a taxing one, and he remarked in later life that rising daily at five o'clock, except on Sundays, had been rather strenuous.

Handsome, rich, good-natured, charming and dazzlingly gifted, Mendelssohn seems to have been truly favoured by the gods. Music was at first only one of the subjects his father set him to study, in all of which he acquitted himself well; but it soon became clear that his talents in this direction were quite prodigious. He first played the piano in public at nine, and quickly became an accomplished violinist and a prolific composer. There were regular Sunday morning concerts at the family house in which he took part with his two sisters and brother and visiting musicians. At these his own music was played as well as other composers'; not only chamber music but also orchestral works were often on the programme. He met Weber and was delighted with *Der Freischütz*; and at this time, aged eleven, he wrote three one-act operettas. He was also entertained by Goethe, to whom he played Mozart and Bach as well as his own music, the boy's intellect as well as his musical skill impressing the great man so much that he was compared to Mozart and rewarded with kisses. In fact, the only mildly critical note struck in accounts of this brilliant childhood was his own mother's remark that her son worked 'harder than he should at his age'.

Mendelssohn was never in the least degree a revolutionary composer. From the very first he respected tradition. He played and studied Bach's music, which his teacher Carl Zelter had been among the first to rediscover, and received from his grandmother a manuscript copy of the St Matthew Passion (which Zelter had bought some years before) on the occasion of his confirmation at the age of fifteen. He utterly deplored the French view that Bach was 'only a wig stuffed with learning'; and he brought about the revival of this great Passion on March 11th 1829, a century after its original performance, thus setting in motion the renaissance of Bach's music while still only twenty.

At the same time, Mendelssohn's own religious feeling grew. He believed that music should be noble and morally uplifting, and his ideal was in some way to unite romantic feeling with religion. It was therefore as characteristic of him to write oratorios like *St Paul* (1836) and *Elijah* (1846) as it was to compose the nature music of *A Midsummer Night's Dream* (1842, though the overture is earlier) and *Fingal's Cave* (1832). With all this, though, he should not be regarded as a paragon who was also a prig. Like Mozart, he had a sense of fun which emerges in his letters as it did in his conversation: coming to England and Scotland in 1829, he announced that he was taking 'a rake for folk songs, an ear for the lovely, fragrant countryside and a heart for the bare legs of the natives.' He enjoyed himself immensely: 'I do nothing but flirt, and that in English.' Not altogether true, for there was also composition, concert-giving, the inspiration of Scottish scenery which brought forth *Fingal's Cave*, and a visit to Sir Walter Scott.

Mendelssohn made several visits to the British Isles, where he met with the most cordial and appreciative reception. *Elijah* was first heard at Birmingham, and his Third Symphony, the 'Scottish' (1842), was dedicated to Queen Victoria; the Queen even played some of his piano music at Buckingham Palace. But his interest in England was awakened earlier, for Shakespeare readings had been a feature of his home life as a boy. One outstanding work of his youth is the overture to *A Midsummer Night's Dream*, written when he was only seventeen. Other composers have showed great talent at this age, but few have produced such a masterpiece. It has been said that the four opening chords represent moonlight as well as sound can represent an object of sight. Hearing them, we are transported at once to a fairy world.

EX.70

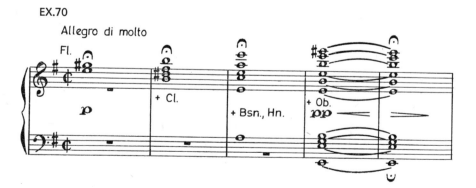

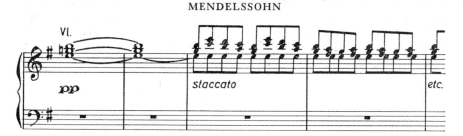

Though he once said that he wished to be thought of as a musician who lived by his profession, which he indeed did, Mendelssohn belonged to a different world from that of any eighteenth-century artist. The poet Coleridge had written in 1810 that beauty served nothing but itself; in this post-Beethovenian era a creative artist was accepted as an aristocrat of the mind, with the status accorded to a philosopher. This was, after all, a post-revolutionary period. Europe was moving into modern times.

The wider public, little by little, was becoming increasingly lettered and cultivated, and Mendelssohn's lifetime saw the foundation of a number of important musical institutions. In 1813 both the Viennese Society of Music-lovers and the Philharmonic Society* of London were founded. These were in the nature of clubs, the subscriptions of the members providing the main part of their income, but they quickly became concert-giving organisations. The German composer-conductor Louis Spohr remarked of one of the Philharmonic concerts in 1820 that, 'Notwithstanding the high price of admission, the number of subscribers is so great that many hundreds who had inscribed their names could not obtain seats.' This society purchased three overtures from Beethoven in 1815 for £75, and several of his symphonies were played at its concerts during his lifetime; he even accepted its invitation to come to England with two new symphonies in 1818, and though this project came to nothing, the Ninth Symphony was actually commissioned by the Philharmonic at a fee of fifty pounds for eighteen months' exclusive possession and it was performed in London in March 1825. At the very end of Beethoven's life the Philharmonic Society sent him a gift of a hundred pounds, hearing that he was in need, and the composer was deeply touched. Mendelssohn conducted at Philharmonic concerts on at least seven occasions. As far as educational institutions were concerned, the Royal Academy of Music in London opened in 1822; and Mendelssohn himself, having become the conductor of the Leipzig Gewandhaus Concerts, founded the Conservatory of Music in that city in 1843. Other such institutions and their foundation include Paris, 1793; Milan, 1807; Prague, 1811; Brussels, 1813; Vienna, 1817; The Hague, 1826; Geneva, 1835; Dublin, 1848; Berlin and Cologne, 1850; and Boston and Chicago, 1867.

Mendelssohn's work as a scholar, administrator and performing musician was remarkable. But he was first and foremost a composer, who wrote

* 'Royal' only after its centenary.

prolifically throughout his short life. Though his youthful works are un-surpassed in charm, it is wrong to think that his talent diminished with maturity: for example, his later incidental music to *A Midsummer Night's Dream* fits perfectly with the overture which he had composed sixteen years before. If there is a certain academic stiffness or archaism about his oratorios, there is none in the Violin Concerto of 1844; and the lovely E minor String Quartet (1837) is among a number of works whose qualities are due for re-discovery. The forty-eight *Songs without Words* for piano, written at intervals throughout his life, include some of the finest short pieces of the piano repertory, beautifully wrought, poetic and charming. Sometimes Mendel-ssohn is thought of as an urbane but essentially small master, but this is too superficial a judgment; and while we cannot place him on the same level as Mozart, it is worth remembering that the same view was once widely held of the earlier master. The time may return when his genius seems more precious than it does now. There have been more thrilling, full-blooded romantic artists, but few have achieved Mendelssohn's blend of classical poise and craftsmanship with tender, subtle romantic feeling.

SCHUMANN

When Mendelssohn opened the Leipzig Conservatory of Music in 1843, he invited his friend Robert Schumann to join the teaching staff. Schumann (1810–56) was the son of a bookseller and author, and he was intended for the legal profession. But though he and his widowed mother agreed that music was an uncertain way of earning a living, he could not resist the claims of his talent and consuming interest, writing to her when aged twenty: 'I am standing at the crossroads and am frightened by the question of which way to choose. My talent points towards art, which is, I really think, the right way . . . "To be, or not to be."'

The quotation from Shakespeare is typical of the man, and indeed of the kind of German romantic artist – Weber and Wagner are others – whose interests were literary as well as musical. 'I learned more counterpoint from Jean Paul than from my music teacher,' said Schumann: a bold remark, since Jean Paul was not a musician but a novelist. The writer-composer Hoffmann influenced him too; so did Goethe and the colourful figure of Lord Byron.

Schumann had none of Mendelssohn's balance and steady purpose. Instead he possessed an intensely poetic, individual quality which his friend lacked, even though he thought Mendelssohn 'the best musician living'. The careers of the two men present a sad contrast. Schumann's talents developed later, and the one important official post he obtained, at the age of forty as municipal director of music at Düsseldorf, ended with his enforced resigna-tion on grounds of inefficiency. As a young man he had had a nervous breakdown, and his career ended with a suicide attempt followed by two years' voluntary incarceration in the asylum where he died. The one really happy part of his life appears to have been his marriage to Clara Wieck, ten years younger and a famous pianist, which however only took place in 1840 after long opposition on the part of her father. In the security of his family circle, with his devoted wife and children, he found protection from a world which he mistrusted.

Schumann is a casualty of musical history, an artist whose heart was too great for his body, or more precisely for his mind. Nearly all his best music was written when he was fairly young; and the fine Piano Concerto of 1846 was his swan-song, or at least the last work to represent his most characteristic genius.

In 1841, Schumann wrote in his diary: 'I am still far from my goal and must strive to do better.' For this was a composer who set himself definite tasks, trying to discipline his artistic development. It was as if he felt himself to be the servant of music in the same way as a priest is dedicated to religion. He used the fairly new medium of musical journalism: in 1834 he founded a *New Music Journal* and as its editor wrote a great deal of fine criticism for nearly twenty years. In two famous and prophetic articles he hailed Chopin and Brahms as coming men of genius.

Before they were married, Schumann wrote to Clara Wieck that he was 'affected by everything that goes on in the world . . . everything extraordinary that happens impresses me and impels me to express it in music.' He wanted to obey the demands of romantic self-expression; but at the same time he was anxious to acquire the craftsmanship of a classical musician, the skill which Mendelssohn, but not he himself, had learned as a boy. But he could not reconcile his different aims. As an intellectual, he was unable to accept musical inspiration with the simplicity of Schubert, though he revered him. So he divided himself into two different imaginary characters with opposing viewpoints, the passionate and impulsive 'Florestan' and the reflective 'Eusebius'; and there was even a third, called 'Meister Raro', to mediate between them. This method made for fascinating musical criticism, but it was dangerous where his own creative work was concerned. An artist must have confidence in what he does, but Schumann was too often incapable of single-mindedness so that, whichever viewpoint he adopted, the ground seemed to slip away from beneath him. At times he would set himself to compose in strict contrapuntal forms, but at others the scholar's skill was repulsive to him. A remark which he made about Berlioz's *Fantastic Symphony* shows this unease; what can one make of it, coming from a symphonic composer? 'I believe that Berlioz, when a young student of medicine, never dissected the head of a handsome murderer with greater unwillingness than I feel in analysing his first movement.'

The first twenty-three of Schumann's published compositions are all for piano, for at one time he intended to be a concert performer himself. *Carnival*, written in 1834–35, is based on a 'motto' spelling out the name of a girl friend's birthplace, Asch, in the German nomenclature:

EX. 71

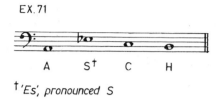

A   S†   C   H

† '*Es*', pronounced S

This is a set of pieces, similar to a series of variations. Clara Wieck, his future wife, is portrayed in a waltz marked 'passionate', and other pieces depict the imaginary Florestan and Eusebius as well as the real Chopin and Paganini. The whole work culminates in a *March of David's Men against the Philistines*, a reference to the crusading zeal of Schumann and his friends when faced with Philistine indifference and misunderstanding of their art. The *Davidsbündlertänze* of 1837 ('Dances of David's Men') has movements signed by Florestan, Eusebius, or both together, according to the character of the music.

Schumann's marriage, which took place in 1840, coincided with a tremendous output of songs. Having suddenly turned to song composition, he found great joy in it, writing no less than a hundred and thirty-eight in that one year. Among these are the *Dichterliebe* song cycle, whose story is Schubertian in that the poet-lover is jilted; though here he finally decides to box up his grief and drop it deep in the ocean. Schumann was a much better pianist than Schubert, and in these songs he uses the instrument with richness and sensitivity: one can no longer speak of a mere accompaniment, and in fact one of the most moving things in the whole cycle is the little piano epilogue which brings it to an end. The *Dichterliebe* covers a whole range of emotions from spring-like tenderness through grief and irony to the strong resolution of the ending. In another song cycle of this same year, 1840, he successfully explored a very different world, for *Women's Love and Life* is written from a woman's standpoint. It tells of courtship and marriage, the blessing of a child ('Only a mother can know what love and happiness are') and final bereavement. In music such as this the composer achieved his aim of writing 'a more highly artistic and profound kind of song'.

Like the songs, Schumann's chamber music has rather a special year, in this case 1842. His three string quartets, written after a study of quartets by Haydn, Mozart and Beethoven, all date from that summer and were followed in the early autumn by a Piano Quintet and Piano Quartet. The Quintet is rightly recognised as one of his best works, but the string quartets are rather neglected. This is a pity, for the craftsmanship is most distinguished. He had, after all, excellent models; and Mendelssohn (to whom these quartets are dedicated) had some influence too, as in the delicate, fairy-like scherzo of the A minor Quartet (No. 1). Yet in spite of the influence of other men which can be traced, the overall effect of the music is unmistakably Schumannesque. The variation-form slow movement of the F major Quartet (No. 2) offers a beautiful example of his mature style: this is Eusebius addressing us with gentle but compelling eloquence.

Schumann wrote four symphonies. Perhaps the most successful of these is the Third or 'Rhenish', which dates from 1850 and was actually the last to be composed, the Fourth being a revision of an earlier work. He left one concerto each for violin and cello, late works of the 1850s. But these concertos are overshadowed by the fine Piano Concerto in A minor, first performed in 1846 by Clara Schumann, which has buoyant high spirits as well as gentle lyricism and which has earned a secure place in the repertory of thoughtful pianists and upon the shelves of music-lovers.

This fascinating man remains a mystery. Reality and fantasy blended in him, so that he could dedicate his first Piano Sonata to his future wife Clara 'from Florestan and Eusebius'. He wrote Fantasy Pieces with titles like *Why?* and *Whims*. Though a fine natural melodist, he sometimes chose to convert the letters of proper names into notes and to use these for themes, or to borrow tunes from other composers or even from his own earlier music. The piano pieces called *Scenes from Childhood* suggest pictures or even literature; the last of them is called *The Poet Speaks*. Schumann wore other faces besides those of Florestan and Eusebius: this creator of musical carnivals sometimes seems himself to be a man in a mask, whose musical personality is elusive as well as enchanting. If romanticism really is Jean Paul's 'beauty without bounds', then it is perhaps right that this most romantic of artists should keep his secrets and remain inexplicable. At the beginning of his C major Fantasy for piano, he placed a motto referring to an all-pervading secret musical sound, and in listening to his music we seem sometimes to overhear an artist's communion with a spirit of beauty, deep within his own soul. We might echo Hoffmann's question: 'Is not music the mysterious language of a far-away spirit world whose wondrous accents, echoing within us, awaken us to a higher and more intense life?'

BRAHMS

Johannes Brahms (1833–97) was Schumann's protégé. The older composer wrote in 1853 that this was a young man 'over whose cradle graces and heroes stood guard' and to whose genius the world would pay homage.

Nothing in Brahms's music tells us that he was born a generation after Mendelssohn and Schumann; for even though they had been traditionalists in their own time (compared to the innovators Liszt and Wagner) Brahms writes like their contemporary. Indeed he turned still further back into the past to become the greatest musical reconstructor of the nineteenth century.

His symphonies, concertos and chamber music are closer to Beethoven than Mendelssohn's or Schumann's are; and in his eleven organ chorale preludes we meet once again, uncannily, the spirit of J. S. Bach. Thus Brahms's First Symphony was heard by some of his contemporaries as 'Beethoven's Tenth'. It matters little that half a century separates it from its predecessor, for from the listener's point of view its intrinsic qualities have nothing to do with its date of composition. But even if Brahms was a disciple of Beethoven – compare their two violin concertos for example – he is always recognisably himself. Like all the romantics, he has a musical personality which is unique. For many people, it is a lovable one.

Brahms was born in Hamburg, the great North German port, the son of an orchestral musician. His mother, whom he loved greatly, was no less than seventeen years older than her husband. After her death in 1865 his father went to the other extreme and married a girl eighteen years younger than himself, with whom Brahms fortunately got on well. But the composer's youth was not happy on the whole. His one great blessing of outstanding musical talent paradoxically accounted for some disagreeable experiences. He used to earn money by playing the piano in sordid cafés frequented by visiting sailors and their women, and this seems in some way to have scarred his mind. None of his biographers has claimed that he was a contented man.

But at least he enjoyed early success. Taken up at the age of twenty by Robert and Clara Schumann, he stayed for some time as a guest in their house. His hosts were delighted with his piano sonatas and songs. Schumann called the sonatas 'veiled symphonies', and in his *New Music Journal* prophesied a great career in choral and orchestral writing for the young composer. These early sonatas belong to a world of full-blooded romanticism, as we see from the opening of the F minor Sonata. Here is a young giant striding out into the world with sternly vigorous keyboard gestures:

EX.72 Brahms *Piano Sonata Op.5*

Schumann had also noted Brahms's modesty, and in fact his musical character soon became a more sober one. It is tempting to see at least a partial cause in the tragic events of Schumann's breakdown in 1854 and death two years later; for Brahms used to visit him in the asylum where he was confined, acting as a go-between for Clara, whom Schumann was not allowed to see. To share in all this suffering must have been a considerable ordeal for a twenty-one-year-old boy. Brahms stood by the stricken family till the end, and his deep affection for Clara lasted all their lives. Upon her death in 1896 he offered her family generous help, and in fact he survived her by less than a year.

Brahms once said that the two most important things which happened during his life were the foundation of the German Empire by Bismarck in 1871 and the completion of the Bach Society's publication in sixty volumes of the works of the great German composer. Actually this second undertaking was not quite finished until 1900, three years after Brahms's death, and in any case his remark was probably a half-humorous one. But the remark remains significant, showing as it does his profound respect for the past, for tradition and for institutions. Not only did he love Bach, he loved German folk song: he used to say jokingly that when in difficulties with melody he would turn to this rich source of themes. He was a cautious, rather reserved man, except perhaps with children, with whom he could unbend and who in return seem to have liked him; once when a child gave him some roses, he laughed and asked, 'Is this supposed to represent my prickly nature?' But though he never married, he was not a recluse. He nearly married a young singer called Agathe von Siebold whom he met in 1858, but then excused himself on the ground that marriage must be postponed until he was fully established; and though in the following year he took on the conductorship of a ladies' choir, this led to no further attempts in this direction. Another post he held was that of director of music at the court of Princess Frederike at Detmold, sixty miles to the south-west of Hanover.

In 1862, aged nearly thirty, Brahms visited Vienna, the home of his great predecessors Haydn, Mozart, Beethoven and Schubert; and in the following year he became conductor of the Viennese choir called the Singakademie. From now on Vienna was his home, and a later conducting appointment there was that of director of the Society of Music-lovers, the Gesellschaft der Musikfreunde. He became a friend of the critic Eduard Hanslick (1825–1904), who contributed articles on music to various Viennese newspapers between about 1850 and 1895.

Hanslick was an influential and enthusiastic supporter of Brahms's music. Unfortunately he was also strongly opposed to the music of Liszt and Wagner: Wagner in reply modelled the character of Beckmesser in *The Mastersingers*, an unperceptive, pedantic musician, upon Hanslick – in fact he was originally named Hans Lich. Brahms thus became the hero-figure of traditionalist musical thought. It was no choice of his own, for he was interested in Wagner's music. 'I shall be called a Wagnerian,' he once wrote to a friend, 'simply because I cannot stand the shallowness of his opponents.' Yet he could not publicly repudiate his friends and strongest supporters, and the result was that he in turn was attacked as old-fashioned by the progressives. The composer Hugo Wolf declared that Brahms was nothing more than an imitator of Beethoven, Mendelssohn and Schumann. On the other hand, academic recognition came Brahms's way: his 'Academic Festival' Overture was written in 1880 for the University of Breslau, which had granted him an honorary Doctorate of Music, while as far afield as England, Cambridge offered a similar honour.*

Brahms's major contemporaries were, of course, more obviously 'romantic' than he. He could never have written, as Liszt did, that 'The artist

* Had it not been for fears of seasickness, Brahms might well have accepted the invitation to visit England, for he liked travel: he visited Italy no less than eight times.

may pursue the beautiful outside the rules of the school;' on the contrary, he thought that music should be 'more strict, more pure'. This most classical among the German romantics acquired his disciplined and craftsmanlike style early in life. He avoided anything suggesting empty theatricality, and was on the whole little attracted by the more literary, programmatic kind of music. He composed no opera or programme symphony, such as Berlioz's *Fantastic Symphony* or Liszt's two works in that form. Instead he distinguished himself in variation writing, chamber music, concertos and symphonies. Whether consciously or otherwise, he was active in those very fields which were neglected by his great contemporary Wagner. Yet to think of him merely as an academic is wrong. The 'St Antony' Variations of 1873 contain contrapuntal feats, yet they owe their popularity not to these but to their tenderly lyrical melody and robust good spirits. Indeed jollity is by no means uncommon in Brahms.

In Brahms's time, the orchestra was fully mature as an instrument in the hands of composers, and had been so from the beginning of the nineteenth century and the symphonies of Beethoven. The standard orchestra was that of Haydn's Symphony No. 101 ('The Clock'), written in 1794: two each of flutes, oboes, clarinets and bassoons, two horns and two trumpets, timpani and strings. Beethoven, while still taking this as his basic orchestral body, occasionally added extra instruments like the piccolo and double bassoon, or additional brass or percussion: it was he who introduced trombones into symphonic writing. These were the orchestral resources which Brahms inherited.

Brahms's use of the orchestra was quite individual, but altogether appropriate to the nature of his musical thought. The fiery brilliance of Berlioz, and even the delicacy and sparkle of Mendelssohn, were rarely for him. But he was not a clumsy orchestrator, and such a movement as the C minor Allegretto of the Third Symphony has an orchestral sound which is wholly Brahmsian in its beauty, mellow and autumnal. He wrote four symphonies, coming to the form rather late in life The First was many years in gestation and appeared in 1876, after which the remaining three followed fairly quickly, within ten years.

Apart from the symphonies, Brahms composed two orchestral serenades and the 'Tragic' and 'Academic Festival' Overtures. The two piano concertos and the Violin Concerto are masterpieces and deservedly popular with performers and audiences alike; while the Double Concerto, for violin and cello, is equally finely wrought if less obviously attractive.

Chamber music features quite prominently among Brahms's works. He loved the rich sound of stringed instruments, and in works like the String Sextet in B flat or the Clarinet Quintet of 1891 (his last chamber work) he is supremely himself. A fine pianist, he also wrote a good deal of piano music, ranging from the early virtuoso works like the sonatas and the Handel and

Paganini Variations to the intimately beautiful short pieces of the 1890s. The opening of the Intermezzo in B minor, Opus 119, is typical late Brahms, unemphatic and subtly melancholy, yet boldly unusual in harmony:

EX.73 Brahms *Intermezzo Op.119*

Brahms was not so sober a composer as to neglect dance forms, for after all he loved folk music. Thus there are Hungarian dances and waltzes for piano, and the *Liebeslieder* Waltzes – literally 'Songs of Love' – for voices with piano accompaniment. Among the other vocal music there are folk song arrangements, over two hundred songs, the *Alto Rhapsody* for voice with orchestra and, not least important, *The German Requiem* (completed in 1868) to words taken from Luther's translation of the Bible.

There is no simple way of summing up Brahms's achievement. To class him with Bach and Beethoven, as was once done, no longer seems possible, for he had neither the purity of the one nor the inventiveness and will of the other. Brahms was a conservative, looking back nostalgically to certain and established values which seemed, and indeed were, in danger of passing away. Yet he forgot, or chose to ignore, the fact that his predecessors too had lived in changing times, creating their own values by the force of genius. Nothing abides but change, it has been said: Brahms knew this, but could not help regretting it, and his work can seem at times like an elegy for the innocent strength of a past age. He had more in common with Mahler, whom he met towards the end of his life, than either he or Mahler could have realised. He bade farewell to classical ideals rather as Mahler, not so very long afterwards. sang the swan-song of romanticism itself.

10

FRENCH ROMANTICISM

Revolution and art. Berlioz. Liszt. Chopin.

REVOLUTION AND ART

The French novelist and intellectual Madame de Staël wrote in 1810 that art should grow from the soil, and in that way become original: instead of seeking clear and elegant forms, art should extend the soul and achieve a 'sublimity of spirit, feeling and action'. Later, and more simply, Victor Hugo defined romanticism as liberalism in art.

This obviously implied a reaction from the formal beauty of classicism, but the word 'romantic' itself derived from the so-called Romanesque art of the Middle Ages. To a classical artist, medieval style had been simply ugly: and Goethe went to Venice to rid himself 'for ever, thank God, of grumpy Gothic saints'. But now the beauties of medieval art were rediscovered, so much so that people constructed new buildings in Gothic style, such as the English Houses of Parliament. Hugo's novel *Notre Dame de Paris* (1831), set in the great Gothic cathedral, symbolised the victory of this revival; while its hunchback hero, too, stood for something oddly homely, grotesque yet not hateful, and in any case altogether un-classical.

French romanticism was more forceful and even violent than its German counterpart. The poet Chateaubriand wrote of moonlight spreading her melancholy secrets among the forest trees; but he was also the author of an *Essay on Revolutions* who claimed full liberty for the artist. The sculptor François Rude created a relief of such forcefulness for the new Arc de Triomphe in 1836 that it was called 'the *Marseillaise* in stone'.

The history of France was turbulent, and passions ran as high in the arts as they did elsewhere. The country had suffered revolution, then, after Napoleon became Emperor in 1804, eleven years of war culminated in defeat. In 1814 the Allies entered Paris and Napoleon retired to Elba; the monarchy was briefly re-established, but then Napoleon returned, only to be defeated at Waterloo. Throughout the nineteenth century rulers and constitutions came and went, and in no civilised country was the structure of authority so unstable. In 1830 revolution was once again abroad in the streets of Paris. When the young Chopin arrived in the city the following year, he wrote home describing a twelve-hour public meeting which ended with everyone singing the *Marseillaise*: 'You can't imagine the impression made by the threatening voice of the people when they are roused.'

But Paris was also an exciting place in a more positive sense. In fact Chopin thought it 'the most beautiful of worlds . . . in this city I have found the leading musicians and the leading opera of the world.' It was at this time that Hugo and his followers claimed that a romantic revolution in the arts had been accomplished. The arts were part of life: indeed in the summer of 1830 an opera by the Frenchman Auber actually started a real revolution in Brussels, which led to the establishment of Belgium's independence. 1830 was also the year of Berlioz's *Fantastic Symphony*. This was music of exuberant and overflowing passion, wild and even bizarrely nightmarish, complete with an execution by the guillotine and a gothically grotesque intoning of the *Dies irae*; yet it also had moments of the most exquisitely delicate and poetic sentiment.

BERLIOZ

Hector Berlioz (1803–69) was born in Isère, a beautiful and mountainous part of France lying to the south-west of Geneva. His father was a doctor, a liberal man who taught his son Latin and gave him a lifelong interest in Virgil, the author of the *Aeneid*. The boy found himself moved to tears by this work and declared long afterwards that Virgil (with Shakespeare's help) had dictated the music of his opera *The Trojans*. He was given a flute and a guitar, and he received piano lessons. But though he became fairly proficient on the flute, he never became a skilled pianist. This handicap held back his boyish attempts to learn harmony, yet even so he was soon composing short pieces to entertain his family. Full of ideas as well as ambition, he submitted music to a Parisian publisher while still in his mid-teens.

But Berlioz was intended for a medical career, like that of his father, and in 1821 he went to Paris to study. As he himself said, he was divided between 'hideous corpses and enchanting dancers': and put in this way, his choice of a musical rather than a medical career was inevitable, though it caused something of a family crisis, and his father may have regretted the extent to which he had encouraged his son's artistic leanings. At any rate, Berlioz entered the Paris Conservatoire. By 1825 he had managed to put on a church performance of his *Solemn Mass*, a work requiring an orchestra of a hundred and fifty players, about three if not four times the normal size. This work elicited the newspaper comment that, 'The young and seething composer pays more attention to his own inspiration than to the narrow rules of counterpoint and fugue,' a criticism which is all the more interesting since it appeared in a paper to which he himself contributed and was in fact either written, or at any rate inspired, by him!

Berlioz was full of intoxicating ideas about his vocation. He called himself a 'Ninevite' and a 'Babylonian', in the latter case no doubt influenced by his teacher Lesueur, a bold musician in both church and theatre who had written an opera called *Alexander at Babylon*. Lesueur told Berlioz, 'You have genius, and I tell you so because it is the truth.'

The flame of this genius burned ever more brightly as new stimuli came, among them being Beethoven's symphonies, Goethe's *Faust* and the plays of Shakespeare. An English theatrical company gave a Shakespearian season in Paris between 1826 and 1828, and Berlioz fell in love with the actress Harriet Smithson, not through personal acquaintance but simply from seeing her performances. He wrote to her, but his letter remained unanswered. The story has a fairly happy ending, for they married eventually in 1833, even if the match was not wholly successful. But in the meantime, as a kind of public revenge upon the indifferent beauty, whom he now regarded as a courtesan, he composed his famous *Fantastic Symphony* (1830).

The German writer Heinrich Heine (1797–1856), who lived in Paris at this time and was at home in both the German and French languages, regarded Berlioz as 'the greatest and most original musician France has produced in a long time,' from whose art even the dullest minds caught fire, whose utterance was that of 'a great nightingale, a lark as big as an eagle, such as must have existed in the primeval world.' His view of the *Fantastic Symphony* was this: 'A fantastic night-piece, which is only occasionally lighted up by the sentimental white of a woman's dress, which now and again flutters through it, or by a sulphur-yellow flash of irony. The best thing in it is a Witches' Sabbath, where the Devil says Mass and Catholic church music is parodied with the utmost in ghastly and bloody ludicrousness.'

The music of the *Fantastic Symphony*, subtitled 'Episode of an Artist's Life', tells a story which Berlioz embodied in a set of programme notes published with the score. The artist-hero suffers and dies for the love of a beautiful but faithless girl, all in the mysterious world of a dream induced by opium. The idea of a literary programme for music was not new, but now it became especially fashionable and gave its name to 'programme music', works of a literary-cum-musical construction which however excluded the actual use of sung words such as one has in opera. Programme music has had many detractors, who argue that the more realistic it is the less musical is the result, adducing the orchestral *Battle of Vittoria* (1813) by Beethoven as an example of even a great composer writing inferior music when adopting this method. Schumann, who liked the *Fantastic Symphony*, still felt that the programme restricted his thought as a listener, taking a similar view even of the programmatic titles to the individual movements of Beethoven's 'Pastoral' Symphony.

Berlioz believed he was carrying out the symphonic aims of Beethoven, whom he deeply admired. He saw these as being the musical embodiment of a poetic idea, such as he perceived in the 'Eroica', Fifth and 'Pastoral' Symphonies, to say nothing of the 'Choral' Symphony. Certainly he did not intend to change all accepted procedures. The first movement of the *Fantastic Symphony* is in classical sonata form, complete with a slow introduction, such as Haydn would have understood and followed without difficulty. What is new is the literary feature which becomes part of the musical structure. This is the *idée fixe*, the theme which represents the beloved.

The *idée fixe* is what we would call in English an obsession, an overriding thought which ceaselessly occupies the mind. The lover in this story is obsessed with the beloved; and thus the *idée fixe* which is her theme is heard in each movement, changing its shape and character according to the circumstances in which she comes upon the musical scene. The effect of the theme is of great spontaneity of style, yet Berlioz marks it meticulously with indications of expression. In fact it has the character of an operatic recitative, and we see here how expressive a purely instrumental language can be in the hands of a romantic composer.*

EX.74   Berlioz *Symphonie fantastique* (idée fixe)

Allegro agitato e appassionato assai

Example continued

* But compare also the Beethoven passage quoted on pages 171–2.

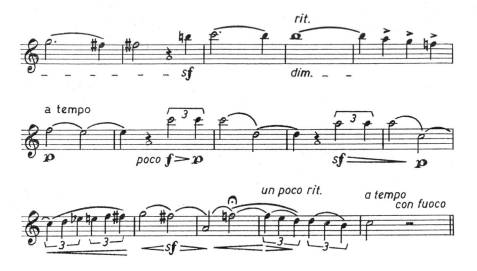

In the *Fantastic Symphony*, as in so many romantic works, Nature has a part to play. In the slow movement, called *Country Scene*, two shepherds' pipes calling to each other combine with the peaceful surroundings to calm the lover's heart; the key is Beethoven's 'pastoral' F major. Yet the thought – the theme – of the beloved returns to trouble him. The first shepherd calls once again, in the plaintive tones of the cor anglais. But now the other no longer replies. The composer's programme tells us: 'The sun sets . . . distant sound of thunder . . . solitude . . . silence . . .'

Berlioz's next symphony was *Harold in Italy*. It is unusual in that there is an important part for solo viola throughout: this was composed with Paganini in mind, for the celebrated virtuoso had a Stradivari viola of which he wished to make use and there was practically no solo music for the instrument in existence at the time. Four scenes inspired by Byron's poem *Childe Harold's Pilgrimage* provided the material of the movements, which like those of the *Fantastic Symphony* are in a recognisably classical order. The remaining two symphonies are *Romeo and Juliet* (1838) and the *Symphonie funèbre et triomphale* (1840). This last commemorated the revolutionary events in France of 1830; Berlioz gave a successful performance of it in the open air to a noisy crowd.

Though all Berlioz's symphonies have their programme, in the last two of them he followed the example of Beethoven in the 'Choral' Symphony and decided to use the more direct, explicit drama of a sung text. But there is an interesting passage in his preface to *Romeo and Juliet* in which he explains why the lovers' scenes at the balcony and tomb are not sung. The sublimity of this love, he wrote, made its musical depiction a hazardous undertaking, and musical freedom would have been restricted by words, with their exact sense; so he turned instead to 'instrumental language, a language which is richer, more varied and free of limitations, and through its very indefiniteness incomparably more powerful in effect.'

What sort of effect was Berlioz aiming at? He said that for him music was 'the art of causing emotion, by combinations of sounds, in those who are intelligent and gifted with unusual and practised abilities of perception.' Music was not only intended to charm the ear and exalt the mind: it might also excite responses beyond the ordinary and carry a listener's thought 'towards infinite regions'. He was in many ways the most extreme of the great romantic composers. He never composed a sonata, quartet or concerto. Even his symphonies are like no one else's, and he seems to have recognised this when he called them 'instrumental dramas', a phrase which Liszt was later more or less to copy when he coined the term 'symphonic poem'.

Much of Berlioz's work uses the human voice as well as instruments, words as well as notes: as well as solo songs, there are brilliant choruses. Indeed he is the chief French composer of romantic opera, though not one of his operas is based on a French story. *Benvenuto Cellini* (1838), with its effective and popular overture, is based on the colourful and picaresque auto-biography of the sixteenth-century Florentine artist, with whom it was easy for Berlioz, an almost equally flamboyant figure, to identify himself. Then came *The Trojans* (1859), with a story drawn from the composer's beloved Virgil, of epic proportions so that it had to be divided into two evenings in the theatre. *Beatrice and Benedict* (1862) takes its much lighter story from Shakespeare's comedy *Much Ado about Nothing*.

Of these works, it is *The Trojans* which is probably Berlioz's operatic masterpiece. Yet it remains a controversial work. In his search for epic and dignified tones appropriate to the subject of the fall of Troy and the flight of Aeneas, the composer took Gluck as a model and employed a style which, though monumental, is not always convincing. For all his dramatic sensitivity, his tragic Queen Dido of Carthage seems less immediately human than Purcell's; the baroque composer here outdoes the romantic in conveying emotion. On the other hand, such a wonderful orchestral set-piece as the *Royal Hunt and Storm* in this opera shows Berlioz's genius unmistakably. Certainly *The Trojans* is a work to be heard, and if possible seen, by anyone wishing to know and respond to this composer.

Berlioz was a master of the orchestra and its instrumental sonorities. He wrote a textbook on the art of instrumentation in 1843 which was of pioneer-ing importance, deriving his teaching from the examples of Gluck, Beethoven and Weber as well as his own discoveries. He was responsible for the establish-ment of the harp, cor anglais and tuba as regular members of the orchestra, but in spite of his enthusiasm for the saxophone, then a brand-new instru-ment, he does not seem to have used it himself. Though he liked to use big orchestral forces, it was equally characteristic of him to write with exquisite delicacy. Passages of this latter kind include the famous 'Queen Mab' scherzo in *Romeo and Juliet*, the ball scene of the *Fantastic Symphony* and parts of the tenderly lyrical oratorio *The Childhood of Christ* (1854).

Mention of religious music leads us to two very different church works, the Requiem and the *Te Deum*. Berlioz said of the Requiem that the text was 'for me a long-coveted prey, upon which I threw myself in a kind of fury. My head seemed ready to burst . . . It is a great affair!' Indeed it is, a work possessing both vocal and orchestral magnificence. The orchestra includes four small brass groups to represent the trumpets of the Last Judgment, which at the première were placed in the corners of the Invalides Church in Paris, sixteen timpani and over a hundred strings. Though destined for church performance, the Requiem was also a national commission intended to honour the heroic dead of the Revolution. Accordingly it has a semi-military splendour as well as abundant romantic fervour. How much of any conventionally religious spirit there is in the work is, however, a matter still open to argument.

Berlioz is an artist who attracts equally vigorous champions and opponents. Schumann likened him to 'a flash of lightning', but did not know 'whether to call him a genius or a musical adventurer'. His own compatriots, on the whole, have been caustic. Debussy called him the favourite composer of the musically ignorant. Ravel, weighing his words significantly, found him 'the worst musician among the musical geniuses', a remark which, after all, falls a long way short of utter condemnation. But it is not the exclusive right of fellow-musicians to decide what is of value. For many people, Berlioz's work is among the most exciting, moving and sensuously beautiful in the concert and operatic repertory. According to the French novelist Théophile Gautier, writing in 1874, Berlioz, with the writer Hugo and the painter Delacroix, together make up a perfect trinity of romanticism: 'In that renaissance of the 1830s Berlioz represents the romantic musical idea, the breaking up of old moulds, the substitution of new forms for unvaried square rhythms, a complex and competent richness of orchestration, truth of local colour, unexpected effects in sound, tumultuous and Shakespearian depth of passion, amorous or melancholy dreaminess, longings and questionings of the soul, infinite and mysterious sentiments not to be rendered in words, and that something more than all which escapes language but may be divined in music.'

LISZT

Franz Liszt and Fryderyk Chopin also brought a new feeling into the romantic climate – one which eventually led to the artistic movement called nationalism. In one of his articles Schumann commented that it was not surprising that a Polish composer like Chopin wished to address his countrymen in their own language: indeed throughout his life, Chopin wrote in Polish dance forms, while Liszt in his turn composed many Hungarian-style pieces. But nationalism was not yet the powerful ideal which it later became; and neither Chopin nor Liszt stayed at home, but came instead to Paris, where so many currents of romanticism met and mingled.

Liszt (1811–86) was born at Raiding, in Austria: the village lies about forty miles south of Vienna and some six or seven from the present-day Hungarian frontier. Neither of his parents was Hungarian, and German was the language spoken at home. But his father served the Esterházy family, over the frontier as it exists now, and certainly Liszt spent a good deal of his early childhood in Hungarian circles. He did not learn the language, though, and to regard him as a Hungarian composer is to over-simplify matters. Nor did he remain in Hungary for long. By the age of ten he had already gone abroad as far as Vienna with his parents, where he studied with Beethoven's pupil Czerny. After a concert in 1823 the brilliant boy pianist was rewarded with an embrace from Beethoven himself, and he also met Schubert during this Viennese stay.

The Liszts next moved to Paris, and all the composer's 'teens were passed there. These formative years gave him French as his main language and, artistically, made him a French romantic. As a young man, his friends included Victor Hugo, Berlioz and Chopin, as well as the liberal philosopher-priest Lamennais, who helped him through a religious crisis following his father's death and who became a second father and his spiritual guide.

At the age of nineteen, Liszt made the prodigious effort which turned him from a merely fine pianist into an unparalleled phenomenon of the keyboard. Having heard the virtuoso violinist Paganini, he decided to develop for himself, if he could, a technical skill which would be equally astonishing in keyboard terms. He practised for up to twelve hours daily. 'Homer, the Bible, Plato, Locke, Byron, Hugo, Lamartine, Chateaubriand, Beethoven, Bach, Hummel, Mozart, Weber are all about me. I study them, meditate on them, devour them furiously. I also practise from four to five hours of exercises – thirds, sixths, octaves, trills, repeated notes and cadenzas. Oh, if only I don't go mad, you'll find an artist in me . . . an artist such as we need today!' Among the results of this intense work were the six 'Paganini' Studies and the twelve 'Transcendental' Studies which Schumann described as 'for at most ten or twelve players in the world'. Music like this symbolised Liszt's dazzling technique and his tremendous personal magnetism, a quality he kept all his long life. Even Clara Schumann, herself a pianist and inclined to think Liszt something of a showman, was deeply impressed. 'He can be compared to no other virtuoso. He is unique. He arouses fright and astonishment.'

In 1833 Liszt made a piano arrangement of Berlioz's *Fantastic Symphony*. This was a real *tour de force*, since obviously the rich orchestral writing is such an important feature of that work. Once, after Berlioz had conducted part of the symphony at a concert, Liszt sat down and played his piano version. Sir Charles Hallé, later founder of the Hallé Orchestra in Manchester, was present and wrote of 'an effect even surpassing the full orchestra, and creating an indescribable *furore*'. This extract from the last movement gives some idea of the breathtaking brilliance of Liszt's keyboard writing.

EX.75 Berlioz / Liszt *Symphonie fantastique*

Above Beethoven walking in the streets of Vienna in about 1823. A contemporary
drawing by Lyfer.

Below An almost illegible, though typical, page from Beethoven's sketchbooks.
This was eventually to become part of the 'Pastoral' Symphony.

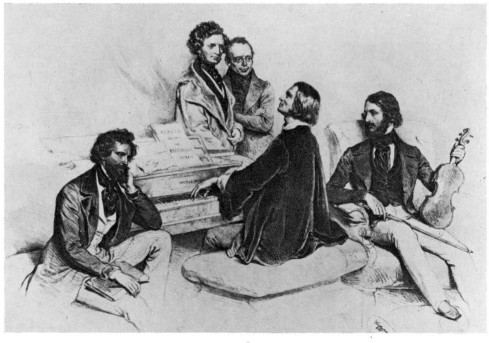

Above A musical evening at Ritter von Spaun's house in Vienna by Schubert's friend Moritz von Schwind. Schubert is at the piano and beside him sits the singer Vogl.

Below Kriehuber's 'An Afternoon with Liszt' shows the great pianist surrounded by rapt admirers including his former teacher Czerny and (*standing left*) Berlioz. The score of a Beethoven sonata is on the music stand.

Liszt was by now quite simply the supreme pianist of his time. He played all over Europe, from England to Turkey. Though he earned large sums, he also gave generously, for example in order to build a Beethoven memorial at Bonn or for various Hungarian causes. He coined the word 'recital', suggesting something more poetic than simple playing, and was to a great extent responsible for the custom of playing piano solos from memory. Accounts of his concerts were often fervent, like this one of 1835: 'I saw Liszt's face assume that agony of expression, mingled with radiant smiles of joy, which I never saw on any other human face except in the paintings of our Saviour by some of the early masters; his hands rushed over the keys, the floor on which I sat shook like a wire, and the whole audience was wrapped in sound.' But there was also a natural reaction against such enthusiasm. One satirist wrote of 'a certain pianist' who paid a woman to faint during his performance of a piece taken so fast that he could not have played the closing passages, and by rushing to her assistance avoided doing so!

Liszt himself tired of public performance. Heinrich Heine wrote of his interest in all kinds of philosophical ideas and his 'unquenchable thirst for light, for the divine . . . that Franz Liszt cannot be a placid player of the piano to peaceful citizens in comfortable nightcaps is easy to understand.' In 1847, aged thirty-five, he gave his last paid public concert; from now on, right up to the end of his life, he accepted no further money for performing or teaching. Encouraged by his friend, Princess Carolyne Sayn-Wittgenstein, he turned seriously to composition, settling at Weimar in Germany, where he accepted a court appointment to take charge of the city's music.

Liszt's view of music was a lofty one. He believed that, properly used, it could lead men to worship; and his two symphonies deal with man's relation with the Divine. *A Faust Symphony* (1854) takes its subject from Goethe: the scholar Faust barters his soul for knowledge and power, but is saved from damnation by the pure love of the maiden Gretchen. This programmatic symphony – significantly, it is dedicated to Berlioz – has three movements, called *Faust*, *Gretchen* and *Mephistopheles*. Liszt uses the Berliozian technique of thematic transformation, and thus the opening tune, representing Faust brooding alone in his study, appears in the finale in a bizarre version which symbolises his near-heedless race to doom. This melody, first heard unaccompanied, is historically important since it uses all twelve notes of the chromatic scale in such a way as to avoid any definite feeling of key, thus anticipating non-tonal music in the twentieth century:

EX.76   Liszt *Faust Symphony*

Liszt's other symphony is the 'Dante' Symphony (1856), which draws its programmatic material from the *Inferno* and *Purgatory* sections of *The Divine Comedy* and ends with a choral Magnificat. Dante was a favourite writer of Liszt's; at one time he thought it would take a Michelangelo to encompass him, then that 'a Beethoven of the future' would be needed to provide an adequate musical setting. This symphony, as well as *Faust*, was in his mind for several years before its completion.

The thirteen symphonic poems are examples of a form which Liszt established, though it was derived from such works as Schubert's 'Wanderer' Fantasy and Berlioz's *Fantastic Symphony*. But in a symphonic poem the different sections are linked not only thematically but also by being continuous. And as the name suggests, there is a programme. The name 'symphonic poem' was Liszt's own invention, and each of these works expresses a poetic or visual idea. So the first is called *What we hear in the Mountains,* the second tells of the life of the poet Tasso, the fourth represents Orpheus and the healing power of music, while the tenth is a character study of Shakespeare's Hamlet.

The third of the symphonic poems is *Les Préludes,* inspired by a poem of Lamartine. 'What is our life,' asks the composer's preface, 'but a series of preludes to that unknown song of which death sounds the first solemn note?' The four sections of the music portray different stages of life, and they are melodically interlinked so that we hear the work as a single movement of varying moods. The main theme introduces the music and sets the scene:

EX. 77 Liszt   Themes from *Les Preludes*

After this, the introduction, *Spring and Love* gives us this version of the theme:

In *Tempests of Life* we hear fragments of the theme and then, as the music becomes calmer, this oboe version:

Consolations of Nature has the theme in a pastoral form. Finally, *Struggle and Victory* begins with a military-sounding variant:

Les Préludes, though effective, is not the most subtle of Liszt's works. In fact it has been this composer's misfortune that his showier pieces are the ones most often played, while some of the best works among his vast output are unknown. For example, he is rarely thought of as a vocal composer. But he wrote about seventy songs, to poems in five languages, German being the commonest, then French, Italian, Hungarian and English. Some of these are fine, but his *Lieder* are at present overshadowed by other great names in this field from Schubert to Wolf. Of his choral works, the oratorio *Christus* is probably the most important: he was a devout man who wrote in all over sixty religious choral pieces.

As one would expect, Liszt wrote an enormous amount for piano, including two concertos. The solo pieces include splendid studies, very difficult but nonetheless music first and valuable exercises only secondarily. There are also pieces evoking different visual or literary ideas. Several are on religious subjects, like the 'St Francis' Legends. Others are travel pieces: *The Bells of Geneva, The Fountains at the Villa d'Este, Venice and Naples*. Others are nature poems: *Feux follets, Chasse-neige, Waldesrauschen, Nuages gris* ('Will-o'-the-wisp', 'Winter wind', 'Forest murmurs', 'Grey clouds'). There is the magnificent B minor Sonata (1853), Liszt's only sonata, dedicated to Schumann and, most originally, cast in one movement lasting nearly half an hour. There are also over three hundred piano transcriptions of other men's music, ranging from Berlioz's *Fantastic Symphony* and all Beethoven's nine symphonies to Bach organ pieces, Schubert songs, and operas from Mozart to Wagner. The idea of a pianist attempting the closing scene of Wagner's *Tristan and Isolde* might seem ludicrous today, but in the hands of a master performer these transcriptions are altogether successful, amazing re-creations of orchestral music in pianistic terms.

Some of Liszt's most interesting piano music is only now beginning to come into the concert repertory. In his seventies, he composed pieces such as the Third 'Mephisto' Waltz, *Nuages gris* and *Csárdás macabre* which opened up new sound-worlds of brilliance and mystery in which various modern devices appear: there is even an *Atonal Bagatelle*, quoted below, which was written in 1885 but remained unpublished till 1956. Both Bartók and Debussy expressed admiration for this musician who, in his old age, had the vision and the courage to anticipate the innovations of men born half a century after him.

EX.78   Liszt *Bagatelle sans tonalité*

Allegretto mosso

CHOPIN

The name Chopin is not Polish, and in fact Fryderyk Chopin's father was a Frenchman of peasant stock who emigrated to Poland as a boy, taught French in well-to-do Polish households and eventually married rather above his original social station. His son was born near Warsaw in 1810, the only boy among four children.

Brought up in a cultivated atmosphere among his father's pupils, Fryderyk was intelligent, hard-working at his ordinary studies and so gifted a musician that he was called 'Mozart's successor'. At fourteen he could play a concerto at a private musical gathering and also persuade a village folk-singer with the aid of a few coins to repeat her mazurka, light-heartedly reporting these events in letters home. Another letter described the playing of a pianist who had just spent six years in Paris: 'He plays the piano better than anyone I have ever heard. You can imagine what a joy it was for the likes of us, who have never heard anything really perfect here.'

This was in 1825. Clearly Chopin, who already liked to mix his father's native French with Polish, was in the process of becoming psychologically ripe for Paris. Acquaintance with the French capital, however, was still six years away. He went first to Vienna, giving two successful concerts there in 1829. It seemed clear that the way to further success lay in the cultivation of 'national' colouring in composition, as well as in his already distinctive piano style. So he wrote Polish-sounding finales for both of his piano concertos; and after the Warsaw première of his *Fantasy on Polish Airs* it was said that he knew 'the songs of the Polish villager' and had united them with skilful and elegant art. His teacher Elsner hoped that he would write a great national opera. But this was not to be. Chopin had to try his wings more fully and further afield, away from the support of friendly fellow-countrymen; and after he left Poland – as it happened, for good – the national characteristics of his style, though remaining important, ceased to be pre-eminent.

Chopin's travels led him through Austria and Germany. At last, in the autumn of 1831, he reached Paris. He was still only twenty-one, an unknown talent in a city abounding in gifted people, and things were not especially easy at first. But the friends whom he soon made were enough to hold him. His first concert took place six months after his arrival. Fortunately an influential critic found 'an abundance of original ideas', a welcome new creative voice, and from then on his name was made. At the same time, the friendly patronage of the Rothschild family opened up the best *salons*. Soon Chopin found himself with a new career as a teacher, indeed the most fashionable and expensive in Paris.

He seems to have enjoyed teaching. But he cared little for concert performance – 'He fears the public,' said his friend George Sand – though his high reputation as a pianist was enhanced by the very infrequency of his public appearances. Even among his friends he was reserved: he revealed little of his musical methods and ideals, and even less of his inner human feelings. Just occasionally he let slip a clue to his enigmatic yet touchingly melancholy personality, as when he wrote in a letter to an old school friend: 'Today I finished the Fantasy [this was the celebrated F minor Fantasy] – the weather is lovely but I am sad at heart – not that it matters. If it were otherwise, my existence would perhaps be of no use to anyone. Let us save ourselves up for life after death . . . Don't deduce any wrong ideas from that, I'm just going to dinner.'

Behind his gentle yet firm barrier of reserve, Chopin lived in surroundings which reflected his love of the exquisitely delicate. He had a connoisseur's taste in furniture and clothes, and liked to fill his flat with the scent of violets. Yet he was far from being a languid aesthete; he had a powerful temper, which he controlled with determination but sometimes with difficulty, and to a pupil who apologised for breaking a piano string, he said that if he himself could 'play that polonaise as it should be played there would be no string left unbroken by the time I had finished!' His personality was certainly magnetic. 'Someone you will never forget,' was Berlioz's description, while Liszt wrote a book praising him. It was Liszt who introduced him to George Sand, the woman novelist who was as close to him as anyone for about ten years, after which they parted when he took her daughter's side in a family quarrel. This was in 1847. In the following year he went abroad for several months, to England and Scotland where he played extensively. He returned to Paris a sick man and died there in 1849 of tuberculosis, a disease from which he had suffered for nearly a decade.

Some years ago a critic wrote that Chopin's music was best suited 'to cultivated and poetic natures . . . those who possess the sensitive chord that the music is intended to touch.' It is true that as a fastidious man Chopin was unhappy in public, and that as a musician he preferred Bach and Mozart to the dynamic Beethoven. Yet the music of this refined artist has in fact reached a wider public than that comment would suggest. There was even a time when Chopin's wide popularity caused his genius to be belittled by self-consciously highbrow critics, a fate which he shared with Tchaikovsky.

Yet perhaps Chopin's public, however large, is a specialised one in a sense that Tchaikovsky's is not. Those who love orchestral music or opera, string quartets or church music, will find nothing in Chopin. Virtually everything he wrote was for piano, and in single-movement forms.* Some pieces are dances, like the mazurkas, polonaises and waltzes. Others, like the ballades and scherzos, have a structure of their own which is sometimes on the rondo principle of a recurrent main theme but always sounds spontaneous. Chopin's form in fact offers a masterly example of the art which conceals art. Everything grows naturally, nothing is too long or too short for the piece as a whole, and the music ranges freely through the keys with extraordinary harmonic certainty.

Chopin's mastery came quite suddenly, and early. The piano concertos of 1829–30 are the work of a master pianist who was also a very gifted composition student, but the Twelve Studies, Opus 10, of 1829–32 are already major works in a mature style. He dedicated them to Liszt, who called them 'marvellous'. (Chopin himself, returning the compliment, said he would like to steal Liszt's way of performing them.) Not only is this passage, from the first of these studies, formidably difficult to play, it is alarmingly bold in harmony also: between two chords on A, it pursues a course which, though purposeful, is as unusual as anything of the period. And where is the melody, unless it is in the top notes of the right hand? The model for this piece, surprising though the thought seems at first, was probably the first Prelude of Bach's 'Forty-eight'; for Chopin's originality was backed by a profound respect for tradition.

EX. 79 Chopin *Study Op.10 no.1*

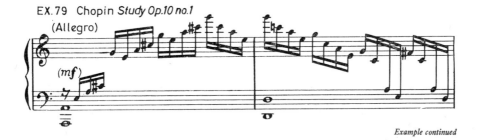

Example continued

* The fine piano sonatas in B flat minor (1839) and B minor (1844) are exceptional.

Though melody may not be obvious in that C major Study, Chopin is also a master in this sphere. To pianistic melody writing he stands in the same relation as Schubert does to vocal melody. In the *Berceuse*, the right-hand tune would be vocally impossible, but it is perfectly in accord with the nature of the piano. The use of the sustaining pedal is of course essential, for the left hand and indeed also for the right. Here, in contrast to the last example, the harmony is absolutely simple, so that all the listener's attention is drawn towards the melodic line.

EX. 80 Chopin *Berceuse*
(Andante) *sostenuto*

The *Berceuse*, as the name tells us, is a lullaby. Chopin's nocturnes, 'night-pieces', explore this mood further. His own piano playing was admired especially for its delicacy and singing tone, qualities not always exploited by more conventional virtuosos. In this respect Chopin influenced Liszt, whose own *Berceuse* was written after the Polish master's death in a style so Chopin-esque that it may have been composed as a tribute, while his D flat *Consolation*, too, one of six pieces begun in the year of Chopin's death, resembles a Chopin nocturne. It was probably due to Chopin more than any other single musician that the intimate and poetic qualities of the piano, as well as its more obvious dramatic power and range, were explored by future composers like Debussy, Scriabin and Rachmaninov, all of whom were pianists and had the invaluable experience of studying and playing Chopin's music for themselves.

Of course Chopin's music is often stirring and vigorous too, as here in the F minor Fantasy:

EX. 81 Chopin *F minor Fantasy*

This has plenty of masculine strength. The same observation is true of the polonaises. Chopin's treatment of this national court dance was heroic and exhilarating. Probably one thinks first of the famous Polonaise in A flat, Opus 53, with its wonderful middle section, neither a march nor a gallop, but suggesting some brilliant imaginary procession.

The mazurkas are examples of another Polish dance form. These fifty or so pieces contain some of Chopin's most beautiful and personal music. The composer seems often to look into his own art, and even his own soul, with a searching eye; and these 'Polish' pieces are among his most revealing, just as his correspondence in that language tells us more about himself than the letters he wrote in French. The opening of the B flat minor Mazurka, Opus 24, No. 4, is puzzling at first hearing even to the ear of an experienced musician:

EX. 82 Chopin *Mazurka Op.24 no.4*

A. Moderato

So is this passage, occurring later, though Chopin makes the second half reassuring after the harmonically disorientating first phrase:

B.

The closing section of this B flat minor Mazurka is also thoroughly Chopin-esque in its unique blend of Slav melancholy, boldness and exquisite grace:

11

FRENCH AND ITALIAN OPERA IN THE
NINETEENTH CENTURY

*France after the Revolution. Gounod, Bizet and their successors.
Rossini, Donizetti and Bellini. Verdi.*

FRANCE AFTER THE REVOLUTION

Post-revolutionary France had three kinds of opera: grand opera, *opéra-comique* and lyric opera. The first of these was a natural outcome of the heroic classicism of Gluck. This had been passed on by Gluck's disciple Etienne Méhul (1763–1817) with a work on a sacred subject, *Joseph* (1807); while *La Vestale* in the same year, by Napoleon's favourite composer Gasparo Spontini (1774–1851) was a work of magnificence and pomp deriving from the same tradition. The Paris Opéra was dubbed by Heine 'the paradise of the hard of hearing', and a joke of the time was that a doctor advised a deaf friend to go with him to *La Vestale* as a cure and when the friend exclaimed delightedly that he could indeed hear the music he found that the doctor himself had been deafened!

Spontini was in fact Italian: he came to Paris at the age of twenty-nine to try his luck and achieved great success. Several other grand operas were also by visiting foreigners; Rossini's *William Tell* (1829) was one, and so was Wagner's *Rienzi* (1842). An important example of grand opera by a Frenchman was *La Muette de Portici* (1828) by Daniel Auber (1782–1871); his only work of this kind, it is sometimes called by the alternative title of *Masaniello*. One dominant figure was the Jewish Berliner Meyerbeer (1791–1864), whose real name was Jacob Liebmann Beer. This friend and fellow-pupil of Weber took up residence in Paris, made the fortune of the Paris Opéra with *Robert le Diable* in 1831, and produced his masterpiece in *Les Huguenots* (1836), which has been called the most vivid chapter of French history ever written. Meyerbeer is usually classified as vulgar, appealing to popular taste at any price. But the fastidious Chopin thought well of him, finding *Robert le Diable* 'a masterpiece of the modern school' with its lavish staging (there was a whole congregation-filled church on stage), organ and huge chorus. And such extracts from Meyerbeer's operas as are occasionally heard show that at his best his style was distinguished. *Les Huguenots* was performed regularly at Covent Garden up to 1912, and lasting success like this cannot be won with shoddy goods.

Just as in Italy, the singers were as important to opera as the music itself. Chopin, newly-arrived in Paris, wrote excitedly: 'But I haven't mentioned the Opéra yet. Never have I heard *The Barber* as last week with Lablache, Rubini and Malibran . . . Now, if ever, I have *everything* in Paris. You cannot conceive what Lablache is like! They say that Pasta has gone off, but I never saw anything more sublime. Malibran impresses you merely by her marvellous voice, but no one *sings* like her. Miraculous! Marvellous! Rubini is an excellent tenor. He sings true notes, never *falsetto*, and sometimes his ornamented runs go on for hours (but sometimes his decorative passages are too long and he deliberately uses a *tremolo* effect, besides trilling endlessly – which however brings him the greatest applause). His *mezza voce* is incomparable.'

Berlioz has already been discussed in the previous chapter. This major composer is difficult to classify in the operatic field. *The Trojans* is certainly a grand opera, possibly among the greatest in spite of its unevenness. Its second part was produced in Paris in 1863; but the first had to wait until 1890 and a German-language performance at Karlsruhe – a sad failure on the part of the French in respect of one of France's great musicians.

Opéra-comique was by no means necessarily humorous, for the French used the term *opéra bouffe* for wholly comic works. But it featured spoken dialogue instead of the recitatives of grand opera and was generally simpler, more homely and on a smaller scale. Composers of *opéra-comique* included Boieldieu, Hérold (whose *Zampa* was produced in 1831) and Auber, though these are best known nowadays outside France for their sparkling operatic overtures rather than the operas themselves. *Opéra bouffe* really came later with Jacques Offenbach (1819–80), another composer of foreign origin, born near Cologne. His *Orpheus in the Underworld* (1858) and *La Belle Hélène* (1864) are rightly celebrated, and influenced two illustrious successors in the younger Johann Strauss and the Englishman Sir Arthur Sullivan. Merely to read the titles of Offenbach's innumerable stage pieces is to smile: *The Cat turned into a Woman, The Bridge of Soup-lovers, Green-green, Snowball* and *Voyage to the Moon. Dick Whittington and his Cat* was to an English text and produced in London in 1874. Offenbach also composed one *opéra-comique, Tales of Hoffmann,* produced in 1881. This was a picaresque trio of Hoffmann's stories with a prologue and epilogue, a favourite work of his on which he worked for some years at the end of his life; but the first performance did not take place until four months after his death at the Opéra-Comique.

The French lyric opera represented a compromise between grand opera and operetta – this latter term being a convenient one for lighter opera in general. It aimed at something more than prettiness and wit, at the same time avoiding the weightiness of the 'grand' manner. In the hands of some composers this kind of middle way could have been dull, a sort of stylistic no man's land. Fortunately two outstanding artists worked in lyric opera, Gounod (1818–93) and his friend and pupil Bizet (1838–75).

Charles Gounod's parents were artistic and comfortably off, his father being a distinguished painter and his mother a good pianist. He took a university degree and then entered the Paris Conservatoire. The Rome Prize took him to Italy, where he found Palestrina's music 'like a translation into song of Michelangelo . . . the art of both these men is, as it were, a sacrament.' His taste was wide-ranging: 'Rossini introduced me to purely musical delight . . . Mozart did more, he added the profound and penetrating influence of expressive truth combined with perfect beauty.'

Like Liszt, this serious young man nearly entered the priesthood. Instead he became a church organist and wrote a great deal of sacred music. But the theatre was the scene of his greatest triumphs. *Faust*, which occupied him from 1852–59, is the most famous of all lyric operas. It is concerned only with the love story in the first part of Goethe's drama, and it has a happy ending. *Faust* was condemned by Wagner as 'nauseatingly vulgar' – which seems hard on Gounod since he was himself accused of Wagnerism – but Berlioz, on the other hand, loved it. With its abundant elegant charm and avoidance of sublimity, *Faust* is lyric opera at its best.

For all its vivacity and brilliant Spanish colour, Bizet's *Carmen* (1875) is lyric opera with a difference: its story is uncompromising and even harsh. Gounod and Bizet have things in common, such as a lively melodic gift; but Bizet has the sharper style, in which rhythmic vitality is combined with sensual richness.* *Carmen* is realistic in a way which looks forward to later composers like Puccini, even to Alban Berg in this century with his *Wozzeck* and *Lulu*: a heroine who works in a cigarette factory is a long way removed from the goddesses of earlier opera. The story of *Carmen* was taken from Prosper Mérimée, a writer who, like Flaubert, began as a romantic but turned towards realism: his style is emotionally powerful but detached in a way which is somewhat clinical. Bizet is too warm-hearted to follow Mérimée altogether here. A fine melodist and a skilled craftsman with a sense of the dramatic, he possessed rich gifts. His admirers have included some distinguished non-French names. Brahms joked that he preferred *Carmen* to anything else in his publisher's catalogue, including his own music; while Tchaikovsky called it 'a masterpiece in the fullest sense of the word'. The philosopher Nietzsche said: 'This music is wicked, refined, fantastic, and yet it retains a popular appeal . . . Have more anguished and tragic accents ever been heard on the stage before?'

Camille Saint-Saëns was born in 1835 and lived on right into the twentieth century, dying in 1921. Like Bizet's *Carmen*, his most important opera made

---

* Gounod, who outlived him by nearly twenty years, made a speech at his funeral and was moved to tears.

friends in Germany: *Samson and Delilah* (1877) was first produced at Weimar under Liszt's auspices. Saint-Saëns had great gifts, even if the scholar Alfred Einstein found this opera 'a draught of "Meyer-beer" strained through Gounod's filter'! He was perhaps only too skilled in all styles, rising to every occasion but not impressing his listeners with any powerful individuality. Romanticism here loses its original vigour; its quality of mysterious vitality has been killed perhaps by sheer commonsense cleverness.

This does not quite happen, though, in the operas of Massenet (1842–1912), the composer of *Manon* (1884) and *Werther* (1892). Massenet's talent for smoothly wistful melody is not matched by any great dramatic strength or musical depth, as his treatment of Goethe's story in the second of these two operas shows. But there is a charm and elegance about his music which keeps it in the affections of opera-lovers and makes it hold a place in the repertory. The composer Poulenc has with justice pointed out 'the Massenet aspect of many pages of Debussy'. Massenet may be a minor composer, but he left a unique mark on French music. With him we reach the sunset of French romanticism. This is no longer the style of wild-eyed, ebullient youth but that of a gently middle-aged lady with an interesting past and drawers full of faintly-scented love letters. Of Bizet and Massenet, it is the former composer who points more firmly to the future.

ROSSINI, DONIZETTI AND BELLINI

Italy is often a special case in European history, for this is a country who can lead more easily than she can follow. Thus the Renaissance began in Italy; but the Gothic style, which originated elsewhere, left her relatively untouched. Nor, naturally, did she have a nineteenth-century Gothic revival. Romantic mystery, even, found little place under what the poet Shelley called 'the bright blue sky of Rome'. Shelley was not the only non-Italian artist to feel Italy to be different from the rest of Europe. Goethe found there 'moonlight brighter than daylight'; and for the Russian Gogol, Europe compared to Italy was like 'a gloomy day compared to a sunny one'. The Italians themselves are aware of their special status and character, and this is a matter of pride. A contemporary Italian writer, Luigi Barzini, has said: 'The pleasures of Italy come from living in a world made by man, for man, on man's measurements.'

This is not romantic but Renaissance thinking: 'measure' is far from being a romantic ideal. And in fact Italian music in the nineteenth century is mainly in that most humanist and explicit of musical forms, the opera. But of course nineteenth-century Italian opera has some romantic features, among these being national feeling and the atmospheric use of nature. Thus Rossini evoked nature to great effect in his last opera, the patriotic *William Tell* (1829), though perhaps it is significant that this tale of the liberator of the

Berlioz had a reputation for excess and so provided rich material for caricature. Here he conducts an orchestra in which the bass players have to compete with the blast of a cannon.

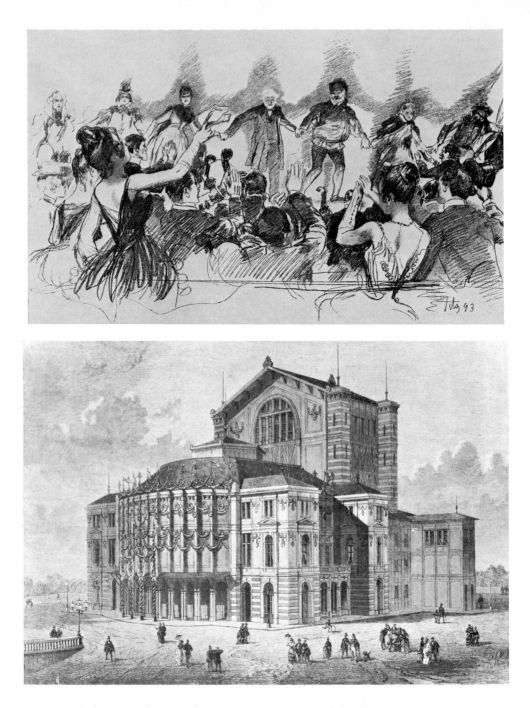

Above Verdi, in his eightieth year, acknowledges the applause of the audience after the triumphant première of his last opera, *Falstaff*, which took place on February 9th, 1893, at La Scala, Milan.

Below Wagner's festival theatre at Bayreuth, in Bavaria: a contemporary engraving.

Swiss cantons was written in French for revolutionary-romantic Paris. He also drew on the same literary sources as Berlioz, so that his opera *Otello* was based on the romantics' hero Shakespeare, and Sir Walter Scott's *The Lady of the Lake* provided him with another operatic plot. On the other hand, *The Barber of Seville* has a libretto based on Beaumarchais' *comédie d'intrigue* of 1775 and is in no way 'romantic' in the nineteenth-century sense of the word.

Gioacchino Rossini was born in 1792 at Pesaro, the son of a town trumpeter, and died near Paris in 1868. He wrote nearly forty operas between the ages of about fourteen and thirty-seven. Then he stopped, for reasons which have never been explained; his *Stabat Mater* of 1842 shows that he had not lost his skill as a composer. He settled down comfortably in his villa near Paris, where he gave splendid dinner parties.*

Rossini was a considerable wit. He advised composers to delay writing an operatic overture until the night before the première. 'Nothing primes inspiration more than necessity, whether it be the presence of a copyist waiting for your work or the prodding of an impresario tearing his hair. In my time, all the impresarios in Italy were bald at thirty. I composed the overture to *Otello* in a little room at the Barbaja palace wherein the baldest and fiercest of directors had forcibly locked me with a single plate of spaghetti and the threat that I would not be allowed to leave the room alive until I had written the last note.' On the subject of hairlessness, there is a story of a visit from his friend Liszt after an absence of some years.† Rossini embraced him and then ran his fingers through his hair, asking if it was really his own. Liszt said it was, upon which Rossini removed a wig from his own head: 'Soon I shall have no teeth or legs either!'

Perhaps it is not surprising that Rossini is at his best in his comic operas, above all *The Barber of Seville* (1816), one of the half dozen or so real masterpieces in this difficult genre. He was a copious and charming melodist; his tunes have an Italian sparkle and bubble like wine, or indeed like happy laughter. He felt himself 'born to comic opera', preferring gaiety to anything savouring of pretentiousness. He distrusted, even in Beethoven, what he called 'oddities, lack of unity and natural flow', and he thought that serious-minded Germans had corrupted musical taste. 'Melody is strangled,' he asserted – and that, for Rossini, was the worst of artistic crimes.

Besides *The Barber of Seville*, Rossini's operas include *The Silken Ladder* (1812), *The Italian Girl in Algiers* (1813), *Cinderella* (1817), *Semiramide* (1823) and *The Count Ory* (1828). Some of these are best known for their

---

* The cookery expert Elizabeth David has written that he was 'almost as famous a gourmet as he was a composer' and thinks it was his love of truffles which has caused his name to be attached to dishes containing them like *tournedos Rossini*, 'on pompous menus all over the world'.

† Liszt arranged the *William Tell* overture for piano.

overtures. To know one of these overtures, with its inevitable long crescendo like a kettle boiling up, is to know a unique and delightful personality. Though he did not choose to plumb the depths of human experience, Rossini is one of the most lovable of composers. As long ago as 1824, the English essayist Leigh Hunt wrote that, while not to be compared with Mozart, Rossini had 'the genius of sheer animal spirits'. He will always be valued by those who love gaiety and love of life in music.

The two most important among Rossini's contemporaries are Gaetano Donizetti (1797–1848) and Vincenzo Bellini (1801–35). Donizetti's first opera was produced in Venice just before his twenty-first birthday. This was *Henry of Burgundy*; and in fact rulers of countries often provide his subject-matter, as in *Peter the Great* (1823) and *Anne Boleyn* (1830), with its important part for King Henry VIII. This last was the work that made his name, and Queen Victoria's Italian singing teacher, the bass Lablache, had his first great London success in the part of the King. *Anne Boleyn* was one of several operas on English subjects, including *Emilia di Liverpool*, remembered more for its title than its music.

Donizetti's love of noble themes was not matched by any corresponding grandeur of style, however, and he was more successful in the vigorous, down-to-earth world of comic opera. In *L'elisir d'amore* (1832), *La Fille du Régiment* (1840) and *Don Pasquale* (1843) he offers delight to audiences whose tastes are not too austere. But it cannot be denied that a good deal of the music, considered as musical invention, is naive and even trivial. Only occasionally, as in the fine sextet of *Lucia di Lammermoor* (1835), are we made aware of the powers he might have developed in different circumstances.

Yet one must be fair. Donizetti wrote for great Italian singers, stars performing to a public which was in turn interested above all in rich streams of vocal melody; and this public had little or no taste for subtleties of harmony, structure or orchestration. So he is not exactly to be blamed if his horizons were limited: perhaps the melancholy which afflicted him at the end of his short life was partly due to a consciousness that he could have done greater things. Still, one of his undoubted achievements was to prepare the way in both serious and comic opera for a greater man, Verdi. He wrote in a letter of 1844: 'My heyday is over, and another must take my place. The world wants something new . . . I am more than happy to give mine up to talented people like Verdi.'

Donizetti gave generous praise also to a composer whom he might well have disliked as a rival. 'Everybody is praising the music of my friend, or rather my brother, Bellini, to the skies . . . The whole score of *Norma* pleases me immensely, and I have been going to the theatre for the last four evenings to hear Bellini's opera . . . Were I to enumerate all the beauties of *Norma* I should never finish this letter. I shall only say that I am completely won over by this moving composition.'

Bellini is sometimes called the Chopin of opera. Both of these composers loved Mozart; and this fact probably accounts more than any direct influence for a similarity between their styles which sometimes strikes one. Certainly this melody from Act II of *La Sonnambula* (1831) would not be out of place in a Chopin nocturne:

EX. 83 Bellini "Ah! non credea"(La Sonnambula)

Bellini's two other well-known operas are *Norma* (1831) and *The Puritans* (1835). He was no composer for comic opera, for his style is notably elegant, lyrical and refined. He was also a master of character-painting, who won even Wagner's admiration, and superior to Donizetti in variety of harmony and orchestration, though he lacks Donizetti's rich humanistic sympathy and wit. With both Donizetti and Bellini we sometimes recognise a new type of semi-serious opera, in which lighter features of picturesque sentiment enliven a basically serious plot; there is a full use of a chorus, since crowd scenes were common. For Bellini, the text was especially important. He said the first requirement for a good opera was a good libretto, collaborating mainly with one author, Felice Romani, a patient man who had to alter Norma's *cavatina* (or short aria) *Casta diva* eight times to satisfy the composer. By helping to repair a rift existing in his time between literature and music, Bellini did as much as Donizetti to lay foundations for Verdi's work, which dominated the Italian operatic stage for the whole second half of the nineteenth century.

VERDI

The long life of Giuseppe Verdi (1813–1901) was almost wholly devoted to opera. His career alone virtually tells the story of Italian music in the latter half of the nineteenth century. When Verdi died, Grieg wrote that with him was gone 'the last of the great ones . . . with Wagner the greatest dramatist of our century.'

Compared to the intellectual and philosophically-minded Wagner, Verdi was untheoretical and uncomplicated. The son of an innkeeper, educated by his parish priest and then through the good offices of a merchant patron, his approach to music was direct and industrious. In the early stages of his career at any rate, he simply composed operas as skilfully as he could to place before the Italian public. After marrying his patron's daughter Margherita Barezzi, whom he had known since childhood, he settled down to *Oberto, Count of San Bonifacio*; this had fourteen performances, in other words a reasonable success, at the Scala Theatre in Milan in 1839.

Then the young composer suffered appalling bereavements: within the space of two years, both his children and then his young wife died. The comic opera, *The Reign of a Day*, produced in August 1840 a few weeks after his wife's death, was a failure. He lost faith in himself as a composer and retired into the gloomy seclusion of his Milan lodgings. But the director of the Scala promised him a performance of any new work he might produce, drawing his attention to a biblical libretto on the story of Nebuchadnezzar which was available and awaiting a composer. Gradually he became interested and set to work. *Nabucco*, produced at La Scala in 1842, was a great success and established his reputation.

The story of the Jewish captivity told in *Nabucco* provided a rallying point for Italian patriotic feeling, directed against Austrian domination of northern Italy. This was also true of the plots of *The Lombards* (1843) and *Joan of Arc* (1845). But Verdi's fame rested on more lasting grounds than the political climate. Though Rossini, Donizetti and Bellini were his first models, he was more serious in intent and more full-blooded in emotional expression than his predecessors; a fine melodist who also possessed an unerring dramatic sense, he was the perfect Italian opera composer, seeming almost to fulfil a historical need. Tunes like this one from *Ernani* (Venice, 1844), abundantly direct in style and even vulgar, set audiences afire with enthusiasm.

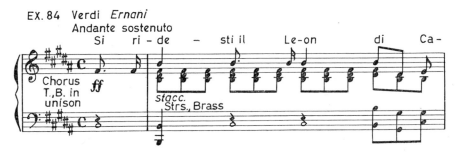

'I do not wish to find in art simply pleasure,' Verdi declared. But when he took the 'romantic' story of Shakespeare's *Macbeth* (1847) as a subject, he attempted a great deal. The various reforms of opera, restoring a more natural balance of drama and music, had had little effect in Italy where vocal brilliance and beauty remained the principal interest. But now Verdi objected to using a conventionally splendid voice for Lady Macbeth: 'Madame Tadolini sings to perfection, but I should like in Lady Macbeth a rough, hoarse and gloomy voice, with something diabolical about it . . . I think it's time we abandoned the conventional formulas and methods.' *Macbeth* was not a great success, for Verdi was ahead of public taste; and while its northern grimness little suited the southern audience, it remained unacceptable equally to literary-minded Shakespearians. Yet it marked a major step forward in the composer's development, offering a degree of psychological tension that was unprecedented in Italian opera.

In the early 1850s Verdi had three notable successes. These were *Rigoletto* (Venice, 1851), *Il Trovatore* (Rome, 1853) and *La Traviata* (Venice, 1853). It is worth noting that the first and third of these took their subjects from French romantic writers, Victor Hugo and the younger Dumas, and that *La Traviata* had a contemporary subject. These are popular works of a blood-

and-thunder and even sentimental type, not calculated to appeal to austere tastes. Yet of their kind they are masterpieces. Not only was Verdi's compositional skill maturing, he knew how to put it to the most effective dramatic use. When Rigoletto hears the Duke whom he thinks to be dead singing a fragment of *La donna è mobile* the dramatic effect is a wholly musical one, for we do not see the Duke: this is a skilful use of something like the Wagnerian leading-motive technique.

Having reached forty, Verdi wrote rather less, and more carefully. He could afford to please himself, and to feel confident that the public would follow him, remembering that *La Traviata* had become popular after an initial failure. In any case, he was philosophical – or simply modest – enough to write, when *Simon Boccanegra* failed at Venice in 1857, 'I thought I had created something passable, but it seems I was wrong.' In the meantime his fame spread widely. *The Force of Destiny* (1862) was first performed at St Petersburg, *Don Carlos* (1867) in Paris and *Aida* (1871) in Cairo, where a new opera house had been built to celebrate the opening of the Suez Canal.

In *Aida* there is a certain amount of musical local colour, with the 'Egyptian' sounds of a drum, harp and low flute melody. Though he was now living the life of a wealthy Italian country gentleman, Verdi had become a universal figure who could move audiences who were not Italian, and indeed to carry them into whatever part of the world the story called for, whether this was ancient Egypt in *Aida* or Shakespeare's Windsor in *Falstaff*.

Verdi composed his Requiem (1874) in memory of the patriotic writer Manzoni, magnificent church music which still remains true to his own dramatic, even theatrical, style. After this further achievement it seemed that he had retired, and in fact this was probably his intention. But there were two more operas to come, perhaps his most masterly of all, *Otello* and *Falstaff*. Both had first-rate librettos taken from Shakespeare by Arrigo Boito, himself a composer as well as a skilled writer. Verdi acquired the libretto of *Otello*, but then did not start work on the music for nearly five years. Finally the opera was finished in 1886 and performed at La Scala, Milan, early in 1887.

In *Otello*, Verdi showed himself aware of Wagner's operatic methods. The melodic lines given to the singers are no longer shaped into recitatives and arias, but instead we have a heightened, lyrical recitative or *arioso* style which a critic of the first performance saw as lying between classical declamatory methods and the rich vocal-orchestral polyphony of Wagner. Verdi felt that the Wagnerians were quite properly the heirs of Bach and a great German tradition, but not to be imitated by the Italians, 'the descendants of Palestrina'; and with him, vocal melody remains supreme and the orchestra secondary even when it is used with great subtlety. There is also in *Otello* a refinement or compression of emotion that is characteristic neither of Wagner nor of early Verdi, but perhaps more of Debussy. Here, in the last moments of the opera, Otello contemplates Desdemona's body before stabbing himself:

EX. 85 Verdi *Otello*

Otello: Adagio

E tu come sei pal - li-da! e stanca, e mu - ta, e

bel - la pia cre-a-tu - ra na - ta sotto maligna stel-la

If *Otello* represents Verdi's highest achievement in the realm of tragic human drama, *Falstaff* (1893) shows us the human comedy; once again it is Shakespeare who provides the starting point, but in creating his triumphant *opera buffa* at the age of eighty the great Italian composer brought his own wit, poetry and humanity to the story. Though bright and indeed brilliant in orchestral colour, it is still a vocal work above all and thus supremely Italian. With a tremendous pace yet full of subtleties, it includes a parody (in the conspiracy scene) of Verdi's own 'serious' style and a final musical jest when the 'academic' form of fugue is used for the closing words, 'All the world's a joke'.

Verdi was a kindly man who founded a rest home for elderly musicians, and he himself was buried there. Two hundred thousand people watched the funeral procession. His librettist Boito wrote: 'He has carried away with him an enormous measure of light and vital warmth. We had all basked in the sunshine of that Olympian old age . . . Never have I experienced such a feeling of hatred against death. It needed the death of this nonagenarian to arouse these feelings in me.'

12

LATE ROMANTICISM AND
NATIONALISM

Wagner. The Russians. Austria. France. Eastern Europe
and Scandinavia: more nationalist composers.

WAGNER

The name of Beethoven dominates musical history in the first half of the nineteenth century. For many people at the time, that of Richard Wagner (1813–83) seemed equally important in the second. Wagner created a new form that combined music and drama, operatic certainly in terms of stage performance, but in structure owing almost as much to Beethoven's symphonies as it did to the operas of Gluck or Weber.

Wagner's father was a minor official of the municipality of Leipzig who died six months after the birth of his son. His mother remarried, and the actor-artist Ludwig Geyer became a kindly stepfather whose surname Wagner took as a young boy, though Geyer, too, died before he left school and he eventually reverted to his original paternal name. While at school in Dresden, he became deeply interested in Greek mythology and was thrilled by Weber's opera *Der Freischütz*, especially its supernatural features; he also wrote poetry and read Shakespeare. At fourteen he became the author of a *Hamlet*-inspired play, of which he later joked that having killed off over forty characters he had to bring them back as ghosts to finish the story. Not only his stepfather but also the father whom he had never known had been theatre-lovers, while his brother and two sisters followed the stage professionally.

Wagner's education continued at Leipzig. One new enthusiasm was the music of Beethoven. He said himself that the effect on him of the Seventh Symphony was 'indescribable . . . in ecstatic dreams I met Beethoven and Shakespeare and talked with them, to awake bathed in tears.' He arranged the Ninth Symphony for piano – a task which, later, even troubled the mature Liszt – and studied hard to become a composer, writing a piano sonata and a string quartet. He also wrote an overture, in three different colours of ink, which was performed on Christmas Day 1830 to a Leipzig audience apparently more amused than enthusiastic. More lessons in fugue and sonata form followed, as did the publication of a Piano Sonata in B flat (1831) and a

Polonaise for piano duet by the Leipzig firm of Breitkopf and Härtel. There were three more overtures and finally in 1832 a Symphony in C major which was performed at a Leipzig Gewandhaus concert.

By this time Wagner had travelled abroad, to Vienna and Prague, and completed his musical studies at Leipzig University. He had also worked on an opera called *The Wedding*, which he left unfinished after his sister told him it would be impracticable to stage; but he soon composed another, *The Fairies*, in conscious imitation of the romantic fairytale world of Weber and Marschner. Both these works had librettos by the composer himself, as all his subsequent operas were to have. His professional career was now set in the world of opera: after being chorus master at Würzburg, he took successive conducting posts at Magdeburg, Königsberg and Riga, the Latvian capital. He married one of his singers, Minna Planer. In 1837 and 1838 he was occupied with *Rienzi*, the story of a Roman tribune taken from an English novel by Bulwer-Lytton, a grand opera with which he had visions of conquering Paris in Meyerbeer style.

It was to Paris that Wagner and his wife went in 1839, leaving behind a number of debts in Riga; his passport had in fact been confiscated and they had to bribe a sentry and cross the frontier illegally. They had a long and uncomfortable voyage, with their large Newfoundland dog Robber, to England in the first place and finally to the French capital. Meyerbeer, who received him affably, gave him letters of introduction to important persons in the operatic world. But nothing came of Meyerbeer's goodwill or Wagner's own enthusiasm and self-confidence; he was reduced to a penniless state, obliged to pawn jewellery and take in lodgers, and he even tried to get a job in an opera chorus but failed for lack of an adequate voice.

Nevertheless, little by little Wagner's situation improved. He composed *The Flying Dutchman* in 1841 and both *Rienzi* and the *Dutchman* were produced in Dresden, at the Court Opera, in 1842 and 1843. Leaving Paris with relief, the Wagners returned to Germany. *Rienzi* was a triumph. The tide had turned, and in 1843, at just under thirty, Wagner became chief conductor of the Dresden Opera. He remained in this post for six years. In 1845 his next opera, *Tannhäuser*, was completed and staged; thoughts of *The Mastersingers* began to occupy him, though it was *Lohengrin* (1848) that he next composed. Already it was the past, and principally the Germanic past, which attracted him above all as a source of operatic subjects.*

But now new factors emerged to affect the course of Wagner's career. In the first place, some friction had arisen between him and his superiors: he seems to have resented the routine of his duties for keeping him from total fulfilment as a creative artist. He neglected to appear at committee meetings

---

* The widely-known stories of Tristan and Parsifal, medieval or even older, were perhaps Celtic in origin; but they were known to Wagner in German forms. Similarly, they existed in English versions, by Malory among others.

and found himself obliged to ask for a salary increase to meet his debts. Secondly, the radical socialist movements in Europe caught his sympathy; he read a paper on republicanism to a large socialist meeting and had dealings with the exiled Russian anarchist-nihilist Bakunin, conceiving the idea of a new opera called *Siegfried's Death*, in which the hero of Germanic legend took on the guise of a socialist revolutionary. In May 1849 there was a violent street demonstration in which Wagner was to some extent involved. Bakunin and others (including Wagner's friend and assistant, Röckel) were sentenced to death – though they were reprieved later – and Wagner fled, pursued by a warrant for his arrest. He went first to Liszt at Weimar, who had already shown friendship and was about to produce his opera *Tannhäuser*. With Liszt's help he then proceeded, separating temporarily from his wife, to Switzerland, where for twelve years he was to remain a political exile. But Liszt's life and his remained linked: Liszt's daughter Cosima left her husband the conductor and pianist Hans von Bülow, to live with Wagner and eventually marry him in 1870, and Liszt actually died at Bayreuth in 1886.

In a letter to Liszt Wagner once referred to himself, Liszt and Berlioz as 'three of us who belong together because only we are alike'. Together they stood for a type of artist symbolised by Beethoven when he called himself not merely a composer but a 'tone poet'. Their music usually has some connection with another art such as literature or even painting. In Wagner's case, there was a real need for words (his own librettos) as well as music to make his fullest artistic statements. As he himself said, he gave up an idea for a 'Faust' Symphony and 'true to my nature, set to work on *The Flying Dutchman*, with which I escaped from all the mists of instrumental music.' In fact he was already working towards the *Gesamtkunstwerk* or 'union of the arts' that was to become his ideal.

Wagner's works after *Lohengrin* were *Tristan and Isolde* (completed in 1859), *The Mastersingers* (1867), *The Ring of the Nibelungs* (1874) and finally *Parsifal* (1882). *The Ring*, which occupied him intermittently for twenty years, is itself made up of the four operas called *The Rhinegold*, *The Valkyrie*, *Siegfried* and *The Twilight of the Gods*. This list of compositions, which omits only some songs, marches and short instrumental pieces, may seem short; but this does not mean that Wagner wrote little music. He dealt with colossal subjects requiring the spread of both music and drama over a vast canvas. *The Ring* takes about sixteen hours to perform: this is the length of five or six ordinary operas, or of twenty or more symphonies. Yet admirers of this work might even echo Professor Tolkien's remark about his own *Lord of the Rings* and find it too short: it certainly needs the full space of time that it occupies. It covers a world of experience in musico-dramatic terms: some even regard it as an allegory of the whole human condition.

The *Nibelungenlied* or *Nibelung Saga* was a thirteenth-century German poem, embodying a story taken from the earlier Norse collection, the Elder

Edda, telling of a hero, Siegfried, of hoarded gold and revenge. In an essay of 1848 called *The Wibelungs: World History from Saga**Wagner explained his artistic preference for myth over history; and he followed this with another essay called *The Nibelung Myth as a Dramatic Scheme*. He told Liszt, who had suggested that he should write an opera with a story from this legend, of the great new project which he had conceived, that of setting to music the whole epic story instead of merely taking an episode of it for a subject, as he had originally intended. He was going, he explained, from a fragment to the whole. His four dramas as now conceived would need to be performed on successive days at a specially-constituted festival. 'If I am to have any regard for my health,' he said, 'the work will take me three years at least.'

But it was to be over twenty years before *The Ring* came to completion and performance in 1876 at the town of Bayreuth in Bavaria. King Ludwig II of Bavaria had been the main helper in getting a special festival theatre built. In addition, Wagner Societies had been formed in centres like Berlin, Vienna and Leipzig; and the composer himself, with Ludwig's support, gave concert after concert to raise money. In spite of press opposition, including one article by a doctor claiming Wagner was mad, the great plan finally came to fruition. Wagner had been theatre designer, stage producer, singing coach and conductor, impresario and press agent, librettist and composer. King Ludwig came by private train, shunning publicity, to the festival: the composer had to meet him in the middle of the night at a remote spot. The Emperor Wilhelm I of Germany was there too for this historic first performance of the 'Ring' cycle. 'I never thought you would bring it off,' he said to Wagner. The composer's great vision had taken on a permanent form. To this day, Bayreuth remains the Mecca of Wagnerians, with the Festival Theatre's performances supervised by the composer's descendants and commanding the services of the most gifted artists.

The German critic Frömbgen wrote in 1929 that, 'High romanticism has made music a language that can express everything, including the artist's views on matters of the world and of life.' Wagner's work occupies a special place in the history of romantic music. Probably the main reason is that for him music was a means to an end and not an end in itself. His ideal was dramatic. Like Beethoven he was a tone poet; but while the drama of Beethoven's Fifth Symphony takes place purely in music, Wagner's has to be seen and felt, indeed perceived with every bodily sense. The perceiver (neither 'listener' nor 'spectator' is an adequate word here) is intended to be involved utterly, to be caught up in the art work as a simple and superstitious Greek peasant might have been drawn willy-nilly into the world of an antique tragedy of Euripides.

'Whatever my passions demand of me, I become for the time being – musician, poet, director, author, lecturer or anything else. Thus I was also

* Wibelung was an alternative name for Nibelung.

for a time a speculative aesthete.' So Wagner wrote to Liszt, and one cannot help noticing that he put music first. It was to philosophy, though, that he turned in order to develop and to justify his theories. The main early influence was Ludwig von Feuerbach, to whom he dedicated his long essay *The Art Work of the Future* (1850). 'As man is to nature, so art is to man,' Wagner claimed in this essay: as nature produces life, so man produces art. Art, therefore, was not artificial but natural, arising from the soul's 'natural morality'. The ancient Greeks, Wagner wrote, put 'our frivolous culture' to shame – 'To the splendid art of the Greeks we look, to learn from intimate understanding of it how the art work of the future must be constituted!' It is fascinating to see him here following the same line of thought as the Florentines who created opera two hundred and fifty years earlier: one can think of him as in some respects a reformer like Gluck, whom he admired and studied. His aim was to make Hellenic art an altogether human art and to seek out the form of 'the great universal art work of the future'.

In spite of Wagner's skill with words, we should still think of him as primarily a musician. Even his own theories allowed him the conclusion that music was the sublimest component of the universal art work. In this he would have been supported by the philosopher Schopenhauer, to whose views he became generally converted, and who found music more powerful than words, calling their association 'the marriage of a prince with a beggar'. The high place accorded to music by romantic philosophers was due to its power to express the otherwise inexpressible. For Schopenhauer, it conveyed the very essence of emotion; it told the secret story of man's 'will'.

And so at last we come to Wagner's musical technique. Since the drama must flow onwards naturally, arias and other set numbers had no place in his scheme for music drama. The singers were also actors whose utterances had to be dramatically convincing. Most important, the orchestra also participated in the drama with its 'leading motives', musical mottoes or phrases which symbolised persons, things and even states of mind. These leading motives thus provided a continuous commentary on the action. Wagner's own term for them was *Grundthema*, 'basic theme', and the concept is clearly related to the *idée fixe* technique used by Berlioz in the *Fantastic Symphony*.

The leading motive (or *leitmotif*) had musical advantages in that it helped to unify the music, to give it continuity and shape. But above all it meant that musical events corresponded indissolubly with dramatic ones in an amalgam of great strength. What was seen upon the stage, and also *felt* by the characters in the drama, was also to be heard, and this applied equally to the music of the orchestra and of the singers. In *The Ring* there are about twenty motives which occur in all four operas of the cycle. Among the most striking and memorable are these, characterising four elements of this Nordic legend:

EX. 86 Wagner *Four motives from "The Ring"*

'In the last whirling of desire, a jubilant kiss brings to an end the last embrace.' This was Wagner's description of the end of Beethoven's Seventh Symphony. But it could also apply to the closing pages of his own *Tristan and Isolde*. This was composed in 1857–59, at the same time as he worked on *The Ring*. The story was once again drawn from legend, the source this time perhaps a Celtic one, and the subject is love. 'I have never written anything like it before,' the composer wrote: 'To me *Tristan* is and remains a wonder! I shall never be able to understand how I could have written anything like it.'

Needless to say, this was no ordinary love story, but one conceived on a Wagnerian level of intensity. It tells of a forbidden and finally doomed love; and it might be thought of as Wagner's *Romeo and Juliet* were it not for the fact that Isolde's dying song over Tristan's body is one of triumph, not tragedy. Her last words, and the last in the opera, are: '*ertrinken, versinken, unbewusst, höchste Lust!*', 'to drown, to sink unconscious in highest ecstasy!' *Tristan* is a hymn to sensual love and longing, yet it is noble too. Even the opening bars of the work are marked to be played in a 'slow and yearning' manner; these chromatic harmonies at once sound unsatisfied, thirsting:

EX. 87 Wagner *Tristan und Isolde (Prelude)*

Example continued

It has been rightly said that the story of *Tristan* symbolises the triumph but also the failure of Wagner's humanistic philosophy. His search for the universal art work to encompass the world failed because it was based on the personal vision of one man only; passion burns itself out in death, a 'Twilight of the Gods' indeed. His one-time admirer, the philosopher Nietzsche, eventually, and cruelly, turned against him and declared his art to be morbid and injurious to music. Certainly the music of the future, as Wagner envisaged it, was not to be. Yet *Tristan and Isolde* remains a unique masterpiece; and its highly chromatic musical language, its harmony, proved immensely influential even if its musico-dramatic ideals did not.

Wagner's next opera was *The Mastersingers*. Here he dealt with real people, not characters drawn from legend; and indeed the shoemaker-musician Hans Sachs (as we noted on page 65) is a historic person of the sixteenth century. In this opera Wagner did something of which most people would have thought him incapable – compose a comedy. And not merely a comedy, but one of rich, mellow humanity, though here too he has a serious message. This time it concerns the power of art. Poetry, says Sachs, is the truth of dreams made manifest; while Walther's *Prize Song* is an artist's banner held on high, a symbol of the belief that new creation comes through reconciling tradition and innovation. But apart from any question of a message, those who think Wagner incapable of lightness and charm should try sampling this work, for example the delightful *Dance of the Apprentices* with its quaint seven-bar phrases.

This composer's attitude towards the past, as we know from his comments on Greek art, was genuinely respectful. Yet Wagner used the past not only as a point of reference but also as a point of departure. This is seen clearly enough in *Parsifal*. With its theme of the Holy Grail and the Grail's knightly guard, it is in a sense a companion piece to *Lohengrin*. But it is more purpose-fully Christian, enough indeed to surprise and offend Nietzsche, who saw in it only 'Christianity arranged for Wagnerians'. Yet by the time of this, his last opera, Wagner had reached certain religious conclusions. In an essay called *Religion and Art*, he wrote: 'We recognise the reason for the fall of mankind in history, as well as the need for its redemption . . . and dedicate ourselves to bringing it about.'

Wagner died in Venice of a heart attack less than seven months after *Parsifal* was produced. With this work he made his farewell to the world, leaving a mysterious masterpiece which will perhaps remain controversial but seems as fitting a culmination as could be imagined to his unique life-work. Wagner's genius was many-sided, yet all his gifts served a single-minded and indomitable will.

THE RUSSIANS

Russia is the world's largest country; yet it was not until the nineteenth century that a recognisable Russian voice made itself heard in European music. When this happened, the effect was to bring about a new artistic movement called nationalism.

There was nothing new about the nationalist artistic theory. Already in his *Dictionnaire de Musique* of 1768, Rousseau had claimed that melody originated from language. 'It is the accent of languages that determines the melody of each nation,' he wrote; and so each nation, or at any rate linguistic group, had its own music.

Of course this is true up to a point. To take one example only, Hungarian words have their first syllable accented, and so folk-song melodies from that country begin on strong beats rather than weak ones. But to elevate simple observations like this to the status of an artistic creed is to exaggerate. Though they are unmistakably Hungarian in flavour, the string quartets of Béla Bartók owe their quality not to their national style but to a musical in-ventiveness having its roots in the quartets of Beethoven.

Nationalism was, however, necessary to the nineteenth century. In the eighteenth, men like Handel and Mozart had been musically at home every-where; but after Beethoven the course of music seemed increasingly to be directed by the hand of Germany, a hand which lay heavily on the helm. Only the French and Italian operatic composers maintained their independence, for sonatas, symphonies and instrumental music generally were in the German sphere of influence.

It was by finding a national voice that other countries managed to assert their individuality. Using a national, historical subject and a consciously Russian style, Mikhail Glinka (1804–57) produced his opera, *A Life for the Tsar*, in 1836. A contemporary of the great Russian poet Pushkin, Glinka lived at a time of growing national literary awareness; and after studying abroad he returned with both the skill and the desire to write Russian music. 'We inhabitants of the North feel differently,' he declared; and he was bold enough to write a quintuple-time wedding chorus in his opera. *A Life for the Tsar* was music which proudly paraded its Russian origin: with its final scene of rejoicing with the Kremlin bells, it would have been inconceivable from a German pen.

No wonder, then, that Glinka is called the 'Father of Russian music'. He brought nationalism into being in a mature form which immediately attracted disciples and created a Russian school of composers. He went further than Russian opera, too, composing instrumental music of a national character such as a *Capriccio on Russian Themes* for piano duet. He even developed what could be called a supra-nationalist style, writing national music of other countries. His 'Spanish' music, including the orchestral *Summer Night in Madrid*, started a fashion for such pieces, Rimsky-Korsakov's *Capriccio espagnol* being the best known of its successors.

Rimsky-Korsakov (1844–1908) belongs to the next generation, and to the group of nationalist composers known as 'The Five': the others are Borodin (1833–87), Cui (1835–1918), Balakirev (1837–1910) and Mussorgsky (1839–81). The greatest among these was probably Mussorgsky, though Rimsky-Korsakov was arguably the most skilled craftsman. Borodin, the composer of the opera *Prince Igor* (1887), is deservedly popular today for his melodic charm and rhythmic vitality, notably exemplified in the celebrated *Polovtsian Dances* from the opera. Cui, the composer of an opera called *The Captive in the Caucasus* (1882), also wrote for musical journals in France which drew European attention to the so-called New Russian School. Balakirev was another advocate of national ideals, the composer of fine piano music and songs as well as the symphonic poem *Tamar* (1882), drawn from a story by his favourite poet Lermontov.

The untimely death of Modest Mussorgsky moved Borodin to set a Pushkin poem (*For the shores of thy fair native land*) to music. Mussorgsky was the son of a landowner who later became an army officer and civil servant, but died a victim of alcoholism at forty-two after an unhappy and rather disordered life. His remarkable gifts may easily be demonstrated: Borodin's peasant chorus in *Prince Igor*, Khan Konchak's people, seem theatrical compared with the yelling mob of rebel peasants who mock a captive general in Act IV of Mussorgsky's *Boris Godunov* (1872). This opera was based on a play by Pushkin and deals with an episode of Russian history concerning one of her Tsars. The realism here is not as objective as that of, say, Bizet's *Carmen*, for the composer cannot remain an observer outside the drama but instead draws us with him into a maelstrom of emotion. He has been called the founder of musical impressionism in the sense of an art of direct impact. Debussy admired him and indeed was influenced by him, saying of his song cycle *The Nursery* (1872), composed to his own words: 'It is a masterpiece . . . No one has given utterance to the best within us in tones more gentle or profound: he is unique and will remain so because his art is spontaneous and free from arid formulas.'

Mussorgsky's other songs include the two cycles *Sunless* (1874) and *Songs and Dances of Death* (1877), both to texts by a young poet called Count Arseny Golenishchev-Kutuzov, a distant relative on his mother's side with whom he actually lived for a while around 1874–75. *Sunless* is pessimistic music, though the subtlety with which the words are given musical substance prevents monotony; the 'Death' cycle is no less subtle but more obviously dramatic, with a *Lullaby* in which Death addresses the mother of a sick child, a *Serenade* which he sings to a dying girl, a *Trepak* (Cossack dance) for a drunken peasant fatally caught in a snowstorm, and finally *The Field Marshal*, in which Death addresses the fallen on a battlefield.

Apart from the sixty or so songs and *Boris Godunov*, Mussorgsky left another opera, *Khovanshchina*, in an unfinished state; it was completed and orchestrated by Rimsky-Korsakov and performed in 1886. Rimsky-Korsakov also produced a new performing version of *Boris Godunov* which though it smoothed out certain characteristic roughnesses of the composer (and so earned the disapproval of later admirers of Mussorgsky) did make this great work more generally acceptable to the public as far afield as Paris and Italy. There is perhaps a parallel here with Ravel's orchestration of the Mussorgsky piano work *Pictures from an Exhibition* (1874), which made this colourful music widely known before it found its present place in the repertory of pianists.

'I have been brought near to everything Russian,' Mussorgsky once wrote, and he was surprised when Liszt admired *The Nursery* with its portrayals of what he thought to be 'purely Russian children'. Yet his best music moves us neither in spite of nor because of its national flavour: its qualities, like those of all great art, are difficult to define and more fundamental.

Rimsky-Korsakov is a simpler and more approachable figure than Mussorgsky. He composed the brilliant quasi-oriental suite *Sheherazade* (1888) and a dozen or so operas of which the most characteristic evoke a dream world; these include *The Snow Maiden* (1881), *Sadko* (1896), set in an undersea kingdom, and finally *The Golden Cockerel* (1907), in which the Astrologer actually tells the audience that the plot has no meaning and that most of the characters are imaginary. Rimsky-Korsakov missed having an academic training as a composer, but he worked hard to perfect his technique and so won the admiration of Tchaikovsky, who assured him of his vocation as 'an artist in the fullest sense of the word'. He became an excellent craftsman, perhaps above all a master of the orchestra – he wrote a textbook on instrumentation. His achievements in the realm of exotic orchestral fantasy strongly influenced the earlier style of his pupil Stravinsky.

Peter Tchaikovsky (1840–93) was not associated musically with 'The Five', whom he regarded as a mutual admiration society. But he remained on courteous personal terms with them; and though not a nationalist, he occasionally used a folk melody, as in the slow movement of his First String Quartet. He recognised Mussorgsky's genius cautiously: 'His gifts are perhaps the most remarkable . . . Mussorgsky, with all his ugliness, speaks a new idiom.' His view of opera, however, was not that of the Mussorgskian realistic school. Nor did he follow Wagner, who in his view had allowed music to disappear in his search for dramatic truth, 'paralysed by theories'; and he liked Wagner's 'rival' Brahms even less, finding him lifeless and inexpressive. In fact, like other highly individual composers, Tchaikovsky is difficult to fit into any obvious historical trend or category. Though he was cultured and articulate about music, he was much more concerned with expression than with theories.

One thing is certain: Tchaikovsky was the first great Russian symphonist. Borodin's two symphonies are good Russian music while falling short of being major symphonic achievements; but Tchaikovsky mastered this hitherto German form by adopting very personal methods. A Tchaikovsky symphony is a sublimated symphonic poem, a transformation of a poetic experience into musical terms requiring no programmatic explanation. It is in the symphonic dramas of the twentieth century, of Elgar, Sibelius and above all Shostakovich, that the importance of his legacy has proved itself.

Tchaikovsky's reputation, formerly rather uncertain with the critics, has steadily gained ground, for these people have found themselves uncomfortably sandwiched between an enthusiastic public and admiring musicians – composers like Stravinsky and Shostakovich as well as performers. No longer is Tchaikovsky regarded as a vulgar emotional exhibitionist, for we recognise that an artist who feels intensely may reasonably write nakedly emotional music without compromising his talent. His 'Pathétique' (Sixth) Symphony (1893) is pessimistic but at the same time noble in its rich outpouring of feeling; and as Professor Tovey says, its slow last movement 'is a stroke of genius which solves all the artistic problems that have proved most baffling to symphonic writers since Beethoven . . . the whole work carries conviction without the slightest sense of effort.' In other words, only the emotionally logical conclusion to the work is structurally right.

In the titles he gave to different pieces, Tchaikovsky acknowledged the flexibility of his forms, which were dictated by the content of what he had to say. Among the orchestral works we find the overture to *Romeo and Juliet* later renamed an 'overture-fantasy'. *Hamlet* also has this designation, but *The Tempest* and *Francesca da Rimini* (on Dante's story) both have the title of 'fantasy'. *The Year 1812*, for all its noisy grandeur, is simply an overture. There is also a 'symphonic ballad', *The Voyevode*, and the unnumbered 'symphony' (in the free, Berliozian sense) on Byron's story of *Manfred* (1885).

Manfred is a complex, individualistic figure, with whom Tchaikovsky identified himself in the romantic manner. 'It is so highly tragic, so complicated and difficult,' he declared of this composition, 'that at times I myself become a Manfred.' A sensitive but lonely man, he found in the act of composition both a challenge and a solace. Too much altogether has been made of his brief disastrous venture into marriage with a girl he did not love, even though the experience was a grim one. For the most part, although undoubtedly neuropathic, Tchaikovsky behaved in a sensible and balanced way. For example, though he suffered badly from nerves before conducting he still undertook this work and carried it out successfully. The period after his marriage was fruitful musically, with the Fourth Symphony and the opera *Eugene Onegin* (1878); he travelled abroad and acquired a pleasant and varied circle of friends; and he won the respect even of the nationalists, including Rimsky-Korsakov and the influential historian and critic Stassov. In time he settled at Maidanovo, between Moscow and St Petersburg, writing to his brother: 'I am contented, cheerful and quiet.' His daily routine included a two-hour walk, a constitutional which also permitted the thinking-out of musical ideas. 'I cannot tell you what a pleasure it has been to watch my flowers grow . . . when I am quite old and past composing I shall devote myself to growing flowers. Meanwhile I have been working with good results, for half the symphony is now orchestrated.' Tchaikovsky, the so-called neurotic, was by no means unacquainted with peace.

The symphony to which he referred in the letter just quoted was the Fifth, which like the Fourth and Sixth (the 'Pathétique') is well known today; so are the First Piano Concerto, the Violin Concerto and *Romeo and Juliet*. The public has its favourites, and performers naturally respond to their demands, but it is a pity that other works are less familiar. For example, there are over a hundred songs, among which are some quite as fine as one might expect from so sensitive and melodically gifted a composer; surely it is only the language problem which has so far kept them from popularity outside Russia, and this situation shows signs of changing. Of the nine operas, *Eugene Onegin* is the only one which is widely known, though *The Queen of Spades* (1890) is gaining in popularity. The splendid ballets *Swan Lake*, *The Sleeping Beauty* and *The Nutcracker* are however rightly recognised as masterpieces. Tchaikovsky may not be among the supremely great composers, but he has abundant vitality and, above all, charm – a quality much to be valued in music.

AUSTRIA

Anton Bruckner (1824–96) takes us back to the German-speaking part of Europe, where he was born in the village of Ansfelden, near Linz, to the west of Vienna. Like Schubert, he was the son of a schoolmaster who taught him music. His father died when he was eleven and Bruckner became a chorister in the great baroque monastery of St Florian overlooking the Danube, studying the piano, organ and composition. After a spell as a schoolmaster and organist, during which he continued to study, he finally became organist of Linz Cathedral in 1856. He was now in his early thirties; but he continued with the famous teacher Simon Sechter, whom eventually he succeeded at the Vienna Conservatory as a teacher of organ and musical theory. His slow development resulted in his F minor Symphony of 1863 being classified as a student work and remaining unnumbered. Yet he was now nearly forty.

Around this time Bruckner made the acquaintance of Wagner's music. He attended the première of *Tristan* in 1865; he also heard Beethoven's 'Choral' Symphony for the first time and he met Berlioz and Liszt. This was the period of his Mass in D minor (1864), and he also composed a symphony in the same key, which however was not published or performed till long afterwards and which, added to the later nine symphonies, is now very confusingly called *Die Nullte* – 'number 0'.

At long last Bruckner was a mature composer. Between now and his death in 1896 at the age of seventy-two, he continued to compose sacred music and symphonies, leaving his Ninth Symphony unfinished. He taught at the Vienna Conservatory till his retirement in 1891, and he had international success as an organist, playing at Notre Dame in Paris and also on the new Willis organ of ten thousand pipes in the Royal Albert Hall in London, then the largest in the world, just after its inauguration in 1871.*

Bruckner's work, like Tchaikovsky's, stands rather on its own in nineteenth-century music. This devout Catholic wrote music of a massive, almost baroque quality, and his symphonies have an atmosphere of power and space. He dedicated the Third to Wagner, whom he revered. Yet his style was not imitative of Wagner: in fact, the opening of the Third Symphony, with its bare fifths, calls to mind Beethoven's Ninth. Beethoven's influence, this time that of his great Mass in D, is felt also in Bruckner's large-scale church music with orchestra. Furthermore, when Bruckner provided a 'programme' for his 'Romantic' Symphony (the Fourth) with the scherzo representing a hunting scene, here too it is of Beethoven's 'Pastoral' Symphony that one thinks rather than of the more richly programmatic music of Berlioz or Liszt.

While Bruckner occupied himself with church music and symphonies,

---

* His programme on that occasion included an improvisation on 'God Save the Queen' as well as pieces by Bach and Handel, though with typical Brucknerian modesty he played nothing of his own.

another Austrian, Hugo Wolf (1860–1903), devoted his great gifts mainly to song. Thus, though Wolf admired both Wagner and Bruckner, his sphere of creation was different from theirs. He began song composition as a boy of fifteen, and continued until the tragic mental breakdown which overtook him in 1897.

Wolf once answered a request for biographical details with the following abrupt statement: 'My name is Hugo Wolf. I was born on March 13th 1860, and am still alive at the moment. That's biography enough.' He preferred people to study his work, putting art before the artist who had produced it. But for the less single-minded, a little more biography may be of interest. He was born in Austria, in the south-eastern district of that country called Styria; in fact his birthplace since 1919 has been Slovenjgradec in Yugoslavia and his mother was partially Slavonic, though his leather-manufacturing father was wholly German in language and culture. The household was a musical one, with five other children, and even had its family orchestra to while away the evenings. It was not intended, though, that Hugo Wolf should become a full-time musician; what his father called 'the learned professions' were a far more sensible choice of career in the eyes of this provincial and fairly prosperous businessman.

Yet the young Wolf turned out to be the most difficult of problem children. He did well at elementary school, particularly at music; but once at the high school at Graz he persistently neglected all studies except music and was dismissed after one term as 'wholly inadequate'. At another school he did little better, though he stayed longer: the teachers found him 'defiant, proud and stubborn' and he was asked to leave. He was then thirteen years old. A third school was tried, with the same result after Wolf had a furious quarrel with a master who sneered at his 'damned music'. 'Music is like food and drink to me,' he declared. Eventually his father accepted the inevitable. Wolf went to live with an aunt in Vienna and entered the Conservatory there in 1875. This was at first deeply satisfying, and he instantly became a committed Wagnerian, even, at the age of fifteen, managing to meet that great composer – who told him with a smile to come back later when his talent had ripened. Then came an unexpected fresh disgrace. He was expelled from the Conservatory for what was called a 'breach of discipline'. At least, that is how the authorities saw it, though Wolf himself maintained he had left of his own accord after informing the director that at his institution he was forgetting more than he learned.

Fortunately Wolf's talents were literary as well as musical: he was a voracious reader, of Scott and Dickens as well as the German classics, and could write well. Because of this, after a period of poverty eked out by teaching for which he had no vocation, he was appointed music critic of a weekly journal. His reviews were lively and provocative, and he quickly made a name for himself, taking up the cudgels on behalf of Wagner and Bruckner,

Berlioz and Liszt, but making enemies by his attacks on Vienna's great musical resident, Brahms, whose music he castigated as artificial and unhealthy, 'music without ideas'.

At this point, things improved for him with regard to composition and recognition as a composer. A well-to-do friend found him a publisher at last, after the better-known firms had declined his work, by guaranteeing them against loss. In 1888 his first published works appeared, a dozen songs for female voice which he had composed at various times over the preceding ten years. From now on he began to pour out songs in great bursts of creativity, for example fourteen Goethe settings in ten days of January 1889. He once wrote: 'Today I've produced a masterpiece – *A Girl's First Love Song* is by far the best thing I've done, compared with this, everything before was child's play.' But the next day he was writing again: 'I take back what I said. What I've written this morning, *A Journey on Foot*, is a million times better still.' Yet between such blazes of inspiration there came periods of distress and despondency, so that in 1891 he wrote to a friend, 'I've no longer any conception of composing. God knows how it will end. Pray for my poor soul.' It seemed that his creative powers had withdrawn themselves: 'I almost start doubting whether the compositions bearing my name are really my own.' Inspiration did return; but eventually there was a tragic mental breakdown. Paralysed and wasted away, Wolf ended his days in an asylum which he entered at his own request.

Apart from the opera *The Corregidor* (1895) and the *Italian Serenade* (1892) for string quartet or small orchestra, Wolf's output is wholly in the field of *Lieder*, German songs for voice with piano. He never used a poem that he considered had been successfully set to music before. This meant that many lyrics by Goethe and Heine were unavailable to him, following as he did both Schubert and Schumann, his earliest models. Still, there was Eichendorff, not set by Schubert and only sixteen times by Schumann. Another favourite poet, Mörike, he had entirely to himself. The collections which he produced of 'Spanish' and 'Italian' songs, over forty of each, were settings of German translations from those languages and they contain some deliberate musical evocation of the South.

The power and quality of Wolf's songs lie in the precision of their word-setting rather than in their melodic charm. Even the titles he gave them, like *Goethe Songs*, are significant, for with other composers we usually fail even to notice who the poet is. Compared to Schubert or even to Brahms, Wolf is a very literal or literary song composer, faithfully following each nuance of meaning in a text. There was of course a price to pay for the resultant powerful fusion of words and music, one that his idol Wagner always just avoided paying; and this is the subordination of music to meaning. Wolf had little use for simple folk-like melody and strophic form. His greatest admirers have always been the most literary-minded among musicians, who find in these songs psychological insights of a subtle type unknown in the 'purer' music of Schubert. It is noticeable how the richly chromatic, Wagnerian language of this music suggests a more complex reaction to words than that of earlier composers:

EX. 88 Wolf *Seufzer*

Langsam und schmerzlich
(Slowly and painfully)

Hab's nicht ge-he – – get und nicht ge-pfle – get, bin tot im
I let it per – ish nor did it cher – ish my heart must

Her – zen, o Höl – len schmerzen!
dead be and Hell doth claim me.

FRANCE

César Franck (1822–90), born at Liège nearly forty years before Hugo Wolf, was nevertheless active at about the same time: Franck's Symphony, for example, dates from 1888, while the Symphonic Variations for piano and orchestra and the Violin Sonata are works of 1885 and 1886 respectively.

Franck was a late developer, a church organist (in Paris) and a teacher of some fame. In all these things he resembles Bruckner; and as with Bruckner, recognition as a composer was for him slow in coming. Vincent d'Indy, a pupil of Franck, said his first success was in his sixty-ninth year! For just as Bruckner, the massive symphonist, had been out of the main stream of German music, Franck, with his church music and his chamber and organ works, had little to offer the opera-loving Parisian public. His organ music includes Three Chorales (1890) which actually remind us of Bach not only in their name but in the notes: they have a dignified spirituality, a quality, due in part to a baroque chromaticism, which can perhaps be called mystical. This feeling is also present in the Chorale of the Prelude, Chorale and Fugue (1884) for piano:

EX. 89 Franck *Prelude, Chorale and Fugue*

Franck's music is by no means all solemn, though; nor was it at all archaic in technique. His Symphony and several other pieces are strongly romantic and use Lisztian thematic transformation, a method which suited him and which is the basis of the sunny Symphonic Variations for piano and orchestra

(1885). We find it too in the Violin Sonata (1886); the finale of this work begins with what must be the most convincing and spontaneously melodious of strict canons, the 'academic' device fitting perfectly into the warmly atmospheric music:

EX.90   Franck   *Violin sonata*

Franck's influence was considerable. His pupils included another Parisian resident, Vincent d'Indy (1851–1931), who wrote his biography. D'Indy is better known in France than elsewhere: an ardent Wagnerian and a distinguished composer of operas and programmatic orchestral pieces, he was also a famous teacher and scholar. As a conductor, he was progressive enough to support his younger rival Debussy and perform his music. Another Franck pupil was Chausson (1855–99), a song composer who also wrote a nobly-proportioned symphony; and a third pupil was also a song composer, Duparc (1848–1933), whose music all dates from before 1884, after which he gave up composition and went into premature retirement.

Camille Saint-Saëns (1835–1921) also had a part to play in the revival of French musical life outside the theatre. A gifted and fertile musician, he may have fallen short of real genius; yet he enriched the repertory in all spheres, from opera and church music to the symphony and string quartet. An infant prodigy who performed all Mozart's piano concertos as a young man, he was organist of the Madeleine Church in his native Paris and also taught the piano for a while. He was only twenty when he composed his First Symphony in 1855; a Second and Third followed in due course, as well as five piano concertos, three concertos for violin and two for cello. Saint-Saëns wrote twelve operas, including one on the subject of *Henry VIII*, produced at the Paris Opera in 1883. Although he visited Wagner's Bayreuth, his music was not much influenced by the great German, but he admired Liszt, whose style and methods are echoed in his symphonic poems, including the popular *Danse macabre* (1874). Saint-Saëns's musical personality tends towards the classical rather than the uninhibitedly romantic: a French writer, Romain Rolland, said he was 'tormented by no passions'. He was a scholar of some achievement who took trouble to bring such great names of the past as Lully and Rameau before the French public; equally notable was his work for modern French music, and he was the co-founder in 1871 of the Société Nationale de Musique which had as its aim the promotion of new works. It is ironic that his best-known work today should be one he would have thought relatively minor, the delightful *Carnival of the Animals* for orchestra that he wrote in 1886.

Gabriel Fauré (1845–1924) was Saint-Saëns's pupil. Fauré composed nearly a hundred songs which stand comparison with those of Brahms, Tchaikovsky or Wolf. These include the cycle of nine songs called *La Bonne Chanson* (1892); this is to words by the poet Verlaine, for as had happened in both Germany and Russia, contemporary native poetry now attracted French composers and the *Lied* or art song was no longer Germany's exclusive property. Fauré also wrote a Symphony (1884) but withdrew it later when he found that it did not altogether satisfy him; in fact his larger instrumental works are mainly chamber music. His Requiem (1887), composed in memory of his father, is unique in its serenity, the *Dies irae* with its Doomsday terrors being simply omitted. Another work which is characteristic of this refined artist is the opera *Pénélope*, which he dedicated to Saint-Saëns. There is also a good deal of piano music, rich yet delicate in feeling: it shows Chopin's clear influence and includes the Chopinesque titles of barcarolles, nocturnes, impromptus and even a mazurka.

Fauré contributed to French musical life first as an organist in Paris – he was one of Saint-Saëns's successors at the Madeleine – and later as Professor of Composition at the Conservatoire, where his subtle command of harmony provided a model for his pupil Ravel. In 1905 he became Director of the Conservatoire, and he held this influential post until his retirement in 1920.

Those qualities of taste and refinement which we often think of as Gallic may also be found in the work of another Saint-Saëns pupil, André Messager (1853–1929). Messager was a friend of both Fauré and Debussy: he was the first conductor, in 1902, of Debussy's opera *Pelléas et Mélisande*.* As Director of the Paris Opéra he was an influential figure; he also spent five years (1901–6) as Artistic Director of the Covent Garden Opera in London and he married an Irish girl. Messager was mainly a composer for the stage: his operettas *Véronique* (1898) with its *Duet on a Swing*, and *Fortunio* (1907), are charmingly written and remain popular light classics in France.

Such composers as these were not consciously fulfilling any nationalist ideal: their music is characteristically French, but its style is spontaneous rather than deliberate. Nationalism as a movement was not needed in countries like Italy or France which had already found their musical identity. We have already seen its rise in Russia; that country was to offer an example to others, until this time less developed musically, in Eastern Europe and in Scandinavia.

EASTERN EUROPE AND SCANDINAVIA: MORE NATIONALIST COMPOSERS

Towards the end of the eighteenth century, the historian Dr Burney had bestowed the name 'Europe's conservatory' on Bohemia, the western part of present-day Czechoslovakia, where the teaching of music in village schools and the skilful making of violins by village craftsmen had impressed him. Hitherto this part of Europe had produced no famous composers, unless we include Gluck and Stamitz, who by both residence and style were non-Bohemian. But now a distinctive Czech voice appeared in music, encouraged and supported by growing national feeling of a political kind directed against Austrian rule and the authorities' use of German as an official language. This voice was that of Bedřich Smetana (1824–84).

---

* The French writer Colette described a friendly gathering of musicians with d'Indy and Debussy present and Fauré and Messager improvising a duet at the piano 'in a perilous rhythm'.

Smetana was a brilliant youthful pianist whose aim, noted in his diary, was to become 'a Mozart in composition and a Liszt in technique'. As a matter of fact, Liszt's compositions also influenced him later; he saw the Lisztian symphonic poem as something new and progressive and wrote an orchestral portrait of *Richard III*, calling it a 'personification of Richard in musical shape'. Later he composed the more obviously nationalist set of six symphonic poems called *My Country*: the second of these is *Vltava*, which evokes the course of the great river upon which stands the city of Prague.

Smetana's life was characteristic of a composer concerned with the development of his country's musical life generally as well as with his own talent. The son of a brewer, he showed early gifts as a string player as well as a pianist and after study in Prague opened a private school of music there. For five years he held a conductorship at Gothenburg in Sweden – this was a self-imposed exile when his strong, politically nationalist feeling made life in Austrian-dominated Prague uncongenial – but then in 1861 he returned for good. When the National Theatre was founded in the following year he at once became associated with it and four years later was appointed its principal conductor. This enterprise, of fierce cultural independence, was linked with the Czech Philharmonic Orchestra and a choral society called Hlahol; Smetana conducted both these bodies, and he also helped to found a Society of Artists. No wonder then that the fine new building for the Opera was inaugurated in 1881 with the première of his opera *Libuše*. The title is the name of the heroine, the foundress of Prague who marries a noble-hearted peasant and in the final scene prophesies a splendid future for her nation.

Smetana's nationalism went deeper than musical local colour. Indeed he said that he never actually imitated folk music but tried instead to show national character at a more profound level. However this may be, *The Bartered Bride* (1866), the second of his eight operas and the most popular by reason of its abundant colour and gaiety, reveals its national origins clearly enough in the music as well as the Bohemian story.

Zdeněk Fibich (1850–1900) composed operas and symphonies which are performed in Czechoslovakia today; but this Leipzig- and Paris-trained musician was more Germanic and less nationalist in style than Antonín Dvořák (1841–1904), and it is Dvořák who is Smetana's obvious successor. He was the son of an innkeeper and butcher of Nelahozeves on the River Vltava, forty-five miles south of Prague. Somehow he managed to learn music as a boy, for as he once said, 'In Bohemia, every child has to learn music, and if possible sing in church; after church, people delight in music and dancing' – and he himself played the fiddle for these occasions.

From 1857 to 1859 Dvořák studied the organ, singing and the theory of music at the so-called Organ School in Prague, founded in 1830 by the Association for the Improvement of Bohemian Church Music. After that he was on his own, and eked out a living as an orchestral viola player. He played under the conductorship of Smetana; and soon he was the musical disciple of the older composer. However, Dvořák did not share Smetana's enthusiasm for the structural ideals of Liszt; in fact he attracted Brahms's attention and admiration and Brahms recommended his *Moravian Dances* (1876) for publication.

Dvořák did resemble Smetana in that he followed not so much the letter as the spirit of his country's national music, though this was often in the German, or Brahmsian, forms of chamber music, concertos and symphonies. When he used the simpler forms, the national flavour is strongest. The musical lexicographer Percy Scholes once wrote of this *Slavonic Dance* (1878) that it 'simply shouts "Bohemia!" at you'.

EX. 91 Dvořák *Slavonic Dance Op. 46 no. 8*

Dvořák's range as a creator of music was a wide one. He composed church music like the fine *Stabat Mater* and Requiem, and his ten *Biblical Songs* (1894) are noble utterances, the culmination of his song-writing art. His style is somehow both mellow and fresh, so that works like the 'New World'

Symphony (his Ninth) (1893) and the Cello Concerto (1895) have rightly become popular. The first and second subjects of the Concerto's opening movement, in which we find the 'folk' characteristics of a flattened seventh and pentatonic outlines, give some idea of the strength as well as the beauty of this composer's ideas:

EX.92 Dvořák *Violoncello concerto*

A few other Slav musicians added their national voices to European music. Stanislaw Moniuszko (1819–72), the composer of the colourful and melodious opera *Halka* and nearly three hundred songs, became the leader of a Polish school, one which Chopin might have headed had he not gone to Paris and developed differently. The same could be said of Magyar music and an equally illustrious expatriate, Liszt: the most significant local Hungarian musician was Ferenc Erkel (1810–93), who wrote the Hungarian National Anthem and the patriotic opera *Hunyadi László* (1844).

The musical soul of Scandinavia was also awakening. The Dane Niels Gade (1817–90) wrote eight symphonies and a violin concerto; and he was also the composer of overtures called *Echoes from Ossian*, *In the Highlands*, and *A Mountain Journey in the North*, as well as *Nordic Tone-Pictures* for piano duet and *Nine Songs in Folk Style* for two voices and piano. It was of Gade that Schumann made the famous remark: 'The North is most decidedly entitled to a language of its own.' Sweden produced a highly original symphonist in Franz Berwald (1796–1868); but no major nationalist figure emerged, though there was a so-called 'Swedish Glinka', Ivar Hallström

(1826–1901). In Finland, the Hamburg-born Fredrik Pacius (1809–91) composed the National Anthem and *Suomen laulu* ('Song of Finland'); having taken Finnish nationality, Pacius began the process of establishing the country's musical style and earned the title of 'Father of Finnish music'.

The most important nineteenth-century Scandinavian musician was the Norwegian, Edvard Grieg – descended from a Scottish merchant called Alexander Greig. Grieg (1843–1907) wrote pieces which have found a secure place in the repertory, like the Piano Concerto and the incidental music to Ibsen's intensely Norwegian, picaresque drama of *Peer Gynt*. He studied at Leipzig and there learned to love Schumann's music, which influenced him more strongly than that of any other composer. Back in Norway, however, he turned firmly to a national language. He even found Gade's music Mendelssohnian, an 'insipid Scandinavianism', though he liked and respected the senior Danish composer personally. When Gade found his Second Violin Sonata 'too Norwegian', he retorted defiantly: 'On the contrary, Professor! The next one will be more so!'

Grieg refused to think of himself as merely a miniaturist. In 1905, near the end of his life, he wrote to a biographer indignantly repudiating a German suggestion that he ' "never reached the ocean but stuck in the fjord" . . . as a matter of fact I owe my name to my larger works.' Yet his larger-scale pieces are few and mainly youthful. Where Grieg really seems to come into his own is in the many short piano pieces and the songs; and here his idiom is often of great freshness. As Fauré said, Grieg is 'fine, strange, always individual'. He was frequently unconventional, especially in his harmony, looking forward to Bartók's *Allegro barbaro* in the *March of the Dwarfs* and to Debussy's *Cathédrale engloutie* in *Bell-ringing*.

EX.93A   Grieg   *March of the dwarfs*

EX. 93 B   Grieg   *Bell-ringing*

Yet Grieg's later nationalism does not have the youthful fervour, or the confidence, which we find in the music of Glinka or Smetana. Already he strikes a wistful, elegiac note, as in *The Last Spring*, a piece which he liked enough to write in three versions: as a song, for string orchestra and for piano. Here he went beyond the accents of Norway to speak a more universal language of autumnal sadness which Tchaikovsky uses also at times. It looks forward to the work of his own disciple, a great poet of nostalgia, Delius.

EX. 94   Grieg   *The last Spring*

13

THE ROMANTIC TWILIGHT AND THE
EARLY TWENTIETH CENTURY

Strauss. Mahler. Debussy. Ravel. Some later nationalists.

STRAUSS

With Richard Strauss (1864–1949) and Gustav Mahler (1860–1911), German music came fully into the twilight of romanticism. Like other twilights, this one possessed the beauty of unhurried parting, of approaching peace. At times there were yearning backward glances from the places of the sunset towards the flushed dawn of youth and innocence: the 'modernist' Strauss turned to old Vienna and even to Mozart, Mahler to Schubert and a fragile Chinese-porcelain world. There was also some anguish: Dylan Thomas's line, 'Do not go gentle into that good night,' would have been understood by Mahler in particular.

Strauss was the son of a musician, the leading horn player of the Munich Opera orchestra. Given a strict musical training, he began composition early, and before leaving university in 1883 he had had performances of a Symphony in D minor, shorter orchestral pieces, choruses, songs and a String Quartet in A. At the age of twenty-one he became a professional conductor at Meiningen, directing the opera there; further experience came at the Munich Opera and at Weimar, and in 1898 he was appointed conductor of the Berlin Royal Opera. Berlin was at this time one of the greatest musical centres of Europe; and Germany herself maintained about a hundred and twenty opera houses, even quite small towns managing to support one (which doubled as a theatre) as well as a chorus and symphony orchestra. Years of peace and economic growth following upon the foundation of the German Empire in 1871 had brought a healthy prosperity to the arts; and though Strauss's early music has been called imperialistic and materialistic, it undoubtedly reflects an attractive youthful confidence which was very much a quality of its time and place.

Since Strauss made his name principally in symphonic poems and operas, he may be said to have had Liszt and Wagner as his spiritual forbears. Yet he began and ended his career as a conservative. His early training had given him a Brahmsian style. But then, the composer said, his friend Alexander Ritter 'urged me on to the development of the poetic, the expressive in music, as exemplified in the works of Liszt, Wagner and Berlioz. My symphonic fantasy *Aus Italien* is the connecting link between the old and new methods.'

Strauss tried to take romanticism to its limit and so open up a path to the future. With his background of classical technique and romantic intention, he was well placed to go forward in the post-Wagnerian world. He was probably the most naturally gifted composer of his generation, and his *Don Juan*, the brilliant and vital symphonic poem of 1888, is a work of almost insolent mastery for such a young man. The series of symphonic poems continued with *Death and Transfiguration* (1889), *Till Eulenspiegel* (1895) and *Also sprach Zarathustra* (1896), whose grandiose opening music was later to be used in the space-fiction film *2001*. Next came *Don Quixote* (1897) and *A Hero's Life* (1898): this latter was autobiographical – and included an acid little section depicting the composer's mean-spirited and small-minded critics!

Even Strauss needed eventually to pause for breath, to check his impetuous progress and consider his course. In fact the *Symphonia Domestica* (1903) – also autobiographical, and including a sequence portraying a baby's bath – and the *Alpine Symphony* (1915) were the last of the symphonic poems. In the meantime, progressively from 1901, Strauss turned his talents to opera, and continued to write operas for forty years.

Salome (1905) tells the biblical story (in *Matthew*, Chapter 14) as treated in the play by Oscar Wilde. In this opera, Salome demands from her stepfather Herod Antipas the death of John the Baptist, who has rejected her, and passionately kisses his severed head, whereupon the horrified Herod has her killed by his soldiers. Strauss undoubtedly found suitable music for his subject: it shifts and seethes like a pit of snakes; the large orchestra is used luxuriantly throughout; and the harmony, at times seductive, can also be very bold in its sinister dissonance. The first of these examples is the music introducing the Baptist, and the second is from the end of the opera, as Salome holds the head and a mysterious darkness falls.

EX. 95 A
Largo

EX. 95 B

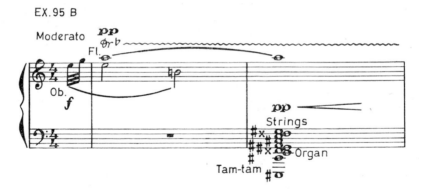

Salome exemplifies a kind of ruthless realism in art which is not at all the same as Wilde's hypersensitive aestheticism: Strauss seems to enjoy above all the powerful drama. *Elektra* (1908), based on the drama of Sophocles, had an equally grisly plot, in which Elektra avenges her father's death by the murder of her mother Clytemnestra and then dances herself to death in insane rapture. The music was even more dissonant than that of *Salome*. But the work found powerful supporters, and the dramatist George Bernard Shaw was enraptured: 'Human emotion is a complex thing: there are moments when our feeling is so deep and our ecstasy so exalted that the primeval monsters from whom we are evolved wake within us and utter the strange tormented cries of their ancient struggles with the Life Force. All this is in *Elektra* . . . not even Beethoven in his last great Mass comprehended so much.'

Elektra is an extreme work, one which could only belong to a period of decadence, and it may be admitted that an interest in extreme or even morbid emotional expression characterises those of the later romantics who are most clearly in the Wagnerian line of succession and who belong to a Germanic tradition that also produced the psychoanalyst Sigmund Freud. *Elektra* marked the beginning of Strauss's important collaboration with the Viennese poet and dramatist, Hugo von Hofmannsthal, in six operas over a period lasting till the writer's death in 1929. Their second opera was altogether different: *Der Rosenkavalier* (1910) is the best known and possibly the finest of Strauss's operas, a tale of love and intrigue in eighteenth-century Vienna which is at one and the same time erotic and delicate, sophisticated and gentle. The variety of characters allowed Strauss to cover a musical range from the coarse though comic Baron Ochs to the innocent, virginal Sophie. And in the sensuous but essentially unspoiled boy Octavian the collaborators created the only operatic companion to Mozart and da Ponte's Cherubino in *The Marriage of Figaro* – a role so stylised that it is taken by a soprano, yet which is convincing here.

Der Rosenkavalier was followed by *Ariadne auf Naxos*, which underwent various revisions before reaching its final form in 1916. In this work Strauss found a new refinement of style, its simplicity reflecting classical or even pre-classical ideals. *The Egyptian Helen* (1927, revised 1933) and the charming *Arabella* (1932) were also written to librettos by Hofmannsthal; but the profoundly symbolic *Die Frau ohne Schatten* ('The Woman without a Shadow'), completed in 1917, is for Straussians the most challenging example of their joint art. Hofmannsthal died in 1929, and after completing *Arabella* Strauss turned to other librettists: of his remaining five operas, the best known are *The Silent Woman* (1935), with a libretto by Stefan Zweig, and *Capriccio* (1941), with words by a fellow-musician, the Viennese conductor Clemens Krauss.

Living on as he did through and beyond the Second World War, Strauss became willy-nilly the observer of great changes, and not only in music. He managed to ride out the storm of Nazism, feeling, like the conductor of the Berlin Philharmonic Orchestra, Furtwängler, that music had nothing to do with politics and doing what he could from his position as Germany's leading musician to help his Jewish friends. But even this untiring, extraordinarily gifted man was worn down and saddened at the end. At the age of eighty, he returned for solace to the spirit of Mozart; and once again the classical forms occupied him, so that his Second Horn Concerto was written sixty years after his First. His Oboe Concerto of 1946 combines romantic warmth with echoes of the long-lost gaiety of rococo style. To the nineteenth century he paid tribute with the *Metamorphosen* for twenty-three solo strings (1945), an elegy perhaps for music itself, whose nature is revealed by the use of a theme from Beethoven's 'Eroica' funeral march. Finally in 1948, the year before his death, Strauss completed the lovely *Four Last Songs*, a farewell to the soprano voice for which he had written so much music, and perhaps to life itself. In one of these songs, *September*, the words end:

> In the dying garden's dream
> Summer still remains within the roses
> Longing for peace;
> Then, slowly, he closes tired eyes.

MAHLER

When Mahler wrote to his wife in 1907 that Strauss's opera *Salome* was a 'masterpiece of our time' – though one had 'to separate the chaff from the grain' – he was nearing the end of his own, much shorter career. And he had himself created masterpieces: eight symphonies (the Eighth only awaited scoring) and all of his songs. There only remained to come *The Song of the Earth*, the Ninth Symphony and the unfinished Tenth.

Gustav Mahler was born at Kališt, Bohemia, into a Moravian Jewish family in poorish circumstances. His childhood was not especially happy, with a delicate mother and a father who treated her harshly; he was one of twelve children of whom only three besides himself survived to the age of thirty. He once said, 'I am three times a homeless man: as a Bohemian among Austrians, as an Austrian among Germans and as a Jew among people the world over.' However, he went from grammar school to the Vienna Conservatory, where he became friendly with Bruckner and especially Wolf – an intimate friend with whom he shared lodgings, though later they lost contact with each other. Various posts as an operatic conductor followed, at first in Austria and Germany (where he was deeply impressed by Wagner at Bayreuth), later in Prague and Budapest – where his performance of Mozart's *Don Giovanni* impressed Brahms. It was Brahms who recommended him for the post of *Kapellmeister* of the Vienna Opera in 1897, and in the same year in which he took up this appointment he became a convert to the Roman Catholic Church. Within a few months he was given a life contract as Artistic Director of the Vienna Opera, and in 1898 he also became conductor of the Vienna Philharmonic Orchestra. This appointment may be said to have marked a summit of achievement in his chosen career. In 1902 he married Alma Schindler, young and beautiful as well as musically gifted and devoted to him; they had two daughters, of whom one died young of diphtheria and scarlet fever. Calling himself a 'summer composer', since he had to compress creative work into holiday periods, he managed to compose fairly extensively nonetheless while fulfilling a career as a distinguished conductor. He was one of the first modern international artists, who conducted in London, Moscow, Amsterdam and New York, travelling four times to the American capital between 1907, in which year he relinquished his Viennese post, and 1911, the year of his death.

Mahler's talents were of a different kind to those of Strauss; his musical fields were those of symphony and song. While still under twenty, he tried his hand at opera and chamber music; but of these works not a single one survives complete. What he called 'my Opus 1, the first of my works in which I found myself', was *Das klagende Lied* (1880). The title means 'Lament'; and this elaborate work for voices and orchestra, on a sinister fairy tale by the Brothers Grimm, sets the tone for much of his music, in which romance, mystery, joy and terror emerge in a strange blend of childlike simplicity and tormented soul-searching.

'Only when I experience do I act as a tone-poet; only as a tone-poet do I undergo an experience,' Mahler admitted. His work is like an autobiography. Listening to the music, we seem to enter the presence of the man himself: the brilliant virtuoso conductor, the unyielding administrator, the touchingly gentle father, the lonely spiritual seeker, the eternal child who loved the countryside. The influence of other composers is sometimes clearly to be heard; yet even in his Schubertian or Wagnerian moments Mahler somehow remains himself, with a style that is individual enough to be recognised in other, later composers influenced by him, like Berg, Shostakovich and Britten.

Mahler's symphonies and songs are closely related. The First Symphony (1888) uses melodies from the cycle called *Songs of a Wayfarer*, a Schubertian idyll of a jilted lover for which Mahler wrote his own words. The Symphony begins with a breathtaking evocation of dawn, marked 'like a sound of Nature': yet this calm does not lull the listener but makes him feel intensely alive. Then we hear the tune of a *Wayfarer* song, bringing movement and a fresh morning brightness. In fact the song version has the words: 'Today I set off through the fields, dewdrops still upon the grass . . . Good morning! isn't the world lovely?'

EX. 96 Mahler *Symphony no.1*

The world was lovely indeed, but for Mahler there were always dark shadows. This First Symphony includes a funeral march, a type of movement common in his music. But here we have macabre humour too: the performers are told to play 'with parody' and one tune is even marked '*keck*', 'cheeky'.

EX. 97 Mahler *Symphony no.1*

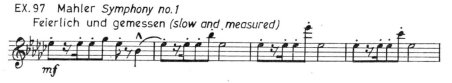

Song and symphony again come together, not only by quotation but literally, in Symphonies Two to Four. In each one the voices are used differently. The Second has five movements, of which the last two use voices; while the Third has six, of which the fourth and fifth are vocal. The Fourth Symphony, Mahler's shortest, has a soprano song for the finale. The words of this depict a child's picture of heaven, and are taken from the German folk anthology called *The Youth's Magic Horn*, from which Mahler often drew his texts.

The Fifth, Sixth and Seventh Symphonies are once again purely orchestral, even though instrumental echoes of the songs are again heard in each of them. The Sixth is Mahler's 'Tragic' Symphony and ends in gloom; but the other two, like the first three symphonies, end optimistically. The cheerful, busy finale of the Fifth is preceded by a short adagietto, scored only for strings and harp yet rich in sonority, music of a luxuriant pathos.

Mahler once said that, 'The creative urge for a musical organism certainly springs from an experience of its author, that is, from a fact which after all should be positive enough to be expressible in words . . . there need be no objections to a programme.' He provided some kind of verbal explanation for several of the symphonies. All of them seem to chart a pilgrimage towards a spiritual goal; and this ideal (not, however, attained in the tragic Sixth) was the victory of faith and love over fear and conflict.

The Eighth Symphony, dedicated to Mahler's wife, represents the culmination of this aspect of his creative personality. It is in two long sections and uses a vast array of vocal and orchestral forces which have earned it the name of 'Symphony of a Thousand', though this is perhaps unfortunate in view of the frequently delicate instrumentation: Mahler was no megalomaniac. It was composed in a mere eight weeks of 1906, and Mahler wrote to the conductor Mengelberg: 'I have just completed my Eighth . . . it is the biggest thing I have done so far . . . Imagine that the universe begins to vibrate and sound. It is a question no longer of human voices, but of planets and suns in rotation . . .' The Eighth Symphony was inspired by Plato's view of the material world as only the image of a greater spiritual reality, but this philosophy was seen through Christian eyes. '*Alles Vergäng-liche ist nur ein Gleichnis,*' 'All that perishes is but a parable': the words come from the second section of Goethe's *Faust*, which together with the Latin hymn *Come, Holy Ghost* provided the text for the symphony.

The monumental Eighth Symphony waited three years for its triumphant first performance in 1910. In the meantime Mahler had composed *The Song of the Earth* and the Ninth Symphony. These were works of a very different kind, written *sub specie mortis*. For a heart complaint had been diagnosed in July 1907; Mahler was told he must change his energetic way of life, and from now on he felt doomed. Yet he wrote to his young friend, the conductor Bruno Walter: 'My thirst for life is keener than ever and I find the habit of life even sweeter than before.'

This state of mind seems to have been perceived by the Viennese composer Alban Berg, as early as 1910 and thus before Mahler's death: 'Once again I have played through the score of Mahler's Ninth Symphony: the first movement is the most heavenly thing . . . the expression of exceptional love for this earth, the longing to live at peace in it, to enjoy nature to its depths before death comes. For he comes irresistibly, the whole movement is permeated by premonitions of death . . .' Mahler made deliberate use of the descending three-note figure which was Beethoven's 'farewell' motto that opened his 'Les Adieux' Piano Sonata (Example 98A). It also appears in the last movement of *The Song of the Earth*, which is actually called *The Farewell* (Example 98B):

EX.98
A. Adagio

Le - be - wohl!

B. Slow

Die lie – – – be Er – – de

The Song of the Earth is, according to Mahler, a symphony. Here in fact the distinction between song and symphony, never very clear in his case, breaks down. The poems for this cycle of six songs were German translations from Chinese poems of the T'ang dynasty: *Youth* and *Beauty* are contemplated with sweet nostalgia, but there are also songs with the titles *Autumn Loneliness* and *Farewell*.

In their last works, both Strauss and Mahler wrote of autumn and twilight. Yet these are part of a cycle: for spring comes, and sunrise too. And, symbolically, in Mahler's last music we witness not only the end of an era but also a foreshadowing of something new. In the song called *Autumn Loneliness* in *The Song of the Earth* the singer has a phrase marked 'without expression': it seems that romanticism has turned to ashes, and yet this very restraint set the tone for more austere kinds of twentieth-century expression. The orchestral writing has become spare and translucent: no longer is this a richly comforting Wagnerian sound, but it has influenced later composers. Finally, the harmonic freedom, which permits strong dissonance or timeless consonance, even the non-harmonic suggestion of bird song, opened paths for Schönberg's atonality and the Eastern vision of Messiaen. The ashes of German romanticism contained the seeds of modern music.

DEBUSSY

In 1839 Wagner arrived in Paris hoping to find success there; but he failed, and eventually left with relief for Germany, though he had to borrow money in order to do so. Half a century later, things were very different, and artistic France was at his feet. There was even a journal called the *Revue wagnérienne*, founded in 1885. Fauré, Saint-Saëns and Messager visited Bayreuth. Another composer, Chabrier, burst into tears at a performance of *Tristan* even before the music began, saying, 'Fifteen years I've been waiting to hear it!' Debussy too, according to a friend, 'literally shook with emotion' on hearing the same work in Paris. He called *Parsifal* 'One of the loveliest monuments in sound ever raised to the serene glory of music.'

However, Claude Debussy (1862–1918), though his opera *Pelléas et Mélisande* shows his debt to Wagner, did not remain in the German camp. Far from aiming at a literary kind of music, he explored sound for its own sake. Yet he was profoundly aware of the other arts. He admired the painter Turner for being 'the finest creator of artistic mystery', and he felt able to describe his own orchestral cloudscape *Nuages* as 'like a study in grey in painting'. Music, he said, is 'all colours and rhythms . . .'

Was Debussy a revolutionary? Certainly he declared that music was 'a young art in technique and knowledge': a strange remark from a musician with centuries of history behind him. But he was no nihilist. He wished neither to deny nor to escape from the past, rejecting only what he called the humbug of lifeless rules invented by pedants 'riding the backs of the Masters'. When asked by fellow-students which rules he did acknowledge, he retorted, 'My taste'. Throughout his career, he relied less upon established forms and procedures than upon his own musical intuition.

Debussy in fact is among the great pure musicians of history. Though his work can be linked with French impressionist painting and symbolist poetry, that is not because it is any the less musical. Rather it is that all these artists, using different media, aspired to a realm beyond all specific subject-matter, beyond articulate thought. This ideal world of pure beauty was symbolised by the 'azure', the infinite heavenly blue of which the poet Mallarmé (1842–98) wrote. Mallarmé's poetry, in the words of the French critic Cazamian,* has 'an intoxicating sense of visionary energy'; but one needs only to think of Debussy's orchestral piece *Fêtes* to realise that the description fits the composer as well as it does the poet. 'Things must be hinted, not said, and suggestion must be the standard method:' once again a remark applied to Mallarmé fits Debussy perfectly. He after all placed the titles of his piano preludes almost apologetically, and in brackets, after the music. He even left some titles ambiguous: for example, *Voiles* can mean 'Sails' or 'Veils', or indeed both of these.

One of Debussy's early successes was inspired by a Mallarmé poem and elicited that poet's delighted praise. This was the orchestral *Prélude à l'après-midi d'un faune* (1894). The poem explores the borderline world between consciousness and dream, reality and imagination. The faun is a mythical creature, half man and half animal; neither we, nor indeed he himself, know whether he sees or only dreams of the nymphs among the trees of his forest on a hazy summer afternoon. The music begins with a flute solo, one of music's most antique and evocative sounds, which steals in unaccompanied upon the consciousness. Though the key is E major, this is only implied in the subtlest way. Even the rhythm is apparently quite free: one notices the change of time signature and the silent bar. Debussy wants, as it were, to bring the scene only gradually into focus.

EX.99

* *A History of French Literature*, Oxford University Press, 1955, pp. 387–88.

Even when key and rhythm are fully established later in *L'après-midi*, we are still far from any 'classical' kind of clarity. Preferring suggestion to direct statement, Debussy did for music, single-handed, what the impressionists had done for painting and the symbolists for poetry, exploring the mysterious world of waking dreams. Even so, we may admit that impressionism had its romantic antecedents, for example in Schubert's *Winterreise* with its remote, hallucinatory aspects. And the romantics' hero Shakespeare had shown the way with the dream world of *A Midsummer Night's Dream*; Debussy, who loved Shakespeare, actually called one of his piano preludes *Puck's Dance*.

We should emphasise here that Debussy's sense of form was strong. Without structure, his music could not have risen above the function of atmosphere-creating sound, which like film music may be effective but lacks independent life and memorability. He knew this from the start. Once he wrote to his publisher: 'It's strange how two "parasitic" bars can bring down the most strongly-built form. This is exactly what has happened to me. Nothing can prevent it, neither long experience nor the finest talent! Only instinct, as old as the world itself, can save you!' In fact he did create satisfactory shapes: his 'instinct' was monitored by such a clear and critical intellect that his music stands up to rigorous formal analysis. One feature of classical form which he nearly always retained was at least a hint of recapitulation at the end of a piece. The closing bars of *L'après-midi* could be an example, though in this particular case they are in fact preceded by a fuller version of the theme. What we hear is not a direct restatement of the opening phrase; yet it has the same effect. And the cadence on to the final tonic chord, in the same way, is both unorthodox and convincing.

EX.100

Très lent et très retenu jusqu'à la fin

Muted horns and violins

Example continued

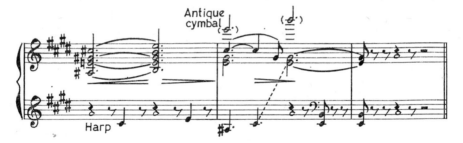

We notice the use here of an unusual percussion instrument, the little antique cymbals. Debussy's orchestral writing is full of subtle colouristic effects. Sometimes a page of this music, for example in *La Mer* or *Jeux*, may look extremely full of notes and thus complex in thought. But this is misleading; for usually the effect is quite unlike that of a busy, Straussian web of sound, and Debussy merely seeks to create a shimmering background against which one melody emerges clearly. His music is hardly ever contrapuntal: it always has a dominating melodic line, and this is a feature which has helped to make it popular. One can literally sing one's way through the most subtle Debussy scores.

Debussy's orchestral music after *L'après-midi* includes three *Nocturnes* (1899), the magnificent 'symphonic sketches' *La Mer* (1905) and three *Images* (1909), as well as the ballet *Jeux* (1912). But this composer was also a fine pianist who wrote a great deal for his instrument. Quite as much as the orchestral works, the piano music shows his great sensitivity to sound itself. His teacher, Madame Mauté de Fleurville, was a Chopin disciple; and he was influenced by the great Polish musician, to whom he dedicated his last solo piano pieces, the *Twelve Studies* (1915).

We can illustrate from the piano music two features of Debussy's general style which are among his most easily recognisable innovations. One is the whole-tone scale, used sparingly to create a fluid, mysterious atmosphere. The other is the use of chords in parallel movement, a way of enriching a melody line and giving it an antique flavour that is probably due to the reminder of medieval *organum* as described in Chapter 3.

EX. 101 A   Debussy *Voiles*

Modéré

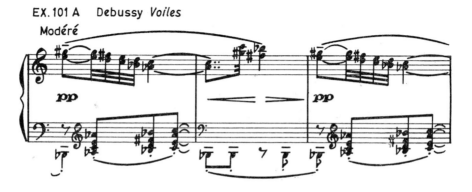

EX.101 B   Debussy *La cathédrale engloutie*
Sonore sans dureté

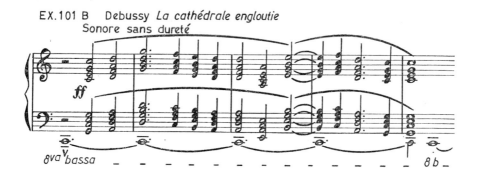

Sometimes block chords such as these were not consonant but dissonant. In conventional harmony dissonance is functional, leading towards resolution on an appropriate concord. But here it was used for expressive reasons and emancipated. This kind of writing opened up a new area of musical language to twentieth-century composers:

EX.102 A   Debussy *La terrasse des audiences du clair de lune*
En animant

EX.102 B Debussy *Et la lune descend*

Debussy wrote only one opera; however, like the single operas of Purcell and Beethoven, it is a masterpiece. *Pelléas et Mélisande* (1902) has a story drawn from the symbolist-mystic Belgian writer Maeterlinck. It is set in medieval times in some coastal kingdom of France. Mélisande is found by Prince Golaud weeping in a forest; but we find out little of her past except that she has run away. Perhaps she is a princess: she had 'the crown which he gave me', but the identity of the giver remains for ever unknown. When Golaud asks her age, she only replies, 'I'm beginning to feel cold' – this, incidentally, is a not unfair sample of the kind of Maeterlinckian dialogue which has attracted good-humoured parody. Golaud leads Mélisande home and they marry. But she and his young half-brother Pelléas fall in love; Golaud kills him in jealous rage, and Mélisande dies bearing Golaud's daughter.

This story, one of suggestion rather than statement, suited Debussy perfectly. The music is gravely mysterious, reticent yet profoundly responsive to every nuance of feeling in the text. The lovers' hushed greeting in Act

EX.103 Debussy *Pelléas et Mélisande*

IV could hardly be further from the wild outcries of Wagner's *Tristan* – though the story itself has striking similarities of which Debussy was surely aware – but the French composer's method, in its context, is equally moving.

Indeed the vocal writing of *Pelléas*, in semi-recitative style and set against the ever-changing background of the orchestra, certainly owes much to Wagner's example. Richard Strauss was quick to point this out when he saw the opera, but regretted the lack of anything that could be called a big scene: 'Is it all like this?' he asked plaintively. However, the musical language is quite different from Wagner's, in whose music the very first six bars would be unthinkable. They employ modal harmony (C natural instead of C sharp), organal consecutive fifths and the whole tone scale (Example 103).

Debussy's career, like that of Beethoven, culminated in a 'last period' with characteristics of its own. And just as Beethoven incorporated the older form of fugue into the contemporary form of the sonata, Debussy too used the past in order to go forward creatively. He came to feel an identity with his predecessors Couperin and Rameau. In Rameau, he declared, there was to be found 'a pure French tradition full of charming and tender delicacy . . . and without any affectation of German profundity.' He regretted 'that French music should so long have followed a course treacherously leading it away from that clarity of expression, that terse and condensed form, which is the peculiar and significant quality of the French genius.'

It seemed that Debussy had become some kind of nationalist. But clearly he was not trying to create a culture through folk music in typical nationalist fashion; nor did he wish to revive the past by imitating earlier masters. He did however turn to more clear-cut and classical forms like studies and sonatas, and achieved new emotional force by intense refinement of style combined with directness of utterance. These together made something of a new tradition in modern music, one which is maintained today in some of the work of Pierre Boulez.

In 1915–17 Debussy composed three of a projected set of six sonatas for various instruments, which remained incomplete at his death in 1918. The first was for cello and piano; and he claimed with pride that its form was 'almost classical, in the good sense of the word.' The third was the fine but elusive Violin Sonata, beautiful by any standards, though some critics claim to detect in it signs of creative fatigue. In between these two works there is an unquestionable masterpiece, the Sonata for Flute, Viola and Harp. Debussy himself said of it that it was 'terribly sad, and I don't know whether one should laugh or cry, perhaps both? . . . How much there is to discover, and then to suppress, before reaching the naked flesh of emotion!'

Once again, as in *L'après-midi* over twenty years before, the composer chose the flute to express his most personal thought: a friend wrote to him that the instrument was like a melancholy Puck 'questioning the hidden meaning of things'. The sonata begins with a movement called *Pastoral*; its opening is mysterious certainly, and yet there is no longer any contrived vagueness about these precisely drawn lines, no delicate orchestral shimmer or piano pedal effect. The clarity is remarkable, but the music remains profoundly Debussyan and poetic.

EX. 104 Debussy *Sonata for flute, viola and harp*

The ending of the second movement, called *Interlude*, is a beautiful passage with a major–minor alternation that remains in the memory. One notes the spacing of the final C – the flute does not play the high note, but its lowest, middle C, with its own strange tone-colour.

EX. 105 Debussy *Sonata for flute, viola and harp*

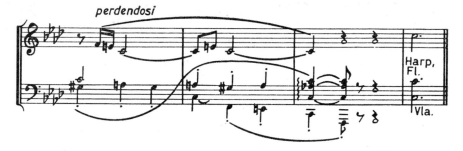

Debussy's death elicited a remarkable tribute from the French critic Romain Rolland, writing in his diary on the day after it occurred: he was, said Rolland, 'The only creator of beauty in the music of our time.' Certainly he was irreplaceable. Among leading composers who had known him, Stravinsky, Ravel and Falla composed music dedicated to his memory. The actual wartime funeral was a simple one. The Minister of Education was present, but few of the composer's friends. One of them, Louis Laloy, attended in military uniform. He heard the distant sound of gunfire, as well as a remark of a Montmartre shopkeeper watching the procession, a kind of epitaph whose understatement Debussy himself might have appreciated. 'It seems he was a musician.'

RAVEL

Maurice Ravel (1875–1937) still suffers from the misfortune of having been Debussy's younger contemporary, coming from the same musical background of training at the Paris Conservatoire. The critics, to say nothing of the public, could not come to meaningful terms with the evolution of two such original talents. Inevitably, Ravel was dubbed as Debussy's imitator, bringing up the rear of the modernist French school which seemed opposed to the Franckian conservatives.

As far as their lives are concerned, Ravel and Debussy do have quite a lot in common. After Conservatoire training, they remained Parisian residents; the villa, *Le Belvédère*, which Ravel bought at Montfort l'Amaury in 1920 near the Forest of Rambouillet, was only a short drive from the French capital. Yet there were differences of a profound kind in their respective psychologies. Debussy married twice, and had a daughter who did not long survive him, dying of diphtheria in 1919; Ravel remained a lifelong bachelor who was never known to have entered into any intimate relationship although he enjoyed the company of a number of loyal friends. Ravel never shared Debussy's mild interest in mysticism, nor the relaxed kind of romantic feeling which is sometimes found in Debussy: both composers loved the poetry of Mallarmé, but it is instructive to compare Ravel's crystalline Mallarmé settings with those of Debussy, softer and gentler, of the same poems. Debussy's 'harmonic chemistry' was not for Ravel, the scrupulous craftsman; yet Ravel called himself with truth an artist of feeling rather than intellect, and Debussy did not surpass Ravel's tenderness in his opera *L'enfant et les sortilèges*. If Debussy can be thought of, fancifully, as an untamed, sensitive faun wandering through the materialistic twentieth-century world, then Ravel by contrast appears a little aloof from it, a dandyish figure, fascinated by the exquisite, the jewel-like, by mechanical toys such as those which he delightedly showed to visitors at his home.

In fact the music of these two composers is no more alike than that of, say, Haydn and Mozart. The main difference is that Ravel was from the start more classically orientated, having a special love for Mozart that Debussy did not share. The titles of Ravel's first piano pieces, written between 1895 and 1905, suggest with one exception his classical affinities: *Menuet antique, Pavane pour une infante défunte, Jeux d'eau* and *Sonatine*. Only the third of these, an evocation of a fountain, could be called impressionistic. And even here the assumption of Debussyan influence cannot hold. For though *Jeux d'eau* probably owes something to Liszt's *Fountains at the Villa d'Este*, it cannot be indebted to Debussy's 'water music' for piano, for the simple reason that the latter composer's *Jardins sous la pluie, L'isle joyeuse, Reflets dans l'eau* and *La cathédrale engloutie* were still unwritten. Debussy recognised that Ravel 'could not be more gifted'; though he was a little touchy about the younger man's success, and was not pleased once when he called on his publisher Durand to find Ravel seated in his usual armchair! Actually Ravel did not enjoy success till he was over thirty. He himself had the greatest admiration for Debussy, called his piano preludes 'wonderful masterpieces' and was found by Romain Rolland to be 'more Debussyist than Debussy himself'. In 1922 he dedicated a major work (the Duo Sonata for violin and cello) to Debussy's memory.

Pianists are grateful to Ravel, as they are to Debussy; for he too wrote magnificently for the instrument, a good deal for piano solo as well as two concertos, of which one is for the left hand alone. *Jeux d'eau* (1901) begins in a very Ravelian way. Though the music is difficult to play, it is also delicate: the composer marks it 'very gentle'. The treble register suggests the fountain's coruscating droplets, and the effect is extraordinarily pure and fresh:

EX.106 Ravel *Jeux d'eau*

Later in this piece there is a harmonically bold cadenza combining the chords of F sharp major and C major, anticipating by ten years Stravinsky's famous juxtaposition of the same two harmonies in *Petrushka*.

Ravel's harmonic daring went a good deal further in the five piano pieces called *Miroirs* (1905). The title was distinctly Debussyan (Debussy was soon to produce his own *Images*); and at least one piece, *La vallée des cloches*, is as impressionistic as Ravel ever became. Its slow, rich chords could even have influenced Debussy in one of his *Images, Et la lune descend sur le temple qui fut* (Example 107), as well as later pieces like the study called *Pour les sonorités opposées*.* To sum up this question of mutual influence, one is tempted to conclude that Ravel, having studied impressionistic technique in Debussy's orchestral music without fully adopting it himself, showed Debussy how it could be applied to the piano.

Ravel's next piano work, *Gaspard de la Nuit* (1908), was larger in scope than anything Debussy wrote for the instrument. In fact, both in length and overall structure there is a parallel with Debussy's orchestral work *La Mer*: that consists of 'three symphonic sketches', while Ravel's *Gaspard* has the

EX.107 A   Ravel *La vallée des cloches*

* Debussy's *Et la lune descend* was dedicated to the one close mutual friend of the two composers, Louis Laloy.

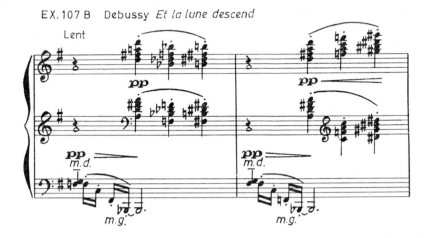

EX. 107 B   Debussy *Et la lune descend*

sub-title 'three poems for piano'. Both composers frequently use this triptych form; for though neither was drawn to symphonic structures, the idea of a work in this 'classical' number of movements, more closely-knit than those of a suite, remained attractive. The subject matter of *Gaspard* is altogether in the romantic tradition. The first piece, *Ondine*, in the exotic key of C sharp major, portrays the fascinating but heartless water-nymph of German folk-lore. *Le Gibet* paints a grim picture of a laden gallows seen at sunset, with a tolling bell (the note B flat) sounding throughout. Finally, *Scarbo* describes the nocturnal visit of some grotesque imp, 'pirouetting round the room like the spindle fallen from a sorceress's loom'. Here the invention explodes in pianistic virtuosity. There is also an even greater harmonic daring. The work ends on a chord of the seventh, A sharp in a chord of B major, and there is a famous twenty-bar-long passage of consecutive major seconds beginning:

EX. 108

As a counterpart to *Gaspard*, Ravel brought out at the same time a work of serene harmonic simplicity, the *Mother Goose Suite* for piano duet, most often played in its orchestral version. His next major piano works were a set of brilliant and poetic waltzes, the *Valses nobles et sentimentales* (1911) and the *Tombeau de Couperin* (1917). In this, his last music for solo piano, he recreated in terms of his own musical style the spirit of an eighteenth-century keyboard suite, with six movements including a forlane, rigaudon, minuet and final toccata.

The use of dances in these works is typical of Ravel, and another of the stylistic features which on the whole distinguish him from Debussy. A large-scale orchestral piece in dance form was *La Valse* (1920). It was originally conceived as a symphonic poem called *Vienna* and is a unique and even shocking amalgam of sensuously charming music and what the composer called 'a fantastic and fatal Dervish's dance'. His capacity for large-scale work of great emotional power is apparent too in the ballet *Daphnis and Chloe* (1912), in which the music is wonderfully written for the orchestra and of unmistakably symphonic stature. Composed for the impresario Diaghilev and his Russian Ballet, on a pastoral tale by the ancient Greek author Longus, this great work is truly a 'choreographic symphony' (the composer's own term); its impetuous finale took him a year to write.

Ravel's vocal music includes three settings of Mallarmé poems (1913) in which the voice is accompanied by a small chamber ensemble. He and Stravinsky were working together at the time of their composition, and the Russian composer said long afterwards that he liked them best of all Ravel's music. They have a modernity coupled with a dazzling precision of thought which together make them landmarks of twentieth-century music. Indeed both Stravinsky (whose *Rite of Spring*, produced in the same year, had moved him to tears) and Schönberg's *Pierrot Lunaire* (1912) were in Ravel's mind when he wrote the Mallarmé songs. From now on, this inventive musician became even more preoccupied than before with a conscious exploration and extension of his style. Bitonal writing (the simultaneous use of two keys) became something of a feature of his music; so did jazz, and the 'Blues' slow movement of his Violin Sonata (1927) illustrates both.

But one of his boldest innovations is scarcely recognised as such. *Bolero* (1928), conceived as a ballet in which more and more dancers join in as the work progresses, is a long orchestral crescendo of some seventeen minutes, in which one melody is repeated without development or even a change of key until just before the end. 'It's musically empty,' Ravel remarked, and he was astonished, or pretended to be, at its public success. Yet he was unjust to himself. *Bolero* is a set of variations, like many highly respected works from Bach's organ Passacaglia onwards. But here the variety is wholly in the realm of instrumental colour. When sound-quality is seen to be an inventive sphere as 'musical' as, say, harmony, *Bolero* may be recognised as a pure but possibly unique masterpiece. It has of course one other indispensable strength, the quality of the melody itself. No ordinary tune would have stood up to this repetition. It is an exceptionally long one – seventy-two bars, if one counts the repeat of each half an octave higher. And though the keynote remains as C, the modality changes considerably, so that four notes of the scale (D, E, A and B) are sometimes flat instead of natural.

While the melodic style of Debussy is somehow open-ended, so that there are few self-contained tunes, Ravel was a fine melodist in the more conventional sense. With this gift, he succeeded brilliantly in vocal music, with all its human implications. The great and sophisticated craftsman in him was matched by an artist of deep though undoubtedly childlike humanity. Of his two operas, the comedy *L'heure espagnole* (Paris, 1911) is the more adult; *L'enfant et les sortilèges* (1925), to a story by the woman novelist Colette, is a feast of sparkling wit and colour, but it ultimately proves to be a moving parable of the human condition in which a naughty child is finally redeemed by one spontaneous kind action. The composer's friend and biographer Roland-Manuel has described the calm choral finale of the opera: 'This ode to kindness gives the work profound significance. It ennobles it; it so enhances it that the last page of the score is one of the composer's most beautiful and most harmonious. Music of the spirit and sensibility, filled with tenderness. Emotion born in the heart of trees and birds and all the little people of the night, which dies with a sob on the threshold of the house of man.'

SOME LATER NATIONALISTS

The music of both Debussy and Ravel represented a reaction against Wagner's ideals and Germanic musical thought; and though it had its roots in the past it broke new ground, not only in compositional techniques but also in aesthetics or musical philosophy – for example in the direction of economy, the avoidance of anything savouring of the grandiose. Of the late nationalist composers that we come to now, perhaps only Janáček and Scriabin were notable innovators; but each wrote distinguished and individual music.

Leoš Janáček (1854–1928) was the successor of Smetana and Dvořák, born in what is today Czechoslovakia. Like Bruckner, he was the son of a village schoolmaster who learned music in a monastery school. In due course he acquired a polished technique, in Prague and later in Leipzig. In 1881 he founded a music school in Brno and married. Soon after this he published at his own expense two organ pieces which were oddly named Concerto-Fantasies; and next he dedicated some men's choruses to his friend Dvořák, who was impressed but confessed to being startled by some of the harmonies.

Janáček was a nationalist through and through. He claimed that, 'A fragment of national life is attached to every word uttered by the people; the melody of their speech should be studied in every detail.' Significantly, he referred to speech itself, rather than song. And it was not only human speech that was part of the countryside, owing its character somehow to the locality, for this was also true of the sounds of birds and animals, of water and wind. Janáček walked through the countryside listening and noting what he heard. He believed that music derived from natural sounds: speech, bird song, and nature herself were the sources of his art. He once noted down the sound of a waterfall in just the same way, and for the same reason, as he did the cry of a page-boy at a London hotel, with the words, 'There is the *real* England!'

Janáček's music bears out his theories. It hardly ever sounds sophisticated or elegant, and it can be strangely repetitive and jerkily unpredictable. But it is not naïve. Like the poet A. E. Housman's Shropshire lad, Janáček's peasant hero in the *Diary of a Young Man who Disappeared* (1919) has deep feelings; in fact this song cycle has something in common with Vaughan Williams's Housman settings in *On Wenlock Edge*, the same sense of keen agonies and fleeting joys which can be expressed only with difficulty in speech. The poems Janáček set were written by a village boy who ran away from home for love of a gipsy girl: a true story of youth brought to life again by the magic of the then elderly composer's art.

Janáček does not manifest the contrast of style which is found in most composers between their instrumental and their vocal music. Perhaps because of his theories, the music remains remarkably consistent. The late Second String Quartet of 1928 – the year of his death – has an almost 'spoken', recitative-like quality, a lack of conventional musical flow which may be disconcerting but is turned to great expressive use. It is therefore no surprise to find that it is called *Intimate Letters* and has an elaborate programme concerning the composer's love for a young girl. 'Youth' is also both the subject and title of the Wind Sextet *Mládí* of 1924. Of this music, the composer said: 'I listen to the birds singing . . . my music remains young through contact with the eternally young rhythm of nature.' The feeling he had for Nature and for natural sounds as well as speech is fully demonstrated in such a work as *The Cunning Little Vixen* (1923), the eighth of his ten operas. It is full of graphically appropriate phrases such as these three:

One of Janáček's late works symbolises his love of his homeland and its traditions: the *Glagolitic Mass* (1926), which was intended for open-air performance with choral and orchestral forces and had a text in Old Slavonic, or Glagolitic as this liturgical language is sometimes called. Yet it was in his operas that he made his deepest exploration into human nature. These include the powerful and realistic *Jenufa* (1903) and *Katya Kabanová* (1921): the second of these was based on the Russian playwright Ostrovsky's drama *The Storm*, which also inspired a Tchaikovsky overture. With *The Makropoulos Case* (1925) we enter a somewhat serious legal world, though the opera is called a comedy, and one which is modern enough to include a telephone call between the law courts and a lawyer's office. His last opera was also on a contemporary subject. This was *From the House of the Dead* (1928). He drew his subject, very freely indeed, from a Dostoevsky novel – not a play, one notices, and in fact there is little that could be called a plot in the ordinary sense. The opera ends with a chorus praising freedom, and is in the great tradition of prison-inspired works of art, from Beethoven's *Fidelio* right up to Alexander Solzhenitsyn's novel of the Soviet labour camps, *One Day in the Life of Ivan Denisovich*.

Giacomo Puccini (1858–1924) was Janáček's exact contemporary, and like him a composer of opera, even though the resemblance does not go much further. To place Puccini with a group of nationalists is perhaps unconventional; nevertheless he is as supremely Italian as any composer could be. Compared to Verdi, his style is blander and less powerful, yet it shows both talent and taste. We may compare the dawn music which begins Act III of *Tosca* with a quiet passage from *The Pines of Rome*, by a fellow-Italian, Respighi (1879–1936): the latter is essentially picture-postcard music, while Puccini, writing two decades earlier, is much more sensitive and evocative. And precise too: he wrote to his publisher asking to know 'the exact tone of the church bells near Castel Sant' Angelo and of the big bell at St Peter's'. Though less than great, he had the sense not to attempt musical settings of Goethe or Shakespeare. Setting his sights lower, he produced excellent though not exalted works of art.

Born into a family of church musicians at Lucca, Puccini soon found his way to the Milan Conservatory. In spite of early recognition of his talent, it took some time for him to achieve complete success. This came with *La Bohème* (Turin, 1896). The opera is based on a novel by the French writer Henri Murger and tells of a group of impoverished students leading their 'Bohemian', hand-to-mouth existence in Paris around 1830. Mimi and the young painter Rudolph meet and fall in love, and at this point comes the famous aria, 'Your tiny hand is frozen'. But then the drama moves on to a plane of cooler realism as they set up home together, quarrel and separate; finally they are reunited as the undernourished Mimi lies dying of tuberculosis. Puccini thought the scene leading up to her death 'very moving', and we can only agree. Though too picturesque for real tragedy, *La Bohème* is still much above the level of melodrama. The same is true of *Tosca* (1900) and *Madam Butterfly* (1904). Once again, these operas have lovable, head-strong and ill-fated heroines. Puccini's heroines, like those of Massenet in France, tend to outshine the heroes in importance so that the music gains in grace, charm and temperament at the expense, perhaps, of strength and deep-rooted passion. Puccini's *Otello* would have been very different from Verdi's – if the subject had appealed to him, which is unlikely. His last opera, *Turandot* (1926), has a heroine with a more powerful personality than ever, giving the work paradoxically the strength and even masculinity hitherto lacking in his operas. Yet when Princess Turandot yields at last to the stranger prince, Puccini is splendidly true to himself.

Puccini once said, half jokingly, that God had told him to 'Write for the theatre – only for the theatre, mind!' When he lacked a good libretto, he was therefore stifled; and he once exclaimed, 'If only I could be a purely symphonic writer!' But at least he learned from his non-operatic contemporaries. He got to know Debussy and Stravinsky and successfully incorporated parallel-chord motion and even bitonal effects into his later operas. His technical and expressive range is wider than superficial acquaintance would suggest. He was capable, for example, of real musical humour. We find it in *La Bohème, Turandot* – the trio of the three ministers, Ping, Pang and Pong, in Act II – the little-known comedy *La Rondine* (1917) and above all the richly comic *Gianni Schicchi* (1918).

Though he had successors like Ermanno Wolf-Ferrari (1876–1948) and Italo Montemezzi (1875–1952), Puccini broadly marks the end of the long line of Italian operatic tradition.* Melody was the strong point of this tradition, and melody – at least of the *bel canto* type – was no longer a prime consideration with the composers born a generation after Puccini and who emerged after the First World War. In 1944, near the end of his life, Montemezzi composed a piece called *My Italy! none shall silence thy song!* But, sad to say, he cannot be said to have been right. The rich vein of Italian melody, explored for so long and to such effect by so many musicians, appears, at least for the present, to have been worked out.

If Puccini's music ends a tradition, so does that of the Russian composer Sergei Rachmaninov (1873–1943); as Puccini stands in relation to a greater artist, Verdi, so does Rachmaninov to Tchaikovsky. Rachmaninov also is a nationalist composer only to the extent that Puccini is: that is, not in a conscious, literary sense.

* The same may be said of his contemporaries Ruggiero Leoncavallo (1858–1919), the composer of *I Pagliacci* (1892), and Pietro Mascagni (1863–1945), best known for *Cavalleria rusticana* (1890).

Rachmaninov was an outstanding pianist as well as a composer, who studied with Liszt's pupil Siloti, and left Russia at the time of the Revolution to become an international star of the concert platform, one of the first of a kind familiar in our own age of rapid travel. He was a taciturn man, not unfriendly but difficult to get to know, who seems to have been at ease only in the intimate circle of his wife and family. Stravinsky once described him, with characteristic wit, as 'a six-and-a-half-foot-tall scowl'. He added, perhaps contradicting himself, that he was the only pianist who did not grimace while performing – 'that is a great deal'. But for Stravinsky, Rachmaninov the composer was 'a very old composer indeed'.

These two men could hardly have been more different. Stravinsky was a boldly confident artist entirely of the twentieth century, while Rachmaninov admitted to feeling uncertain of himself, wrote relatively little and only used traditional forms. But one of his biographers goes much too far in maintaining that all his music might have been written before 1880. His harmony is subtle and quietly adventurous; and individuality is proved, as with Mahler, by his style's capacity to be recognised even when adopted by later composers.

Rachmaninov's attraction for the musically untutored has resulted in his being distrusted and even condemned by some critics, those who believe that popularity is only to be achieved at the expense of quality. But at the very least he deserves to be judged by his best work; and not all of this is known, much less popular. There is distinguished church music, as well as works for the theatre, other choral pieces and songs. Of his three symphonies, the Second (1907) is perhaps the most characteristic, although the much later Third (1936) and the Symphonic Dances (1940) are more strikingly original. Yet even in such an early work as the symphonic poem *The Isle of the Dead* (1907) the mysterious scene is skilfully evoked in a lapping quintuple rhythm and rich orchestral sonorities. Of the four piano concertos, the Third (1909) at least is a masterpiece. Its themes, or rather short motives, are well organised in a form which uses thematic transformation, so that the opening theme appears in all three movements; there is a surprising economy in view of the luxuriance of the emotional effect. In the brilliant finale in the example opposite a galloping theme is transformed in a grand final apotheosis. This music has abundant energy and harmonic 'bite'.

Besides the concertos, Rachmaninov composed a masterly set of variations for piano and orchestra called *Rhapsody on a Theme of Paganini* (1934), terse and vital music quite innocent of overblown romanticism. There are also two sonatas and a number of shorter piano pieces. The ending of the A minor Prelude, Opus 32, does credit to the masterly virtuoso pianist-composer. One notes the almost casual use of the whole range of the keyboard, the richly pedalled sonorities alternating with drily laconic utterance. The passage begins with consecutive fifths, hardly nineteenth-century in style, and ends with a distinctly original cadence (Example 111):

EX.110 A Rachmaninov *Piano concerto no.3*

EX.110 B Rachmaninov *Piano concerto no.3*

EX.111 Rachmaninov *Prelude in A minor, Op.32*

Another Russian composer, more original though not necessarily finer than Rachmaninov, was Alexander Scriabin (1872–1915). He too was a pianist of uncommon skill, and though his orchestral *Poem of Ecstasy* (1908) and *Prometheus: the Poem of Fire* (1910) are unique in their strength of personality and late-romantic fervour, it is perhaps in his ten piano sonatas that his qualities of craftsmanship as well as inspiration are most clearly to be seen. The last six of these, despite superficial similarities of style, offer a wide range of emotional expression, often of an esoteric kind – who but Scriabin would ask a performer to convey 'poisoned sweetness' as he does in the Ninth Sonata? They seem more or less to have established themselves in the piano repertory, and rightly so. Scriabin contemplated a highly post-Wagnerian artistic enterprise, a 'Mystery' involving all the arts, including that of perfumery, which failed to come to fruition owing to his untimely death at the age of forty-four.

At the end of the nineteenth century, two countries were ready to emerge from relatively uncreative periods in movements of belated nationalist feeling. One of these was Great Britain, whose musical renaissance will be discussed in the next chapter. The other was Spain.*

Felipe Pedrell (1841–1922) composed an opera called *The Pyrenees*: it was finished in 1894 but had to wait till 1902 for its première in Barcelona, in Italian! Pedrell was also a teacher and a scholar who wrote copiously on his country's music, devoting much time to a four-volume study of Spanish folk song that remained unfinished at his death. He also served the cause of Spanish art music by preparing a scholarly edition of Victoria's complete works, holding the view that national characteristics were to be found in the music of the great masters of the past in spite of their not being conscious nationalists.

Enrique Granados (1867–1916) was Pedrell's pupil. With Isaac Albéniz (1860–1909), another gifted pianist and a Liszt pupil, he created an important Spanish school of keyboard writing which has affiliations with the piano music of Debussy and Ravel. Albéniz's *Iberia* is an important set of twelve Spanish scenes for piano, composed during the last three years of his life. Another Pedrell pupil, Manuel de Falla (1876–1946), was, however, the composer who did most to give back to Spanish music some of the European prominence it formerly enjoyed but lost during more than a century of Italian influence.

Twenty years ago, Falla's reputation in serious musical circles stood much higher than that of, say, Rachmaninov. But where the latter's standing has risen, Falla's has rather fallen. His residence in Paris from 1907–14 and his friendship with Debussy, as well as his work for Diaghilev's Russian Ballet, helped to bring his name before a wide public. People responded enthusiastically to his vigorous and atmospheric music, with its strong Spanish flavour. *Nights in the Gardens of Spain* (1916), for piano and orchestra, is typical of his earlier work. Yet this attractive piece really owes too obvious a debt to Debussy's orchestral *Ibéria* and Ravel's *Rapsodie espagnole*, exploiting the same 'Spanish' effects used by the Frenchmen; while its form lacks originality and subtlety and even the piano writing is not especially idiomatic. The ballet *Love, the Magician* (1915) is much stronger, harsher and genuinely Spanish. Falla's increasing individuality shows too in another ballet, *The Three-cornered Hat* (1919) and the puppet opera called *Master Peter's Puppet Show*

---

* This is perhaps also the place to mention the Jewish music of Ernest Bloch (1880–1959), a native of Geneva who made his home in the United States. Works like *Schelomo* ('Solomon') for cello and orchestra (1916) and the *Sacred Service* for voices and orchestra (1933) are powerfully expressive.

(1923), the libretto of which he wrote himself, basing it on an episode in Cervantes's *Don Quixote*.

Having escaped from a style in which somewhat Europeanised Spanish musical features were too easily exploited, Falla now produced his Harpsichord Concerto (1926), written for the Polish woman player Wanda Landowska. As well as being one of the first works to rehabilitate the long-neglected harpsichord as a living instrument, the concerto, with its reminders of Scarlatti, has a suitably classical character. It represented a final turning away from obvious nationalism, as well as a reaction against romanticism and impressionistic vagueness. But the independence which Falla finally achieved at the age of fifty did not bring forth much fruit. For about twenty years he sketched a vast oratorio on the subject of the legendary lost continent of Atlantis, but at his death it was still incomplete.

With Albéniz, Granados and Falla – to whose names we should perhaps add those of Turina (1882–1949) and Rodrigo (b. 1902), the composer of a Guitar Concerto (1939) – Spanish nationalism was born, lived and died. Nationalism itself continued elsewhere, however, as a powerful artistic force amid the uncertainties of post-Wagnerian music in the twentieth century, notably in England and Scandinavia.

14

THE ENGLISH RENAISSANCE
AND NORTHERN EUROPE

*Victorian and Edwardian England. Delius, Vaughan
Williams and Holst. Nielsen and Sibelius.*

VICTORIAN AND EDWARDIAN ENGLAND

England's musical renaissance came at the end of the nineteenth century, after a long period of relative unfruitfulness. In the first place, there was a notable rise in the quality of British music; then, rather later, came the conscious assertion of a national voice.

English music had for a long while been dominated by the spirit and even the style of Handel. The great German composer had established artistic norms, as well as actual forms such as the oratorio, which proved as satisfying to musicians and audiences in the mid-nineteenth century as they had done in the eighteenth; Mendelssohn, on his numerous visits to England, continued the oratorio tradition with his *St Paul* and *Elijah*, the latter composed for the 1846 Birmingham Festival. Just as the royal house itself remained somewhat Germanic in outlook, so did the musical establishment. The critic George Hogarth, the father-in-law of Dickens, wrote in 1835 that national music was 'more a matter of enquiry and speculation than history' and that England simply lacked creative talent The music critic of *The Times* newspaper, Francis Hueffer, himself German-born, declared in 1889 that the Hanoverian culture had 'killed English music' and offered only the small consolation that, 'The race of great composers is, with one or two exceptions, extinct in other countries as well as ours.'

England, furthermore, did not possess the state orchestras and opera houses which were a feature of the German-speaking part of Europe, and she had as her state music only that of the Chapel Royal and the armed services. Her universities offered a form of teaching which produced church musicians almost exclusively, so that the best music was thought to be sacred. But even here, and in an Anglican environment, the visitors outshone the native composers.* Some kind of national inferiority complex was inevitable; perhaps in self-defence, the view came to be held that skill in music was somehow incompatible with 'gentlemanliness'.

* England heard oratorios by Gounod and Dvořák besides those of Mendelssohn.

This was a deadlock; but fortunately it was broken by a group of men born around the middle of the century. These were Arthur Sullivan, Hubert Parry, Charles Villiers Stanford and Edward Elgar. Parry (1848–1918) was an Etonian, a sportsman and country squire who became Professor of Music at Oxford and later Director of the Royal College of Music: writing oratorios and cantatas within the English choral tradition, he won his fellow-country-men's respect. Stanford (1852–1924), born in Dublin, came also from a wealthy background and became a composer as well as an influential teacher at the Royal College, where his pupils included Vaughan Williams and Gustav Holst. Sullivan's father, on the other hand, was an army bandmaster, and Elgar's the owner of a music shop; but their less affluent origins did not prevent them from achieving still greater distinction and individuality.

The collaboration of Arthur Sullivan (1842–1900) with the humorist W. S. Gilbert, whom he met in 1870, marked a clear step forward for English music. The Savoy Operas, named after the London theatre where the last eight of them were first performed, were their joint creations and in the line of topical operatic comedy which may be traced back to *The Beggar's Opera* of 1728. A skilled craftsman, Sullivan drew his ideas from the best models: Handel for craftsmanship, Offenbach for wit, Schubert for melodic style and Mozart for all of these qualities. Though we miss in Sullivan the outstanding qualities of invention and depth of feeling which we expect of a major composer, there is no doubt of his music's attractiveness. The Savoy Operas, which include *Iolanthe* (1882), *The Mikado* (1885) and *The Gondoliers* (1889), are very enjoyable. At times, as in Jack Point's final song in *The Yeoman of the Guard* (1888), we are moved as well as charmed. But more of the emotional weight lies in the words than is usually the case, even in comic opera: Gilbert's contribution was at least half of this partnership.

Romanticism in its more full-blooded forms had left England nearly un-touched, although she welcomed visitors such as Liszt, Weber, Mendelssohn, Wagner, Berlioz and Chopin. But now one outstanding romantic composer emerged. This was Edward Elgar (1857–1934). Elgar's style was derived not only from German music – Mendelssohn, Schumann, Brahms and Wagner – but also from other models, including Rossini, Franck and Tchaikovsky. This mainly self-taught composer gave himself a lengthy course of instruc-tion tailored exactly to his own requirements, creating an individual, highly expressive style. Sullivan used to regret not having fulfilled himself in serious works; Elgar, however, set about creating large-scale choral and orchestral music as soon as he had acquired the necessary skill.

Elgar's background could hardly have been more suitable for the develop-ment of his gifts. While the professional training that young Purcell had received two centuries before had been altogether beneficial, because in the context of a flourishing musical culture, such academic training as Elgar might have received in London or some German city would have left him a different composer from the musician we know – and, one inevitably feels, an inferior one. As it was, his parents could not have afforded to send him away to study. His father kept a music shop in Worcester and tuned pianos, also playing the organ in the local Roman Catholic church: in fact Elgar, often thought of as a typical upper-class Englishman, was rather of the lower-middle class and, as a Catholic, not a member of the established church. The latter point made a difference culturally, too, for the plainchant singing and the use of liturgical Latin led away from the German-English style which was the church-going background of his contemporaries. Another influence was that of his mother, who had strong literary interests. But it was the music in his father's shop which was his constant study, and he made orchestral arrangements of compositions by various composers from Corelli to Wagner. He took part in almost every local concert or other musical occasion as a violinist, organist or conductor, playing the bassoon also in a wind quintet, and writing a number of short pieces. Finally, he made a point of following the music at Worcester Cathedral, in other words the English repertory of sacred music. Everything was grist to his mill: no mere theoretical study could have formed this many-sided artist, for whom expression and enthusiasm were synonymous with the nature of music itself. He married in 1889, into a military family; his wife's devotion was a constant background to his slow rise to fame.

Elgar's public career, in the larger sense, began with the orchestral overture *Froissart* (1890), a tribute to fourteenth-century chivalry expressed in the vigorous, leaping melodies and glowing orchestral colours which were henceforth to be features of his style. *The Black Knight* (1893), a setting for chorus and orchestra of a German poem translated by Longfellow, continued this particular vein of pageantry, which was to find further expression in *King Olaf*, *The Banner of St George* and *Caractacus*, all works for chorus and orchestra which were composed between 1896 and 1898. This characteristic of Elgar, which we also find in his fine 'Pomp and Circumstance' Marches, has inevitably caused his name to be linked with a kind of blustering patriotism or 'jingoism' which thoughtful Englishmen find distasteful. Yet this is as unfair as to blame Wagner for the rise of Nazism in Germany; and as it happens, the First World War and the militaristic use of his music deeply saddened Elgar, who had many German friends.

The spirit of friendship had drawn from Elgar music of a much more introspective and delicate kind earlier in his career with the 'Enigma' Variations for orchestra (1899); his expressive range was thus enlarged in a way which was necessary for the future symphonist and oratorio composer. These variations marked a turning point in his career: they are a set of musical portraits of friends beginning with one of his own wife Alice and ending with one of himself. The 'enigma', or puzzle, seems to have been the philosophical question of the nature of friendship itself, while the portraits in variation form probably had their model in Schumann's *Carnival*. Like the subjects of that work, some are introspective (Variation IX, *Nimrod*) and others briskly extrovert, like Variation XI, *G.R.S.*, which depicts the Hereford Cathedral organist out for a walk with his bulldog Dan.

In 1900, Elgar produced a vocal masterpiece whose stature is unquestionable. *The Dream of Gerontius* is a work of major dimensions on a level befitting the subject of Cardinal Newman's text, that of a Catholic soul's pilgrimage after death, guided by his guardian angel into the presence of God. In spite of potentially bathetic stages of the journey, such as a chorus of demons, and the comparative anticlimax of the oratorio's ending with Purgatory rather than Heaven, *Gerontius* is a moving and, for some, even a sublime work. It impressed Richard Strauss when he heard it in Germany in 1902: Elgar's music had by now won a hearing abroad, and Strauss hailed the composer as 'the first English progressivist, Maestro Edward Elgar of the young progressive school of English composers.' The renaissance of English music, we may observe, was already a recognised fact.

Elgar went on to write two more oratorios, *The Apostles* (1903) and *The Kingdom* (1906); two symphonies (1908 and 1911); concertos for violin and for cello (1910 and 1919), the latter strongly elegiac in character; and two 'English' orchestral pieces, *Cockaigne* (*In London Town*) and *Falstaff* (1901 and 1913). Some of these at least have won a place in the international repertory, for Elgar's capacity for noble emotional utterance, for vigour not unmixed with sadness, have brought him deserved popularity. But however he may be regarded in England, on the continent he is seen as a Straussian kind of composer: one whose Edwardian, late-romantic opulence was destined inevitably to give way, with the advancing twentieth century, to nostalgia and final silence. His last years, after his wife's death, were uncreative.

DELIUS, VAUGHAN WILLIAMS AND HOLST

Elgar was a nationalist in some senses. He loved England, her institutions and her history. But he did not draw on her folk music in the traditional way of nationalist composers The heritage of folk music, and also of the compositions of Tudor and later musicians, was to inspire the next generation, led by Ralph Vaughan Williams.

However, another composer, Frederick Delius (1862–1934), should be mentioned first. Delius used folk song, for example in *Brigg Fair: an English Rhapsody* (1907). But he was a universal nature poet: he was equally at home in Paris (of which city he composed an orchestral picture), in Scandinavia or across the Atlantic with Whitman's *Sea Drift* (1903). This last work, for baritone with chorus and orchestra, deals with a boy observer, a seascape and the sadness of nature, and is one of the best to be composed by this uneven, technically ill-equipped but often movingly poetic artist. It was first heard in Germany, and in fact the composer's name was known in Europe, where he studied, before it reached English musical circles.

Delius's cosmopolitanism was not surprising. Though he was born at Bradford in Yorkshire, his father was a German wool merchant who had made his home there some years before and who brought a wife from his native Bielefeld in 1859 to bear him a large family; the children had German as well as English as mother tongues, following their strict father's decree. Delius was given an expensive education that included music, but when it appeared that he was becoming deeply involved with the art his father made it clear that the family business was his destiny. When he was sent to Germany at the age of nineteen to represent the family firm, he found himself within reach of great musical centres like Leipzig and Berlin, taking violin lessons and hearing Wagner's *Mastersingers*. After returning home, he persuaded his father to let him travel abroad again: Norway and France were supposed to initiate him further into wool, but rather served to increase his appetite for music as well as the civilised artistic life which he found in Paris. It was in France that he eventually made his home, with the German painter Jelka Rosen whom he married in 1903. What brought them together in the first place was a mutual admiration for the music of Grieg, who had helped and encouraged Delius and who was to remain his favourite composer.

Grieg, for all his charm and individuality, could not really be called a major composer: his expressive and intellectual ranges are not great enough. Delius himself, though a complex personality, also achieved a unique stylistic flavour by restricting himself to the exploration of a narrow emotional range. As for the intellectual aspect of composition, he claimed to be relieved at not having undergone formal instruction. What he called 'traditional technique' was, he said, of little use to him, for learning killed instinct. 'A sense of flow is the main thing, and it doesn't matter how you do it as long as you master it.' That he did master a compositional technique suitable for his own purposes is undeniable. Furthermore it served him in large-scale works, such as the *Mass of Life* which he composed to Nietzsche's words in 1905, or indeed his opera *A Village Romeo and Juliet* (1901). His nostalgic, late-romantic style is not for those with severe musical tastes perhaps; but it has attracted many musicians, including the conductor Sir Thomas Beecham, whose promotion of Delius over a period of twenty years and more made his reputation secure, at least in his native country.

Ralph Vaughan Williams (1872–1958), the son of a Gloucestershire clergyman, received precisely the kind of thorough academic training that Delius did without. He was slow to mature as a creative artist; but by the age of thirty he was a highly qualified scholar with the Royal College of Music and a Cambridge doctorate behind him. His academic qualifications proved a stimulus, however. The bicentenary of Purcell's death in 1895, with its reawakening of interest in that composer, as well as a three-year period as a church organist and the important job of music editor for the *English Hymnal* (1906), all contributed to his awareness of England's great musical past; and in 1904 he joined the English Folk Song Society, itself a fairly new body founded in 1898. The Purcell revival, and that of folk song, were in themselves only manifestations of a greater musical awareness generally; the famous London Promenade Concerts were founded in 1895 by Robert Newman who, their conductor Sir Henry Wood tells us, 'wanted the public to come to love great music'.

Vaughan Williams's creed was typically nationalist and aware of the public. 'Art, like charity, should begin at home . . . Have we not all about us forms of musical expression which we can take and purify and raise to the level of great art? For instance, the lilt of the chorus at a music-hall joining in a popular song, the children dancing to a barrel-organ, the rousing fervour of a Salvation Army hymn . . . Have all these nothing to say to us? . . . The art of music above all other arts is the expression of the soul of a nation.'

We should guard against thinking Vaughan Williams to be a deliberately blinkered provincial, remembering that he went to Berlin to study with Max Bruch and (having discovered Debussy) to Paris in 1908 to work with Ravel, who was actually slightly younger than he. The idea of a composer having roots was for him not the same thing as provincialism; and he used to cite the long residence in Leipzig of J. S. Bach, a universal genius, as an example others might follow in this respect.

Vaughan Williams wrote operas, ballets (notably *Job*, 1930) and film music; church music of all kinds including the unaccompanied Mass in G minor (1922), with its consciously archaic beauty; many songs; and orchestral works including the *Fantasia on a Theme by Tallis* (1910) as well as nine symphonies. Only chamber music is rather poorly represented in the long catalogue of his compositions. The first three symphonies are semi-programmatic, and have the sub-titles 'Sea', 'London' and 'Pastoral'. The powerful and dissonant Fourth (1935) shocked those of his admirers who, ignoring Satan's music in *Job*, thought him essentially a gently dreaming, pastoral artist. He himself said of it: 'I don't know whether I like it, but it's what I meant.' It is based on two contrasted short motives, one, as it were, horizontal and the other vertical:

EX. 112 Vaughan Williams   *Motives from Symphony no. 4*

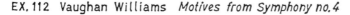
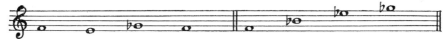

There is a parallel here with the finale of Mozart's 'Jupiter' Symphony, which also uses a four-note motive. Like that work, this Fourth Symphony is contrapuntal rather than harmonic, and in fact it ends with a fugal epilogue.

Music had now entered a period of neo-classicism, in which some of the ideals held prior to the romantic period were reinstated. The symphony and sonata form were, perhaps surprisingly, re-established as major modes of expression. In spite of the nineteenth century's discoveries in the realm of form, much new music after 1920 followed the example of Debussy in his last works, turning to the remoter past in order to go forward. In broad terms, neo-classicism represented a rediscovery of counterpoint with its energy and strength, and an alliance of classical form with modern harmony. Vaughan Williams provided a fugal conclusion for his Fourth and Sixth Symphonies, while the finale of his Fifth is a passacaglia and that of his Eighth a toccata. His Violin Concerto in D minor (1925) has the subtitle 'Academic' and clearly takes Bach as its model.

Yet it would be misleading to leave the impression that Vaughan Williams was an austere musician. On the contrary, he is often playful: to write concertos for harmonica and tuba, as he did, is no act of a musical puritan, and the Eighth Symphony (1955), written when he was over eighty, is youthfully lavish in its use of percussion instruments.

Both Vaughan Williams and Gustav Holst (1874–1934) contributed to English musical life by teaching as well as composing: after the First World War they joined the staff of the Royal College of Music in London, the institution founded in 1883 at which they themselves had first met as fellow-students. In fact they used to teach each other, or at any rate exchange ideas and criticisms at regular meetings, arranged for this purpose, which they called 'field-days'. Holst was Vaughan Williams's most distinguished English contemporary; and though his career was less consistent, his gifts were in some ways more original. His talent for brilliant orchestral writing was shown in the highly imaginative suite that he called *The Planets* (1916); this was Straussian in its instrumental opulence, yet *Neptune*, the final piece of the suite, has Debussyan impressionistic features with its deliberately vague washes of gentle sound and its mysterious alternation of the unrelated chords of E minor and G sharp minor (Example 113). More striking still are the features of *The Planets* which are unmistakably Holstian: the quintuple rhythms of *Mars* and *Neptune*, the parallel block chords, the marching basses and bitonal effects.

Born the son of a Cheltenham music teacher, with experience as a village church organist and choral society conductor, Holst cared deeply for folk music. His early works include a *Cotswolds Symphony* and a *Somerset Rhapsody*. But the folk idiom did not come to dominate him. He sometimes drew his inspiration from the East, so that even *The Planets* took its inspiration from the ideas of Chaldean astrology; the chamber opera *Sāvitri* (1908) and a *Japanese Suite* for orchestra (1915) are among other such works. But Holst was equally at home in the Shakespearean world of his opera *At the Boar's Head* (1924), in Thomas Hardy's country, the West of England, with

EX.113 Holst *The Planets (Neptune)*
Andante

the orchestral *Egdon Heath* (1927), and even writing for a military band. Like Vaughan Williams, he was attracted by neo-classicism, composing a *Fugal Overture* (1922), a *Fugal Concerto* (1923) for flute, oboe and strings, and an interesting Terzetto (1924) in which the austere texture of flute, oboe and viola is offset by daring polytonal effects. To the last, Holst remained an inventor and a visionary who was not content to repeat himself. Once the barrier of unfamiliarity is overcome, a work like the *Twelve Songs* of 1929 may be very moving. Though not like Debussy's music in their sound, these masterly songs resemble the French composer's last works in their combination of extreme refinement and profound feeling.

NIELSEN AND SIBELIUS

Carl Nielsen (1865–1931) and Jean Sibelius (1865–1957) were born within six months of one another in 1865, Nielsen being the elder. Both came from Scandinavia, both were principally symphonists, and both were apparent conservatives whose style, on investigation, proves to be far from unadventurous.

Nielsen was the son of a South Danish working man, a house-painter who also played the fiddle for local dances, and a folk-singing mother; he joined a military band at the age of fourteen and eventually found his way to the

Copenhagen Royal Conservatory, where he became a pupil of Gade. A spell of several years as a violinist in the Royal Opera Orchestra was interrupted by a state-subsidised trip abroad from 1890–91, during which he met and married his sculptress wife. Increasing experience of conducting led to his being appointed a conductor at the Opera and later of the Copenhagen Musical Society; finally he became the Director of the Conservatory.

Sibelius's career was no less distinguished. His father was a doctor; but the advantage of being born into an educated family circle was, as so often happens, somewhat outweighed by parental intentions to prepare him for a more conventional profession than music. He abandoned the law, however, for musical studies at Helsinki; further study in Vienna and Berlin was followed in 1897 by tangible recognition of his gifts in the shape of a life annuity from the Finnish Government permitting him to compose without financial worry – an enlightened step which has few parallels even in more affluent societies. Sibelius did continue with some composition teaching at the Helsinki Conservatory, though he declined a professorship at Vienna in 1912; and he travelled a good deal, conducting his own works, making visits to Germany and France, the United States in 1914, and England – a country where he had warm admirers and which he visited five times. He married in 1892 and twelve years later moved with his family to Järvenpää about thirty-five kilometres from Helsinki. There he lived and worked; but after the age of sixty he composed less and finally became musically silent for nearly thirty years. He died, of a cerebral haemorrhage, at Järvenpää in 1957, aged ninety-one.

Like Debussy and several other composers of their generation, Nielsen and Sibelius reacted against the influence of Wagner. Nielsen admired his genius but deplored his taste, calling it 'excessive and unwholesome'; and he declared that the only right course lay in the rediscovery of basic musical ideas in all their strength. Sibelius, in his turn, undertook to offer the public 'pure water' instead of elaborate concoctions. The implications of this purist philosophy were twofold. First, music should become less chromatic, literally less highly coloured. Secondly, it should separate itself from the other arts, particularly literature, and gain in power through this act of purification. It is significant that Nielsen, though taking the concept of human love as the subject of his first choral work, the *Hymnus Amoris* (1896), sought an escape from 'too subjective and personal feelings' by having the Danish text translated into Latin.* Similarly, Sibelius admired Palestrina's counter-reformationist combination of purity with fervour: this stirring nature poet was ill at ease when his musical landscapes were humanly inhabited. Finally, in turning to the un-Wagnerian form of the symphony, both Nielsen and Sibelius exemplified their own kind of neo-classicism.

Nielsen composed six symphonies between 1894 and 1925. When he
_____
* He thus anticipated by thirty years Stravinsky's similar procedure in *Oedipus Rex*.

conducted the Fourth in London in 1923, the critic Edwin Evans found it 'austere, even bleak music, such as will not appeal to the sensuous . . . It is of northern character throughout.' His colleague on *The Times* wrote: 'Mr Nielsen's music has behind it the solidity of classical tradition, together with the evidences of an enterprising invention . . . there is a cold northern feeling about the orchestration.' This rather conventional and generalised praise nevertheless sums up certain aspects of Nielsen's gifts and style fairly enough. What is notably missing, though, is a mention, necessary in any account of this composer, of his warmly assertive optimism and humanity. Nielsen is neither nostalgic nor pessimistic; and it is right that another *Times* critic, writing much later (1951) of this same symphony, pointed out 'the vigour which propels it from the beginning to the end of a vast and impassioned musical sentence.'

That same critic liked 'the flow of Nielsen's enthusiasm'. For as all good symphonists must be, Nielsen was a master of growth and movement. He once said himself: 'If my music has any value, it lies in the one fact that it has a certain flow, a certain motion.' But this claim is too modest, for of course there is more to him than this. In the splendidly conceived Fifth Symphony we have a musical drama quite worthy to stand in Beethoven's company: this is a modern 'Eroica', in which man faces conflicts and finally emerges triumphant. In its originality – it has only two movements – as well as the subtlety of its key structure and its contrapuntal mastery, the Fifth Symphony offers evidence of Nielsen's stature as a major composer.

Sibelius was once heard to say – though probably not too seriously – that he preferred Nielsen's music to his own. The Finnish composer achieved a high reputation in the English-speaking world long before Nielsen. How high this was may be judged from some critical writing of the 1920s and 1930s, in which Sibelius's achievement as a symphonist appears to cause even Beethoven to tremble on his pedestal. The reason for this was clear even at the time. In a period dominated by the unpredictable Stravinsky and the baffling Schönberg, Sibelius's music offered sanity and sense while still clearly possessing stature and individuality. An adventurous conservative such as he, a careful innovator, has much to attract those who know the need for originality in art but who deplore anything savouring of eccentricity. Times have changed, though; and with the general acceptance of Stravinsky and even Schönberg there has been some danger of Sibelius being relegated to the status of an unfashionable minor figure, with critics quick to point out that in countries like France he was never especially admired. But on the whole common sense has prevailed; and Sibelius is seen as a master whom one may respect alongside others whose aims were different.

Sibelius took seven years longer than Nielsen to produce his First Symphony (1899). It proved a more conventional work than Nielsen's First, which begins and ends in different keys; and while Nielsen showed some indebtedness to Brahms, Sibelius wrote a broadly romantic, somewhat Russian-sounding work closer in style to Borodin.

Yet Sibelius later achieved a more original form of symphonic thought, possessing what he called 'severity of style and the profound logic that creates an inner connection between all the ideas'. His development was steadily directed towards greater economy and unification of ideas, until eventually he reached the one-movement form of the Seventh Symphony (1924), his last. His technique was motivic: that is, he built up an extended piece of music from an idea or motive, usually too short or incomplete-sounding to be called a theme. This method was not of course entirely new: Palestrina's counterpoint is made up of the imitative interplay of motives, and so are Bach's fugues, while Beethoven had shown in his Fifth Symphony that a motive could retain its identity through rhythm alone, so that the figure of three short notes followed by a long one unifies both the first movement and the scherzo of that work. However, Sibelius went to the extreme of this technique by basing his Fourth Symphony (1911) on a mere interval, that of the augmented fourth or tritone. This is the opening:

EX. 114   Sibelius   *Symphony no.4*

Tempo molto moderato, quasi adagio

The tritone is a fascinating if disturbing interval.* It is richer than any other in possibilities for development – which is no doubt why Sibelius chose it for this work.

In the Third Symphony (1907), Sibelius compressed a scherzo and finale into one continuous movement, and in the Fifth (1915) he did the same with the first movement and scherzo. The Sixth (1923) has the conventional four-movement form, but there is an extraordinary purity of thought resulting in a compression which is disconcerting: there are few if any symphonic movements which end as abruptly as the first two here, though their musical logic can be demonstrated. This was an extreme position; and the Seventh Symphony, though in a single movement, has on the contrary a feeling of rich expansiveness. The symphonic poem *Tapiola* (1925), growing like the Fourth Symphony from a single idea, has equal grandeur, though of a starker

---

* Exactly these same notes are used as a motivic basis in Britten's *War Requiem*, and in the Debussy example quoted on pages 272–3 (where we read G flat instead of F sharp); but the effect in terms of key is different in each case. This ambiguous interval also outlines the 'magic' opening theme of Stravinsky's *The Firebird* (Example 115, p. 301).

kind befitting the supernatural subject matter, the legendary spirits of the northern forests.

Sibelius cannot be thought of, any more than Nielsen can, simply as a nationalist composer, for all the recognisably northern sound of his music. This is not only because he avoids using folk song. He was too complex a man to devote himself entirely to the discovery and exposition of a national spirit. Perhaps he was too self-doubting, even. He said that his Fourth Symphony described 'experiences of an introspective, spiritual nature, arising from pondering over the most important problems of existence, life and death'. Not long after writing that symphony, he was moved to tears by Bruckner's Seventh. Here, he said, was a profoundly religious spirit which in his own time had been lost, or set aside. 'How much pathos there is in our time. We are approaching a looked-for religious epoch. But it is impossible to define a religion, least of all in words. Yet perhaps music is a mirror.' So it is perhaps not surprising that he called his last three symphonies 'professions of faith'.

As far as orthodox religion is concerned, Sibelius, like Debussy and Delius, perhaps even Vaughan Williams, had what has been called 'a religious sensibility without a faith'. Working, in this sense at least, in a sort of no man's land, these men were to a large extent alone, having neither obvious predecessors nor even followers. After *Tapiola* Sibelius seems to have silenced even himself; he had followed his lonely path as far as it would go. Twentieth-century music was to need, and in the nick of time to find, another kind of creator. The next big advance in music was made by an immensely vital artist, forward-looking yet aware of the past, iconoclastic yet as religious as Bruckner. This was Stravinsky.

15

TRADITION AND INNOVATION IN THE TWENTIETH CENTURY

Stravinsky. Schönberg. Berg and Webern. Hindemith.
Bartók. Messiaen.

STRAVINSKY

Igor Stravinsky (1882–1971) was the son of a bass singer of the St Petersburg Opera. Imperial St Petersburg was Russia's most beautiful city, and an exciting place in which to grow up. As a boy of seven or eight Stravinsky sat in a box of the Maryinsky Theatre to hear Glinka's opera *A Life for the Tsar*; and this first hearing of an orchestra was, he said, 'perhaps the greatest thrill of my life'. At the Imperial Opera House he caught a glimpse of Tchaikovsky a fortnight before his great predecessor died. He studied the piano, and at the same time he listened to the village songs near his birthplace, the family country house at Oranienbaum.

Stravinsky's father intended him for the law, which he studied at St Petersburg University. But music was his greatest interest. He worked at harmony and counterpoint, eventually becoming a pupil of Rimsky-Korsakov. 'I was at his house almost every day of 1903, 1904 and 1905 . . . he made me the most precious gift of his unforgettable lessons.' The lessons took place twice weekly and were mainly in orchestration. This was unorthodox, for although Rimsky-Korsakov was expert in this branch of technique, it is not really a basic part of a composer's training. At any rate, in the meantime Stravinsky continued working on his own at counterpoint, and of course in the process of orchestrating Beethoven piano sonatas he learned about classical forms. His own unpublished Piano Sonata of 1904 was the fruit of these studies, and so was the Symphony in E flat (1905–7) which he dedicated to Rimsky-Korsakov.

An orchestral *Scherzo fantastique* (1908) was music of a much more exotic kind, brilliant and lightweight. Indeed, it was highly balletic, and at this point we come to the other main stimulating figure of Stravinsky's youth, Sergei Diaghilev. Diaghilev, the wealthy son of an army general, was an intellectual impresario who organised art exhibitions and founded an art journal as well as a ballet company. The progressive climate of Diaghilev's circle had a profound influence on Stravinsky's development, as he himself acknowledged. It was the Diaghilev group that opened up to him the world of French music, including Debussy's. An orchestral fantasy called *Fireworks* showed this new influence, and at the same time convinced Diaghilev that his young compatriot had a future.

With the dancer Mikhail Fokine, Diaghilev had founded the celebrated Russian Ballet Company and had a great success with its first season in Paris in 1909, impressing French audiences with the high dramatic and scenic level of the performances as well as the dancing itself. Now he asked Stravinsky to compose the music for a fairy-tale ballet on the legend of *The Firebird*. A single musical motive, that of a tritone, begins this work and unifies the entire score:

EX.115   Stravinsky *The Firebird*
Lento

The Firebird was a great success at its Paris première in 1910. One critic wrote: 'Here at last is a work that is absolutely beautiful, completely new and deeply significant.' He was wrong in thinking it wholly original. For Rimsky-Korsakov's influence is clear, and even the pounding energy of the *Infernal Dance* had a model of a sort in Borodin's *Polovtsian Dances*. But even so, Stravinsky outshone his models. This work was a masterpiece. Besides its intrinsic merits, furthermore, it gave a new lease of life to ballet as a musical art form; for Stravinsky's ballet music, though not conventionally symphonic, had from the first an increasingly independent status, being perfectly adequate for concert performance, without the stage action.

Petrushka (1911) actually originated in a concerto-like work for piano and orchestra, but Diaghilev persuaded Stravinsky to turn it into a new ballet set in a Russian fairground about a Pierrot puppet endowed with human feelings; the title role was taken by the celebrated dancer Nijinsky. Here the composer found himself completely, going far beyond *The Firebird* in imagination and technical resource: even the orchestra, with its prominent piano part, sounds new and more percussive. The rhythmic freedom of the opening section is remarkable. So is the bitonality of the famous passage for two clarinets in F sharp major and C major. Ravel had done this already in *Jeux d'eau*, but not so boldly:

EX.116   Stravinsky *Petrushka*

Bitonality, the simultaneous use of two keys, has nothing to do with chromaticism, the use of extra notes in one. After the chromatic wizardry of *The Firebird*, the harmonic novelty of *Petrushka* lay in a diatonicism (plain scales) which was equally fresh. Where Debussy had used block dissonances moving in parallel (see the examples on pages 269–70), this had been for subtle colouristic effects and never with the defiant open-air vigour we find here:

EX.117 Stravinsky *Petrushka*

Stravinsky's technical novelties were not an end in themselves. What was important was that he had found himself as an artist. Debussy, thanking him for the score of *Petrushka*, wrote that he found in it 'a kind of sound-magic, a mysterious transformation of mechanical into human souls, by a spell whose invention seems to me so far to be yours alone.'

Stravinsky's third ballet, *The Rite of Spring* (1913), was described by a delighted Diaghilev as 'the twentieth century's Ninth Symphony'. No brief description can hope to do justice to this extraordinary and thrilling masterpiece. The dramatic idea was once again the composer's own: a series of pagan rituals of a primitive tribe culminating in a young girl's voluntary sacrifice, dancing herself to death to propitiate the gods. As with *Petrushka*, the original idea was for a concert piece, in this case a programmatic symphony. The work is in fact as much symphonic as balletic, and the composer later in life preferred it to be performed without the stage spectacle. Lasting about half an hour, it is in two parts: there is a tonal orientation (towards D), so that this large-scale work sounds even more firmly structured, less episodic, than the two earlier ballets.

In spite of his modernity, Stravinsky thought in terms of key, or at any rate of tonal centres. 'Composing, for me, is putting into an order . . . a search for the centre upon which the series of sounds involved in my undertaking should converge . . . The discovery of this centre suggests to me the solution of my problem. It is thus that I satisfy my very marked taste for such a kind of musical topography.'

Debussy declared that with *The Rite of Spring* Stravinsky had 'enlarged the boundaries of the permissible in the empire of sound'. Yet this great work had no apparent sequel. The outbreak of war in 1914, a year after its première, ended an era. Money became short and lavish productions were difficult to mount, though Diaghilev put on one brilliant show in 1915 for the British Red Cross. But apart from this the composer himself was changing. He was about to become an expatriate. When the war began, he settled with his wife and family in Switzerland, and the Russian Revolution of 1917 lengthened his self-imposed exile. It was to be nearly half a century before he returned again to Russia in 1962 after his eightieth birthday, a visit which moved him deeply. But now in post-war Europe, although his music was still often based on Russian subjects, his style became more consciously international.

A new post-war aesthetic had as its leader the French poet Jean Cocteau, who declared that he had had enough of Wagnerian mists and even of Debussy's 'clouds, waves, aquariums, water-sprites and perfumes of the night'. Cocteau admired the composer Erik Satie (1866–1925) for his bold simplicity, his ability to recapture 'the poetry of childhood'. Clarity, sophistication, elegance and even a certain cheekiness were among the new values of Cocteau and *Les Six*, a group of young musicians which included the delightfully gifted song composer Francis Poulenc (1899–1963) as well as Darius Milhaud (born 1893) and Arthur Honegger (1892–1955), both of whom developed quite independently later. Cocteau's artistic creed was highly artificial, so that he claimed to prefer the painted harlequins of Cézanne and Picasso to Harlequin himself. In fact this was essentially an aesthetic movement of the theatre, stylised or even masked, lacking any element of self-revelation on the artist's part.

The greatest music of this new movement was not French, however, but by Stravinsky, who indeed made his home for some years in France. *Pulcinella* (1920) was a ballet based on eighteenth-century Pergolesi tunes which became in this composer's hands something unmistakably Stravinskian. *Pulcinella* is full of good humour and vitality, and it swept aside the last mists of romanticism. Pulcinella is the character of popular Italian comedy whose nearest English equivalent is Punch; and this new work was of a disconcerting lightness, coming as it did from a notoriously 'difficult' composer with whose earlier style the critics and public were just coming to terms.

Stravinsky always remained one step, or several even, ahead of his public: in fact the only predictable thing about this artist was his endless capacity to surprise. For example, when he eventually collaborated directly with Jean Cocteau, it was a deeply serious work that emerged, the opera-oratorio *Oedipus Rex* (1927). Here too, however, the style is theatrical, though in the best and most classical sense: the characters even wear masks as in classical tragedy. The text, sung in Latin, was derived by Cocteau from the Greek tragedy written in the fifth century BC by Sophocles.

Perséphone (1934), for speaker, voices and orchestra, also drew its story from the ancient world. Here once again Stravinsky collaborated with a leading French writer, this time André Gide. The words are French; and the music too has a certain Couperin-like elegance and dignified tenderness. These were baroque-rococo characteristics, and indeed there is more than an echo of the Elysian Fields music of Gluck's opera *Orfeo*, as befits the subject. Persephone questions the shades in the underworld, and their reply is lightly accompanied by the orchestra, with a prominent flute part:

EX. 118   Stravinsky   *Perséphone*

Perséphone is one of Stravinsky's most beautiful and moving works, a hymn to compassion: it thus has a Christian quality even though the story is of course pre-Christian. Stravinsky was a deeply religious man. His church music includes the magnificent *Symphony of Psalms* (1930) for chorus and orchestra, the *Mass* (1948), the *Canticum Sacrum*, written for St Mark's, Venice, in 1956, and finally the *Requiem Canticles* (1966). All these works manifest an austere solemnity combined with a quiet glow of deep feeling which together perhaps betray the composer's nationality, for we find the same qualities in the anonymous medieval ikon-painters of the Orthodox Church. The final chorus of the very late *Requiem Canticles* – of which his wife wrote, 'He was writing it for himself' – is a plea for divine mercy at the Day of Judgment. Doubled by four muted horns, a quartet of singers intones the text in modern, but in a sense ageless, harmonies. There is neither crescendo nor diminuendo, so that 'human' expression is kept to a minimum, and the rest of the chorus speak the text at the same time but in a faster and freer tempo:

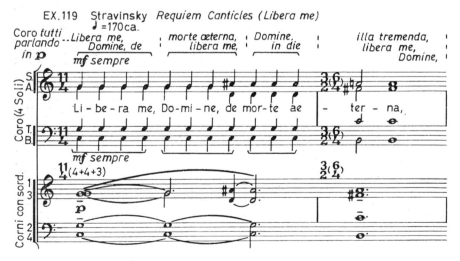

EX.119   Stravinsky   *Requiem Canticles (Libera me)*

Above Bruno Walter talking to Mahler (*left*) in Prague, 1907.

Below The critic, Eduard Hanslick, tells the composer Richard Wagner how not to compose. Silhouette by Otto Böhler.

Two remarkable faces: Debussy (*standing*) and Stravinsky, not long before the outbreak of World War I. This was the time of *Petrushka* and *The Rite of Spring*, both of which received their premières in Paris.

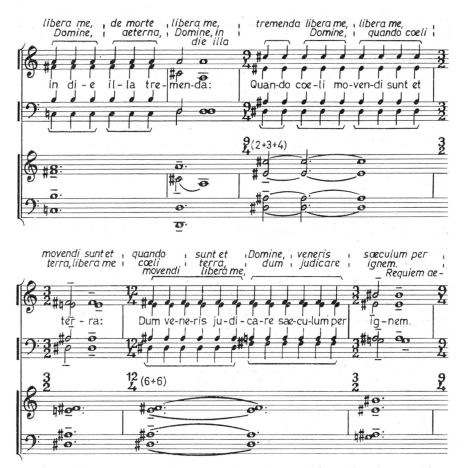

So far we have said little about Stravinsky's use of the more conventional large-scale instrumental forms of sonata and symphony. Did his early studies of Beethoven lead to nothing more orthodox than, say, the choral *Symphony of Psalms*? In fact instrumental symphonies, concertos and sonatas do feature among his compositions; but these works prove to be closer to the baroque tradition than to the classical. Stravinsky was stimulated, he said, by turning 'back to John Sebastian Bach, whose universal mind and enormous grasp upon musical art has never been transcended'. His Piano Concerto (1924), whose orchestra altogether eschews the 'romantic' sound of strings, has a busy Bachian energy. Both the 'Dumbarton Oaks' Concerto in E flat (1938) and the Concerto in D for strings (1946) – one notes the deliberate naming of keys – have affiliations with Bach's 'Brandenburg' Concertos. So, for that matter, has the *Ebony Concerto* for jazz band (1945) – the composer's ability to make other styles his own even extended to jazz, the authentic music of his last adopted country of residence, the United States. Even the fine *Symphony in Three Movements* (1945), though as forceful as Beethoven, reflects the baroque *concerto grosso* in its structure, and the name seems to have been chosen to emphasise this.

As a creator of music, Stravinsky dominated the twentieth century for fifty years: none has had greater influence. He was wider-ranging than Debussy or Ravel, more daring than Sibelius or Bartók, more accessible in human terms than Schönberg or Webern. He was also among the most articulate of artists: generations of scholars and music-lovers will find sustenance and stimulus in his writings and recorded conversations.

Stravinsky died in 1971, aged nearly ninety, and at his own request his body was flown across the Atlantic to Venice to be buried near Diaghilev. It was a touching desire. This adopted citizen of the New World had his roots in Europe. The great composer was drawn at the end by the beauty and gentle dignity of this loveliest and most civilised of European cities, itself perhaps dying. Just as they had done for Wagner in the nineteenth century, the funeral gondolas moved slowly down the Venetian canals: the sounds of water and voices, proper sounds for human environment, are more fitting for the interment of a musician than that of city traffic.

In his small frame, Stravinsky carried not only the acutest artistic mind of our time but also a great heart. This intellectual was also an intuitive artist, whose intellect was a means to an end, the creation of some musical magic. He said of *The Rite of Spring*: 'I heard, and I wrote what I heard. I am the vessel through which *Le Sacre* passed.' Before such a mystery, that of inspiration itself, one can only be silent.

SCHÖNBERG

The music of Arnold Schönberg (1874–1951) was more consistent in its development than Stravinsky's and more defiantly, even doggedly, radical. The two composers were interested in each other's work around 1912; then they drifted apart, and Schönberg satirised Stravinsky as 'little Modernsky' in 1925 in a piece for mixed chorus. (Stravinsky drily commented years later: 'I almost forgive him, for setting it to such a remarkable mirror canon.') One of the unpredictable Stravinsky's greatest surprises was his adoption, for the first time and at the age of seventy, of serial methods. For serial composition was Schönberg's discovery and the basic method of the Schönbergian school, whose leading figures were Schönberg himself and his pupils Alban Berg and Anton Webern.

Schönberg was born in Vienna and started to play the violin at the age of eight, writing little pieces which he played with his teacher. He did not study music on a full-time basis, but instead took a few counterpoint lessons with his future brother-in-law, Alexander von Zemlinsky. In 1897 he provided the libretto for Zemlinsky's opera *Sarema*; like his German predecessors, Schumann and Wagner, he had literary gifts and later he was to be his own

librettist for the opera *Moses and Aaron*. 1897 also saw the production of a
String Quartet. This was successfully performed; but in 1900 the performance of some new songs caused a mild scene, and in the composer's own
words, 'Since then the scandal has never ceased.'

The work which established Schönberg's international fame was *Pierrot
Lunaire* (1912). Stravinsky heard an early performance and declared himself
impressed by what he called the 'instrumental substance' of the music. But
its originality made it very difficult to perform. It is written for voice and a
five-piece chamber ensemble, and the vocalist declaims the text in *Sprechstimme* or speech-song. The singer Maggie Teyte studied the part with
expert help but eventually admitted failure; while the composer said that no
less than two hundred rehearsals were needed for the first recording! Only
in the last few years has *Pierrot Lunaire* become more accessible. Pierre
Boulez, who has conducted it many times, finds it 'continually rewarding,
theatrically effective, intellectually stimulating and altogether convincing in
spite of certain insoluble problems for the vocalist.'

The text of *Pierrot Lunaire* is a German translation of intense and even
lurid symbolist poems by the Belgian Albert Giraud (1860–1929). And in
spite of the composer's unguarded comment in a letter that musical listeners
'would not bother about the text, but would whistle the melodies instead',
the words do help to lead us into the strange world of this music. In *The Sick
Moon*, the voice is only accompanied by a flute. The vocal notation, with a
cross on the note-stems, indicates the speech-song technique:

EX.120

Example continued

fie - bernd ü - bergroß bannt mich, wie fremde Melo-

- die.

What was baffling about Schönberg's music was not so much its high level of dissonance as its apparent lack of structure. Since the classical period, musical form had been indissolubly based on three things. These were tonality (key itself), harmonic movement within and between keys, and finally the kind of melodic or motivic development which provided a meaningful, natural flow of thought. But all this was eschewed by Schönberg in the non-tonal style he was now using. The last of his *Six Little Piano Pieces*, Opus 19, is a case in point. He called it a bell tolling for Mahler's death – Mahler had championed him without, however, claiming to understand his work – and it is atmospheric, even beautiful. But it is hard to imagine this music being prolonged, for its brevity and epigrammatic character seem part of its very nature.

EX.121

Sehr langsam *(very slow)*

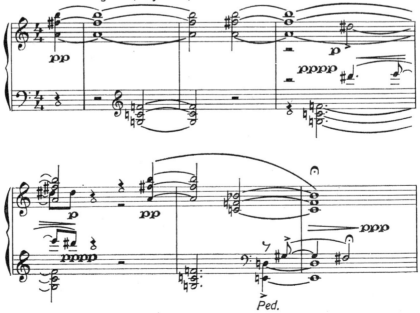

mit sehr zartem Ausdruck

genau im Takt

wie ein Hauch

If this music had any precedent at all, it was to be found in Debussy: perhaps, for example, *Canope* in the second book of Preludes, though that particular piece is not earlier but exactly contemporary. Schönberg had studied Debussy and he declared that impressionistic 'moods and pictures' might in themselves become constructive elements in music. Now, he said, there was a new 'sort of emotional comprehensibility; in this way, tonality was already dethroned in practice.'

Yet extended form remained a problem. Debussy himself, as we have seen, compromised with tradition in his last sonatas; and while his ballet *Jeux* has greater formal freedom, there a dramatic element provided coherence and order. The same dramatic coherence exists in Schönberg's *Erwartung* (1909), which is in effect an opera with one character only. The title means 'Expectation': a woman wanders through a forest anxiously seeking her lover, fearing his desertion and finally coming across his murdered body. Even so, the work ends in a kind of peace. It was written in a few days of white-hot inspiration. It is even possible to see the composer's own search for musical fulfilment symbolised in the story. 'I felt as if I had fallen into a sea of seething water . . . I do not know what saved me, why I did not drown or become water-logged. Perhaps my only merit was never to give up . . . At least I couldn't swim with the current. All I could do was to go against the current.'

Schönberg had found a style which already made him a major figure in contemporary musical thought. Yet he came to a nearly complete halt around 1914; and during the war years and even afterwards he seemed preoccupied with literary work. He wrote the texts for a projected trilogy of oratorios; and he also taught in Vienna and began conducting and lecturing. Then at last, in 1923, two works appeared using a new serial technique of composition: the *Five Piano Pieces*, Opus 23, and the *Serenade* for chamber ensemble.

The serial – or twelve-note, or dodecaphonic – technique must be explained. The basis for a serial composition is a specially selected arrangement of all the notes of the chromatic scale. This acts rather as the key, with its own scale and harmony, does in traditional music. The twelve-note series or 'row' chosen by a composer for a piece does resemble a scale in that melodies are drawn from it. But it can just as well be presented chordally, and in fact the note-row governs every note of the music, not merely those of the melody. A basic rule is that the twelve notes which together make up the row (or series) must be heard in their proper order: for example, notes seven and eight may be heard simultaneously in a chord or consecutively, but not preceding note six – this rule makes sense, for after all it is the particular *order* of the twelve notes which forms the basis of the music.

Once the row has been established in the listener's mind, however, certain specific variants of it become recognisable, or if not precisely that, at any rate meaningful. These are the inversion (upside down), the retrograde (backwards) form, and the retrograde form of the inversion. An example will make this clear. This is 'real' music and has a rhythm, which for simplicity's sake is kept the same in each permutation; but the rhythm is quite free and could of course have changed:

EX.122

This is Schönberg applying his serial technique in the last of the *Five Piano Pieces*. The row itself is shown, and then its use in four bars of the music:

Schönberg's method, being that of an artist, was of course a means to an artistic end and not an end in itself. Whatever one's reactions to such unfamiliar music may be, this is an undoubted fact. The composer himself was anxious to make it clear. 'I cannot say it often enough: my works are twelve-note *compositions*, not *twelve-note* compositions.' What mattered to him was 'what it *is*', not 'how it is *done*'. And his technique, though both new and difficult to assimilate, is perhaps not in itself more contrived or intellectualised than the traditional diatonic method of the past.

Having created his new technique, Schönberg proceeded to acquire increasing mastery in its use. Dance forms helped with formal problems, but soon extended works were possible without their aid, and this marked an important step forward. The Wind Quintet of 1924 was followed by a Suite for seven instruments and a Third String Quartet (both 1926). The Variations for orchestra (1928) had a stormy reception when Furtwängler conducted them in Berlin. There was a one-act opera called *Von Heute auf Morgen* ('From Today till Tomorrow', 1929), with saxophones and jazz rhythms, while the Violin Concerto and Fourth String Quartet both date from 1936.

But the next decade brought something of a surprise. Schönberg had produced alongside his serial music occasional, and exceptional, tonal music, like the Suite in G (1934), written for a New York student orchestra. Now he relaxed, even mellowed, in the use of the twelve-note technique. He used it with great freedom in the *Ode to Napoleon* (1942), which actually ends with a chord of E flat major. Here, as well as in the Piano Concerto of the same year, there are many tonal effects which suggest a nostalgia for the triads and cadences of the traditional system. In fact he admitted this in a collection of essays called *Style and Idea* (1951): 'A longing to return to the older style was always vigorous in me; and from time to time I had to yield to that urge. This is how and why I sometimes write tonal music. To me stylistic differences of this nature are not of a special importance. I do not know which of my compositions are better; I like them all, because I liked them when I wrote them.'

Schönberg seems to have been an excellent teacher. (There is a marked contrast here with Stravinsky, who said: 'I have very little gift for teaching, and no disposition for it: I am inclined to think that the only pupils worth having would become composers with or without my help.') But Schönberg had perforce to teach his new method of composition to those wishing to use it: nobody else could do so. His most famous pupils, Berg and Webern, never ceased to praise his discoveries and his teaching ability. This is almost a pity, for it tends to turn our attention to the theorist rather than the musician that Schönberg was. Like any other composer, he deserves to be remembered first and foremost for his music, culminating in the unfinished opera *Moses and Aaron*, a work of religious force and powerful humanity.

BERG AND WEBERN

Both Alban Berg (1885–1935) and Anton Webern (1883–1945) were Schönberg's pupils in Vienna. In the words of another pupil, Erwin Stein, 'They actually experienced the absolute necessity that gave birth to a new music, and could therefore not help making Schönberg's style their own.'

Berg came to Schönberg in 1904 with a bundle of songs, many written before he was fifteen. Soon he produced the so-called *Seven Early Songs* (1905–8), which he later orchestrated before publishing them in 1928. They are rather unadventurous in word-setting, reminiscent of Debussy's *Pelléas* and at moments also of Richard Strauss. Yet for all that, this was music of promise. Next came a Piano Sonata (1908), Berg's only music for solo piano, a String Quartet (1910) and *Three Orchestral Pieces* (1914).

Berg's opera *Wozzeck* took shape slowly in his mind between 1914 and 1921; and the libretto, based on Georg Büchner's drama, was his own. He dedicated the opera to his friend Alma Mahler, the widow of the composer whom (as did Schönberg) he revered. This work made him famous. In the decade following its first performance in Berlin in 1925 it had about a hundred and fifty performances in twenty-nine different towns. In England, Sir Adrian Boult conducted a broadcast in 1934; while Leopold Stokowski performed it in New York and elsewhere. Such a success for a difficult and uncompromising modern opera is evidence of its effectiveness. Part of this may be attributed to its sheer dramatic force. From the moment the curtain rose, Berg said, 'There should be nobody in the audience who is aware of any of these fugues and inventions, suites and sonata movements, variations and passacaglias: nobody filled with anything but the idea of this opera.' In telling the story of a poor, unhappy soldier, he felt what he called 'the need to provide folk-like tuneful elements . . . something that in tonal music is quite taken for granted; it was not easy to distinguish these levels so clearly in this so-called atonal harmony. I believe I succeeded . . .'

Berg did succeed. He felt the need to reconcile the serial method with more familiar elements. Of the three leaders of the so-called Second Viennese School, he is thus the most approachable. His best known work besides *Wozzeck* is a Violin Concerto, which he wrote in 1935 when already suffering from the illness that caused his early death. It is based on a twelve-note series and yet is strangely tonal in effect, so that he even managed to incorporate a Bach chorale into the music in a way which is altogether convincing. In this elegiac work written in memory of a young girl, Berg achieved an emotional intensity which has provided more than one listener with the key to genuine enjoyment, and even love, of twelve-note music.

Stravinsky met Berg on one occasion, in Venice in 1934, and was 'quite taken with his famous charm and subtlety'. Webern's personality, too, had charm; his pupil Humphrey Searle tells us that he was 'simple, direct and charming, and like Goethe he was a passionate student of nature'. Yet the resemblance between these two friends and fellow-pupils of Schönberg does not go much further. To quote Stravinsky again, Berg 'is at the end of a development' in terms of form, the melodically-based structure of his music; but 'Webern, the Sphinx, has bequeathed a whole foundation, as well as a contemporary sensibility and style.'

Webern is indeed sphinx-like. Most people's first contact with his music is baffling. 'Art must be simple,' he told his friend Berg; yet his intensely felt music, economical to the point of being laconic, puzzles a listener accustomed to free-flowing melody – of which there is little or none in his mature work. This passage is taken from one of the *Three Songs*, Opus 23 (1934), called *The Dark Heart*. The notation is of a type sometimes used by twelve-note composers, with an accidental for every note including naturals:

EX.124 Webern *Op.23 no.1*

Example continued

Of course it is quite impossible to 'understand' this music if one approaches it in terms of traditional technique. With Schönberg and Berg, there seem at least to be some familiar features, such as chords which can be heard tonally or recognisable rhythmic patterns. But here there is nothing familiar except the individual notes, time-signature and expression marks; though the music can be shown to be logical, the logic is not that of tonality but of an uncompromising serialism. To a large extent this is another musical language, unintelligible until it becomes familiar. But just as one can learn a spoken language by the 'direct method' – as we all have learned to follow traditional music – one can learn to make sense of Webern through familiarity. A study of the grammar, the syntax, of this style will speed up the process, as with a language. But of course listening experience is essential. The effort is worth while, so that we may learn to respond to what Stravinsky called Webern's 'dazzling diamonds'. This music also provides a gateway to the understanding of a great deal of the music written by advanced-style composers in the last twenty years or so. In the words of Pierre Boulez, one of the leaders among these, Webern was 'the one and only threshold'.

One feature at least of Webern's work facilitates familiarity: it is not extensive. Though perhaps he 'says' more in thirty seconds than another composer might in three minutes, it is still true that all his music could be performed in an afternoon. Even his Symphony (1928) only lasts about nine minutes, as does his last chamber work, the String Quartet (1938). Here, as in the *Concerto for Nine Instruments* (1934), his concentration reminds us of certain features of early Netherlandish music, a subject, significantly, in which he was an expert scholar.

In a lecture, Webern once said: 'The style that Schönberg and his school seek is a new saturation of the musical material in the horizontal and the vertical dimensions, a polyphony that formerly found its high points with the Netherlanders and with Bach . . . it is not a matter of the reconquest or re-awakening of the Netherlanders, but rather of a new filling out of their forms by way of the classics.' Thus like Stravinsky, and Schönberg too, this most radical-sounding of composers rooted his fearlessly inventive art firmly in the past.

Not all the German-speaking musical world sympathised with the methods of Schönberg's school. Paul Hindemith (1895–1963), though he conducted Webern's Symphony near the end of his life in 1962, was essentially opposed to serialism. 'With this method,' he declared, 'no pieces can be produced which could fill big spaces with broad symphonic colours, or which could satisfy many people's demands for simplicity, directness, and personal sympathy.' True: but after all, a composer such as Debussy does not satisfy our demands for Bachian counterpoint or spirituality, and yet this does not invalidate his work. There is room in the world for all kinds of music.

As a theorist and teacher with a reputation comparable to Schönberg's, Hindemith also faced the problems of modern musical thought in an individual way and developed a kind of compositional system. Though far less radical than serialism, it was also concerned with harmony, rather than, say, rhythm; but it was a tonal technique, one which he claimed was based 'entirely upon the natural laws of sound'. His students could therefore build upon classical harmony. But the idea was to extend it: and this was mainly done by emancipating and giving prominence and new functions to the interval of the fourth, which, although theoretically less dissonant than the thirds of classical harmony, had for some centuries not been treated as such. Strong-sounding fourths give Hindemith's music a characteristic vigour. In this passage from the opera *Mathis der Maler* (1934), accidentals abound; yet the effect is a tonal one, C being an unmistakable keynote although we cannot describe the music as 'in C major':

EX.125 Hindemith *Mathis der Maler*

Among twentieth-century composers, Hindemith was one of the most gifted in practical music-making, for he was a competent player of most orchestral instruments as well as the piano. His career began in café bands, including dance bands. Then in 1916 he became leader of the Frankfurt Opera Orchestra and remained in that post till 1923. As a viola player he rose to international virtuoso standard and was the soloist in the first performance of William Walton's Viola Concerto in 1929. But it was as a composer that he was best known, and he taught at the Berlin High School for Music, the city's main conservatory. Then, under Nazi rule, his 'modernistic' compositions were no longer played, and he left his post in 1934. From 1939 he made his home, as both Stravinsky and Schönberg had done, in the United States; and from 1942 onwards he directed the activities of the Department of Music at Yale University.

Hindemith's best-known works include the opera *Mathis der Maler* (1934), to his own libretto on the life of the painter Matthias Grünewald, and a ballet *Nobilissima visione* (1938) on the subject of St Francis of Assisi. There is also a song cycle on the life of the Virgin Mary called *Das Marienleben* (1924), and the big-scale contrapuntal piano work *Ludus tonalis* (1943). These are large, impressive subjects. Yet certain features of his work have tended to give him a reputation for dryness, or more precisely *Kapellmeister*ishness. These are his theoretical and teaching achievements, his athletic contrapuntal style, his willingness to write for every conceivable instrumental combination (who but he could have composed a Trio for Viola, Heckelphone and Piano?), his sheer size of output, and worst of all his unfortunately-named 'utility music'. It was impossible to forget 'this silly term', he later complained: '*Gebrauchsmusik*' was after all only a name he coined for music that he wrote specially for amateurs. These pieces were 'play' music written for practical enjoyment; the colourless implication of the English translation is entirely wrong, and 'practical music' or even 'everyday music' convey his meaning better.

For Hindemith's creed was one of communication. Reminding us of Beethoven's 'Be embraced, ye millions', a message of which 'we are all so terribly in need', he was disturbed by the widening gap between composers and the public. Yet though anxious to bridge it, he would tolerate no lowering of standards. He said that a composer must find the moral strength to maintain standards of technique and style distinguishing him from mere commercial entertainers. So much for the 'capitalist' world; but it was no solution either, in Hindemith's view, to submit to political demands in a state like the Soviet Union, for this could only result in 'the stunting of all imagination'. His own opera *Mathis der Maler* embodied an indictment of political authorities who take it upon themselves to interfere with an artist's creative freedom: it was of course banned in Nazi Germany.

A few years before his death, Hindemith told a touching story of his youth. As a German soldier in the First World War, he and three other string players prepared a performance of Debussy's String Quartet for his commanding officer, a lover of French music and culture. While they were playing it, just after the elegiac slow movement, an officer arrived and told them that news of Debussy's death had just been announced. 'We did not go on to the finale. It was as if the breath had been knocked out of our playing. But here we felt for the first time that music is more than style, technique, and expression of personal feeling. Here music reached out over political boundaries, over national hatred and the horror of war. On no other occasion has it ever been so clearly revealed to me in which direction music should be developed.' He never forsook his ideal: one of his late pieces was a *Song of Hope* (1955) composed for the United Nations Organisation.

BARTÓK

Béla Bartók (1881–1945) shared Hindemith's ideal, though his music is quite different. He once wrote: 'Ever since I found myself as a composer, I have been fully conscious of the brotherhood of peoples . . . and I try to serve this idea in my music.' Bartók loved people, the country folk of several countries among whom he collected folk music; and, with equal strength, he hated all forms of political and cultural oppression. But unlike Hindemith, whose last work was a Mass, Bartók as a young man rejected religious belief. Even so, we remember the profoundly spiritual feeling of certain passages of his later music, like the slow movement of the Third Piano Concerto (1945) – his last completed work – which is actually marked *religioso*.

Bartók was born in Hungary and had his first music lessons from his mother. At the Budapest Academy of Music he became a fine pianist, and he eventually taught the piano there from 1907–34. Richard Strauss's music impressed him; so did that of Liszt, his fellow-Hungarian, whose importance he was among the first twentieth-century musicians to recognise. In about 1907 he also got to know Debussy's music; this was through his friend Zoltán Kodály (1882–1967), himself a distinguished composer, scholar and teacher.

When he was about twenty-two, Bartók discovered folk music, which became a lifelong interest. 'Folk music studies,' he said, 'are as necessary to me as fresh air to other people.' And it was the rhythms and melodic shapes of Eastern European folk music which gave an unmistakable flavour to Bartók's music. Like Vaughan Williams and Falla, he arranged folk songs for concert performance, and he treated his material, itself unfamiliar to Western ears, with great harmonic boldness, amazing in that for all its modernity the music is appropriate and convincing. In the *Ballad*, from the *Fifteen Hungarian Peasant Songs* (1917), a simple four-bar phrase is given a dissonant harmonisation. Yet the effect is not chromatic, but still diatonic, with an open-air freshness. And, as with Hindemith, the keynote – in this case G – is never obscured:

EX.126 Bartók *Ballad*

This same piece, a few bars later, shows the original phrase in two variants, one on E and the other, more extended and for left hand, on C sharp. Here Bartók is much freer in his treatment of the phrase, both melodically and rhythmically. This music serves as the middle section of the piece. In this tiny example we can see how a sophisticated compositional technique, such as he was to use in his sonatas and string quartets, could perfectly well evolve or be forged from the semi-raw materials of folk music.

EX.127

'The study of all this peasant music,' Bartók wrote in 1921, 'had the decisive significance for me that it led me to the possibility of a complete emancipation from the exclusive rule of the traditional major–minor system.' But he did not take Schönberg's way, the abandonment of tonality, any more than Hindemith had done. The old modes, he said, although 'disused in our art-music, had by no means lost their vitality. Returning to their use, moreover, made possible novel harmonic combinations.' Bartók often used key signatures. But these were sometimes unconventional, so that the passage with E as its keynote in the example above has a C sharp in the key signature for the good reason that the mode has this particular note; occasionally with Bartók one even meets flats and sharps together in the same key signature.

The character of Bartók's music, particularly his earlier work, is often energetic to the point of aggressiveness. The piano piece called *Allegro barbaro* (1911) is unashamedly percussive, with dynamics covering a range from quadruple *piano* to triple *forte*; and its harshness is enhanced by the fact that its theme, a wholly white-note melody, is harmonised in something like F sharp minor. The primitive, even wild effects Bartók creates, like those of Stravinsky's *Rite of Spring*, are often frankly attractive. There is something exhilarating about the furiously grating repeated dissonances which open the finale of the Fourth String Quartet (1928), or the headlong chase constituting the middle section of the slow movement of the Second Piano Concerto (1931).

Like other composers drawn to folk music, Bartók possessed a powerful melodic gift. The fine opening movement of the *Music for Strings, Percussion and Celesta* (1936) is that most melodically-based of forms, a fugue. Yet here too, out of a polyphonic technique, characteristically Bartókian harmony emerges. Finding the conventional perfect cadence, dominant followed by tonic chords, 'contrary to the music of today', he was able to create new and meaningful cadences with a craftsman's precision and an inspiration that goes beyond craftsmanship. The ending of this movement provides an example: two parts, the lower an exact inversion of the upper, converge with convincing finality upon the keynote.

EX.128

Melodies became more lyrical, more simple even, in Bartók's later music, written in the decade between the mid-1930s and his death; so it is usual to say that his style mellowed, and this seems fair comment. The Violin Concerto of 1938 and the Divertimento for string orchestra composed in the following year are more attractive and approachable than some of his early works, so much so that one can easily overlook their mature skill. For example, the whole finale of the Concerto is a variant of the first movement, while the slow movement that separates them is itself a set of variations. This was one of the 'arch' forms, symmetrical structures that the composer favoured: the Fifth String Quartet (1934) is another example, with five movements, of which the first and fifth as well as the second and fourth are related to each other. The *Concerto for Orchestra* (1943) has rightly become popular, but even here there is more to find than the obvious charm and vivacity of a colourful score.

Bartók's last years were not crowned with material success. He spent them in self-imposed exile in the United States; and although he received some academic honours there, he suffered illness and even poverty, writing once to a friend that he had neither pupils nor a job and was in 'a horrible position' that was daily worsening. This was in 1942; and alongside the comic 'interrupted intermezzo' of the *Concerto for Orchestra* written in the following year there is an intense lament, an *Elegy*. But his disillusionment went back

Paul Hindemith was a skilled practical musician as well as a composer. It was he who gave the first performance of Walton's Viola Concerto in 1929.

Ravel in 1915. He composed at the piano, and enjoyed smoking cigarettes made of characteristically strong French tobacco.

Benjamin Britten, listening intently, conducts. Recently he has won a high reputation in this capacity.

Pink Floyd: a modern pop group whose electronic techniques are inseparable from their style and public image.

a few years further. His last string quartet, the Sixth (1939), composed even before he left Hungary, deeply shaken by his country's alliance with Germany, has a motto theme marked *mesto*, 'sadly', which dominates the finale.

This Sixth Quartet is by any standards a masterpiece. Bartók's works in this form, spread over thirty years, are certainly the most important since Beethoven's. It is of Beethoven more than any other composer that Bartók in his last years reminds us; and it is without surprise that we learn that he carried around with him scores of the late Beethoven quartets. One commentator has suggested that Bartók's art was neither incomprehensibly novel nor reactionary; for his explosive rhythms and intense feeling are contained, as with Beethoven, within a perfect formal order. But where Beethoven looks forward to some kind of musical advance and even liberation, Bartók foresees a disintegration of the musical tradition and so is pessimistic. This is thus music of threatened order: yet it stands fast, challenging us to do likewise. The quietly sad ending of the Sixth Quartet, in the view of the American scholar William Austin, is thus closer to the spirit of Greek tragedy than anything in Schönberg or Stravinsky.

MESSIAEN

Where Bartók believed in the brotherhood of man and had to cling as best he could to that belief while living his last years under the shadow of war, Olivier Messiaen (born 1908) believes in God. Not only is Messiaen an orthodox and devout Catholic,* he is also a lover of nature to a degree which shows the intense devotion of the mystic. 'Just as Bartók scoured Hungary to collect folk songs, I have wandered at length in the different French provinces to note down bird song.' For Messiaen, birds are God's creatures, and their voices incorporate a divine message. Their music colours the *Quartet for the End of Time* (1941) and the *Turangalîla Symphony* (1948), and it forms the main basis of other works including the *Oiseaux exotiques* for piano and chamber ensemble and above all the *Catalogue d'Oiseaux* for piano solo.

Messiaen has explained this interest in natural things. When music seems 'reduced to the meritorious product of patient studies, while nothing behind the notes justifies so much work, what is there left but to rediscover the true forgotten face of music somewhere in the woods, in the fields, in the mountains, by the sea, among the birds? . . . The bird is the symbol of freedom. We walk, he flies. We make war, he sings . . . I doubt that one can find in any human music, however inspired, melodies and rhythms that have the sovereign freedom of bird song.' He is quite explicit in his use of this source. So, in the words of his own programme note to the *Vingt Regards sur l'Enfant-Jésus*, the glory of heaven descends upon the Holy Child 'like a lark's song':

* For many years the organist of the Trinité Church in Paris, he has composed extensively for this instrument, mainly on sacred subjects.

EX.129 Messiaen *Vingt regards* (*L'alouette*)

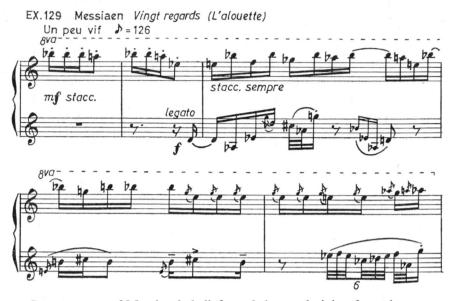

Some aspects of Messiaen's beliefs, and the art deriving from them, may be related to oriental mysticism, particularly that of the Hindu priest-philosophers. In point of fact several of his works have been inspired by non-European art: the *Turangalîla Symphony*, *Harawi*, vocal settings of love poetry (1945) and the *Cantéyodjayâ* for piano (1948). To anyone who thought this accorded oddly with his devout Christianity, he might well reply that Western faith had its origin in the East, and that the East had remained closer to nature, and thus to God, than modern Europe.

But God is the Eternal Being: for Messiaen, as for other mystics, time must cease to flow if communion with God is to take place. Time, or rather its abrogation, is a crucial factor in his art. It is significant that he wrote, as early in his career as 1941, a *Quartet for the End of Time*. Again this may be related to Indian art; for Indian music is contemplative as opposed to eventful, and one sees no special reason why a treatment of a *raga* should ever end since form in the Beethovenian sense of 'architecture' is absent. Messiaen's form too is differently conceived from that of most Western music. Some of his works are extremely long. The *Vingt Regards sur l'Enfant-Jésus* (1944) lasts over two hours, and another piano work, the three-hour *Catalogue d'Oiseaux* (1959), must approach the limits of the psychologically possible from the listener's point of view. That is, while we do not expect to devour a book at one sitting, we do on the whole approach music as a single experience and not a piecemeal one, and our powers of sustained listening are limited. Messiaen's view may be different, of course; yet he has been practical too. Thus, in a note prefacing the *Turangalîla Symphony*, he points out that he conceived this one-and-a-quarter-hour work 'as a whole' and wants it played without interruption, but then goes on to say that there may be an interval between the fifth and sixth movements, even adding that 'if the long duration frightens a conductor' certain selections from the movements, or indeed the fifth movement alone, may be performed instead of the whole work.*

Messiaen is a composer of extremes. Some would say of excesses, not least in sheer volume of sound. Stravinsky, with characteristic wit, remarked of *Chronochromie* that 'its "strike power" is so great I wonder the marimbas, xylophones and gongs did not collapse from metal fatigue.' The *Turangalîla Symphony* sometimes seems like a technicoloured assault on the senses, complete with the wildly wobbling swoops of the electronic instrument called the *ondes Martenot*, of which the composer is dangerously fond. In some works there is an extreme harmonic simplicity, which is either banal to a high degree or daring in its directness, depending on the listener's taste. This example, taken from *The Kiss of the Child Jesus* in the *Vingt Regards*, does not seem unfair:

EX.130 Messiaen *Vingt regards (theme of the Enfant)*
Très lent, calme (♪=88)
(Le sommeil)

(Thème de Dieu en berceuse)

But even if Messiaen shocks those whose artistic ideals include moderation, his intellect and integrity command respect. In the field of rhythm, especially, he has made innovations of importance. Drawing on Indian rhythmic theory, he has used durational patterns having something in common with the Western rhythmic modes of the twelfth century (*see* page 48).

---

* It appears, too, that the thirteen pieces of the *Catalogue d'Oiseaux* have not said the last word. Messiaen tells us that this is 'a work without an end. If death does not put a stop to my plans, this first catalogue of birds should be followed by a second and possibly a third.'

His rhythmic style is instantly recognisable. One feature is what he calls 'added values', tiny units of time added on to a rhythmic group, as in the *Theme of the Star and the Cross* in the *Vingt Regards*:

EX. 131 Messiaen *Vingt regards*
(theme of the Star
and the Cross)

Besides this, in a piano study in durations and dynamics (1949) he used series or rows in the Schönbergian sense which governed both the length and the loudness of notes, whereas the Schönbergian row had only applied to their pitch. This particular music opened the way to a technique of total serialism explored for a while by several younger composers, notably his pupil Karlheinz Stockhausen (born 1928).

Stockhausen, Pierre Boulez, Luigi Nono, Bengt Hambraeus and Alexander Goehr are now leading figures among the younger composers of Germany, France, Italy, Sweden and England – and all of these have been Messiaen's pupils. It is possible that he has been the most stimulating teacher of our century, for his students have developed more independently than Schönberg's or Hindemith's. He never proposed that others should adopt his own style, which is in any case intensely personal. But in giving his pupils both skill and dedication he has earned their respect and even devotion, as well as ensuring his place in any history of twentieth-century music.

16

NEW COUNTRIES AND SOCIETIES: THE PRESENT DAY

The United States. The Soviet Union. Britten and English music.
The avant-garde and the contemporary musical climate. Epilogue.

THE UNITED STATES

For all practical purposes, the history of music in the United States begins with the arrival of the first white settlers and colonists in the seventeenth century. There was church music which reflected their European customs; patriotic songs appeared later with the feeling of nationhood itself. But even by the nineteenth century the most distinguished American composer, Edward MacDowell (1861–1908), wrote music mainly reflecting his European training. He was influenced by Mendelssohn and Grieg and, knowing this, once admitted: 'The weakness of our music is in its borrowing.' America's music had to find its identity in a spirit of independence, ignoring or even rejecting, at least for a time, the European stylistic heritage.

The first distinctively American composer was Charles Ives (1874–1954). Though a musician's son, he nevertheless pursued a successful career in business and was for fourteen years a director of an insurance firm which bore his name. Ives's bold, even wild, modernity of musical style contrasted markedly with his well-ordered external Connecticut career. Yet his early training and compositions were traditional and craftsmanlike; he was no mere eccentric or simple experimenter.

Unlike his romantic predecessors, Ives did not think of music as self-expression. Rather it was a language of 'sounds approving and reflecting . . . moral goodness'. Ives's uncompromising idiom was, as he knew, challenging. 'Beethoven,' he wrote in 1920, 'had to churn to some extent, to make his message carry. He had to pull the ear, hard, and in the same place and several times.' He saw in the opening of Beethoven's Fifth Symphony 'the Soul of humanity knocking at the door of the Divine mysteries, radiant in the faith that it *will* be opened – and the human become the Divine!'

Ives certainly lived up to his visionary ideals. Sometimes the very appearance of his music, which he had to publish at his own expense, seems to defy the performer, to say nothing of the listener. The piano part of the song called *Soliloquy* (1907) is literally impossible for one player. How can it be realised in terms of sound? Ives's answer was simple, though hardly helpful: 'My God! What has sound got to do with music?'

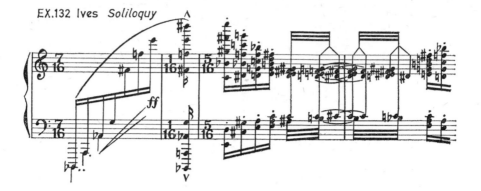

EX.132 Ives *Soliloquy*

There are similar performance difficulties in some of Ives's orchestral music. *Central Park in the Dark* (1907) requires two conductors, for he liked mixing up different musical ideas, each with its independent rhythm, tempo and key. The results are profoundly startling, predictably. But even if one sometimes feels Ives to be uninhibited to the point of frank irresponsibility, his vitality is always to be recognised. His final stature may remain doubtful, but at least we may find in him, as Stravinsky did, 'a new awareness of America'. His independence of spirit, which earned him also the admiration of Schönberg, has stimulated a number of his compatriots seeking liberation from traditional methods. At the time of its composition, Ives's music was unknown: Aaron Copland, raising the question whether American music might have developed differently had it been otherwise, answers himself with the regretful phrase, 'Perhaps he was too far in advance of his own genera-tion.' Though this unique artist's creative work was halted by illness after he was about fifty, it is good that he lived on to find himself acknowledged by his countrymen as a figure of major importance.

Jazz also brought its unique flavour to American music, from the begin-ning of the present century onwards. So much has been written about it that we may lose sight of a simple fact. Jazz is a form of folk music just as much as Neapolitan song or Scottish dance tunes, and we may disregard the mystique propagated by devotees and frankly admit that like all folk music it is 'good', at least if our main criteria of quality are sincerity and vitality. It is essentially simple, but there is nothing wrong in that.

Jazz was created by Negro musicians in America, whose forefathers had been among the most cruelly treated slaves in modern history and who were themselves semi-exiles and secondary citizens. The blues is a song of sorrow, even though it normally possesses a tough, defiantly courageous quality. The special flavour of jazz is an emotional one, and though it is not unique in being a folk music created in political subjection – the Jews for centuries made their music under similar conditions – it has reacted in such a special way to its white urban-industrial environment that it has become not only a musical but a sociological phenomenon. Yet its great individual names – such as those of the clarinettist Johnny Dodds (1892–1940), the pianist Jelly Roll Morton (1885–1941), the trumpeter Louis Armstrong (1900–71), even such a recent figure as the trumpeter Miles Davis (born 1926) – seem now to belong to an artistic movement of the past. And this is even more true of blues singers like the celebrated Bessie Smith (about 1900–37). The 'white' commercial elements which were present from the 1930s onwards in swing bands have changed jazz into what is usually called popular music, a form which with its self-conscious world outlook appeals to an uneasily affluent younger generation in many countries besides America. But in ceasing to be folk music, jazz ceases to be itself.

The Negro jazzmen named in the preceding paragraph are performers rather than composers. The leading jazz composer is one of the elder statesmen of the movement, 'Duke' Ellington (born 1899). Ellington was one of the first jazz musicians to be seriously studied by scholars. Yet as a composer, with written-out arrangements for his band, he is exceptional. Like all folk music, jazz is improvisatory; its musicians are thus instrumentalists or singers. The improvisation is melodic, like that of classical sets of variations: and here we find a special inventiveness like that of Dodds's clarinet weaving brightly through a texture, or Davis's cool yet lyrical trumpet on the record *Kind of Blue* (1959). Dodds is a master of the characteristic jazz 'blue' notes, flattened thirds and sevenths which impart poignant 'minor' expressiveness to basically major harmony. Yet harmonic and even rhythmic resources are limited and even stereotyped in jazz. More recently, academically educated white musicians like Dave Brubeck (born 1920) have rather self-consciously sought a greater freedom, and Debussyan chords and hitherto-unused triple rhythms appear, even though the quintuple time (three beats plus two) of Brubeck's *Take Five* or the 3 + 3 + 4 of his *Nomad* (on the record *Impressions of Eurasia*, 1958) sound tame compared with their real models, Bartók and oriental music. Experiments in instrumentation, again fairly recent, have also taken place. The flute, soft by jazz standards, has found its way into small groups: the traditional jazz group, originally consisting of a trumpet and clarinet plus banjo or piano, has always been small, the big bands of swing being an offshoot of the authentic style.

Jazz has influenced several composers, and not only American ones, for it somehow represents urban life, its very sound symbolising modernity. Schönberg, Stravinsky, Ravel, the German Kurt Weill (1900–1950) and most recently the Englishman Peter Maxwell Davies (born 1934) are among those who have employed its flavour, though they have done so more sparingly than some reference books imply and, with the possible exception of the last two, none has made jazz an essential feature of his work. For it really offers little in the way of novelty, except perhaps for the improvisatory element. And even this is an old feature of Western music, which, though for a while disused, is now reappearing rather through Eastern influence than through that of jazz.

George Gershwin (1898–1937) was not really a jazz composer – jazz being in any case not composed in the sense of 'written down' – though his music is closely linked to jazz. His style is closer to that of the more sophisticated white composers of the commercial musical world called 'Tin Pan Alley', who used a New York–Hollywood idiom. His *Rhapsody in Blue* (1924) was written for the 'symphonic-jazz' Paul Whiteman Orchestra; the Piano Concerto in F (1925) was a stage nearer classical models, among them Rachmaninov, but at the same time, inevitably, further from jazz. Gershwin rightly saw a more feasible link between classical and jazz methods in the fields of song and opera, and his songs for various shows are often distinguished and subtle. His Negro opera *Porgy and Bess* (1935) is a minor masterpiece owing something to Bizet's *Carmen* and deserving its place among those few folk operas possessing both musical skill and humanity.

Aaron Copland (born 1900) came from a similar Brooklyn background to Gershwin's. But he is demonstrably a musician of far wider range. Copland rounded off his training with three years in Paris and came home admiring European culture and Stravinsky, the possessor of a fine technique. Having hitherto ignored jazz, he now tried it out as a potential source of inspiration. The orchestral *Music for the Theatre* (1925) was the effective result and brought him critical praise; and there were also *Two Blues* for piano (1926).

However, after a few years Copland found the jazz interest too narrow, though he still sought a musical language 'which, as language, would cause no difficulty to my listeners'. Folk material in a wider sense helped him to achieve this aim. There are echoes of cowboy songs in *Billy the Kid* (1938) and *Rodeo* (1942), bugle calls in *Fanfare for the Common Man* (1942), and Latin-American popular music in *El Salón México* (1936); while the beautiful ballet *Appalachian Spring* (1944) has a harmonic purity combined with poetic feeling that has led one American critic to compare it with Vaughan Williams's 'Pastoral' Symphony. Of course, the clean sound of these diatonic dissonances is also Stravinskian:

EX.133 Copland *Appalachian Spring*

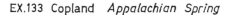

Copland's music ranges from popular to quite complex pieces like the Piano Quartet (1950) in which he uses serial technique, though in an individual way. He himself has remarked that critics note a distinction between his 'simple' and 'severe' styles but denies that this exists in his own mind: 'Different purposes produce different kinds of work, that is all.' What matters to him is that music should keep open 'the irrational doorways' through which we may glimpse 'the wildness and the pang of life'. Copland is America's best-known composer and one of her most skilled musicians, as well as being a distinguished and remarkably clear writer on musical subjects.

Although Copland's musical personality is an attractive one, perhaps the outstanding figure in this respect is Leonard Bernstein (born 1918). Bernstein, born in Massachusetts, attended school in the New England capital of Boston and then studied composition at Harvard with the distinguished teacher and composer Walter Piston (born 1894); he also acquired skills as a conductor and pianist. Appointed an assistant conductor of the New York Philharmonic Orchestra in 1943, he achieved overnight fame when he took over a concert following the illness of a visiting conductor; and since that time much of his professional life has been spent conducting as a modern-style international artist to whom travel among the world's musical centres is a way of life.

Like Mahler, whose music he often conducts, Bernstein has not allowed his career as a performer to silence his creative gift. Two programmatic symphonies, the 'Jeremiah' Symphony and *The Age of Anxiety*, were successfully performed in the nineteen-forties; though Bernstein reached his widest public with the sophisticated, energetic and touching musical *West Side Story* in 1957. His concern to bridge the gap between the contemporary creative musician and audiences has marked virtually all his work, and probably reaches its most intense expression in the Mass (1971) composed at the request of President Kennedy's widow for the opening of the Kennedy Arts Centre in Washington. This Mass for voices and instruments mixes the traditional Latin liturgy with contemporary words and an idiom incorporating modern 'hard rock' jazz as well as more symphonic styles: its stature remains controversial, but there is no doubting its burning sincerity.

Two other composers belonging roughly to the generations of Copland and Bernstein respectively are Elliott Carter (born 1908) and Lukas Foss (born 1922). Paradoxical though it may seem, their music has attracted less attention outside America because it is less obviously American in character. Like Bernstein, Carter studied at Harvard with Walter Piston; and like Copland, he went on to Paris for three years' work with the distinguished teacher Nadia Boulanger. He developed slowly, writing music for a ballet company which he directed and showing a predilection for classical subjects and sources; but in due course his individual style emerged strikingly with a Piano Sonata (1946) which is both rhythmically free and tonally ambiguous. Two string quartets (1951 and 1959) show remarkable originality of structure as well as a high degree of independence between the four instruments. Formal originality and strength are also features of the Variations for orchestra (1956), of which Carter said, 'As in all my works, I conceived this one as a large, unified musical action or gesture.' The same characteristics of powerfully organised form and differentiated instrumental roles are found in the Double Concerto (1961) for harpsichord and piano with two chamber orchestras, in connection with which Carter has written of a 'formation of the physical universe by the random swervings of atoms, its flourishing and its destruction'. Carter's music is among the most difficult being written today; but its intellectual strength commands respect.

Lukas Foss was actually born in Berlin and began his musical studies in Europe. In the United States, where he arrived at the age of fifteen, he went on to study with Hindemith, but like Copland and Carter, he finished his training in Paris. A fine pianist and the composer of two piano concertos, Foss has also written a good deal of vocal music, sometimes with Jewish–oriental affiliations. More recently, he has moved into improvisation placed alongside 'written' music, which he describes as representing 'chance corrected by the will': he himself plays the piano in his improvising ensemble.

THE SOVIET UNION

There is something in common between the music written by the Americans Copland and Bernstein and that of Russian composers such as Prokofiev and Shostakovich. We find in the work of all these artists a certain feeling of space and open-air freshness, a directness of utterance too, that seem appropriate to large and powerful countries. Both Shostakovich and Bernstein have had the confidence to compose splendid light music, something which some more uneasily self-conscious Europeans could never have done. Prokofiev's *Peter and the Wolf*, written for children in 1936, was ahead of its time in its tunefulness and certainty of touch.

Yet although Sergei Prokofiev (1891–1953) is a popular composer, he remains misunderstood and to a large extent even unknown, for his fame rests on a small number of works. In fact he wrote eight operas and seven symphonies, cantatas and ballets, nine each of concertos and piano sonatas, two string quartets and a great deal of other music besides. It is rewarding to make the acquaintance of this music, for the composer of the *Classical Symphony* (1917) and of *Peter and the Wolf* possessed ample personality, wit and skill.

One aspect of his wit is easily exemplified, namely his combination of the familiar with the new. The opening tune of *Peter and the Wolf* begins with conventional harmony and suddenly takes a completely unexpected turn, so that we gasp for breath at the tonal shock; but then, just as we are getting our new bearings, we are put neatly back into the home key to be left wondering just what happened. The same kind of thing occurs in the gavotte of the *Classical Symphony*:

EX.134   Prokofiev   *Gavotte (Classical Symphony)*

Prokofiev's modernity is apparent enough, but he always shows an aware-ness of what is both comprehensible and palatable. Like Stravinsky he was taught by Rimsky-Korsakov, though not, however, on the same individual basis, and he too worked later with Diaghilev. But whereas Stravinsky in his self-imposed exile came to be distrusted and unplayed in the new Soviet Union after the First World War, Prokofiev was gradually tempted back to Russia after some years of residence abroad. The composer of a ballet called *The Prodigal Son*, he himself now played that role: it was this younger man, not the older exile Stravinsky, who became the flattered major figure of Soviet Russian music.

Like everything in the Soviet Union, music was the subject of government policy; and there was an Association of Proletarian Musicians which aimed to purge Russian music of the bourgeois, decadent influence of the West. Prokofiev's own talent was fortunately of a kind which combined officially-approved positive qualities with both freshness and integrity. 'All my work,' he said, 'is founded on melody. Of course I have used dissonance in my time but . . . it must be relegated to its proper place as one element in music.' He wrote his Fifth Piano Concerto (1932) in a spirit of search for a new directness, hoping that it would 'seem as simple to the listener as it was to me'. Even so, the Concerto had a cool reception in Moscow and Leningrad. This was intellectual stuff, it was said; what could it do for peasants and working people? Prokofiev's answer was firm and sensible. Good music, he said, did not consist of 'cheap little tunes' that quickly wore thin, but 'melodies with their roots in classical music and folk songs. Only by aiming ahead will you catch and hold the public: we don't want the old simplicity but a new one.'

However, the struggle to preserve artistic freedom in Soviet Russia was only beginning. Prokofiev was too eminent for open attack, or at any rate for outright condemnation. He was later to suffer from political pressure; but in the meantime the storm broke over the head of the most gifted among the younger composers, Shostakovich. Dmitri Shostakovich (born 1906) had called on Prokofiev in 1927 at the Leningrad Hotel and immediately impressed him with his music. A quietly serious, even melancholy young man, by 1936 Shostakovich had become famous, and his name even known abroad. Then an article appeared in *Pravda* called 'Not Music but a Mess'; the subject was Shostakovich's opera *Lady Macbeth of Mtsensk* (1934), and the composer was accused of adopting the worst of decadent Western manners and so producing music that was offensive and even harmful to Soviet citizens. A few days later his ballet *The Limpid Stream* (1935) was similarly attacked. His Fourth Symphony, in rehearsal but awaiting its première, was hastily withdrawn. It was not heard in public till long after, in 1961, when it proved to be a long, masterly and highly original piece with an unusual structure, seemingly loose but in effect convincing.

The nature of the Fourth Symphony is tantalising. How Shostakovich might have developed under other circumstances we cannot know. As it was, with a heroic effort of will he changed his artistic direction. The Fifth Symphony (1937) is headed with the words 'A Soviet artist's response to just criticism'. It would be easy to see a simple backward step in the clear outlines, straightforward melody, rhythm and orchestration of this work. Yet Shostakovich is an artist who in depth of feeling goes beyond Prokofiev (whose tragic Sixth Symphony is exceptional); and this dramatic Fifth Symphony never sounds like a work conceived in a spirit of compromise and apology. It is what he called it, an artist's 'response' but not a recantation; and though not innovatory in any technical sense, it is fine music whose emotional impact is positive and direct.

However, it would be misleading to leave the impression that Shostakovich's later achievement has been easy or consistent. In fact, it is frankly uneven. A few works of deliberately 'popular' intent, like the Twelfth Symphony (1961), celebrating the 1917 Revolution and dedicated to the memory of Lenin, are, to a Western ear at least, banal, with commonplace populist ideas that receive inflated and repetitious treatment. But one should not forget the difficult situation of this patriotic artist, of whom so much is demanded by the society of which he is the leading musical representative, yet who is so individual and even introverted by nature.

At least one can turn to a more positive note with other works by Shostakovich, for there is more than enough first-rate music to ensure this composer's reputation. The two violin concertos and the Cello Concerto (1959), the Second Piano Trio (1944) and the autobiographical Eighth String Quartet (1960) are works of high quality to stand beside the Sixth, Eighth and Tenth Symphonies. More recently he has written a Fourteenth Symphony (1969), for voices and orchestra; the subject of this beautiful and moving work is that of death and the work is dedicated to the composer's English friend Benjamin Britten, who in 1970 conducted its first performance outside the Soviet Union. His Fifteenth Symphony (1971) is quite different, purely orchestral and somewhat enigmatic in its use of quotations from Rossini's *William Tell* Overture, Wagner's *Ring* and Shostakovich's own works.

Prokofiev and Shostakovich stand well above their Russian contemporaries. However, when we compare them with Schönberg, Stravinsky or Messiaen we have to acknowledge that they are not among the great explorers of the twentieth century. On the other hand – to return to a theme argued elsewhere in this book – an artist's importance as an innovator is not the only standard by which he is to be measured: Bach and Brahms were in some respects old-fashioned in their lifetimes, but to us this matters little if at all. One may be confident therefore that these two Russians will take their place alongside their more adventurous compatriot Stravinsky in the affections of future generations of music-lovers.

BRITTEN AND ENGLISH MUSIC

Benjamin Britten (born 1913) also belongs in the category of the traditionalists. That is, he does not appear to have sought consciously to extend the technical aspects of the musical language. It is instructive to compare him with Stravinsky, whom he admires but who himself appears to have regarded Britten with respectful distrust. For Stravinsky, harmony 'has had a brilliant but short history . . . harmony offers no further resources in which to enquire and from which to seek profit. The contemporary ear requires a completely different approach to music.' But to whose ear does he refer? To witness the delight of the children and adults who both perform and listen to Britten's *Noye's Fludde* (1957) – a subject Stravinsky himself later treated quite differently – is to ask if any 'completely different approach to music' is possible, or for that matter desirable. Human psychology does not change, a fact that Stravinsky with his feeling for the past would surely have conceded – so is there really such a thing as 'the contemporary ear'?

Britten's own view with regard to performers and listeners is clear: 'I certainly write music for human beings, directly and deliberately . . . it is the composer's duty, as a member of society, to speak to or for his fellow human beings . . . it is insulting to address anyone in a language which they do not understand.' All art is for him a form of communication, and Britten describes music in terms of musical experience requiring a 'holy triangle of composer, performer and listener'. As a self-confessed communicator, his success has been outstanding. Yet he is not merely a popular composer. In fact his music is by no means all easy to follow or even to enjoy. T. S. Eliot once remarked that a complex thought cannot be expressed in a simple way: Britten's thought is sometimes complex and the music correspondingly 'difficult'. The children who enjoy *Noye's Fludde, The Young Person's Guide to the Orchestra* (1946) and *Saint Nicolas* (1948) would be unmoved, probably bored, by the adult utterance of the two suites for unaccompanied cello (1964 and 1967), fine and rewarding though these are to a sophisticated listener.

Similarly, the mood of Britten's music, its subject-matter, is quite frequently sombre. The international success of *Peter Grimes* (1945), the opera which made his name, was achieved in spite of the near-absence of a love story and a protagonist who is forced into suicide by the fatal interaction of his pride and ill-fortune with an unsympathetic society. The principal characters of later operas, *The Rape of Lucretia* (1946), *Billy Budd* (1951), *The Turn of the Screw* (1954), *Owen Wingrave* (1970) and *Death in Venice* (1973) are equally ill-fated. Even in the comedy *Albert Herring* (1947) one is made conscious of the tension which exists between the desires of an individual and society's demands upon him.

This particular tension, and the problem of suffering in general, have preoccupied Britten. But he is a Christian, and one remembers that the theme of suffering, of innocence betrayed, is central to Christianity and thus to the accepted Western moral code. In *Billy Budd*, the paradox is succinctly put: 'The angel of God has struck and the angel must hang.' The composer has from his youth been a pacifist; and it is obvious that war, representing suffering on the largest scale, must cause the artist in him, as well as the man, to speak out.

Thus Britten's *Cantata Misericordium* (1963) is on the parable of the Good Samaritan and was written for the International Red Cross, while *Voices for Today* (1965) is for the United Nations; one of his largest and most powerful works, the *War Requiem* (1961), places the bitter anti-war poems of Wilfred Owen alongside the timeless and universal Latin text of the Mass for the Dead. More recent is *Children's Crusade* (1968), written for the fiftieth anniversary of the Save the Children Fund. Its text, an English version of a poem by Bertolt Brecht, describes the wanderings of a group of lost children through the winter landscape of war-torn Poland, where they finally disappear without trace. The music for boys' voices, piano and percussion, is tough and without charm; yet its emotional effect is overwhelming. Beethoven once told a pupil to study Handel in order to learn 'how to achieve great effects with simple means', and Britten too knows how.

We need not overlook the fact, however, that Britten's music can be abundantly gay and attractive: for example, the *Cantata Academica* (1959), for voices and orchestra, composed for Basle University in Switzerland, quite belies its serious name. Qualities of lightness and humour are all the more to be valued in the music of our time, in that they are comparatively rare.

Britten is the outstanding figure among a group of by no means undistinguished English composers born in the forty years or so after Vaughan Williams and Holst. Sir Arnold Bax (1883-1953) is best known for his orchestral music, which includes seven symphonies. He called himself 'a brazen romantic', and works like the symphonic poems *Tintagel* (1917) and *The Tale the Pine Trees knew* (1931) explore the poetic aspects of Britain's Celtic history, heroic yet remote and dreamlike. Two others drawing inspiration from the mysterious past of legend were John Ireland (1879-1962) and E. J. Moeran (1894-1950), composers respectively of, among other things, *The Island Spell*, an evocative, impressionistic piano piece (1912), and *In the Mountain Country*, an orchestral 'symphonic impression' (1921). Frank Bridge (1879-1941) was Britten's principal teacher, but deserves to be remembered for more than this, for he was not only a fine craftsman but a bold and poetic artist. Less overtly romantic or impressionist than his contemporaries, a fine string player and conductor, Bridge wrote a good deal of chamber music, including four string quartets, and is on the whole better known to performers than the general public.

Arthur Bliss (born 1891), William Walton (born 1902) and Michael Tippett (born 1905) are more in the European mainstream than some of their predecessors. Both Bliss and Walton had made their reputations by the 1920s. They reacted not only against Wagner but also against the English-Celtic school – though not specifically against its most distinguished figure, Vaughan Williams – in favour of the kind of clear modernity exemplified at its best by Stravinsky. Bliss's *Colour Symphony* (1922), *Music for Strings* (1935) and Piano Concerto (1939) have a vigour and astringency combined with a certain quasi-romantic richness. Walton's wit is drier: *Façade* (1922), in which Edith Sitwell's poems are recited to the accompaniment of a small instrumental ensemble, is a youthful masterpiece. His Viola Concerto (1929), the oratorio *Belshazzar's Feast* (1931) and the First Symphony (1935), though they have a more traditional format, are still distinguished and vital. But Walton does not seem to compose easily, and his later music is less challenging, breaking no obviously new ground.

Tippett developed much more slowly than Walton, and did not make his name until the Second World War. The oratorio *A Child of our Time* (1941) is a passionate protest against war; for Tippett is a pacifist, having this in common with Britten. But he does not possess Britten's unerring artistic judgment: the texts that he writes himself, for oratorio and opera alike, are curiously ineffective, while even in such a purely musical matter as orchestral balance he can miscalculate. Tippett's music covers a wide range, from string quartets to a fine Piano Concerto (1956), three symphonies, songs and choral music, and three impressive operas, the most recent being *The Knot Garden* (1970). The most intellectually adventurous among senior English composers, he seems perpetually willing to explore and to take risks in spite of the inevitable occasional failure.

THE AVANT-GARDE AND THE CONTEMPORARY MUSICAL CLIMATE

With Alexander Goehr (born 1932), Peter Maxwell Davies (born 1934) and Richard Rodney Bennett (born 1936) we reach a generation of English musicians who link up with a whole international group. For each has consciously worked within a post-Schönbergian aesthetic. Nationalism in all its forms seems a thing of the past; and it is significant that Goehr and Bennett studied with Messiaen and Boulez respectively.

Two Messiaen pupils are among the most influential musicians of their generation, the Frenchman Pierre Boulez (born 1925) and the German Karlheinz Stockhausen (born 1928). Boulez's *Le marteau sans maître* (1954) had, in 1958, attracted Stravinsky most of all the younger generation's music. To some extent it resembles *Pierrot Lunaire*, though it is more complex in layout. For Boulez regards *Pierrot* as one of the century's 'great source works' and has often conducted it. Indeed his reputation as an orchestral conductor now, regrettably, eclipses his composing; for the last decade he has been much in demand all over the world to conduct not only those moderns whom he admires – such as Debussy, Bartók, Stravinsky, Schönberg, Berg and Webern – but also earlier music, such as Wagner's *Parsifal* in Bayreuth.

Boulez's own style is essentially non-melodic. 'Purely thematic writing has no future,' he has declared; 'it was adapted for certain kinds of situation: the situation is over when a theme can take place.' The same applies to form in the conventional sense. But he recognises the need to 'make a junction' between the musician and the listener, and for 'necessary recognition points'. These, however, are now provided not by themes but by contrasts of speed, pitch and tone colour.

Both Boulez and Stockhausen have applied serial technique to duration, tone colour, dynamics and tempo as well as pitch. This method is frighteningly single-minded; for once the serial patterns are decided on, their application during the course of a composition leaves the least possible room for spontaneity. Soon, as it happened, human performing skills were overtaxed by such complexities as rapid runs of notes each of slightly different duration and loudness. In this passage from a Stockhausen piano piece, one bar has five crotchets; but eleven quavers have to be played in the time normally taken by ten, and of these the last five must be divided into seven quavers, a septuplet of which, however, the notes are subject to further variation – and so on:

EX.135

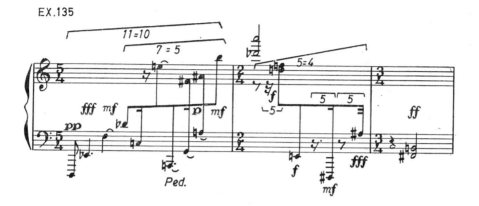

Ped.

This sort of music, for reasons both technical and human-perceptional, led to an impasse. From this difficulty Stockhausen found two quite different ways out. One was in the field of electronic music, which dispensed with performing difficulties simply by requiring no performers: the music was built up little by little on magnetic tape, a recording without a performance. *Gesang der Jünglinge* ('Song of the Youths', 1956) is a montage on tape of boys' voices and electronically produced sounds. It tells the Biblical story of the three Jews cast by Nebuchadnezzar into a fire; and in fact the effect is neither inhuman nor mechanical, but highly imaginative, even moving. His other solution was in the direction of indeterminacy or improvisation, which gave back to the performer a great deal of freedom, more indeed than that to which his training accustomed him.

Though it was not obvious at the time, Stockhausen was steadily moving towards a mystical, even religious, creative standpoint. The improvisatory tendency was now to predominate. A *Piano Piece* (1957) consisted of a series of fragments; but the order in which they were heard was the performer's to choose. Boulez used a similar technique in his Third Piano Sonata (1960), and other musicians followed; so that total serialism was an ideal quickly forgotten. Determinedly 'indeterminate', some musicians, among them the pioneering American John Cage (born 1912), went so far as to abandon written notes altogether. Cage has written the total-silence piece called 4' 33" (1952), as well as *HPSCHD* for seven harpsichords and fifty-one tapes (1969). But Stockhausen himself remains the most interesting, provocative and convincing of avant-garde composers. In his work at least, indeterminacy seems here to stay.

In Stockhausen's *Stimmung* ('Mood' or 'Atmosphere') six vocalists produce into microphones for seventy-five minutes various musical sounds such as syllables, vowels, and occasional spoken passages of verse while the sound is electronically manipulated; in a 1971 London performance this control was exercised by the composer himself. The performers have no music, and since the entire work is derived from one six-note chord the effect is 'overwhelmingly static . . . here sound is at rest'. This was the view of Peter Heyworth, the *Observer* newspaper's critic, who added that *Stimmung* was 'totally remote from the dynamic tradition of the West'. Of this same performance another critic, John Warrack, wrote in the *Sunday Telegraph*: 'Clearly we are dealing with something that lies quite outside any tradition of music as an account of human experience . . . Perhaps what is reflected is a genuine evolution out of a moribund Western tradition. Perhaps not: there have been many false dawns and postponed dusks.'

One thing is certain: Stockhausen offers some kind of challenge. It may – though I do not personally accept this view – merely be the invitation to 'turn off your mind and float downstream', to quote a Beatles lyric. If we do this, we are clearly renouncing most of the heritage and achievement of Western tradition. It is perhaps a portent that incense, with its oriental associations, was burned at the London Promenade Concerts 1971 performance of Stockhausen's *Mantra*, with its Indian title meaning 'Prayer'.

In Britten's church parable called *The Prodigal Son* (1968), the false friends tempt the Younger Son with the words: 'Come and try, come and taste,/Taste and drink, and drink again,/Float for ever on the flowing/Stream of glad forgetfulness.' And they fall into a drunken stupor. Here we are shown that it is bad, or at any rate foolish, to stop thinking. Britten and Stockhausen evidently represent different attitudes both to art and to life. Britten of course writes in musical notation, though even with him there is a greater improvisatory element than ten years ago: in him, too, the East has sounded a responsive chord. Stockhausen no longer see notes as essential; and when he was asked in a radio interview in August 1971 how he communicated his intentions to his performers, he replied, 'I emit waves, unifying waves.'

An American scholar, William W. Austin, the Professor of Music at Cornell University, has written (1966): 'If Britten's work is as important as his admirers believe, then Cage and Stockhausen are at best marginal elements . . . the present writer is deliciously tormented by a vacillating judgment of this question. Every new work of Britten's is exciting, partly because this question stays alive.'

And so we end with a question, or at any rate without a conclusion: there are no certainties in musical history. Indeed, someone has said that the only lesson we learn from history is that history teaches us nothing. Stravinsky, in 1958, made a similarly enigmatic comment. Asked if he thought the masterpiece of the next decade would be written in the serial technique, he replied: 'Nothing is likely about masterpieces, least of all whether there will be any.' But he added that developments in the musical language could not be ignored, and that a composer might lose 'the mainstream' by failing to take account of them. Style is a living, changing thing, and the creation of music remains the challenge that it has always been. That Stockhausen's present activities constitute a development in language, in the articulate sense in which Stravinsky used the word, is of course not necessarily the case.

EPILOGUE

At least, music is happening. All over the world, though naturally more so in the wealthier societies, people make music with varying degrees of elaboration. In the more popular field, the division between composers and performers has to a large extent broken down; and this represents the reinstatement of the oldest musical traditions, in which improvisation rather than written-down composition was standard practice. Popular music, furthermore, often goes a long way towards making up in vitality what it lacks in subtlety and sophistication. There are genuinely creative pop groups such as Pink Floyd and the Beatles; though inevitably their life may be short, their influence may be far-reaching and, through recordings, lasting.

Recording has gone from strength to strength over several decades; yet it has not, as is periodically feared, made live performance obsolete. Nor has the accessibility at all times of professional music-making via recordings, radio and television dimmed the enthusiasm and talents of the active amateur musical public, from members of choral societies and brass band players to pop guitarists and folk singers: rather, it seems to act as a stimulus, and in this sense there is a parallel with sport. Music is taking on a steadily larger role in the school curricula of most countries, since it has come to be recognised that active music-making is enjoyable, demanding and educationally worthwhile – a fact known to Plato but which has often been forgotten. One result has been an increase in the number of qualified professional musicians. Unfortunately these are sometimes unable to find adequate employment in cases where the output of universities and conservatories has outpaced the expansion of the work field.

Indeed, the economic side of music still gives cause for concern. Besides composers and performers, there are many musicians whose interests and qualifications lead them towards teaching, criticism, publishing, or the recording and broadcasting fields, and except in education the available jobs are few. The creative musician, without whom music cannot exist, is perhaps especially hard pressed to make a living – that is, unless he lives in a country such as the Soviet Union where State support is given to professionals at some cost to their independence. Since Beethoven's time, we have universally recognised the value of an artist's freedom of thought, the very state which permits him to fulfil himself best and thus ultimately to do most for the society in which he lives. However, a fully independent musician must provide for his own retirement or for uncertain times, and even in the well-paid popular field fashions change rapidly and fortunes may vanish as quickly as they were made.

Individuals must, inevitably, incur problems from time to time in any flexible social environment. But institutions, some well-established, seem hardly better placed. It is regrettable that musical organisations of size and lasting repute, like famous orchestras in major cities throughout the Western world, frequently have serious financial problems, and that smaller groups like theatre orchestras have simply disappeared. Public money for the arts is sometimes available, but in many cases the amount is small and the distribution uncertain; not until there is genuine public demand for a proper support of music by the society which it serves will this situation be remedied.

Music is at least to some extent valued in our industrial society, one which undoubtedly needs the arts as much as any of its predecessors – possibly still more urgently than they. There are good signs from both sides, which may be noted here and there: a city council may come to build an arts centre, properly staffed, or a 'difficult' composer may take trouble, while still not compromising himself artistically, to make his music meaningful and valuable to the community in which he lives. What seems essential is that music, in Britten's words, 'shall be accepted as an essential part of human activity, and human expression', and in those of Stravinsky, 'is at the centre of human culture'. As long as we have civilisation, we need music for people to play, sing or simply hear. Messiaen has said that birds sing with 'the surplus energy that bubbles up with love and joy, for filling time and space'. Birdsong, while our world lasts, is hardly to be silenced. Equally, while people find music in their hearts, we may be sure that the human spirit remains in the fullest sense alive.

Acknowledgments

Thanks are due to the following for permission to reproduce photographs: the Trustees of the British Museum, facing pages 33, 48, 128 and 208 (bottom); the Rijksmuseum van Oudheden, Leiden, facing page 32; Musée Royal des Beaux-Arts, Antwerp, facing page 49 (bottom); the Bibliothèque Nationale, Paris, facing pages 49 (top) and 144 (bottom); the Royal Institute of British Architects, facing page 129 (top); the Victoria and Albert Museum, facing page 129 (bottom); Galerie Liechtenstein, Vienna, facing page 145 (bottom); Mozart Museum, Salzburg, facing page 145 (top); Gesellschaft der Musikfreunde, Vienna, facing page 144 (top); the Royal College of Music, London, facing page 208 (top); Historisches Museum der Stadt Wien, Vienna, facing page 209 (top); the Mansell Collection, London, facing pages 209 (bottom) and 225 (top); Österreichische Nationalbibliothek, Vienna, facing page 304 (bottom); Festspielleitung, Bayreuth, facing page 225 (bottom); the Bettmann Archive, New York, facing pages 305, 320 (top and bottom); the Decca Record Company Ltd., facing page 321 (top); Hipgnosis, facing page 321 (bottom); John Murray Ltd. and Donald Mitchell for a photograph from *Gustav Mahler: Memories and Letters* by Alma Mahler, facing page 304 (top); Dover Publications and Donald Mitchell an illustration from *Liszt* by Sacheverell Sitwell, facing page 224. The jacket photograph shows a sixteenth-century painting of an open-air concert attributed to Veronese, from the Musée Lallemant in Bourges.

Thanks are also due to the following for permission to reproduce copyright material: Mrs Fürstner and Boosey & Hawkes Ltd., London, for two extracts from *Salome* by Richard Strauss on pages 259 and 260; Editions Durand & Cie, Paris, for an extract from *Scarbo* from *Gaspard de la Nuit* by Maurice Ravel on page 276; Editions Max Eschig, Paris, for extracts from *Jeux d'Eau* and *La Vallée des Cloches* by Maurice Ravel on pages 274 and 275; Universal Edition A.G., Vienna, for extracts from *The Cunning Little Vixen* by Leoš Janáček on page 279; Boosey & Hawkes Ltd., London, for extracts from Sergei Rachmaninov's Third Piano Concerto on pages 283 and 284, and Prelude in A minor, Opus 32, on pages 284-5; the Oxford University Press for an extract from the Fourth Symphony of Ralph Vaughan Williams on page 293; Faber Music Ltd., London, on behalf of J. Curwen & Sons

Ltd., for an extract from *The Planets* (*Neptune*) by Gustav Holst on page 295; Breitkopf & Härtel (London) Ltd., for an extract from the Fourth Symphony by Jean Sibelius on page 298; Schott & Co. Ltd., London, on behalf of B. Schott's Söhne, Mainz, for an extract from *The Firebird* by Igor Stravinsky on page 301; Boosey & Hawkes Ltd., London, for two extracts from *Petrushka* on pages 301 and 302, one from *Perséphone* on page 304, and one from *Requiem Canticles* on pages 304–5 by Igor Stravinsky; Universal Edition (Alfred A. Kalmus Ltd.) for an extract from *Pierrot Lunaire* on pages 307–8, one from *Six Little Piano Pieces* on pages 308–9, and one from *Five Piano Pieces* on page 310 by Arnold Schönberg, and for an extract from *Three Songs*, Opus 23, by Anton Webern on pages 313–14; Schott & Co. Ltd., London, on behalf of B. Schott's Söhne, Mainz, for an extract from *Mathis der Mahler* by Paul Hindemith on page 315; Universal Edition (London) Ltd. and Boosey & Hawkes Ltd., London, for extracts from *Fifteen Hungarian Peasant Songs* on pages 318 and 319, and from *Music for Strings, Percussion and Celesta* on page 320 by Bela Bartók; Editions Durand & Cie, Paris, for three extracts from *Vingt Regards sur L'Enfant-Jésus* by Olivier Messiaen on pages 322, 323 and 324; Universal Edition (London) Ltd., for an extract by Karlheinz Stockhausen on page 337; Theodore Presser Co. (Alfred A. Kalmus Ltd.) for an extract from *Soliloquy* by Charles Ives on page 326; and Boosey & Hawkes Ltd., London, for an extract from *Appalachian Spring* by Aaron Copland on page 328, and one from the *Classical Symphony* by Sergei Prokofiev on page 331.

The publishers have made every effort to trace the owners of copyright material appearing in this book. In the event of any question arising as to the use of such material, the publishers, while expressing regret for any error unconsciously made, will be pleased to make the necessary correction in any future edition.

Bibliography

GENERAL

GROVE'S DICTIONARY OF MUSIC AND MUSICIANS, 5th Edition, *ed. Eric Blom*, Macmillan 1954

THE HARVARD DICTIONARY OF MUSIC, *ed. Willi Apel*, Heinemann 1970

THE OXFORD COMPANION TO MUSIC, *Percy A. Scholes*, 10th Edition, OUP 1970

A HISTORY OF WESTERN MUSIC, *Donald Jay Grout*, Dent 1962

MUSIC IN WESTERN CIVILISATION, *Paul Henry Lang*, Dent 1942

MAN AND HIS MUSIC, Alec Harman, Anthony Milner, Wilfrid Mellers, Barrie & Jenkins 1969

MUSIC, HISTORY AND IDEAS, *Hugo Leichtentritt*, Harvard 1964

MUSIC AND THE EUROPEAN MIND, *Wilfrid Dunwell*, Jenkins 1962

A SHORT HISTORY OF OPERA, *Donald Jay Grout*, Columbia 1966

SOURCE READINGS IN MUSIC HISTORY, *Oliver Strunk*, Faber 1952

MUSICAL INSTRUMENTS THROUGH THE AGES, *ed. Anthony Baines*, Pelican Books 1961

CHAPTERS 1-4

THE NEW OXFORD HISTORY OF MUSIC, VOL. I, ANCIENT AND ORIENTAL MUSIC, *ed. Egon Wellesz*; VOL. II, EARLY MEDIEVAL MUSIC UP TO 1300, *ed. Dom Anselm Hughes*, OUP Vol. I 1957, Vol. II 1954

MUSIC IN THE MIDDLE AGES, *Gustave Reese*, Dent 1941

MUSIC IN THE RENAISSANCE, *Gustave Reese*, Dent 1954

A HISTORY OF BRITISH MUSIC, *Percy M. Young*, Benn 1967

CHAPTERS 5-6

MUSIC IN THE BAROQUE ERA, *Manfred F. Bukofzer*, Dent 1948

VIVALDI, *Marc Pincherle*, Gollancz 1958

MUSIC IN PURCELL'S LONDON, *John Harley*, Dobson 1968

CHAPTERS 7-12

MUSIC IN THE ROMANTIC ERA, *Alfred Einstein*, Dent 1947

A HUNDRED YEARS OF MUSIC, *Gerald Abraham*, 2nd Edition, Duckworth 1949

BIBLIOGRAPHY

CHAPTERS 13-16

MUSIC IN THE 20TH CENTURY, *William W. Austin*, Dent 1966

THE ENGLISH MUSICAL RENAISSANCE, *Frank Howes*, Secker & Warburg 1966

A COMPOSER'S WORLD, *Paul Hindemith*, Anchor Books, New York 1961

DEBUSSY: HIS LIFE AND MIND, *Edward Lockspeiser*, Cassell, 2 Vols. 1962 and 1965

MUSIC IN A NEW-FOUND LAND, *Wilfrid Mellers*, Barrie & Jenkins 1964

MUSIC AND MUSICAL LIFE IN SOVIET RUSSIA 1917–1970, *Boris Schwarz*, Barrie & Jenkins 1972

STRAVINSKY: IN CONVERSATION WITH ROBERT CRAFT, Pelican Books 1962

STYLE AND IDEA, *Arnold Schönberg*, Williams & Norgate 1950

AUTHOR'S NOTE: It may seem curious that few books are listed for the popular period of classicism and romanticism covered by Chapters 7–12. There is an abundance of material, yet it is difficult to single out individual works of outstanding usefulness. The Second Edition of Professor Abraham's book, listed above, offers a good bibliography (though only up to 1949) of the romantic period. One general series of books on composers deserves recommendation: THE MASTER MUSICIANS (edited by Sir Jack Westrup, Dent). COMPOSERS ON MUSIC (edited by Sam Morgenstern, Faber 1958) is a valuable anthology of composers' writings on their art.

INDEX

Abbatini, Antonio Maria 95
accordion 43
Aelred of Rievaulx 52
aeolian harp 42
Aeschylus 19, 167
Albéniz, Isaac 286, 287
Alexander III, King of Scotland 42
Alexander, King of Macedonia 20, 23, 166
Alexander Severus, Roman Emperor 21
Alfred, King of the West Saxons 41
Alypios 17
Amati family 108
Ambrose, Saint 24, 25
Amos 22
Anglican chant 70
Anhalt-Cöthen, Prince Leopold of 124, 126
Anne, Queen 120
anthem 65, 74-5, 118
Antinous 21
Antoninus Pius, Roman Emperor 21
Arabic music 13, 15
Aristophanes 19
Aristotle 18, 19, 25, 92
Aristoxenos of Tarentum 17
Armstrong, Louis 327
Arne, Thomas 134
Aryans 14
Assyrian music 12
Aston, Hugh 80
Auber, Daniel François Esprit 201, 221, 222
Augustine, Saint 24, 25, 27
Augustus, Roman Emperor 176
aulos 16, 18, 19, 20, 22, 23, 26
Austin, William 321, 338

Babylonian music 12
Bach, Carl Philipp Emanuel 133, 137, 139-40, 141, 142

Bach, Johann Christian 137, 146
Bach, Johann Christoph 123
Bach, Johann Jakob 124
Bach, Johann Sebastian 9, 59, 60, 66, 67, 79, 81, 89, 91, 99, 105, 108, 109, 110, 115, 120, 122-7, 128, 129, 130, 132, 133, 136, 137, 138, 145, 146, 149, 155, 158, 173, 179, 187, 188, 194, 195, 196, 199, 207, 212, 215, 230, 244n, 248, 277, 293, 294, 298, 305, 312, 314, 315, 333
Bach, Maria Barbara 124
Bacon, Roger 49
bagpipe 13, 16, 42
Bakunin, Mikhail 234
Balakirev, Mili 240
ballade 56
ballet: *see under Dance and dance forms*
bands, instrumental: *see under Orchestra*
Banister, John 104
bars 108
bards 41
Bartók, Béla 9, 156, 212, 239, 255, 306, 317-21, 327, 336
Barzini, Luigi 224
Basil, Saint 25
Bax, Arnold 335
Beatles, the 338, 339
Beaumarchais, Pierre-Augustin Caron de 135, 154, 225
Becket, Thomas à 41, 52, 166
Bedford, Duke of 57, 62
Beecham, Thomas 292
Beethoven, Johann van 157-8
Beethoven, Karl van 175-6
Beethoven, Ludwig van 9, 44, 89, 92, 109, 117, 125, 127, 130, 132, 134, 137, 138, 139, 140, 144, 145, 147, 149, 155-76, 177, 178, 179, 180, 182, 183, 184, 189, 192, 194, 196,

197, 199, 202-3, 204, 205, 207, 209, 210, 212, 215, 225, 232, 234, 235, 237, 239, 242, 244, 260, 262, 264, 270, 271, 280, 297, 298, 300, 302, 305, 316, 321, 322, 325, 334-5, 339
Beethoven, Maria Magdalena 157, 158
Bekker, Paul 174
Bellini, Vincenzo 178, 226-7, 228
bells 14, 15, 42, 43
Bengali music 18
Bennett, Richard Rodney 336
Berg, Alban 223, 263, 264, 306, 311, 312-13, 314, 336
Berlioz, Hector 132, 136, 156, 167, 168, 178, 179, 191, 197, 201-6, 207-8, 210, 212, 214, 222, 223, 225, 234, 236, 243, 244, 246, 258, 289
Bernard of Ventadour 39, 41
Bernstein, Leonard 167, 329, 330
Berwald, Franz 254
Bible, the 12, 13, 15, 21, 25, 29, 55, 62, 66, 207
Binchois, Gilles 58, 60
bird song 85, 117, 121, 131, 170, 321-2, 340
Bismarck, Prince Otto Eduard Leopold von 195
bitonality 277, 281, 294, 302
Bizet, Georges 222, 223, 224, 241, 328
Bliss, Arthur 335
Bloch, Ernest 286n
Blondin de Nesle 41, 134
Blow, John 103, 105
blues 326, 327, 328
Boccaccio, Giovanni 55
Boethius 28, 32
Böhm, Georg 123
Boieldieu, François-Adrien 222

Boileau, Nicolas 97
Boito, Arrigo 230, 231
Boleyn, Anne 62, 226
Bordoni, Faustina 121
Borodin, Alexander 240, 242, 298, 301
Boulanger, Nadia 330
Boulez, Pierre 156, 271, 307, 314, 324, 336, 337
Boult, Adrian 312
Bourgeois, Louis 67, 69
Brahms, Johannes 178, 193–9, 223, 242, 246, 250, 253, 258, 262, 289, 298, 333
Brecht, Bertolt 334
Brentano, Antonie von 174
Breuning (von) family 158
Breuning, Stephan von 175
Bridge, Frank 335
Britannicus 21
Britten, Benjamin 31, 106, 263, 298n, 333–5, 338, 340
Britton, Thomas 104
broadcasting of music 312, 339
Brosses, Charles de 135
Brubeck, Dave 327
Bruch, Max 293
Bruckner, Anton 244, 245, 248, 262, 278, 299
Bruno, Giordano 91
Büchner, Georg 312
Bull, John 81
Bülow, Cosima von (née Liszt, later Cosima Wagner) 234
Bülow, Hans von 234
Bulwer-Lytton, Edward 233
Burgundian music 57, 58, 59, 60–1, 62
Burney, Charles 14, 122, 128, 129, 139, 143, 251
Burns, Robert 144
Buxtehude, Dietrich 110, 123
Byrd, William 63, 74–5, 81, 85
Byron, Lord George Gordon 177, 190, 204, 207, 243
Byzantine music 24, 26

caccia 55–6, 89
Caccini, Giulio 93
cadences 56, 61, 75, 267, 284, 320
Cage, John 337, 338
Caldara, Antonio 128
Calvin, John 67, 69
Calzabigi, Ranieri da 136
Cambert, Robert 96
Campion, Thomas 102

canonic style 53–4, 142, 249, 306
cantata style 124, 126
cantilena 51
canzona 80
Caracalla, Roman Emperor 21
Carissimi, Giacomo 95, 129, 130
Carter, Elliott 329–30
Cassiodorus 27–8
castanets 43
Castro, Fidel 155
Cavalieri, Emilio de' 94
Cavalli, Pietro Francesco 95–6, 127
Cazamian, L. 266
Cellini, Benvenuto 205
cello 135
Cervantes, Miguel de 287
Cesti, Antonio 96, 127
Cézanne, Paul 303
Chabrier, Emmanuel 265
chaconne 80, 108
Chaldean music 12–13, 14, 18
chamber cantata 129–30
Chandos, Duke of 120
chanson 60, 78, 85
chanson de geste 37, 40
Charlemagne, Emperor of the West 29, 37, 42, 43
Charles I, King 75
Charles II, King 103
Charles VI, Germanic emperor 128
Charpentier, Marc-Antoine 129
Chateaubriand, Vicomte François-René de 200, 207
Chaucer, Geoffrey 57, 58, 59
Chausson, Ernest 250
ch'in 14
Chinese music 13–14, 15
choirs 20, 23, 24, 26, 28, 33, 49, 58–9, 60, 63, 67, 70, 74, 75–7, 97, 99, 103, 104, 123, 124, 141, 142, 179, 196, 244, 252
Chopin, Fryderyk 177, 192, 200, 201, 206, 207, 213–20, 221, 222, 227, 251, 254, 268, 289
chorale 65, 66–7, 78, 126, 128
chorale prelude 80, 109–10, 123
Christ 23, 31, 166
chromaticism 82, 87, 124, 210, 237, 238, 247, 248, 296, 302

church musical drama 30–1, 99
Cicero 20
clappers 11
Clarke, Jeremiah 24
clausula 49–50
clavichord 63, 79, 108, 123
Clement of Alexandria 21, 25
Cocteau, Jean 303
Coleman, Edward 102
Coleridge, Samuel Taylor 189
Colette 251, 278
Cologne, Elector Max Franz of 158, 159
concert-giving organisations 104, 147, 189, 250, 293
concerto form 114, 115, 117, 121, 137–8
concerto grosso form 115, 121, 306
conducting 97, 143, 172, 243, 262, 296, 329, 336
conductus 50, 52
Confucius 14
Cooke, Captain Henry 103
Cooper, Martin 166n
Copland, Aaron 326, 328–9, 330
Corelli, Arcangelo 111, 115, 116, 119, 121, 290
Corneille, Pierre 92
cornet 78
cornett 78–9, 103
Cornyshe, William 63
Couperin, François 129, 131, 132, 271, 276, 304
Cranmer, Thomas 69, 70
Cretan music 15, 16
criticism of music and journalism 149, 191, 195, 196, 201, 214, 215, 240, 242, 243, 245–6, 259, 265, 273, 284, 288, 297, 301, 328, 332, 338, 339
Croce, Giovanni 86
crumhorn 78
crwth 42
Cui, César 240
cymbals 19, 22, 23, 26, 41, 43
Czerny, Carl 172, 207

dance and dance forms 19, 37, 39, 42, 44, 51, 55, 80, 96, 102, 132, 135, 199, 206, 215, 218, 243, 268, 277, 286, 293, 300, 301, 302, 311
Daniel, John 82

Dante 40, 84, 93, 210, 243
Dauvergne, Antoine 134
Davenant, William 102
David, Elizabeth 225n
David, Jewish king 22, 62
Davis, Miles 327
Davy, Richard 99
Debussy, Claude 127, 169, 170, 206, 212, 217, 224, 230, 241, 250, 251, 255, **265-74**, 275, 276, 277, 278, 281, 286, 293, 294, 295, 296, 298n, 299, 301, 302, 303, 306, 309, 312, 315, 316-17, 327, 336
Delacroix 206
Delius, Frederick 257, **291-2**, 299
Delius, Jelka (*née* Rosen) 292
Dent, Edward 90
descant 49, 52
Descartes, René 91, 132
Diaghilev, Sergei 277, 286, **300-1**, 302, 306, 331
Dickens, Charles 245, 288
Dodds, Johnny 327
Doles, Johann 137
Donizetti, Gaetano **226**, 227, 228
Dostoevsky, Feodor 280
Dowland, John 79, 81, 100-1, 102
Druidic music 39, 41
drum 11, 14, 25, 41, 103, 104
Dufay, Guillaume 58, 59-60
dulcimer 42
Dumas, Alexandre (the younger) 229
Dunstable, John 57-8, 62
Dunstan, Saint 42
Dunwell, Wilfrid 140
Duparc, Henri 250
Durand, Jacques 274
Dvořák, Antonín **252-4**, 278, 288n

echoi 24
economics of music 147-8, 159-60, 175, 183, 258, 302, 320, 339-40
education, music in (teaching of music) 18-19, 28, 33, 59, 63, 109, 116, 123, 128, 132, 141, 144, 146, 157-8, 159, 179-80, 189, 201, 205, 228, 232, 233, 242, 244, 245, 250, 251, 252, 258, 278, 286, 288, 289-90, 292, 294, 296, 300,

309, 311, 315, 316, 317, 324, 329, 339
Edward I, King 42
Edward II, King 42
Egyptian music 11-12, 13, 16, 20
Eichendorff, Joseph 246
Einstein, Alfred 89, 224
Elagabalus, Roman Emperor 21
Eleanor of Aquitaine 39, 41
electronic music 337, 338
Elgar, Alice (*née* Roberts) 290, 291
Elgar, Edward 242, **289-91**
Eliot, Thomas Stearns 334
Elizabeth I, Queen 74, 79n, 81, 86, 118
Ellington, 'Duke' 327
Elsner, Ksawery Józef 213
equal temperament 125
Erkel, Ferenc 254
Eskimo music 13
Esterházy family 141, 207
Esterházy, Prince Nikolaus 141-2
Esterházy, Prince Paul Anton 142
Euripides 19, 235
Ethelbert, King of Kent 27
Eusebius of Caesarea 22, 23
Evans, Edwin 297
Evelyn, John 118

Falla, Manuel de **273**, **286-7**, 317
Farnaby, Giles 81
Fauré, Gabriel **250-1**, 255, 265
Fayrfax, Robert 63
Ferdinand IV, King of Naples 143
Ferrabosco, Alfonso 85
Feuerbach, Ludwig von 236
Fibich, Zdeněk 252
fiddle 42, 55, 103, 252, 295
Fielding, Henry 134
figured bass 93, 111
flageolet 103
Flaubert, Gustave 223
Fleurville, Madame Mauté de 268
Flotow, Friedrich 129
flute 11, 14, 15, 19, 25, 42, 66, 105, 114, 116, 201
Fokine, Mikhail 301
folk music 13, 38, 46, 60, 103,

107, 144, 196, 199, 213, 239, 242, 251, 254, 271, 286, 291, 293, 294, 295, 299, 300, 312, 317, 319, 320, 321, 326, 327, 328, 332
form (musical structure) 44, 56, 61, 79-81, 89, 108, 177, 203, 236, 242, 266, 267, 275-6, 284, 308, 309, 314, 320, 321, 322, 329-30, 336
Förtsch, Johann 98
Foss, Lukas 329, 330
Francis, Saint 40, 49, 212, 316
Francis I, King of France 63
Franck, César **248-50**, 273, 289
Franck, Johann 98
Franco of Cologne 48, 50
Frederick the Great, King of Prussia 139
Frederike, Princess of Detmold 196
Frescobaldi, Girolamo 110
Freud, Sigmund 260
Froberger, Johann Jacob 111
Frömbgen, H. 235
fugue form 60, 108, **125**, 146, 156, 173, 231, 320
Furtwängler, Wilhelm 261, 311
Fux, Johann 128

Gabrieli, Andrea 75, 76, 81
Gabrieli, Giovanni 76, 81, 98, 99, 114
Gade, Niels 254, 255
Galilei, Vincenzo 92-3
Galileo 92
Gaukler 41
Gautier, Théophile 206
Gay, John 131, 134
Gebrauchsmusik 316
Geminiani, Francesco 115, 116
Genzinger, Marianne von 144
George I, King (formerly Elector of Hanover) 118, 119, 120
George II, King 122
George III, King 144, 146
George, Prince of Wales (George IV, King) 143, 144
Gershwin, George 328
Gesamtkunstwerk 234, 236, 238
Gesualdo, Carlo, Prince of Venosa 82-4

Geyer, Ludwig 232
Giacobbi, Girolamo 98
Gibbons, Orlando 75, 81, 86, 103
Gide, André 303
Gilbert, William Schwenck 289
Giorgione 116
Giotto 55
Giraud, Albert 307
gleemen 41
Glinka, Mikhail 240, 254, 256, 300
Gluck, Christoph Willibald 132, 134, 135–6, 159, 206, 221, 232, 236, 251, 304
Goehr, Alexander 324, 336
Goethe, Johann Wolfgang von 156, 157, 164, 178, 180, 187, 190, 200, 202, 210, 223, 224, 246, 264, 280, 313
Gogol, Nikolai 224
Golenishchev-Kutuzov, Count Arseny 241
goliard songs 38
Goudimel, Claude 67, 69
Gounod, Charles 77, 178, 222, 223, 224, 288n
Granados, Enrique 286, 287
Greek music 13, 15–20, 42
Gregory I, Pope 28–9
Greig, Alexander 255
Grétry, André 134
Grieg, Edvard 45, 146, 151, 228, 255–7, 292, 325
Grimm, the Brothers 262
Grout, Donald Jay 18n
Grove, George 132
Grünewald, Matthias 316
Guarneri family 108
Gudea, ruler of Lagash 11
Guido of Arezzo 32–5, 36, 47
guilds of musicians 38, 42, 108–9
Guiraut de Bornelh 39
guitar 79, 103, 201

Hadrian, Roman Emperor 20, 21
halil 22, 23
Halle, Adam de la 51
Hallé, Charles 207
Hallström, Ivar 254–5
Hambraeus, Bengt 324
Handel, George Frideric 9, 91, 92, 95, 98, 99, 105, 110, 118–22, 123, 125, 127, 128,
129, 130, 132, 133, 135, 143, 145, 147, 155, 168, 173, 197, 239, 244n, 288, 289, 335
Hanslick, Eduard 196
Hardy, Thomas 294
Harman, Alec 36n
harmonic series 12
Harmonides 18
harp 12, 22, 23, 39, 41, 42, 58
harpsichord 42, 79, 80, 105, 108, 119, 121, 123, 124, 125, 131–2, 135, 139, 152, 164, 287
Harris family 108
Hasse, Johann Adolf 121, 128, 133
Hassler, Hans Leo 67, 75, 85
hautboy 108
Haydn, Joseph 91, 118, 122, 130, 133, 137, 139, 140–5, 146, 147, 149, 150, 152, 156, 158, 159, 160, 161, 167, 175, 177, 179, 184, 192, 196, 197, 203, 274
Haydn, Maria Anna (née Keller) 140, 141, 144
hazozra 20
Hegel, Georg Wilhelm Friedrich 185
Heine, Heinrich 202, 210, 221, 246
Heinichen, Johann David 92
Henry II, King 41
Henry V, King 57, 58, 62–3
Henry VI, King 63
Henry VIII, King 63, 69, 70, 226, 250
Henry IV, King of France 93
Henze, Hans Werner 155
Hérold, Ferdinand 222
hexachord 33–5, 36
Heyworth, Peter 338
Hiller, Johann Adam 135, 140
Hindemith, Paul 315–17, 319, 324, 330
hocket 52
Hoffmann, Ernst Theodor Amadeus 177, 184, 190, 193
Hofmannsthal, Hugo von 260, 261
Hogarth, George 288
Holst, Gustav 289, 294–5, 335
Hölty, Ludwig 178
Homer 15, 167, 173n, 207
Honegger, Arthur 303
Housman, Alfred Edward 279
Hucbald 36, 37, 46

Hueffer, Francis 288
Hugo, Victor 200, 201, 206, 207, 229
Humfrey, Pelham 103
Hummel, Johann Nepomuk 207
Hunt, James Henry Leigh 226
hurdy-gurdy 41
Hyagnis 16

Ibsen, Henrik 255
idée fixe 203, 236
imitative counterpoint 60, 70, 105, 109, 298
improvisation 122, 158, 327, 330, 337, 338
Indian music 13, 14–15, 16, 31, 322, 323
Indy, Vincent d' 248, 250, 251n
Ingegneri, Marc Antonio 85
inversions 52
Ireland, John 335
Isaac, Heinrich 60, 61, 78
Isidore of Seville 32
isorhythm 56, 57
Ives, Charles 325–6

Janáček, Leoš 278–80
Jannequin, Clément 85, 86
James II, King 92, 103, 118
jazz and popular music 277, 305, 311, 326–8, 329, 339, 340
Jean Paul 177, 190, 193
Jesse 22
Jewish music 13, 15, 21–3, 286n, 326
John XXII, Pope 52
John, King of Bohemia 56
John of Salisbury 52
jongleurs 38, 39, 40, 41, 42
Jonson, Ben 102
Joseph II, Austrian Emperor 147, 148
Josquin des Prés 60, 61–2, 75, 78, 84–5, 90
jubilus 25, 29, 30
Julius III, Pope 76

Kant, Immanuel 167, 178
Keiser, Reinhard 98, 129
Kempis, Thomas à 167
Kennedy, President John F. 329
kinnor 22

kithara 16
Köchel, Ludwig von 149
Kodály, Zoltán 9, 317
Krauss, Clemens 261
Kuhnau, Johann 111

Lablache, Luigi 222, 226
Lalande, Michel Richard de 129
Laloy, Louis 173, 175n
Lam, Basil 142
Lamartine, Alphonse de 207, 211
Lamennais, Félicité Robert de 207
Landi, Stefano 95
Landini, Francesco 56, 82
Landowska, Wanda 287
Lang, Paul Henry 70n, 92n, 137n, 154, 178n
Lanier, Nicholas 102
Larkin, Edward 176
Lassus, Roland de 78, 85
laudi 40
Lawes, Henry 102
Lawes, William 102
leading motive technique 230, 236–7
Leibniz, Gottfried Wilhelm 136
Lenin 332
Leo III, Pope 29
Leoncavallo, Ruggiero 281n
Léonin 49
Lermontov, Mikhail 240
Lesueur, Jean-François 202
Lichnowsky, Prince Karl 159
Liszt, Franz 140, 156, 170, 173, 178, 182, 193, 196, 197, 205, 206–13, 214, 215, 217, 223, 224, 225, 232, 234, 235, 236, 241, 244, 246, 248, 250, 252, 253, 254, 258, 274, 283, 286, 289, 317
Lobkowitz, Prince Josef Franz Maximilian 160
Locatelli, Pietro 116
Locke, John 207
Locke, Matthew 105
Longfellow, Henry Wadsworth 290
Longus 277
Lortzing, Gustav Albert 184, 187
Louis VII, King of France 39
Louis XIV, King of France 96, 116, 129

Louis XV, King of France 118, 133, 146
Louis XVI, King of France 136, 144
Löwe, Johann Jakob 123
Lucian 18, 23
Ludwig II, King of Bavaria 235
Lully, Jean-Baptiste 96–7, 114, 116, 129, 132, 133, 250
lute 55, 58, 63, 67, 79, 80, 93, 100, 103
Luther, Martin 61, 65–8, 76, 90, 109, 123, 199
lyre 12, 16, 17, 19, 20, 22, 23, 26, 27, 36, 37, 42

madrigal 78, 81–9, 90, 130
Maeterlinck, Maurice 270
Mahler, Alma (*née* Schindler) 262, 263, 312
Mahler, Gustav 199, 258, 261–5, 284, 308, 312, 329
Malibran, Maria Felicita 222
Mallarmé, Stéphane 266, 273, 277
Malory, Thomas 233n
Mannheim, Duke of 138
Manzoni, Alessandro 230
maqam 15
Marazzoli, Marco 95
Marcabru of Gascony 39
Marcus Aurelius, Roman Emperor 20
Marenzio, Luca 84, 86, 100
Maria Barbara, Queen of Spain 132
Maria Theresa, Austrian Empress 160
Marie-Antoinette, Queen of France 136, 144
Marini, Biagio 111
Marschner, Heinrich August 186, 233
Marsyas 16
Martinez, Marianne 141
Martini, Giovanni Battista 146
Mascagni, Pietro 281n
masque 102, 105
Massenet, Jules 224, 281
Mattheson, Johann 119
Maximilian I, Holy Roman Emperor 61
Maxwell Davies, Peter 327, 336
Mazarin, Cardinal Jules 95, 96

Mazzocchi, Virgilio 95
Medici, Lorenzo de' 59
Medici, Maria de' 93
Méhul, Etienne 221
Meistersinger 65, 66, 67
Menander 19
Mendelssohn, Felix 127, 178, 184, 187–90, 191, 192, 193, 194, 196, 197, 255, 288, 289, 325
Mengelberg, Willem 264
Merbecke, John 70
Mérimée, Prosper 223
Merulo, Claudio 80–1
Mesomedes 21
Messager, André 251, 265
Messiaen, Olivier 265, 321–4, 333, 336, 340
Metastasio 135, 141
Meyerbeer, Giacomo 221, 224, 233
Michelangelo 61, 89, 210, 223
Midas, King of Phrygia 16
Milhaud, Darius 93n, 303
Milton, John 95, 102, 145
Minnesinger 40–1, 65
minstrels 26, 37, 39, 40–2
modes 18n, 24–5, 29, 33–4, 40, 61, 74, 105, 107, 319
modulation 74, 87, 215
Moeran, Ernest John 335
Molière 96, 97, 129
Moniuszko, Stanislaw 254
Montemezzi, Italo 281
Monteverdi, Claudio 78, 82, 84–5, 90, 92, 94, 95, 96, 99, 100, 101, 114, 116
Montpensier, Anne-Marie-Louise, Duchess of 96
Mörike, Eduard 246
Morley, Thomas 75, 81, 85–6, 87
Morton, Jelly Roll 327
Morzin, Count Ferdinand Maximilian 141
Moses 21
motet 50–1, 52, 56, 67, 74, 76, 78, 90–1, 129
Mouton, Jean 85
Mozart, Constanze 144, 147, 152, 153
Mozart, Leopold 145, 146
Mozart, Wolfgang Amadeus 95, 109, 127, 128, 130, 133, 134, 135, 136, 137, 138, 139, 140, 142, 143, 144, 145–54, 155, 156, 158, 159, 161, 167,

173n, 177, 179, 180, 182, 183, 184, 187, 190, 192, 196, 207, 212, 213, 215, 223, 226, 227, 239, 250, 252, 258, 260, 261, 262, 274, 289, 293
Murger, Henri 280
musica reservata 61
Mussorgsky, Modest 240–1, 242

Napoleon I (Bonaparte), French Emperor 149, 156, 166, 200, 221
Nebuchadnezzar II, King of Babylon 12, 337
Neefe, Christian Gottlob 158
Neri, Saint Philip 76
Nero, Roman Emperor 20–1
neumes 32, 33
nevel 22
Newman, Cardinal John Henry 291
Newman, Robert 293
Nicetas of Remesiana 24
Nicolai, Otto 187
Nielsen, Carl 295–7
Nietzsche, Friedrich Wilhelm 223, 238, 239, 292
Nijinsky, Vaslav 301
nomes 16, 18
Nono, Luigi 324
North, Roger 92
notation 32–3, 36, 39, 48–9, 307, 313, 338
Notker Balbulus 30

oboe 16, 105, 114, 116, 121
Obrecht, Jacob 60
Ockeghem, Johannes 60, 61
Offenbach, Jacques 222, 289
Olympos 16
opera, development of 92–6, 97, 120–1, 127–8, 133–6, 177, 184, 222, 224, 227, 229, 230, 232, 236, 242, 271, 281, 289
Opitz, Martin 98
oratorio form 76, 94–5, 121–2, 129, 188, 288
orchestra and other instrumental bands 14, 16, 20, 26, 67, 76, 78, 94, 96, 97, 103, 104–5, 114, 115, 121, 126, 132, 138–9, 142, 152, 159, 197, 201, 205, 206, 242, 245, 259, 264, 265, 268, 294, 301, 327

Orff, Carl 93n
organ 12, 14, 20, 26, 27–8, 42, 43–4, 58, 67, 74, 75, 76, 79, 80–1, 97, 103, 108, 109, 116, 121, 122, 123, 124, 135, 139, 244, 252
organum 43, 46–7, 49, 52, 268, 271
Orpheus 15, 37, 171, 211
Ossian 37
Ostrovsky, Alexander 280
Owen, Wilfred 334

Pachelbel, Johann 109, 123
Pacius, Fredrik 255
Paganini, Niccolò 192, 198, 204, 207, 284
Paisiello, Giovanni 134
Parry, Hubert 289
passacaglia 80, 124, 294
Passion music 99, 122, 126, 127, 129
Pasta, Giuditta 222
Pater, Walter 177
Paul, Saint 23
Peacham, Henry 84
Pedrell, Felipe 286
Pépin III, King of the Franks 43
Pepusch, Johann Christoph 131
Pepys, Samuel 102, 103
Pergolesi, Giovanni Battista 131, 133, 303
Peri, Jacopo 93, 94
Pérotin 49
Petrarch 38, 84
Petrucci, Ottaviano dei 80
Pherecrates 19
Philidor, François-André 134
Philip IV, King of France 55
Philip, Duke of Burgundy 58, 59
pianoforte 33, 108, 139, 152, 164, 177, 182, 192, 197, 207–10, 212, 216–18, 284
Picasso, Pablo 303
Piccinni, Niccolò 134
Pink Floyd 339
pipe 12, 14, 15, 16, 22, 204
Piston, Walter 329
plainchant 23–5, 28–9, 30, 31, 35, 36–7, 39, 44, 49–50, 54, 55, 57, 60, 70, 77, 99, 290
Plato 18, 19, 20, 207, 264, 339
Pliny the Younger 23
Plutarch 166

Ponte, Lorenzo 260
popular music: *see under Jazz and popular music*
Porpora, Nicola 141
Poulenc, François 224, 303
Praetorius, Michael 67, 109
Prato, Giovanni da 56
programme music (descriptive music) 18, 82, 85, 86–8, 111, 117–18, 123–4, 126–7, 132, 142, 170, 180–1, 185, 188, 197, 202–5, 210–11, 212, 244, 250, 252, 259, 263, 264, 265, 266, 274, 276, 284, 290–1, 293, 299
Prokofiev, Sergei 330–2
psalm singing 22–3, 67
psaltery 42
publication of music 160, 232–3, 246, 253, 339
Puccini, Giacomo 223, 280–1
Puchberg, Michael 148
Purcell, Henry 103, 104–7, 108, 111–13, 129, 205, 270, 289, 292, 293
Puritanism 67, 102
Pushkin, Alexander 240, 241
Pythagoras 13, 17, 18, 27

Rachmaninov, Sergei 217, 281–5, 286, 328
Racine, Jean 92, 136
rackett 78
raga 16, 322
Rameau, Jean-Philippe 132, 133, 135, 155, 250, 271
rattle 11, 15
Ravel, Maurice 170, 206, 241, 251, 273–8, 286, 293, 301, 306, 327
rebec 42
recitative style 93–4, 100–1, 102, 129, 171–2, 203, 271, 279
recorder 42, 78, 103, 121
recording of music 307, 337, 339
Redford, John 80
Reinken, Johann Adam 81, 123
Respighi, Ottorino 280
rhythmic patterns (modes), medieval 36, 39–40, 48, 54, 323
ricercar 80
Richard I, Coeur de Lion 41
Richardson, Samuel 134

Rimsky-Korsakov, Nikolai 240, 241-2, 243, 300, 301, 331
Rinuccini, Ottavio 93
Riquier, Guiraut 39
Ritter, Alexander 258
Robert the Bruce, King of Scotland 42
Röckel, August 234
Rodrigo, Joaquín 287
Roland-Manuel, Alexis 278
Rolland, Romain 250, 273, 274
Roman music 13, 20-1
Romani, Felice 227
rondeau 44, 51, 56
rondo form 138, 164-5, 215
Rore, Cipriano de 82, 85
Rosenmüller, Johann 114
Rospigliosi, Cardinal Giulio (Clement IX, Pope) 95
Rossini, Gioacchino 95, 221, 223, **224-6**, 228, 289, 333
Rothschild family 214
Rousseau, Jean-Jacques 132, 133-4, 155, 239
Rubini, Giovanni Battista 222
Ruckers family 79, 108
Rude, François 200
Rudel, Jauffre 38, 39
Rudolph, Archduke of Austria 174

Sachs, Hans 65, 66, 187, 238
St Martial *organum* 47-8
Saint-Saëns, Camille 223-4, 250, 251, 265
Sakados 18
Salomon, Johann Peter 143
Salzburg, Archbishop of (Hieronymus, Count von Colloredo) 147
Samuel 22
Sand, George 214
Satie, Erik 303
Saul, Jewish king 22
Sayn-Wittgenstein, Princess Carolyne 210
scales 13-14, 17, 24, 27, 32, 33, 35, 40, 44, 61, 74, 82, 107-8, 210, 268, 309
Scarlatti, Alessandro 114, 119, 127, 129, 130, 138
Scarlatti, Domenico 131, 287
Scheidemann, Heinrich 81
Scheidt, Samuel 109-10
Schein, Johann 110

Schiller, Johann Christoph Friedrich von 173
Schindler, Anton 172
Schober, Franz von 181
Scholes, Percy 70n, 253
Schönberg, Arnold 265, 277, 297, **306-11**, 312, 313, 314, 315, 316, 319, 321, 324, 326, 327, 333, 336
Schopenhauer, Arthur 236
Schroeter, Rebecca 144
Schubert, Franz Peter 178, 179-84, 185, 191, 192, 196, 207, 210, 211, 216, 244, 246, 247, 258, 262, 263, 267, 289
Schulz, Johann Abraham Peter 137
Schumann, Clara (*née* Wieck) 191, 192, 193, 194, 195, 207
Schumann, Robert 177, 178, 190-3, 194, 195, 196, 202, 206, 207, 212, 246, 254, 255, 289, 306
Schütz, Heinrich 98, 99, 123, 129
scops 41
Scott, Walter 188, 225, 245
Scriabin, Alexander 217, 278, 285-6
Searle, Humphrey 312
Sechter, Simon 183, 244
Seikilos 18
Seneca 20
sequence 30
serial technique 306, 309-11, 312, 314, 315, 324, 328, 336, 337, 339
service, Anglican 74, 104
Shakespeare, William 59, 74, 80, 85, 89, 100, 101, 102, 103, 142, 150, 155, 173n, 178, 184, 187, 188, 190, 201, 202, 205, 211, 225, 229, 230, 231, 232, 267, 280, 294
Shaw, George Bernard 260
shawm 16, 43, 78, 103
Shelley, Percy Bysshe 224
shofar 21
Sibelius, Jean 242, 295-9, 306
Siebold, Agathe von 196
Shostakovich, Dmitri 156, 242, 263, 330 ,332-3
Sigismund, King of Hungary 63
Silbermann family 108
Siloti, Alexander 283
Singspiel 135, 136, 140, 184

Sitwell, Edith 335
Smetana, Bedřich 251-2, 253, 256, 278
Smith, Bessie 327
Smithson, Harriet 202
Socrates 166
Solomon, Jewish king 22
Solzhenitsyn, Alexander 280
sonata da camera 111
sonata da chiesa 111, 115
sonata form 80, 111, 114, 115, 121, 125, 137-9, 151-2, 160-2, 169, 182, 203, 232, 271, 294, 305
song, accompanied solo 100-2, 136, 148, 179, 180-2, 192, 199, 205, 211-12, 243, 245, 246-7, 250, 253, 254, 263
Sophocles 19, 260, 303
Spangler, Johann 141
Spartan music 13, 19
Spohr, Louis 189
Spontini, Gasparo 221
Sprechstimme 307-8
Staden, Sigmund 98
Staël, Madame de 200
Stamitz, Johann 138-9, 140, 251
Stanford, Charles Villers 289
Stassov, Vladimir 243
Steffani, Agostino 127
Stein, Erwin 312
Stendhal 153
Stockhausen, Karlheinz 156, 324, 336-8, 339
Stokowski, Leopold 312
Stradella, Alessandro 129, 130
Stradivari, Antonio 108, 204
Strauss, Johann (the younger) 222
Strauss, Richard 151, 258-61, 262, 265, 268, 271, 291, 294, 312, 317
Stravinsky, Igor 82, 157, 242, 271, 275, 277, 281, 283, 284, 296n, 297, 298n, 299, 300-6, 307, 311, 312, 313, 314, 316, 320, 321, 323, 326, 327, 328, 331, 333, 335, 336, 338-9, 340
Strungk, Nikolaus 98
suite form 80, 110-11, 276
Sullivan, Arthur 222, 289
Sumerian music 11, 12, 13, 16
Süssmayr, Franz Xaver 148, 153

Sweelinck, Jan 81, 109
symphonic form 105, 114, 137–9, 142–43, 167, 202–4, 210, 242, 248, 263–5, 297, 298, 305, 322–3, 332
symphonic poem, form 182, 183, 210–11, 250

Tacitus 21
Tadolini, Madame Eugenia 229
Taillefer 41
Taliesin 41
Tallis, Thomas 63, 70–3, 74, 81, 85, 89, 293
tambourine 11, 22
Tartini, Giuseppe 116
Tasso, Torquato 84, 211
Tate, Nahum 106
Taverner, John 63–4
Tchaikovsky, Peter Ilyich 151, 156, 178, 215, 223, 242–3, 244, 250, 257, 280, 281, 289, 300
Telemann, Georg Philipp 127, 129, 132–3
Teresa, Saint 78
ternary form 138
Teyte, Maggie 307
Theile, Johann 98
Theodoric the Ostrogoth, King 28
Thibaut, King of Navarre 39, 40
Thomas Aquinas, Saint 49
Thomas, Dylan 258
Tieck, Ludwig 184
Timotheos of Miletos 19–20
Tintoretto 116
Tippett, Michael 156, 335–6
Titian 116
toccata form 81, 109–10, 124, 294
tof 22
Tolkien, John Ronald Reuel 234
Tomkins, Thomas 75
tonadilla 135
Torelli, Giuseppe 115
Tovey, Donald 170, 242
triads 52
triangle 43
trombone 78, 103
trope 30–1, 32
troubadours 38–9, 40, 41
trouvères 39–40, 51

trumpet 21, 22, 25, 42, 43, 58, 78, 103, 105, 114
Turina, Joaquín 287
Turner, William 265
Tutankhamun, King of Egypt 21–2
Tutilo 30
twelve-note technique: see under Serial technique
Tye, Christopher 74

ugab 22
Urien, King of Rheged 41

Vadé, Jean-Joseph 134
variation form 80, 81, 109, 138, 156, 193, 197, 277, 320
Vaughan Williams, Ralph 125, 279, 289, 291, 292–4, 295, 299, 317, 328, 335
Venice and Venetian music 75–6, 80, 81, 92, 95, 96, 98, 99, 114, 116, 119, 306
Veracini, Francesco Maria 116
Verdi, Giuseppe 105, 178, 226, 227–31, 280, 281
Verdi, Margherita (née Barezzi) 228
Verlaine, Paul 250
Veronese 116
Vespasian, Roman Emperor 21
Vicentino, Nicola 92
Victoria, Queen 188, 226
Victoria, Tomás Luis de 78, 85, 91, 286
vièle 42, 58
viol 74, 78, 79, 93, 103, 111
viola 159, 204
viola da gamba 79, 125
violin 42, 79, 108, 111, 115, 125, 135, 139, 141, 146, 251
violoncello: see under Cello
virelai 44, 56
Virgil 201, 205
virginals 63, 79, 81
Vitry, Philippe de 49, 54
Vivaldi, Antonio 116–18, 119, 127
Voltaire 150

Wagner, Minna (née Planer) 233
Wagner, Richard 65, 151, 156, 174, 185, 186, 187, 190, 193,

196, 197, 212, 221, 223, 227, 228, 230, 232–9, 242, 244, 245, 246, 247, 250, 258, 260, 262, 265, 271, 278, 285, 289, 290, 292, 296, 303, 306, 333, 335, 336
waits 103, 108
Waldstein, Count Ferdinand 158–9
Walter, Bruno 264
Walther, Johann 99
Walther von der Vogelweide 40–1
Walton, William 316, 335
Warrack, John 338
Watteau, Antoine 131
Weber, Carl Maria von 170, 178, 184–6, 187, 190, 205, 207, 221, 232, 233, 289
Webern, Anton 306, 311, 312–14, 315, 336
Weelkes, Thomas 86–8
Weill, Kurt 327
Weimar, Duke Wilhelm Ernst of 124
Whiteman, Paul 328
Whitman, Walt 291
Whyte, Robert 74
Wilbye, John 86, 87
Wilde, Oscar 259, 260
Wilhelm I, German Emperor 235
Willaert, Adrian 75–6, 82, 85
William, Duke of Aquitaine 39
William, Duke of Normandy 41
Winckelmann, Johann Joachim 136
Wither, George 102
Wolf, Hugo 196, 211, 245–7, 250, 262
Wolf-Ferrari, Ermanno 281
Wolsey, Cardinal Thomas 63–4
Wood, Henry 293
Wordsworth, William 155–6, 177
Wright, Orville and Wilbur 109
Wulstan 43
Wycliffe, John 55

Zelter, Carl 187
zelzlim 22
Zemlinsky, Alexander von 306
Zweig, Stefan 261